THE AMERICAN STRAVINSKY

THE AMERICAN STRAVINSKY

The Style and Aesthetics of Copland's New American Music, the Early Works, 1921–1938

Gayle Murchison

THE UNIVERSITY OF MICHIGAN PRESS :: ANN ARBOR

TO THE MEMORY OF MY MOTHERS ::

Beulah McQueen Murchison and Earnestine Arnette

First paperback edition 2013

Published in the United States of America by
The University of Michigan Press
Manufactured in the United States of America
∞ Printed on acid-free paper

2016 2015 2014 2013 5 4 3 2

A CIP catalog record for this book is available from the British Library.

ISBN 978-0-472-09984-9 (cloth : alk. paper)

ISBN 978-0-472-06984-2 (pbk. : alk. paper)

Publication of this book was supported by a grant from the H. Earle Johnson Fund of the Society for American Music.

"Excellence in all endeavors"

"Smile in the face of adversity . . . and never give up!"

Acknowledgments

Hoc opus, hic labor est.

I stand on the shoulders of those who have come before. Over the past forty years family, friends, professors, teachers, colleagues, eminent scholars, students, and just plain folk have taught me much of what you read in these pages. And the Creator has given me the wherewithal to execute what is now before you.

First, I could not have completed research without the assistance of the staff at various libraries. I express gratitude to the library staff at Tulane and Yale universities and the University of Arkansas. At the Music Division of the Library of Congress, Wilda Heiss and Lloyd DePinchback made available to me the Aaron Copland Collection, which in the early 1990s was uncataloged. Thanks also go to the attorney for the Copland Estate, the late Ellis Freedman, who granted permission to use the collection, which was not open to the public at the time I conducted my research. I also am indebted to the Aaron Copland Foundation and Boosey and Hawkes. The staff at the American Composers' Alliance and the American Music Center in New York opened their files to me. Any work on Aaron Copland owes much to Vivian Perlis, for her vision in founding the Oral History Project in American Music at Yale, and because she so generously shares her memories of her dear friend. Mrs. Perlis, I hope this study does justice to Copland and all he accomplished. This book could not have been published in its present form without the support of the Earl Johnson Bequest for Book Publication Subvention awarded by the Society for American Music and a Publication Subvention from the American Musicological Society. I am immensely grateful to these societies for their support.

I have not worked in a vacuum. Many professors have lit my path. I thank Michael Friedmann and Reinhard Strohm. The late Claude V. Palisca provided a sterling scholarly model. I coined the term *Paliscare* when studying Italian in graduate school; it means to work hard, thoroughly, and productively. I hope that this present work does justice to the word. I also wish to thank V. Kofi Agawu, Carol Oja, and William Lowe. I also express immense gratitude to Josephine Wright and Kay Kaufmann Shelemay. When I first began work on Copland, I had few colleagues working in this area, unlike today. I acknowledge and thank my Copland colleagues Sally Bick, Elisabeth Crist, Jennifer DeLapp, Howard Pollack, and Marta Robertson. I also wish to thank Gayle Sherwood. Special thanks is due my extraordinarily patient and understanding editors at the University of Michigan Press, Chris Hebert, Marcia LaBrenz, and Ellen Bauerle.

So many dear friends have offered support along the way: I wish to thank Dr. Merlyn Hurd and the late Hugh Hurd; Denise Hurd for housing me during the New York stage of the research; and Pam Potter for the many kitchen table conversations. I also apologize for the impositions: to Miriam Jaffe and Karen Robinson in Baltimore; to Pamela Jaffari and Kimberly Williams in Washington, D.C.; to Ned Lochaya, Ellie Murphy, and Kelly Parr in New York; to John Gough in Glasgow and London; to Claire Detels and Lewis Chamness in Arkansas; and to Jacqueline McLendon and Hermine and Don Pinson in Williamsburg. I also thank my Tulane colleagues Felipe Smith and Amy Koritz. Michael Cunningham, Pam Franco, Joy V. Fugua, and Rosanne Adderley have been tremendous; you cannot find better. Und auch, veilen Dank, Herr und Frau Herrmann, Karin Herrmann, und Baerli. Joan Capra also opened her home to me, welcoming my many boxes and papers. Violet Fitzpatrick, Hillary, and Buster played a major part in the early stage of this work. Jerise Fogel went above and beyond: without her love and support, my dissertation would not have gotten to Yale on time during that week when my mother died.

I thank other friends for their support: C. Evelynn Hawkins, Tammy Kernodle, Georgiary Bledsoe, and Lisé de Lay. Special thanks go to Wayne D. Shirley and the late Catherine Parsons Smith. I cannot express how important it has been to say that you are my friends. Two others are now no longer with us in this life, but their work and memories live on: Mark Tucker and John Blassingame. "Blass" is my Du Bois. Ingrid Monson and Okolo Ewunike listened in many telephone conversations, especially during a time when I lost my parents a year apart, and moved halfway across the country—twice. And Angus, feline, who played kitten on the computer keys.

I finished this manuscript in New Orleans in August 2004 and edited it over the next year. In August 2005 Hurricane Katrina devastated New Orleans and the Gulf Coast. Fortunately, I had left the city several days earlier, but many of my relatives and friends suffered through the hurricane and its aftermath. Work on the final edits was interrupted as I watched events unfold and I tried to wrap my mind around what was happening in the Crescent City. Key people in New Orleans welcomed and accepted me when others did not. They have touched my life forever. Though dispersed, the Millennium Band lives on: Charles Baker, Richard Fultz, Ed Wills, Rial Diles, Brian Alexander, and Alvin "Apple"

Battise. I give a nod to trombonist Doc Lewis and the Hot Sauce Band, Zion Trinity, and the other musicians I had an opportunity to perform with or just sit in with. Thanks for keeping it real. The members of Cornerstone United Methodist Church buoyed me during my years there, especially the mothers of the church, Mrs. Marian Roussel, Mrs. Cora Charles, Mrs. Janet Jackson, and the late Mrs. Laura Good. I am a fourth-generation educator. Mrs. Roussel taught generations of schoolchildren in New Orleans. Miss Cora and Miss Laura taught generations of nursing students at Dillard University. Thank you for reminding me how far we have come.

Work could not have been pursued without my family and teachers, who first encouraged my interest in music. Never forget the bridge that carries you over. Thanks to my first piano teachers, Mrs. Brown and Carol Sykes. Special praise goes to my high school piano teacher, the late Mrs. Judith Aycock, who first said I could be a(n) (ethno)musicologist. My late godparents, Mr. Isaiah and Mrs. Mildred Jones, told me, "Take God with you." I also thank my aunt, Gay A. Killens—blood *is* thicker than water. My late father, Theodore W. Murchison, set an example of how to live life. Most importantly, this book is dedicated to the memory of my mothers: Beulah McQueen Murchison, who both made numerous sacrifices (now I understand what you were teaching me—you were my rock) and prescribed the simple edict of excellence in all endeavors; and to master musician Earnestine Arnette—pianist, choral conductor, church musician—who saw that I gravitated to the piano when I was three and who gave me my first musicology test when I was eight (you were my inspiration). Teen, your indomitable spirit, tenacity and perseverance will forever be unmatched. "Smile in the face of adversity . . . and never give up."

—Ama, New Orleans, August 2004/Williamsburg, December 2011

Contents

Tables

Musical Examples

Introduction

The twentieth century has often been called the "American" century, which aptly suggests how extensively traditions and genres of American music grew and influenced music globally over those years. Beginning in the 1920s, Aaron Copland built his career during the years American art and popular music gained international prominence. By the mid–twentieth century, he had become the composer most strongly associated with Americana, or the self-conscious use of American folk idioms in art music. For nearly sixty years audiences easily recognized works such as *Billy the Kid, Rodeo, Appalachian Spring, Fanfare for the Common Man,* and *Lincoln Portrait* as somehow American. Yet long before the Brooklynite was pegged as a composer of Americana and identified with cowboys and the open range, he was considered one of the United States' most promising modernist composers, a purveyor not of an American style but of an international, modernist one. While audiences of the latter twentieth century viewed Copland as the quintessential composer of Americana, audiences during the 1920s and 1930s viewed him primarily as an upstart, bad boy of American music—full of brash dissonances and bold rhythms.

American Musical Modernism

At the New York premiere at Aeolian Hall, January 11, 1925, of Copland's *Symphony for Organ and Orchestra,* New York Symphony Orchestra conductor Walter Damrosch quipped, "Ladies and gentlemen, I am sure you will agree that if a gifted young man can write a symphony like this at twenty-three, within five years he will be ready to commit murder!"[1] Two years later the Eastman Philharmonic performed the symphony in Rochester as part of Howard Hanson's series American Composers Concerts.[2] In 1933 an article by Copland appeared in *American Composers on American Music,* edited by Henry Cowell. The concert series and the book publication occurred within a short span of time, and a historian's first inclination is to schematize each forum, viewing the Hanson concerts as nationalist and the Cowell book as modernist. The nationalist forum offered the American composer a venue to solve the difficult problem of securing performances of new works. The modernist forum gave him or her an opportunity to explain the new stylistic and aesthetic orientation of the first generation of twentieth-century North American and Latin American composers. These venues, one in publishing, one in performance, illustrate two of the means by which Copland disseminated his music and aesthetic and critical ideas. However, this simple dichotomy obscures how Copland perceived himself as composer and as critic. The book and the concert series were both forums for the modern American composer, and Copland did not consider himself solely American or solely modernist, but as a *modern American* composer.

What Was Modernism?

Debussy's *Prelude to the Afternoon of a Faun* (1892–95), often marked as the first masterpiece of modern music, broke with the aesthetics and style of German Romanticism, particularly Wagnerism. By the 1920s Europe remained an attractive place for the young composer to receive a musical education, but now the exciting destination was no longer Germany. France emerged as an international music center, where not only Debussy but also Stravinsky was active. During the late teens and the early 1920s, the New Music, or the new styles and musical aesthetics from Europe began to reach major urban American music centers such as New York and Boston, emerging international polestars.

There were contemporaneous attempts by composers and critics to classify and define the new music. Today, the term *twentieth-century music* is objective, and generally applied to all styles and aesthetics of music composed during this period. However, during the 1920s and 1930s, Copland's own time, two terms were in general use, *modernism* and *ultramodernism;* only the former is still in use today. Copland used these two terms extensively, though today their meanings are considered imprecise. According to Paul Griffiths, American writers used both terms to refer to the music of composers such as Varèse, Schoenberg, Bartók, Stravinsky, Cage, Antheil, Webern, and Copland. The term *modernism* suggests a "conscious pushing-back of the frontiers, and so is not inappropriate in connection with composers who have seen this as their aim."[3] Willi Apel, however, found the term applied "so loosely that it is virtually meaningless. The dates of the period so described vary with each writer." Some date the beginning of modernism in music to the period during which "Elgar, R. Strauss, and Sibelius (all born c. 1860) produced their first significant works. Others would restrict it to the music of contemporary (living) composers."[4] Lexicographer Nicholas Slonimsky defines modern music simply as "that written since 1900. The variants are

20th-century music, New Music, Music of Our Time, Music of Today and Contemporary Music." All these writers generally agree that *modernism* applies to the music of composers who depart from Common Practice harmonic and tonal conventions.

The term *ultramodernism* is equally difficult to define. Ultramodernism is a radical aesthetic position as much as a musical style. Slonimsky applies the term to "music beyond the limits of traditional modernism." As he expounds, "Certain attributes of ULTRA-MODERN MUSIC have retained their validity: dissonant counterpoint, atonal melodic designs, polymetric and polyrhythmic combinations and novel instrumental sonorities."[5] In his *Dictionary of Contemporary Music,* John Vinton attributes the origin of this term to American critics and composers who used it to describe the style and aesthetic of those such as Stravinsky and Schoenberg. In her 1921 study, *The Relation of Ultramodern to Archaic Music,* Katherine Ruth Heyman characterizes ultramodern music as departing from modal, melodic, harmonic, and rhythmic conventions.[6]

Perusal of writings by contemporary composers helps clarify the terminology and confusion of modernism with ultramodernism. In *Music Here and Now,* Ernst Krenek, like the lexicographers already mentioned, defines contemporary music as "whatever is written by contemporaries of the person using the term." Noting that musicians in both the United States and Europe used the word similarly, Krenek adds that it describes more than just the date of composition. Modern music is "that part of our contemporary music which emerges from the whole by a visible deviation from tradition in its material, its style, or in some other essential feature."[7] The descriptions and definitions offered by composers and critics whose writings appeared in the American journal *Modern Music* define modernism and ultramodernism more narrowly and precisely. Cowell, in "New Terms for New Music," focuses on the terms *atonal, polyharmony, polytonality, dissonant counterpoint, polyrhythm,* and *polymeter.* In doing so, he linked these techniques with "new music," leading one to deduce that modern music was a function of new harmonies and rhythms.[8]

Recent scholars have attempted to clarify these terms as well. Elliott Antokoletz defines ultramodernism as the aesthetic of Ives, Cowell, Ruggles, Stravinsky, Schoenberg, and Rudhyar. Stylistically, he links the term with "the Stravinskian ostinato technique—based on constant rhythmic reinterpretations of narrow-ranged modal layers." With respect to American composers, he associates the style with "the open quality found in American symphonic works of Harris and Copland—octave pedals in low instruments" and modality."[9] David Metzer considers modernism not only a musical-stylistic and aesthetic movement, but a cultural and historical one. Borrowing extensively from historian Peter Gay, Metzer understands modernism to coincide with the post-Victorian era, a historical and cultural period of major cultural, social, and revolutionary change. Modernism changed all arts and thought—it changed ways of knowing, of "thinking, feeling, and seeing," challenging Western civilization to change its aesthetic sensibility, philosophical style, and social life. Modernism dawned in reaction around 1910 in the United States, creating a new zeitgeist here, as it had in Europe. Modernism broke free of the genteel Victorian tradition in the arts and culture, separating idealism and morality from art.[10]

Thus, modernism can be viewed both culturally and musically. Culturally, modernism is the period from around the turn of the century onward, in which British and American society left behind genteel artistic and social traditions. Musically, *modernism* describes music contemporary with the lives of composers, critics, and musicians who were active during the years encompassed by this study, 1920–41. *Ultramodernism,* in contrast, is applied to experimental music, exemplified by the works of composers such as Schoenberg, Stravinsky, and Varèse, that self-consciously broke with the musical conventions of the Common Practice.

Henry Cowell's *American Composers on American Music* (1933)

Cowell's *American Composers on American Music* sought to inform the public of new directions in American music from a source other than music critics, who usually were not composers and who, as Cowell wrote, "do not understand in the least what is taking place in either feeling or technique, but give out vague personal impressions which have little relation to the reality and which differ widely with each individual critic." Cowell sought to counter the detrimental effect of such critics and to give a fairer description of contemporary composers' aims. His book provided a forum for the young American composer to speak for himself, to explain new stylistic and compositional trends, directions, and developments. Cowell presented a representative sample of the range of ideas Copland's peers held on American music at the time. Cowell included both the "progressive" or modern composer and the more conservative composer.[11] The volume's first twenty essays were devoted to composers analyzing and discussing the music of their peers.

Cowell selected and grouped by criteria of stylistic orientation and influence, delimited first according to nationality (American, German, Russian, etc.). His second criterion was national influence on an individual composer's style: whether he or she was influenced by European music. Cowell subcategorized composers according to a perceived French or German (Cowell used the term *Teutonic*) influence. He also

TABLE INTRODUCTION 1 Cowell's Categories of American Composers According to Style and Aesthetic

Modern	Progressive	Conservative
European influence		
French influence		
German influence		
American idioms		

identified composers whose music had traces of Americanisms, or, as he put it, whether they used "indigenous materials or are specially interested in expressing some phase of the American spirit in their works."[12] Conservative composers were represented as well (see table intro.1). As the table suggests, Cowell's taxonomy was biased: he was interested in modern composers foremost. He did not bother to further categorize and devise subcategories for moderate or conservative composers. His categories symbolized a wide range of aesthetic and stylistic choices that the first generation of twentieth-century American composers faced. The American composer was conservative, progressive, or modern; European influenced or lacking in European influence; if European influenced, French or German influenced; interested in American vernacular idioms or not; of American birth or an émigré. The American composer could be one, or any combination, of these.

Copland represented one of Cowell's group of "progressive" or "modern" American composers, those who "do not attempt to develop original ideas or materials but who take those which they already find in America and adapt them to a European style."[13] Others in this category adapted American vernacular idioms such as jazz, popular music, and Native American music to European style, primarily French, or in the case of George Gershwin, a combined nineteenth-century German Romantic, Italian late nineteenth-century operatic, and French style as represented by Stravinsky.

Copland's Path

Cowell's categorization of Copland was accurate and astute. During his formative years as a teenager in New York, Copland discovered Stravinsky, and the Russian's style left an indelible mark on both his own early style and overall musical aesthetic. As did many American composers, Copland went to Europe—in his case, Paris after World War I—where he absorbed the aesthetics and various styles of the neoclassicism of Milhaud and others of Les Six, a group of young French composers. His study in Europe shaped his embrace of jazz, an identifiably American idiom in vogue throughout Europe. Following his return to the United

States in 1924, Copland continued to combine stylistic elements borrowed from Stravinsky, French neoclassicism, and American jazz and popular song. A major stylistic shift occurred during the Great Depression as he simplified his musical language and reached out to a broader, populist American audience beyond the modern music aficionados and cognoscenti.

How Copland began as a brash modernist and later came to be identified as the quintessential American composer is the subject of this book, which traces the development of both his aesthetic ideas and his musical style, situating both in the context of European and American musical modernism, as well as broader social and cultural changes of the 1920s and 1930s. The first chapter, "*Scherzo humoristique (Cat and Mouse):* Copland's American *Petrushka* and His Debt to Stravinsky," treats the younger composer's development of a modernist musical style by dividing his progress into two stages: (1) his tutelage in New York with Rubin Goldmark, and (2) his study at Fontainebleau and later in Paris with Nadia Boulanger. This chapter begins by looking at Copland's style as a teenager and his early interest in European modernism, at first Debussy, Scriabin, and Stravinsky. This chapter also provides a detailed analysis of two early compositions, "Jazzy" from *Trois Equisses (Three Moods)* and *Scherzo humoristique (Cat and Mouse),* begun in New York and completed in France. In the former, one sees Copland's first mature use of jazz in a modernist work. In the latter work, one also sees the influence of Stravinsky, especially his *Petrushka* and octatonic technique, combined with Debussy's pentatonicism.

The second chapter, "Boulanger and Compositional Maturity," finds Copland in France studying with Nadia Boulanger, first during the summer of 1921 at Fontainebleau and over the next three years as one of her private students in Paris. One work, "Rondino" from *Two Pieces for String Quartet,* looks back to Boulanger's own teacher, Gabriel Fauré, while simultaneously embracing the more recent styles and techniques of Debussy and Stravinsky. This chapter shows how under her tutelage he became influenced by a group of young French neoclassical composers collectively called Les Six. Copland's first American premier of a major orchestral work, the Symphony for Organ and Orchestra, also owes its genesis to Boulanger. Copland's first American breakthrough, this work established his reputation as a promising American modernist. It is also the most Stravinskian of his works from the 1920s.

The next two chapters, chapter 3, "Popular Music and Jazz: Authentic or Ersatz?" and chapter 4, "Paris and Jazz: French Neoclassicism and the New Modern American Music," further explore how Copland conceived of and used jazz. Before he left for France Copland had begun to experiment with jazz in short pieces. In France he embraced the aesthetics of Jean Cocteau and French neoclassicism, which encouraged the young composer to draw upon the music of everyday life as part of a move away from German Romanticism. Copland observed how Milhaud and Auric had used American jazz, which had had a grand reception in France since its arrival via James Reese Europe during World War I. Copland noted how these composers had combined blue notes (as the flatted third and flatted seventh scale degrees), dotted rhythms (to imitate the swung eighth notes of jazz rhythm), and other techniques imitative of 1920s American jazz and ragtime with modernist harmonic techniques. His stay in Europe also awakened a nationalist impulse within him, not the old-fashioned type of American composers such as George Chadwick and his former teacher Goldmark, who both essentially combined German Romanticism with melodies—often quotation of folk song—based on Native American and African-American folk music. Rather, Copland desired to see American *modernist* music represented beside European new music. Like other American expatriates he began to see the United States through a new lens, colored by his European experience. Boulanger also helped Copland see that the United States' musical idioms, particularly jazz, were distinct from those of Europe. Intrigued by the rhythms of jazz, Boulanger stressed that it could be another compositional resource for Copland as an *American* modernist composer.

Copland returned to the United States in 1924, which marks the beginning of his American career and the focus of the next seven chapters. Chapter 5, "Back in the United States: Popular Music, Jazz, and the New American Music," develops Copland's use of jazz and the influence of Milhaud, as seen in *Music for the Theatre.* Chapter 6, "European Influence beyond Stravinsky and Les Six: Hába and Schoenberg," examines the influence of Schoenberg and his twelve-tone method and Alois Hába's influence on Copland during the late 1920s. Chapter 6 explores how he combined music from his ethnic heritage with eastern European modernist techniques. Aware of Jewish composers such as Ernest Bloch, who did use Jewish themes, Copland also explored his own ethnicity. After hearing a folk tune while attending the play *The Dybbuk,* Copland was inspired to compose *Vitebsk,* which also shows the influence of Alois Hába and his use of quarter tones. Copland also lent a composition to a collection in support of Palestine, a hora, "Banu (We've Come)"; however, through most of his career, Copland rarely composed explicitly "Jewish" works (yet critics such as Virgil Thomson wrote about the "Jewishness" of his music—here one detects perhaps anti-Semitic stereotyping). The seventh chapter examines how Copland's style evolved to become more accessible, first seen in his pieces influenced by Paul Hindemith's aesthetic of *Gebrauchsmusik.* Copland also composed *Schulmusik,* works intended for students and young musicians. During this stage of his career, Copland did not abandon the techniques he had borrowed from Stravinsky, Debussy, and Milhaud; rather, he simplified his textures and created works that were less technically demanding on the performers and listeners.

The next two chapters focus on the influence of Copland's involvement in leftist politics on his aesthetic and musical style during the early years of the Popular Front. His political engagement deepened his interest in composing music easily accessible to a broad audience, as discussed in chapter 8. Involved in the Popular Front movement, he became active in leftist composers' organizations. At first, influenced by the ideas of Ernst Krenek, he sought to compose an American mass music; yet even this style was infused with Stravinskian modernist techniques, as was "Into the Streets May First," the winner in a *New Masses* song competition. Copland's writings also appeared in leftist publications. The Left developed an interest in American folk music tradition, as folklorists traveled throughout the country and recorded traditional folk music practitioners. Several performers, such as Leadbelly and Aunt Molly Jackson, were brought north to perform at meetings, hootenannies, union meetings, and such. Anthologizers such as Carl Sandburg and Lawrence Gellert issued collections of folk music closely linked to the Left and leftist causes. Chapter 9 addresses Copland's most extensive use of folk music in the late 1930s, first seen in *El Salón México*. In composing this work, Copland turned to several published music collections, as he would for later works in which he quoted folk tunes. However, he did not use them in the way European nationalist composers such as Dvořák or American nationalist composers such as his teacher Goldmark did. Rather, he used Stravinsky as his model and applied the same techniques heard in Stravinsky's so-called Russian works such as *Rite of Spring*. *El Salón México* also demonstrates how Copland applied his ideas about music and politics and used Stravinskian techniques with folk music in this work. Copland's next major composition to incorporate folk music, the ballet *Billy the Kid* (as well as the suite), followed on the heels of *El Salón México,* and used folk music in the same way, as is discussed in chapter 10. This chapter also makes use of materials found in the Copland Collection at the Library of Congress to establish a new chronology for this ballet.

CHAPTER ONE

Scherzo humoristique (Cat and Mouse) :: Copland's American *Petrushka* and His Debt to Stravinsky

> Who wrote this fiendish "Rite of Spring,"
> What right has he to write the thing,
> Against our helpless ears to fling
> Its crash, clash, cling, clang, bing, bang, bing?
> —NICHOLAS SLONIMSKY, *Music Since 1900*

Copland's path to a modern neoclassical musical style has two stages of training, American and European. The first began during the late teens in New York with compositional studies with Rubin Goldmark; the second began in 1921 in France with his study with Nadia Boulanger. His American training offered him mastery of styles and techniques of the Classic-Romantic period; his European training provided him with mastery of those of music then current in Europe. Past studies of Copland's life and career have conventionally credited Boulanger with shaping his ideas about modernism and with the maturation of his musical style. However, before Copland departed North American shores, he had ideas of his own—ones clearly formed in New York independent of Goldmark that reflect a level of maturity that would be refined by Boulanger. Copland showed an acute and analytical interest in the music of Igor Stravinsky, Aleksandr Scriabin, and French composers such as Debussy and Ravel.

Early works composed during his studies with Goldmark and Boulanger illuminate Copland's understanding of ultramodernism and modernism. These compositions reveal his interest in and mastery of the new techniques of Stravinsky and, limitedly, Scriabin, seen first in his earliest mature composition, *Scherzo humoristique (The Cat and the Mouse)*. *Cat and Mouse* was also the work that brought Copland his first public success. He took it with him to Paris, where it was publicly performed and became his first published composition.

New Music in New York

The new music of both American and European composers during the second decade of the twentieth century was variously referred to as modern and as ultramodern music. As Carol Oja writes in her study of the rise of modern music in New York, during the time the music of European modernists began to arrive in the United States, through the early years of the Great Depression, *modernism* was something of an umbrella term that encompassed the works of composers who "explored an imaginative range of styles and ideologies." Styles and compositional methods varied among composers who emerged during the 1910s and 1920s, and "difference and diversity were at modernism's core." There was no common musical style or language; no single school of composition dominated. The one uniting principle was freedom, innovation, and reaction to—if not rejection of—the nineteenth-century German Romantic tradition in a new century marked by technological, economic, and social change. Pianist-composer Leo Ornstein's early public performances (from 1915 to the end of the decade) of both his own works and those of other modernists introduced New York audiences to highly dissonant music marked by tone clusters and a new conception of piano technique. Other prominent modern composers emerged as leaders of the movement. Bartók received some performances; Scriabin (who had visited in 1906) and Erik Satie were well received in the United States. The music of Arnold Schoenberg was sporadically programmed during the century's second decade, his String Quartet in D Minor premiered by the Flonzaley Quartet in January 1914 in New York. His orchestral works also received major performances: in December 1914 the Boston Symphony Orchestra performed *Five Orchestral Pieces* under the baton of Karl Muck. Months later the New York Philharmonic Symphony Society premiered *Pelleas und Melisande*. Ornstein also introduced New York audiences to Schoenberg's music, performing *Opus 11* in recital. One influential modernist, Edgard Varèse, first arrived in late December 1915, and became what Oja terms the "matinee idol of modernism" in New York during the 1920s. Other Europeans soon followed: Ernest Bloch, E. Robert Schmitz, and Dane Rudhyar. By the second half of the 1920s, two Americans would emerge as modern music leaders: Henry Cowell and Aaron Copland.[1]

While many styles were considered "modern" during this time, critics referred to the dissonant, innovative music of composers such as Schoenberg and Stravinsky as "ultramodern." Composers of this ilk sought to break free of the tonal system, embraced an aesthetic of experimentation, and liberated dissonance in their works. Stravinsky made an early and major impact on American concert life. The BSO performed *Fireworks* in December 1914. American audiences were further introduced to his works *via* the Ballets Russes' 1916 Metropolitan Opera–sponsored American tour. Other New York performances of *Firebird* and *Petrushka* took place in January 1916. *Petrushka* appears to have captivated New York audiences, inspiring sisters Irene and Alice Lewisohn to present it at Grand Street's Neighborhood Playhouse later that year. A production of *Petrushka* choreographed by Adolph Bolm (based on Michel Fokine's) choreography was staged at the Met in 1919. Concert performances of Stravinsky's works also took place. Although his *Three Pieces for String Quartet* was poorly received in 1915, Olga Haley and the London String Quartet successfully presented *Pribautki* in New York in the spring of 1918; the Flonzaley Quartet premiered Concertino for String Quartet in November 1920.[2]

Early Piano and Composition Studies

Most of Copland's exposure to contemporary music during his youth was the product of autodidacticism and study of the piano literature. There was amateur music making in his home: his mother played piano and sang; his uncle played the violin, and occasionally his brother and sister would play violin and piano duets. Their selections consisted mostly of "potpourris from operas—but their top accomplishment was a fair rendition of the Mendelssohn *Violin Concerto,*" Copland recalled. Other music performed in his home included ragtime and selections from popular shows. Copland started piano at the age of seven, learning the basics from his sister Laurine. His father, Harris, finally consented to formal lessons when Copland was thirteen; he studied with three prominent New York pedagogues: Victor Wittgenstein, Clarence Adler, and Leopold Wolfsohn. From Adler, Copland learned both technique and the core piano repertoire—Chopin waltzes; Haydn, Mozart, and Beethoven sonatas; Hugo Wolf songs, Debussy preludes, and Scriabin tone poems. In the fall of 1917, his senior year of high school, Copland began composition studies with Goldmark. After a year of study, together they agreed that Copland had learned about as much as he could from Wolfsohn; Goldmark recommended Wittgenstein. Copland had hoped to learn more about the contemporary piano literature, but like Wolfsohn, Wittgenstein was, in Copland's view, a musical conservative and considered Copland something of a radical. The most modern work he performed during his study with Wittgenstein was Ravel's *Sonatine.* The teen studied two years with him before moving on to study with Adler, with whom he remained from the winter of 1919 to the spring of 1921.[3]

On his own Copland began to discover new music, that of Scriabin, Debussy, and Ravel. Modern music emerged before the phonograph and sound recordings became mainstays in American homes, initially disseminated through live performances and scores, published reviews, and simply word of mouth. Similarly, Copland encountered modern music by attending concerts in Manhattan, which he began in earnest after commencing studies with Goldmark. During World War I and following, the popularity of German music declined in the United States due to anti-German sentiment. This led to increased performances of works by French composers, the United States' ally. Thus, Copland was exposed to a range of new French music. He heard Walter Damrosch and the New York Symphony Orchestra, and Debussy's *Nocturnes* performed by the Philadelphia Orchestra; he attended a Chicago Opera production of *Pelléas et Mélisande*. He also attended concerts by both Prokofiev and Paderewski, who inspired Copland to become a composer around 1915. Copland also subscribed to the Metropolitan Opera, where he heard his first opera, *Boris Godunov*. He also enjoyed dance, attending performances by Isadora Duncan and the Ballets Russes. He is known to have attended a performance by Ornstein in 1919.[4]

Copland gained further exposure to modern music through the study of scores, either through purchase or by borrowing them from Manhattan's Fifty-eighth Street branch of the Public Library. Among works from the standard repertoire, he was drawn to the music of Chopin, Grieg, and Tchaikovsky rather than to the German Romantics. Bloch's Violin Sonata inspired Copland to study more of his works. Independent of either Goldmark or his piano teachers, Copland studied several Debussy piano works, Scriabin's "Vers la flamme" (1914) and his Tenth Sonata (1913); and the works of Ravel, Mussorgsky, and other contemporary composers.[5] Thus, before he had even graduated high school, Copland had been exposed to the music of the leading European modernists, ranging from Debussy to Stravinsky, from the 1890s to works composed shortly (sometimes just months) before Copland first heard them.

In his autobiography cowritten with Vivian Perlis, Copland reminisced that at the age of eight and a half, he began his earliest attempts at composition. Copland's biographer, Howard Pollack, documents that by the age of twelve Copland had begun notating melodies. By the time he began study with Wolfsohn, Copland had begun an opera, a setting of *Cavalleria Rusticana,* but lacked the skill to complete more than just a few bars. As Copland neared the end of his studies with Wolfsohn, he also began a Schubert-influenced piano work, *Valse Impromptu* (1916). Realizing he had a limited knowledge of harmony, he first attempted to improve his compositional technique through a mail-order harmony course. Despite following this course of study, Copland began but was unable to complete an ambitious *Capriccio* for piano and violin. He also worked on an early *Theme and Variations* for piano; a Victor Herbert–

style nostalgic song; and planned a biblical oratorio. By spring 1917 Copland completed a solo piano work, *Moment Musicale—a Tone Poem,* influenced by Beethoven, Liszt, and Tchaikovsky, and Jewish music. Copland's primary deficiency was his inability to modulate, which prompted him to seek a composition teacher. Wolfsohn referred him to Goldmark.[6]

Copland found Goldmark an excellent teacher of the fundamentals of musical composition (harmony, form, and counterpoint) and stayed with him for four years. He consistently praised Goldmark's sound mastery of Common Practice styles and techniques. His studies progressed, but Copland experienced the same problems with Goldmark that he had with his piano teachers. Goldmark was limited: he had little use for new music and openly discouraged Copland from playing such works and composing in this style. Rather than resigning himself to studying exclusively the works of past masters, Copland pursued the study of modern music and the latest works coming from Europe on his own rather than with the assistance of an instructor.[7]

Through independent study of scores and reading contemporary music criticism, Copland began to shape his own modernist aesthetic. His first efforts to discuss modern music dates to a student performance in Adler's studio. Before performing Ravel's *Sonatine,* Copland explained the work to his audience of fellow students. "It was my first talk about a musical 'modernist.' Without being aware of it, I was embarking here for the first time on the role of musical commentator."[8] His earliest ideas about modern music can be gleaned from his articles on the music of his contemporaries. One appeared in Cowell's groundbreaking *American Composers on American Music,* in the section "Composers in Review of Other Composers." In "Carlos Chávez—Mexican Composer," a reprint of an article first published in the *New Republic,* Copland wrote about another composer who would be identified with both international modernism *and* national and ethnic, self-conscious cultural definition, or nationalism. Praising several features of Chávez's music, Copland, by then a member of the League of Composers, placed his peer among a small group of "forward-looking musicians" that included composers who were not known beyond the modern music concerts of the International Composers' Guild.[9] Not only did Copland describe Chávez's style, but in the course of the article he also indirectly explained the new musical developments generally applicable to all composers. In doing so, Copland attempted to define the new music in general.

Copland was direct and to the point: Chávez's music exemplified "the complete overthrow of nineteenth-century ideas which tyrannized over music for more than a hundred years."[10] Copland saw all twentieth-century music as this departure from nineteenth-century romanticism. "The entire history of modern music, therefore, may be said to be a history of the gradual pull-away from the Germanic musical tradition of the past century."[11] This led eventually to two revolutions, one aesthetic and one technical, thereby delimiting definitions of modernism along these two lines, aesthetic and stylistic.[12] Copland characterized the technical revolution, via a departure from music of the past, as an aesthetic of innovation, which had led to new techniques, new harmonic languages, and new styles. As the years progressed and Copland assessed the developments of the thirties, his writings became more specific and moved beyond general references to "nineteenth-century Germanic ideals." He presented considerations of style, theory, chronology, and aesthetics upon which to base his definitions.

Copland's later ideas on modernism remained consistent with those formed during his twenties and early thirties. One unifying thread he wove through his music criticism in articles written in the 1930s and early 1940s was the innovation of French modernists. He later specifically referred to German romanticism as the ideal that composers had rejected. Copland cogently summarized the Romantic aesthetic as one of the composer striving for emotional expression. "The German Romantic was highly subjective and personal in the expression of his emotions. The 20th-century composer seeks a more universal ideal. He tends to be more objective and impersonal in his music."[13] The "subjective" was the primary feature of romanticism—a subjective/objective dichotomy often also articulated by other writers. Modern music was "objective"—it sought no deep philosophical meaning. It did not strive for metaphysical transcendence or the prima facie expression of the artist, but was "matter-of-fact, more concise—and, especially, less patently emotional."[14] It was, to borrow from Stravinsky, autonomous and expressed only the musical idea itself. Copland identified two composers who had inaugurated the move away from the styles and aesthetics of Wagner: "Modernism is generally taken to mean the Debussy-Ravel aesthetic."[15]

Copland accepted the then-current new music categories "ultramodern music" and "modern music," noting that many different styles of music were pigeonholed as ultramodern by critics and audiences. He wrote, "A great many different kinds of music were grouped indiscriminately together, and especially today the newer music may be said to include an unusually variegated experience."[16] Modern and ultramodern music, however, were not synonymous, though the terms were often used interchangeably. Both trends did spring from the same source—the rejection of the aesthetics and styles of the German Romantic past—but there were aesthetic, stylistic, and chronological differences that permitted Copland to differentiate between them. He devised a chronology, separating the way the terms were used at the beginning of the century from their use from the mid-twenties to World War II. In a 1928 article, "Music Since 1920," Copland summarized new musical developments that had taken place in the United States, acknowledging that there was no crystal-clear, precise meaning of the term *modern music.*

> It is important, first, to point out that the term modern music has a variety of meanings. We can distinguish at least three different classes of so-called modern music. The oldest generation think of Strauss and Debussy as the last examples of a long line of great composers. As revolutionists they paved the way for the complete overthrow of nineteenth century harmonic laws. Their tonal innovations, so startling when *Salomé* and *Pelléas* were new, are now entirely assimilated and universally accepted. For the large mass of music-lovers these two men represent modern music; after them, all is chaos. This takes us no further than the decade 1900–1910.[17]

Copland identified the period 1910–20 as belonging to Schoenberg and Stravinsky.

Copland had additional criteria for differentiating between modernism and utlramodernism. In defining ultramodernism, he retrospectively identified innovation and iconoclasm as supplanting the Romantic aesthetic during the early 1920s. Ultramodern music of the first three decades of the century was "an attempt to free music from the conventions and ideals of Romanticism—rhythmical, harmonic, formal—that had gradually been stifling all freshness."[18] The ultramodern music of the 1920s was self-consciously experimental.

> The very word "modern" was exciting. The air was charged with talk of new tendencies, and the password was originality—anything was possible. Every young artist wanted to do something unheard of, something nobody had done before. Tradition was nothing; innovation everything.[19]

In the article on Chávez, Copland further characterized this ultramodern music:

> Among many other kinds of interest, the ironic and grotesque seemed to exert a particular fascination. No combination of instruments was too outlandish to be tried at least once. There were experiments in jazz, in quarter-tone music, in music for mechanical instruments. Composers vied with one another in damning all conservative music.[20]

An article on George Antheil published in *Modern Music* in 1925 along with various articles published during the late 1920s and in the 1930s further illuminate what Copland saw as the difference between ultramodernism and modernism.[21]

> The watchword in those days was "originality." The laws of rhythm, of harmony, of construction had all been torn down. Every composer in the vanguard set out to remake these laws according to his own conceptions. And I suppose that I was no exception despite my youth—or possibly because of it.[22]

Ultramodern music possessed a certain "shock value" through the use of rhythmic techniques borrowed from outside art music; it invented new instruments and explored microtonality. Ultramodern composers sought new tonal systems or procedures other than functional tonality, new ways of constructing and handling of harmony, and new forms. They formulated new "laws" for the treatment of all conventional musical parameters. Aggressively avant-garde and innovative in the handling of conventional musical parameters, the formulation of new musical systems, the use of nondiatonic scales, twelve-tone techniques, or nonfunctional harmony or polyrhythms, ultramodern music questioned very basic assumptions about the aesthetic and technical nature of music. In other words, ultramodern music sought to redefine music as sound and experiment.[23] In Copland's own method of categorizing the new music according to its systems, Schoenberg's atonality and twelve-tone method and Stravinsky's tonal techniques (what theorists have identified as octatonicism) and the style of his "Russian" period would make them composers of ultramodern music.

In his critique of Chávez's style, Copland obliquely defined modernism: "Without consciously attempting to be 'modern,' his music indubitably succeeds in belonging to our age."[24] His idea of the variety of styles subsumed under modernism is suggested by the composers he considered modern: Scriabin, Debussy, Ravel, and Stravinsky. In Copland's view, the modern music movement was born in Europe; specifically, in Paris with Debussy and Ravel and the impressionists, in Vienna with Schoenberg, and in St. Petersburg with Stravinsky.[25] In retrospect, Copland saw both ultramodernism and the modernism of Stravinsky's neoclassicism as a reaction against impressionism. Stylistically different from ultramodern music, modern music featured harmonic and rhythmic innovations that could return to older forms or even use conventional-sounding harmonies. Copland believed it was even possible to compose atonal or polytonal music, to use polyrhythms and unconventional forms, yet not be an ultramodernist. In other words, modernism did not necessarily bar the conventional. The modern composer dispensed with functional tonality and relied on no theoretical harmonic system, yet retained the supposition that harmony was still a viable musical parameter that could be stretched but not completely broken. The composer dispensed with all preconceived theories, making "his ear the sole judge of right and wrong in harmonic wisdom, whether or not the theorist were able to explain the resultant harmonies logically."[26] Modern music's second major stylistic innovation, in Copland's schema, was polytonality that did not bar triadic harmony.[27]

Thus, for Copland, modernism lay in both stylistic innovation and a shift in musical aesthetics. He linked modern music with both exploration of new styles and techniques *and* the desire to break from Romanticism and imitation of past conventions. So when at midcentury Copland offered a concise, summary definition of modern music, it represented how he conceived both ultramodern and modern music:

> Modern music in a word, is principally the expression in terms of an enriched musical language of a new spirit of objectivity, attuned to our own times. It is the music of the composer of today—in other words—our music.[28]

Music could sound conventional harmonically or melodically, but still be deemed modern if composers treated harmony and melody in ways that did not adhere strictly to previous styles and exhibited innovative traits in other areas.

Study with Rubin Goldmark and Beyond

Copland's ideas about modern and ultramodern music were formed during the years he completed secondary school and after graduating in 1921. Although he decided against attending college (a decision he later regretted), during these private studies in theory and composition with Goldmark from fall 1917 to spring 1921 Copland "essentially charted out his own three-year program roughly comparable to a conservatory education."[29] Published accounts of what Copland studied with Goldmark remained sketchy for years; Copland never provided details about these lessons. His most extensive writing about his former teacher is found in a tribute, but he reveals nothing about what he learned.

Archival sources document some of what Copland learned from Goldmark. The primary source materials dating from these years are a series of seventeen notebooks, each labeled "Music Composition Notebook," and a second set of seven Schirmer manuscript books spanning the years 1916 through 1921 in the Aaron Copland Collection at the Library of Congress. The first, "Music Composition Notebook 1: Exercises and Early AC Compositions, 1916–1917,"[30] contains exercises, sketches, and compositions, as do the remainder of these notebooks (except 6 and 14 through 16, which primarily contain sketches and complete compositions).

According to Copland's own account, Goldmark primarily provided him with thorough instruction in harmony, species counterpoint, eighteenth-century counterpoint, and classical forms, especially sonata form.[31] He started Copland on a systematic course of study, beginning with the basics—bass clef, scales, intervals, triads and their inversions, modulations, and harmonic exercises. Notebook 1 also has thematic ideas and melodies, some with Goldmark's blue-pencil corrections. Sketches for several short pieces are also found here: a Chopinesque "Nocturne" in G minor; the vocal line of the song, "My Heart is in the East"; the text for "Burial of Moses"; a second theme in G minor; and, a sketch for "Amer-tune." This notebook contains finished as well as uncompleted compositions: a "Theme and Variations in B minor" (dated November 23, 1917, four variations on a five-measure theme); "Romance-Barcarolle"; and *Valse Impromptu* (February 6, 1916, predating study with Goldmark). The title at the head of page 12v is "Selections from an Imaginary Oratorio," Copland's biblical oratorio. He worked as far as planning two movements. As seen in Notebook 2, marked "Scrap Book, Fairmont Hotel, Aug. 1916," Copland continued learning his minor scales and studying modulation (most of the remainder of Notebook 2 is filled with modulation exercises).[32]

These notebooks chart Copland's progress with Goldmark as both theory student and composer. Goldmark thoroughly trained him in sixteenth- and eighteenth-century counterpoint, and Copland produced didactic two- and three-part inventions, fugues, song forms, and a sonata. Notebook 3 (1918–19) contains counterpoint exercises: a "Theme (Experiment in Ground Motive)," a fugue, and double fugues. Notebook 4 is filled with fugues, showing Copland's progress from two-voice to three- and four-voice fugues. By September 19, 1919, Copland had mastered the rudiments of a fugue for three voices; by October, 28, 1919, he had completed a fugue for four voices. He also continued harmony exercises. The Schirmer manuscript books are undated, but like the notebooks, contain Goldmark's corrections. Schirmer Manuscript Book 1 contains notes on species counterpoint and parallel thirds and sixths; Schirmer Manuscript Book 2 contains more species counterpoint and free counterpoint. By this stage Copland was capable of writing canons and applying the techniques of diminution, augmentation, double counterpoint, contrary motion, and stretto. Goldmark continued drilling Copland in modulating through the circle of fifths and the use of various cadences (Notebook 12). These exercises are the equivalent of the first two years of conservatory studies in harmony and counterpoint.[33]

Goldmark further trained Copland through model composition. By the next year, as documented in Notebook 5, dated 1919–20, Copland had progressed to composing simple and rounded binary forms, all the while continuing his counterpoint studies. Goldmark also had Copland compose binary dances. He began to prepare Copland to write a piano sonata, beginning with the first movement, "Allegro." Goldmark further drilled Copland in the basics of harmony and counterpoint, with Notebook 8 (undated) containing exercises in harmony, figured bass, chorale harmonizations, and four-part writing. The Schirmer manuscript books more extensively document Copland's progress at this point. He made a diagram of what he called "2 part binary form," showing simple binary form as having two parts of sixteen measures and rounded binary as twenty-four measures. Rather than understanding rounded binary as a two-part form, Copland seems to have understood it as "3 part primary" form or A–B–A, a precursor to the ternary forms he later used for many pieces, A–B–A or A–B–A′ (see table 1.1). Copland continued writing more binary dances and a scherzo and trio for string quartet. Schirmer Manuscript Book 5 shows Copland mastering rondo form. He also began sonata form, understanding it as a three-part structure (see table 1.2). Next, Copland completed an extended first movement of a sonata, found in Schirmer Manuscript Book 7; he had also progressed to composing in four parts, as seen in a slow movement for string quartet (notated on a piano grand staff!). This notebook spans his final months with Goldmark and the beginning of his studies in France: page 16v is dated "Fountainebleau, JUNE 1921," clearly marking the end of his American studies.[34]

Goldmark taught from two harmony books, *Richter's Manual of*

TABLE 1.1 Copland's Diagram of Rounded Binary Form (3-part primary form in 24 measures)

Part 1	Part 2	Part 3
8 [Period w. phrase]	8 New	8 Repetition

Source: Schirmer Manuscript Book 3, n.d., Box 117C, Folder 4, ACC, p. 22v.

TABLE 1.2 Copland's Diagram of Sonata Form ("Notes On Sonata Form")

Part 1	Part 2	Part 3	Part 4?
Exposition 1. Theme in tonic 2. Repetition of theme (flowing) or Episode, leading to 3. Dominant of dominant, return establishment takes place 4. *Second or lyric theme in dominant* or relative major 5. Closing theme in key of second theme	Developments or free fantasia or Durchführung	Recapitulation of part 1 with harmonic modification	(Coda 2)

Source: Schirmer Manuscript Book 5, n.d., Box 117C, Folder 5, ACC, p. 25v.

Harmony and the Foote and Spaulding *Modern Harmony in Its Theory and Practice.* The latter, published in 1905, encompassed nineteenth-century chromatic harmony. It also included theoretical treatment of many harmonic advances associated with music from the turn of the twentieth century, such as the use of ninths, elevenths, and thirteenths, explaining their theoretical construction. Examples from the contemporary repertoire included excerpts from Debussy's *Pelléas et Mélisande* in a discussion of the thirteenth.[35] Copland's early notebooks contain evidence that Goldmark used these texts with him. Notebook 11, "Exercises in Harmony" (undated), contains a note, "see Richter Table." This notebook also contains notes on chromatic and extended harmonies. Copland continued studying free counterpoint and was learning the use of suspensions and anticipations.[36] These studies from 1917 to 1920 covered basic compositional styles and techniques of the Common Practice, while those from 1920 to 1921 covered chromatic and extended harmony. Thus, from Goldmark Copland received a thorough grounding in music from Bach to Debussy.

In Copland's view, Goldmark represented the outmoded American nationalist composer. The elder composer had written works based on Native and African-American themes, a superannuated musical nationalism.[37] Copland felt he was working in a vacuum. Although the new music of Europe was performed in the major American musical centers—New York, Boston, Chicago, and Rochester—Copland thought the United States then lacked a substantial modernist art music repertoire. He knew little of the American music that had preceded him and apparently was not influenced by the nationalist or Americanist styles of earlier composers, even Goldmark himself. "My own generation found little of interest in the work of their elders: MacDowell, Chadwick or Loeffler; and their influence on our music was nil. (We had only an inkling of the existence of the music of Charles Ives in the Twenties.)"[38] Goldmark was sympathetic to the idea of identity—national or ethnic—in musical composition, and many of his works bear Americanist titles: Pollack lists *Hiawatha Overture, Negro Rhapsody, The Call of the Plains,* and his best-known composition, *Requiem,* suggested by Lincoln's Gettysburg Address.[39] Goldmark studied at the Vienna Conservatory and had been a student of Dvořák at the National Conservatory. He followed Dvořák's lead in using Native American and African-American musical materials, rather than being motivated by a broader consciousness or deeper understanding of the musical traditions they represented. Goldmark did not influence Copland to write Americanist music, but rather instilled in him technical mastery as defined in the German Romantic tradition.

A musical conservative, Goldmark espoused conventional tonal music, forms, and genres, leading Copland to describe Goldmark's compositional style as "in the familiar idiom of his day."[40] An admirer of

German Romantic music and the more contemporary, Strauss, Ravel, and Debussy, Goldmark rejected the modernism of Schoenberg, Stravinsky, and Ives, warning Copland to avoid modern music lest he become "contaminated." Copland's style of his student days, by his own account, was beginning to show traces of the moderns. Goldmark had no interest in Copland's more modern pieces. Copland remarked, "I had a little trouble with him because I was beginning to write pieces that, from where he sat, seemed rather avant-garde and he couldn't apply any of his conventional harmonic ideas to them because they didn't have any conventional ideas in that sense."[41] Goldmark refused to critique these independently composed "radical" pieces, as he called them, admitting he did not understand the new language.[42] Nonetheless, Copland pursued the newer styles that Goldmark considered "modernistic experiments" or "avant garde."[43] So during the Goldmark years Copland produced two types of compositions, conventional model compositions submitted for lessons and modernist ones pursued independently.[44]

Several "modern" works from these years survive, mostly two-page songs and piano pieces.[45] Goldmark little influenced Copland's stylistic development in them. As Howard Pollack's recent overview of Copland's juvenilia shows, Copland had already begun developing his own style and compositional voice during high school. The music composition notebooks from Notebook 2 on are filled with sketches and completed compositions dating back to at least 1917. They contain sketches for art songs (Notebooks 2, 3, 6, 7), solo instrumental works (for cello, violin, piano, "B♭ instrument" and piano) (Notebooks 3, 6, 5, 13), and a trio (Notebook 7). They also contain several finished compositions, showing that Copland was quite prolific and ambitious at an early age. Obviously drawn to Chopin, the teenager made transcriptions of two etudes for cello and piano (Chopin, op. 10, no. 4 and op. 25, no. 7), though only the cello parts are found in Notebook 3 (transcribed June 27, 1919). Copland also made another arrangement for piano and cello, *Schumanniana,* a medley of *Papillons, Carnival,* and *Kreisleriana* themes, presumably for Copland and his friend Arne Vainio, who was both a cellist and clarinetist. It is probable that Copland arranged the Chopin etudes as duets for himself and Vainio.

These early works show the youth influenced by composers ranging from the Europeans, Debussy, Ravel, Scriabin, and Bloch, to Americans such as Carpenter and Griffes. His solo piano work, *Moment Musicale—a Tone Poem* (inspired by a poem by his new friend, Aaron Schaffer), shows the influence of Beethoven, Liszt, Tchaikovsky, and what Pollack describes as "Jewish-sounding meanderings" that illustrate Schaffer's text.[46] Stylistically, these early works show Copland beginning to move beyond functional tonality and triadic harmony and exploring seventh chords and chromatic harmony along with the tritone. Furthermore, these works are often tonally ambiguously, with unexpected harmonies, cadences, and frequent modulations.

Although struggling to find his own compositional voice, by fall 1917 (shortly after his studies with Goldmark began) Copland clearly showed signs of having assimilated techniques borrowed from Debussy and Liszt. His first accomplished works from this fall—three songs—are influenced by Debussy: "After Antwerp" (text by Emile Cammaerts), "Spurned Love" (text by Thomas Bailey Aldrich), and "Melancholy," subtitled "a Song a la Debussy" (text by Jeffrey Farnol). Copland progressed rapidly in his next art songs composed over the next three years: *Three Songs* (1918; text by Aaron Schaffer); "Simone" (1919; text by Remy de Gourmont); "Music I Heard" (1920; text by Conrad Aiken); "Old Poem" (1920; translated from the Chinese by Arthur Waley); "Pastorale" (1921; translated from Kafiri by Edward Powys Mathers); and "My Heart Is in the East" (text by Schaffer). His early instrumental works, *Waltz Caprice* for piano (1918) and *Poème* for cello and piano (1918), *Sonnets* I and II for piano (1919, 1920), and *Preludes* I and II for violin and piano (1919, 1921) show the influence of both Liszt and Debussy.[47]

Night

By the time Copland left for Paris, he had composed numerous pieces, varying from juvenilia to technically accomplished works.[48] One student work, the art song "Night," shows a teenaged Copland composing in an Impressionist style à la Debussy. Although Goldmark could inculcate in Copland his admiration for the German Romantics, he did indeed impart to his student solid grounding in harmony and counterpoint, as "Night" attests. Beginning it on July 1, 1918, in Marlboro, New York,[49] Copland finished it on December 16 back home in Brooklyn.

"Night" shows how far and how quickly Copland had progressed during less than a year's study with Goldmark. Only in the previous year had he reached the point where he could actually complete short works, rather than abandon them for lack of technique. Goldmark, versed in French Impressionism, had taught Copland the use of ninths, elevenths, and thirteenths (as per Spaulding's *Modern Harmony*). He had also drilled Copland in chromatic harmony. Both are evident in "Night," which begins on a $D^{\flat 9}$, and features the liberal use of ninths and parallel harmony. A letter from his friend Aaron Schaeffer, who wrote the poem Copland set, makes numerous references to traces of Debussy and Scriabin in the piece, such as the whole-tone scale.[50] Analysis of the short piece supports Schaeffer's observations and reveals the influence of Debussy. Copland introduces the whole-tone scale (which returns throughout the song) in the right-hand piano motive appearing at the outset and when the voice enters. With its dominant ninth harmony, whole-tone scales, and harmony built thereupon, "Night" is rather conventional and imitative of the French composer.[51] Yet Copland's own musical personality had begun to emerge, for this work displays more than extended harmonies and half-diminished sevenths used as harmonic color rather than functionally. By this time, Copland had finally learned to modulate and makes a bold shift from D♭ to A major, a whole tone away. Again, this suggests Debussy, for example, *Prélude à l'après-midi d'un faune,* with its exploration of melodic and harmonic whole-tone relationships.

Copland displays sensitivity to the text in supplying a burst of thirty-second-note pianistic figuration to paint the phrase "gentle murmur of the lake / is silvered by a fountain's play." Yet he is awkward and inexperienced when writing for voice. The principal vocal motive requires an upward leap of octave followed by a downward leap of a diminished fourth, chromaticism, and a descending augmented second at its close. Pollack interprets the prominent use of augmented seconds as suggesting a Jewish musical influence, but regardless, the vocal melody is rather difficult to sing. Nonetheless, the work compares favorably with the songs of Debussy and shows that the eighteen-year-old had made striking progress under Goldmark. Copland had developed a strong, French-influenced musical personality of his own. Unpublished for seventy years, "Night" never garnered public recognition for Copland.

Copland's "Ultramodern" Style: *Scherzo humoristique (The Cat and the Mouse)*

The piano works *Scherzo humoristique: Cat and Mouse*[52] and "Jazzy" from *Trois Equisses* (*Three Moods*) further exhibit Copland's exploration of an unconventional harmonic style as a teenager and during his twenties. With its extensive dissonance and atonality, *Scherzo humoristique* fits Copland's description of ultramodernism and can be taken as an example of his beginning exploration of the style in 1920. Composed during the final year of his study with Goldmark, the work undoubtedly reflects Copland's interest in the moderns about which he wrote so many of his articles and whose scores he studied on his own during high school. Like many of his early instrumental works, *Cat and Mouse* is based on a poem, Jean de la Fontaine's "Le Vieux Chat et la Jeune Souris" ("The Old Cat and the Young Mouse"). Full of symbolism, the poem is about the vain attempts of a young mouse in the grasp of an old cat to convince the feline to release him.[53] Whether interpreted as programmatic or impressionistic, *Scherzo humoristique,* nonetheless, is one of Copland's first "ultramodern" works, that is, one in which he explored new tonal procedures and new means of tonal organization. The piece uses nondiatonic scales, nonfunctional harmony, and new rhythmic techniques, and departs from classical forms. Bridging youthful study and early public success, it shows Copland's highly sophisticated and personal modernist style at the end of his studies with Goldmark and at the beginning of his professional career.[54]

Debussy's Influence: Pentatonicism and Whole Tones

The influence of Debussy is seen primarily in Copland's pentatonic and whole-tone scales, formal organization, and the means by which he establishes tonality. In *Scherzo humoristique,* Copland moved beyond the sonata form Goldmark required of all his students and used a tripartite form similar to Debussy's. The work divides into three major sections, A–B–A′, plus an Introduction and Coda (see table 1.3, cf. table 1.2).

Scale Systems

Copland's *Scherzo* exhibits pentatonicism and whole tones as alternate scale systems to escape the tyranny of diatonicism. In the Introduction, he immediately establishes the overriding architectonic principle of the work: the alternation of the minor pentatonic scale with the whole-tone collection. The work begins with an ascending pentatonic scale, the source of the melody (see example 1.1). The generative principles of the work all derive from the opening two measures. Pentatonic melodies and ostinati return throughout, first in mm. 21–30 in the left hand (see example 1.2) and later in mm. 38–39, both times starting on G♭. The left-hand ostinato of mm. 21–30 begins with a G♭-D♭ dyad in the bass for the first three measures of this passage before expanding to encompass the complete pentatonic scale in mm. 38–39. The pentatonic scale also occurs

TABLE 1.3 *Scherzo humoristique (The Cat and the Mouse),* Overall Form

	Section				
	Introduction	A	B	A′	Coda
Melody	Pentatonic/ whole-tone alternation	x–y–x–chromatic	x–pentatonic–y–diatonic–x	x–y–x–x–whole tone	Whole tone–simultaneity
Collection	4-24/5-35	4-24/5-35	5-35/7-35	4-24/8-28/ 5-35	4-24/5-35
Measures	1–4	5–20	21–39	40–72	73–end
Harmony		I-I	♭V-IV	V-I	I
Tonal center	D	D	C	D	D

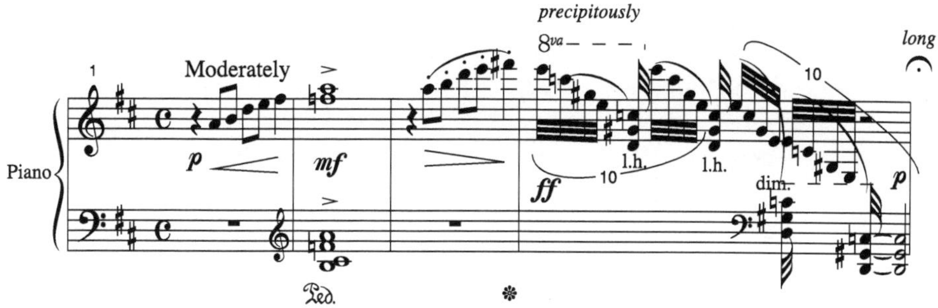

EXAMPLE 1.1 Copland, *Scherzo humoristique (The Cat and the Mouse)*, mm. 1–4

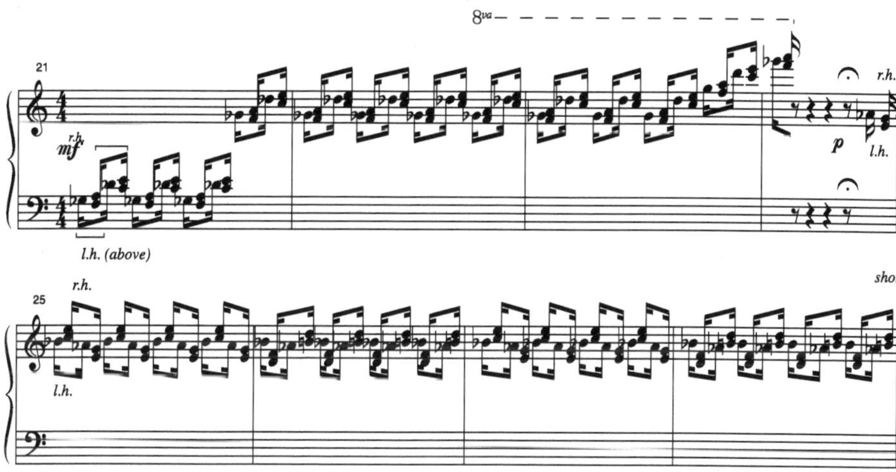

EXAMPLE 1.2 Copland, *Scherzo humoristique (The Cat and the Mouse)*, Pentatonic occurrences in section B, mm. 21–30

in mm. 25ff., on A♭, and is also found in m. 29, beginning on C♯, enharmonically D♭. Copland also uses the whole-tone scale, as discussed below.

Harmony

Copland does not just create melodies with the whole-tone and pentatonic scales; they are also the sources of his harmonies. Immediately following the introduction of the pentatonic scale in m. 1, the F whole-tone collection appears, and Copland uses it to generate a vertical sonority, a whole tone "chord" 4-24—or, if thought of diatonically, an augmented triad to which is added an augmented sixth (enharmonically, minor seventh; see example 1.1). In m. 4 Copland draws upon the other whole-tone collection, the one built on C-natural (6-35, t = 0). Unlike the second measure, where Copland uses tertiary harmonies, here he *seems* to create quartal harmonies: using D as the root, he "stacks" an augmented fourth above it, and a diminished fourth above that. However, his harmonies are in reality tertiary, for C—rather than D—is the root of the chord, with E occurring as a major third above. The D is introduced as a pedal tone. It is this sonority in m. 4, 4-24, t = 0, I = 0, or a whole-tone triad built upon C, that serves as the harmonic pedal in mm. 5–8. Whole-tone passages recur throughout the piece: mm. 14–18, 31–37, 40–48, 55–58, 70–72, and 73–79 (again alternating F and C whole-tone collections).

This organizational principle—the alternation of the pentatonic scale and the whole-tone collection—not only generates both melodies and harmony, but also guides the overall formal scheme (see table 1.4). Each of these primary divisions is further subdivided into sections that are predominantly pentatonic or whole tone. Copland strives for symmetry and balance, reversing the order in which the pentatonic and whole-tone collections follow each other from section to section. Although in the Introduction Copland begins with the pentatonic scale, he begins the first subsection of A with the C whole-tone collection (see table 1.5). This section closes with a collection that is a superset of the whole tone (6-35) and the pentatonic scale (5-35): the chromatic scale (12-1).

Octatonicism

Scherzo humoristique features Copland's first use of the octatonic scale in a finished composition. Section A′ begins like section A, with the whole-tone collection, 6-35 in mm. 59–62. He quickly introduces the octatonic collection (see table 1.6; cf. table 1.5). The outer X subsections frame a single internal octatonic y subsection. Copland closes A′ with the

TABLE 1.4 *Scherzo humoristique,* Introduction

Melody	Pentatonic	Whole tone	Pentatonic	Whole tone
Collection	5-35	4-24	5-35	4-24
Measure	1	2	3	4
Tonal center	ambiguous	ambiguous	ambiguous	ambiguous

TABLE 1.5 *Scherzo humoristique,* Section A

	Subsection			
	x	y	x	
Melody	C whole tone	Pentatonic	C whole tone	Chromatic scale
Collection	4-24/6-35	5-35	4-24/6-35	
Measures	5–8	9–14	15–18	19–20
Harmony	I, D pedal	I, D pedal	I, D pedal	I, D pedal
Tonal center	D	D	D	D

TABLE 1.6 *Scherzo humoristique,* Section A′

	Subsection				
	x	y	x	x	
Melody	F whole tone	1212 octatonic	F whole tone chromatic	A♭ pentatonic	C whole tone
Collection	4-24	8-28	4-24	5-35	4-24
Measures	55–58	59–62	63–67	68–69	70–72
Harmony	V	IV-V♯	V♯	♭V	V-I
Tonal center	D	D	D	D	D

return of the pentatonic and the C whole-tone collections. Copland's interest in scale types extends to section B, where he briefly juxtaposes pentatonicism with diatonicism (see table 1.7). Each scale type is associated with characteristic melodic and thematic motives. There are two basic melodic figurations, X and Y, each tonally, rhythmically, and texturally distinct. The melodic ideas help to delimit both the form and the tonal system undergirding a particular section. The X material first occurs in mm. 5–8; characterized by a sixteenth-note rhythm that traverses three octaves, it recurs throughout the piece, appearing in either a pentatonic configuration (as it does at mm. 21–30, see example 1.2; mm. 51–54; mm. 68–69), or an F whole-tone configuration (mm. 55–58; see example 1.1). Rhythmically static rather than propulsive, the Y material is characterized by sustained pentatonic sonorities.

Copland eschews functional tonality, establishing nonfunctional tonal centers by other means. In sections A and A′, he establishes D as the tonal center, first by using the whole-tone and pentatonic scales, whose properties defeat the pitch centrism of diatonicism. The pentatonic scale lacks the half-step between scale degrees 3 and 4 and the pitch-defining centrism of the leading tone of the major scale; Copland's pentatonic is comprised of alternating whole steps and minor thirds. Similarly, the whole-tone scale, comprised solely of successive whole steps, also lacks a leading tone. By using the pentatonic and the whole-tone scales, Copland

TABLE 1.7 *Scherzo humoristique,* Section B

	Subsection				
Melody	x	Pentatonic scale	y	Diatonic	x
Collection	5-35	5-35	4-24	7-35	5-35
Measures	21–37	38–39	40–44	45–50	51–54
Harmony	♭V	♭V	I-IV$^6_4$ alternation C-A dyad	I D major harmonic pedal	VI B major harmonic pedal
Tonal center	C	C	C	D	D

can escape the gravitational pull of diatonicism and avoid functional tonality.

Copland fully exploits the atonal implications involved in using the whole-tone scale by basing his harmonies upon it, particularly the 4-24. He also generates harmonies from the pentatonic scale, as he does in subsection Y (see example 1.1, mm. 9–12). The final two measures of the piece confirm that the whole-tone collection and the pentatonic collection are the sources of his harmonies. In m. 81 the left hand plays the pentatonic scale solely on the black keys; the right hand plays a portion of the diatonic scale in parallel thirds. In the final two measures of the piece, Copland combines the pentatonic dyad comprised of C♯ and D♯ with the pair of thirds F-A and G-B to complete the F whole-tone collection. Thus, the pentatonic and whole tone are sounded simultaneously, yet distinctly, following a passage where diatonicism and pentatonicism are sounded together.

Throughout *Cat and Mouse,* Copland avoids the V–I progression by establishing tonal centers by other means, first through the use of pedals, which establish tonal poles to further subvert functional tonality. He establishes D and C as tonal centers in A and B, respectively. The overriding tonal center of section A is D, which is confirmed in m. 5, where D is introduced as a rhythmic pedal. Copland repeats this pitch in mm. 5–6 in the left hand as he introduces whole-tone sonorities built on C. A similar figure reappears in mm. 40–48. The primacy of D as tonal center is later asserted in mm. 9–12 and returns in mm. 47–51 and the Coda (mm. 73–79). The Coda returns to the pedal, now D^1, the lowest note in the piece, occurring in the lowest octave of the piano. Above this, Copland reintroduces whole-tone harmonies. In section B (beginning m. 21), Copland establishes C as the tonal center, but more subtlely. Rather than use a single unambiguous pedal point, section B uses ostinati that oscillate between two pitches or two pairs of pitches, thereby shifting from one tonal center to another. This section also contains discernible harmonic progressions, in contrast to the outer sections. Copland initiates this section with the dyad G♭-D♭, which suggests ♭V of C; this changes in mm. 22–25 to B♭-A♭. Simultaneous with the left-hand dyad, pairs of thirds alternate in the right hand, F-A and C-E, and later C-E and E-G, suggesting an F-major seventh chord, or IV^7 of C major. Over the span of mm. 29–31, Copland even alludes to the dominant of C major (see example 1.2). The diatonic thirds above the pentatonic scale of the left hand fill in the perfect fifth, G and C, thereby setting up these two pitches as two diatonic poles, the dominant and the tonic, the pillars of the tonal system. Yet functional tonality is absent. Neither a functional tonic nor dominant appears in this work—just the piling up of dyads ripe with tonal implications, including bitonality. While C major is the overarching tonal focal point, the G♭-D♭ ostinato suggests G♭ as a tonal center at the micro level, with G♭ as the tonic and D♭ as the dominant. The ostinato involving the pairs of thirds F-A and C-E alludes to F major (which itself lies a fourth above C major).

The Provenance of Copland's Tonal Experiments

One may wonder about the precocity of a nineteen-year-old composer who developed not only a personal style before reaching the age of majority, but also a means of controlling tonal flow and organization that has at its basis extremely sophisticated theoretical thinking. Is it possible that Copland, like Athena, sprang from the head of a compositional Zeus? No, rather, at this stage in his development, Copland aspired to be the spitting image of his hero, Stravinsky. We know that Copland had enthusiastically and independently studied the music of a French Impressionist and the Russian "modernist" Scriabin. Copland clearly knew *of* Stravinsky's music: he regularly read music critic Paul Rosenfeld's articles in *The Dial.* Rosenfeld wrote of the new European composers and readily championed their music, including Stravinsky. As Carol Oja has shown, Stravinsky enjoyed popularity in the United States during this time.[55] We can now say with certainty that Copland knew the music of Stravinsky. He had ample opportunity to hear the elder composer's music while he was in high school. Regularly commuting into Manhattan for his Saturday morning lessons with Goldmark, the teenager also took a subscription to the Metropolitan Opera. Pollack has documented that Copland attended performances by the Ballets Russes, which presented both *Firebird* and *Petrushka* in New York in January 1916 under the auspices of the Metropolitan Opera. Copland would have had a second opportunity to see the ballet in 1919, when the Metropolitan Opera again presented it. Furthermore, one of Copland's unfinished efforts, "Sketch for Song 'Music I Heard with You,'" which displays a brief octatonic scale in the right hand of the piano accompaniment, shows that Copland had begun experimenting with octatonicism as early as 1919.[56] By the time he composed *Cat and Mouse,* Stravinsky had replaced Debussy and Scriabin as the composer after whose music Copland modeled his own.

Noting the extensive and deep influence French music had on Copland's contemporary Virgil Thomson (whose ideas were shaped by exposure to the music of composers such as D'Indy, Debussy, and Satie), Carol Oja challenges the original conventional wisdom that the first generation of American twentieth-century composers were *tabulae rasae* when they went to Paris, to be shaped almost exclusively by their experiences there. "Often writers have assumed that American composers of Thomson's generation presented Paris with a clean slate, that there they gained sophistication and encountered contemporary musical developments."[57]

When he went to Paris, Copland, too—like Thomson—had ideas of his own. However, rather than D'Indy and Satie, Copland, in contrast to Thomson, was influenced by the Russian-in-Paris Stravinsky.

Previous Copland scholars have generally accepted that Copland was influenced by Stravinsky, exposed to his music by Nadia Boulanger. In a 1950 article David Matthews noted that Stravinsky's *Rite of Spring* influenced Copland's *Dance Symphony,* and the elder's neoclassical Octet influenced the younger's large orchestral works and musical development.[58] In his germinal article "Stravinsky and the Younger American Composers," Arthur Berger argues from his personal experience as a composer that Stravinsky exerted a strong influence on American composers of the second and third quarter of the twentieth century and that the influence on Copland was particularly strong, witness Copland's sobriquet "the Brooklyn Stravinsky." Berger writes, "It was Nadia Boulanger, no doubt, who was a key figure in solidifying the kinship between Copland and Stravinsky, and my account of the parentage of our school would be very incomplete, indeed, if she were not mentioned."[59] But Copland was first influenced by Stravinsky independently of Boulanger. In this work he created while still studying with Goldmark, Copland borrows directly from the second tableau of Igor Stravinsky's ballet *Petrushka* in four specific and telling ways.

Octatonicism

Richard Taruskin, in *Stravinsky and the Russian Traditions: A Biography of the Works through "Mavra"*[60] and several recent articles on Stravinsky's Russian music, has identified a Russian modernist style. It is characterized by a harmonic language developed by Mussorgsky, Rimsky-Korsakov, and his students (Stravinsky among them), whom Taruskin refers to collectively as the St. Petersburg school of composers—those associated with the conservatory. Although *Scherzo humoristique*'s harmonic foundation rests on the pervasive use of the whole-tone scale and pentatonicism to generate both melodic and harmonic formulations, octatonicism is present. As shown in table 1.6, it is found in the single internal octatonic Y subsection of section A′. However, octatonicism alone is not conclusive proof of a connection between Stravinsky and Copland in this work.

Black Key/White Key Division

In numerous places in *Scherzo humoristique,* as we saw, Copland assigns the left hand and right hand specific duties. Evidence suggests that the model for this piece was the second tableau of Stravinsky's *Petrushka.* With respect to figuration and pianistic idiom, *Scherzo humoristique* reflects the black-key/white-key division found in the second or *Konzertstuck* tableau. At [50] and at [51], the famous "Petrushka chord" occurs. Stravinsky assigns the left hand and right hand of the solo piano specific duties: the left hand plays the black keys and the right hand the white keys. The effect is more than visual, it is also aural: playing on the black keys (left hand) forms pentatonic scales, and playing on the white keys (right hand) forms diatonic scales. In numerous passages in *Cat and Mouse,* Copland's assignments are identical: the left hand plays on the black keys and the right hand on the white keys in the passages at mm. 21–31 and mm. 81–end.

Tritone

Copland's interest in octatonicism extends beyond melodic application. In *Cat and Mouse* he also explores the tritonic properties of octatonicism. The black-key/white-key division has harmonic implications identical to those in Stravinsky's *Petrushka.* It stresses the tritone as more than a dissonant sonority: the tritone serves a harmonic and architectonic purpose. In his article "*Chez Pétrouchka:* Harmony and Tonality *chez* Stravinsky," Taruskin calls the tritone "octave bisecting"[61] because it divides the whole-tone scale (and the diatonic scale). The black-key/white-key division in *Petrushka* reflects the importance of the tritone as the midpoint dividing the octatonic scale, a means by which the octatonic scale may be organized into tetrachords. This "common tritone" also has bitonal implications in *Petrushka.* The black-key/white-key bifurcation throughout the second tableau, for example, at [50], and at [51], the "Petrushka chord," anchors around the tritone C-F♯ (enharmonically G♭). Copland borrows this common tritone and uses it in a similar fashion. This "octave bisection," or the use of tritonic organization, occurs in *Cat and Mouse* in section B, where tritones are formed by the G♭ of the dyad and the C of the pair of thirds (reinforced by the key change to C major!) in m. 21; B♭-E in m. 25 and m. 27; and D-A♭ in m. 26 and m. 28.

Tonal Coherence

Copland also borrowed from Stravinsky harmonic progressions that use tonal relationships other than tonic-dominant or tonic-subdominant. In "*Chez Pétrouchka,*" Taruskin discusses tonal coherence in the second tableau, pointing out the importance of the ii–I and VII–I harmonic progressions as Stravinsky's Russian modernist harmonic alternatives to the

V–I progression of the conventional tonal system first identified by Rameau. True, similar scales (whole tone and pentatonic) are also found in the works of French impressionist composers, whose works Copland also studied. But the likelihood of *Petrushka* being the model for Copland's *Scherzo humoristique* increases when one takes into consideration the tonal coherence (Taruskin's term) of both works. The tonal organization of Copland's piece closely resembles that of this ballet's second tableau. First, both works have D and C as tonal centers. Stravinsky's *Petrushka* moves from C to D, and eventually E and F♯. Copland's work reverses the polarity, moving from D to C and back to D (C being the tonal center of section B, with a C triad in the right hand and use of the C whole-tone collection). In section B, while the left hand plays G♭-D♭ or B♭-A♭, the right hand is anchored about the C-E pair. Furthermore, the whole-tone sonorities that close the first subsection of B are built on C. Taruskin has identified the vii^7–I progression, along with ii–I, as an important cadential progression in *Petrushka.*[62] Copland's *Scherzo* also features the VII–I progression. Although the Introduction is tonally ambiguous, D is established as the tonal center of both sections A and A′. Section B is cast in C. The overall tonal flow (again Taruskin's term) is D–C–D, or I–VII–I, a mirror or inverse of the ii–I Petrushka progression. The simultaneous use of the whole-tone and pentatonic scales, the juxtaposition of octatonicism with diatonicism, the prominence of the tritone, the black-key, white-key bifurcated roles assigned to the left and right hands, and the use of VII–I as a modification of the vii^7–I to provide tonal coherence lend overwhelming support to the thesis that Stravinsky's *Petrushka* served as a direct model for Copland's *Scherzo humoristique (The Cat and the Mouse).*

Assimilating Stravinsky

Scherzo humoristique shows the extensive early influence of Igor Stravinsky on the young Copland. One of the works Goldmark would not critique, *Cat and Mouse* is representative of both Copland's individual musical voice and his relatively mature style. It shows complete control over form and over what were astonishingly new techniques for American composers in 1921—certainly for someone just out of his teens! It shows Copland at the age of twenty composing a work with clear tonal centers yet free of functional tonality. He fully realizes rhythmic, programmatic (that of a mouse being chased by a menacing cat across the piano keyboard, in the manner of Zez Confrey and his popular song "Kitten on the Keys"), harmonic, and formal ideas.[63] The work shows Copland as autodidact: he has clearly advanced beyond the teachings of Goldmark and his requisite sonata form. This dissonant, whole-tone/pentatonic alternation represents Copland's ultramodern style from the period he finished his studies with Goldmark, antedating his study in Paris. Thus, not only is *Scherzo humoristique* a work from Copland's first maturity, it also represents one of his earliest encounters with ultramodern music as he later identified it in his article of the mid-1920s, associated with the music of Stravinsky and Schoenberg.

We know that Copland had enthusiastically and independently studied the music of Debussy and Scriabin. We know that Copland knew *of* the music of Stravinsky from reading Rosenfeld's *Dial* articles. We know from Oja's research that Stravinsky had won over New York and American audiences by 1920, and that *Petrushka* proved to be popular in New York. Pollack has shown that Copland attended performances of Stravinsky during those years he studied with Goldmark, thereby encountering his music directly in New York before departing for Paris. Stravinsky replaced Debussy and Scriabin as the composer after whose music he modeled his own. Analysis of *Scherzo humoristique (The Cat and the Mouse)* illuminates what Copland considered ultramodernism and reveals the techniques he explored during his study with Goldmark just prior to his trip to Paris. Throughout this work, Copland explores the fundamental nature of the tonal system and of diatonicism. The young composer used the whole-tone and octatonic scales not only to create melodies but also to fashion nonfunctional, nondiatonic ambiguous harmonies. Copland combined these scale systems and nontertian harmonies with other techniques such as the use of tonal poles, pedals, and ostinati to establish tonal centers. Copland also uses the tritone as dominant, and uses subdominant substitution. All these techniques allow Copland to establish a tonal center without resorting to the conventional means of diatonicism or functional harmony.

It is true that in his *Scherzo* Copland uses techniques derived from Debussy, particularly the suggestive, impressionistic title and the melodic and harmonic interaction of pentatonic–whole-tone formations. However, evidence shows that *Petrushka* must have been the model for the *Scherzo*. The tonal organization of Copland's piece closely resembles that of *Petrushka*'s second tableau. Copland's *Scherzo* clearly shows the black-key/white-key division, with dedicated roles assigned to the left and right hands. As did his model Stravinsky, Copland juxtaposes octatonicism with diatonicism, and uses tonal pedals, prominent tritone, tritonic octave bisection, and nonfunctional harmonic progressions that provide the tonal coherence that models the Russian modernist Stravinsky's harmonic alternative to the V–I progression, either ii–I or VII–I. All these allow Copland to construct a piece that is highly dissonant, atonal, and based on a system of tonal organization other than diatonicism. It is within these parameters, alternative harmonic progressions and innovative means by which to establish tonal centers—

the use of pedals, avoidance of leading tones—that one can see the influence of Stravinsky.

Clearly, the similarities between *Scherzo humoristique* and the second tableau of *Petrushka* are too striking to be ignored. But the implications extend beyond this single piece. Copland composed this work while he was studying with Goldmark and took it with him to Paris. The harmonic and tonal organization of this work suggests that by 1921, when Copland departed New York, he had already come under the influence of Stravinsky in his independent search for a new system of tonal and harmonic organization, and that the discovery of Stravinsky and his influence upon Copland's style began prior to the American's study with Nadia Boulanger.

CHAPTER TWO

Boulanger and Compositional Maturity

> While walking about the streets of Paris on that first day, I noticed on the billboards that there was to be a premiere performance of a new ballet by Darius Milhaud, *Les Mariés de la tour Eiffel,* performed by the Ballet Suédois at the Théâtre des Champs Elysées the night of 19 June. Of course, I decided to go. It was a show put on by Cocteau and a group of composers called *Les Six*. . . . The audience was shocked by the modernity of the music and the fanciful nature of the production; they whistled and hooted each time the curtain descended. I recall seeing Milhaud take a bow from the stage to mixed applause and hisses. It was the perfect way to spend one of my first nights in Paris—to get right into the action, where controversial music and dance were happening.
>
> —COPLAND

Copland initially planned to work in musical theater after high school and continue his piano and composition studies. After graduating he played in dance bands in the Catskills and Brooklyn. His friend Aaron Schaffer (then a twenty-two-year-old graduate student in literature on the Johns Hopkins University faculty), whom he met the summer of 1916 at the Fairmont Hotel in Tannersville, New York, advised him against going into popular music, believing it would not help him build a career in art music but would only be a dead-end grind. Urging him not to compromise his goals, Schaffer encouraged him to pursue his "high ideals and great ambitions" and "to be firm in your resolution to enter one of the most glorious professions in the gift of God and not to be deterred by the carping of small-minded people." Copland felt he had learned all that he could from Goldmark and was aware that if he wanted to pursue a career in art music, he would have to go to Europe for further study.

> It was a foregone conclusion around 1920 that anyone who had serious pretensions as a composer would have to go abroad to finish his studies. Before the war it was taken for granted that "abroad" for

> composers meant Germany. But I belonged to the postwar generation, and so for me "abroad" inevitably meant Paris.[1]

Both Goldmark and Adler had studied in Germany.[2] Goldmark's music reflected his training; he composed in essentially Romantic style. Copland belonged to the next generation, those born near the turn of the twentieth century and reaching maturity during the twenties and drawn not to Vienna or Berlin but Paris. For Copland, "Paris was an international proving ground for all the newest tendencies in music."

Schaffer had spent a postdoctoral year in Paris and while there had corresponded with his young composer friend. Schaffer promised to "let you know about the big concerts which take place here, and imagine, when I attend any of them, that you are sitting beside me." In letters written August 1919 through February 1920 Schaffer chronicled Paris's musical life, sending programs and detailed descriptions of the concerts he attended. He wrote Copland in late November 1919, "And now for music in Paris. I know you would enjoy this city if you were here; the concerts are simply countless and of every conceivable character." These included attending a performance of the opera *Salomé* by Marriotte and as well as the Concerts Touche, where he heard works by Debussy, d'Indy, and Fauré. Early in 1920 he also attended the Ballets Russes' performance of Stravinksy's *Petrushka.* Schaffer also heard works by Rimsky-Korsakov, Moussorgsky, and Scriabin. He purchased scores to send his friend back in Brooklyn, including Debussy's *12 Preludes* and *Pelléas et Mélisande,* works by Scriabin, and whatever else Copland requested.[3] Copland's own interest in new music (no doubt further piqued by Schaffer's reports of Parisian musical life) drew him, not to study with a particular teacher, but to be in the midst of the latest musical trends. Copland later revealed why he had decided to go to Paris: "And also very much because of Debussy and Ravel and also the fact that we knew that Stravinsky was in Paris. Debussy and Ravel were very fresh and different in the early 20s, as they were, and so you just wanted to go where the action was."[4] Having come across an announcement in a music journal proposing the establishment of a music school for Americans at Fontainebleau commencing the summer of 1921, Copland wrote Schaffer early in 1920 about the possibility of Copland remaining in Paris after the summer session had ended and finding work as a musician. Bolstered by Schaffer's support of his ambitions and excited about the music coming from Paris, Copland submitted his Fontainebleau application, hoping to find a way to remain in France past the summer (by the fall of 1920 Schaffer had returned to the United States and was then on the faculty of the University of Texas).

In summer 1921 Copland left New York for Paris to study at Fontainebleau, hoping to find a composition teacher with whom he could continue his studies and remain in Paris at the close of the summer.[5] There, in the City of Light, he encountered the teacher who would be most influential on his development as a modernist. Thus, the second stage of Copland's modern style gradually evolved under the musical midwifery of Nadia Boulanger.[6] He became her student and mentee, remaining with her until 1924. Exactly what Copland learned from Boulanger and experienced in Paris is not fully understood—not only stylistically, but aesthetically, intellectually, and culturally.[7] As has already been shown above, Copland did not arrive in Paris a tabula rasa, completely without his own aesthetic and stylistic ideas and emergent personal style. Nonetheless in Paris an important transformation took place. Copland advanced from being a student composer who intuited the harmonic language of Stravinsky to become a mature one who embraced the new aesthetic of a young generation of French composers, his European contemporaries known as Les Six.

An American Composer in Paris

Copland was among the first class of students at the American Conservatory at Fontainebleau, as it was originally known. Intended for the "élite of American students only" or those whose talent and advanced training showed their promise, the school provided students with training that was essentially French. This "new American-French School of Music in Fontainebleau," as Mabel C. Tuttle referred to it, was a summer school whose "course will be similar to that of the famous Paris Conservatoire and will be directed by many of the same teachers."[8]

That first summer at Fontainebleau, Copland did not begin study with Boulanger. When he first arrived in June, he initially studied piano with Ricardo Viñes (from summer 1921 to spring 1922) and composition with Paul Vidal (who often sent his assistant, André Bloch, to teach his class). Vidal, the head composition teacher at the Paris Conservatory, was conservative like Goldmark and had little sympathy for contemporary music. Copland even described him as a "French Goldmark."[9] Initially Copland was not interested in studying harmony with Boulanger because he had already studied harmony in New York with Goldmark, but during that summer the reputation of the brilliant young harmony teacher spread. Copland was persuaded to visit one of her classes by a fellow student, harpist Djina Ostrowska. After just one visit Copland was so impressed by the enthusiasm and clarity of her teaching and vibrancy of her personality that he regularly began to attend her harmony and analysis classes. The following fall, on October 26, he showed Boulanger some of his scores and performed "Jazzy" from *Trois Equisses.* She accepted him immediately for private composition studies. Copland remained in Paris to study with her until 1924.[10]

Study with Nadia Boulanger

Copland was often elliptical in describing exactly what he learned from Boulanger. He believed she had two unique qualities: her love of music and her ability to inspire confidence in her students.[11] She also had an encyclopedic knowledge of music history. Under Boulanger's tutelage he progressed from writing two-page pieces to writing large-scale works. Unfortunately, Boulanger had effectively ceased composing by the time her American students arrived at Fontainebleau, and she was then known primarily as a pedagogue, organist, and conductor. There exists little of her oeuvre to compare with the works of her students. Copland's recollections, and those of other Boulanger students, have to be carefully scrutinized to reconstruct what Copland learned from her.

Boulanger sought first and foremost to develop technique. Copland, in his autobiography, remarked upon her emphasis on solid technique, ear training, mastery of all styles of music and knowledge of music from all periods, and on counterpoint, score reading, and orchestration.[12] He often referred to her extensive knowledge of music history, technical mastery, ability to facilitate the process of composition for a student, and critical acumen as part of her skills in developing a student's compositional talent.[13] A study by Caroline Potter, based on archival materials, provides insight into Boulanger's pedagogy. She was quite systematic, her pedagogy varying little over more than seventy years. She stressed the study of works by past masters, placing the "masterpiece" on a pedestal. Yet she refrained from imposing her own or any singular style on her students (though she disdained Schoenberg's serial method). She transmitted to her students much of the training she herself had received from the Paris Conservatory.[14] Harmony, counterpoint, and ear-training drills and exercises were central to her pedagogical method. According to Pollack, "Boulanger's prescribed regimen" entailed "study of choral works from the Renaissance through the nineteenth-century; requiring students to compose a passacaglia for piano and eventually a complete ballet; orchestration assignments ranging from arrangements of the works of other composers to composing small works for a specific combination of instruments."[15] According to Teresa Walters, Boulanger recommended study of four major treatises: Andre Gedalge, (1856–1926), *Traîté de Fugue;* Vincent d'Indy (1851–1931), *Traîté de Composition;* Maurice Emmanuel (1863–1939), *L'histoire de la Lange Musicale;* and Marcel Dupré (1886–1971), *Traîté d'improvisation.* Well-read in twentieth-century music treatises, Boulanger also used Alfredo Casella (1883–1947), *Histoire de l'harmonie;* and Charles Koechlin's *Encyclopédie de la Musique.*[16] These all served to develop both excellent musicianship and technique.

Copland specifically described two ways Boulanger instructed him.

The single idea that most represented Boulanger's teachings, concepts, and aesthetic was that of *la grande ligne:*

> At the period when I was her pupil, she had but one all-embracing principle, namely, the desirability of aiming first and foremost at the creation of what she called "la grande ligne"—the long line in music. Much was included in that phrase: the sense of forward motion, of flow and continuity in the musical discourse; the feeling for inevitability, for the creating of an entire piece that could be thought of as a functioning entity. These generalizations were given practical application: her eye, for instance, was always trained upon the movement of the bass line as controlling agent for the skeletal frame of the harmony's progressive action. Her sense of contrast was acute; she was quick to detect *longeurs* and any lack of balance. Her teaching, I suppose, was French in that she always stressed clarity of conception and elegance in proportion.[17]

Copland's remarks and definitions are corroborated by both former students and scholars.[18] Alan Howard Levy describes her *grande ligne* as a horizontal approach to music that emphasizes melody and rhythm across the bar line; the vertical elements of harmony and instrumentation are de-emphasized.[19] Thus, Boulanger's concept of *la grande ligne* was essentially that of forward linear progression and formal clarity.

Boulanger's concept of *la grande ligne* was also, however, of vital importance in her understanding of the interrelationship of musical elements and form.[20] More than just a drill master and gifted pedagogue, Boulanger was a theorist, aesthetician, and critic, writing and speaking about music outside her classrooms and private lessons throughout her career.[21] She herself explained *la grande ligne* in November 1919 in *Le Monde Musical.*

> The work, short or long, unfolds itself between two determined points; the interpreter must choose the general curve by analysis and intuition, and be aware of these two fixed points. Even while calculating, he must not forget that to show the partial images of a whole does not permit the concept of the whole, while the poor yet faithful reproduction of a work of art makes us better understand than the original exposed in pieces.[22]

Sixteen years later, in a July 1936 *Le Monde Musical* article, Boulanger wrote:

> That which generally is lacking in performance, is the establishment of the *grandes lignes* and meanwhile, that is the essential thing, it is this which ought to be the most perfect. Therefore, find the long lines within the architecture; give them all their value.[23] . . . The essential

> consideration with regard to line is to proceed by the extended structures, especially not to proceed by little phrases. It is necessary to achieve understanding, to feel the music internally.[24]

This definition and conception of *la grande ligne* remained consistent through the end of Boulanger's career. Her explanation of this concept is consistent with how Copland (and later scholars) understood the term.

Two Pieces for String Quartet, "Rondino"

Boulanger instilled in her students a sense of the importance of clarity of form and the interrelationship of form with rhythm, harmony, and melody. She urged the performer—the interpreter—to keep in mind how the smaller divisions and subdivisions fit together in the overall formal design. David Ottenberg devises his own description of what he terms a "Boulanger-influenced composition." Resorting to the words of her students, Copland and Virgil Thomson, Ottenberg enumerates:

> 1) These compositions would be, to quote Copland, "in the idiom of the day," i.e. highly contrapuntal, rhythmically vital, and harmonically bold;
> 2) they would be tonally based, regardless of the colorfulness of the harmonies employed, and notwithstanding the inclusion of polytonal elements;
> 3) . . . an uncomplicated texture, a characteristic for which the French have always been noted, would be the norm;
> 4) . . . the typical works—if one may use the word in light of Boulanger's "virtually infinite tolerance of the variety of artistic expression"[25]—might be comprised of an eclectic mix of Gallic, folk, archaic, popular, and other materials;
> 5) . . . a Boulanger-influenced composition would exhibit the objective, problem-solving approach and decidedly unsentimental, and anti-Teutonic bias of its creator;
> 6) . . . one would expect a well-structured, solidly-crafted creation—one which exhibits careful attention to detail, and conformity to the principles of *la grande ligne.*[26]

These characteristics are all evident in Copland's works during and following his study with Boulanger.

Copland composed prolifically under Boulanger's tutelege. His first work composed completely in Paris was *Sonata Movement on a Theme by Paul Vidal* for string quartet, recently discovered by Vivian Perlis in the Fontainebleau library. He also set two French texts by Victor Hugo and Fernand Gregh, "Une Chanson" and "Reconnaissance," respectively, both songs influenced by Debussy. Copland had gained little in technique from Vidal. Upon studying with Boulanger, he undertook her regimen, composing the requisite contrapuntal vocal works, *Four Motets* (fall 1921) and the de rigeur *Passacaglia* for piano (winter 1922), which demonstrate his mastery of counterpoint.[27] Another short work for string quartet, *Movement,* also dates from his Boulanger years.

Representative of the stylistic and aesthetic principles Copland received from Boulanger is "Rondino," the second movement of *Two Pieces for String Quartet.* It was composed near the end of his study with Boulanger in 1923; Copland added the first movement five years later in 1928 to form *Two Pieces for String Quartet.* Copland also completed *Movement,* which dates from about 1923 and was possibly originally intended as part of a larger string quartet that included "Rondino." In his discussion of "Rondino," Pollack considers rhythm its "principle novelty," particularly syncopation, that is, groupings of three and five eighth notes (which are subdivided into patterns of three and two).[28] Focusing on rhythm, however, overlooks "Rondino's" chief technical traits and leads one to miss exactly how far Copland advanced under his new teacher. Boulanger taught using compositions by past and recent masters as models. She especially held her own teacher, Gabriel Fauré (1845–1924), in high esteem. Copland used him as a model for the "Rondino," which indeed began as an "Hommage à Fauré." This movement displays stylistic traits and compositional techniques that suggest how Boulanger influenced Copland during his first two years of study with her. It is academic as well as "ultramodern," displaying both Boulanger's classicism and Milhaud-Stravinsky neoclassicism. Furthermore, Copland drew upon the trademark styles of two composers: the classicism and modality of Fauré and the ostinato technique of Stravinsky. The "Rondino" shows how Copland combined these disparate elements in forging his personal style.

"Rondino" is Copland's most academic work, as it looks back several centuries, first to the sixteenth century: Copland adapts what is known as a *soggetto cavato dalle vocali.* This technique dates back to the Renaissance and to Josquin, who first used it in *Missa Dux Hercules Ferrarie.*[29] The theme of the "Rondino" spells its honoree's name, "Gabriel Fauré," in solfège syllables, albeit with chromatic alterations (see table 2.1).[30] From this Copland derives both the tonal center and the scale types that provide the melodic and harmonic ideas for the piece. The first letter of Fauré's Christian name is taken as the tonal center, G minor.

TABLE 2.1 *Two Pieces for String Quartet,* "Rondino," Soggetto cavato, Fauré

G	A	B	R	I	E	L	F	A	U	R	É
sol	la	si	re	si	mi	sol	fa	la	sol	re	mi

Copland chooses minor because fa, pitch name F, is used to begin Fauré's last name, rather than fi, or F♯, which would create a G major scale. The pitch F♯ is used, however, as a leading tone to G, resulting in harmonic minor. To this he adds the tritone D♭ and generates the scale from which he creates the movement's primary theme: G–A–B♭–C–D♭–B♭–E♭–F♯–G (see example 2.1). From this theme, which functions as a source set, Copland derives diatonic, modal, and octatonic scales to be used as source material (see table 2.2). Copland used the 2121 ordering of the octatonic scale: G–A–B♭–C–D♭–E♭–E–F♯–G (he also experimented with octatonicism in *Movement* for string quartet). From this collection, he derives two transposed modes with chromatic alteration.

EXAMPLE 2.1 Copland, *Two Pieces for String Quartet,* II. Rondino, Canon Subject (T[1])

TABLE 2.2 *Two Pieces for String Quartet,* "Rondino," Scale Types Derived from Subject

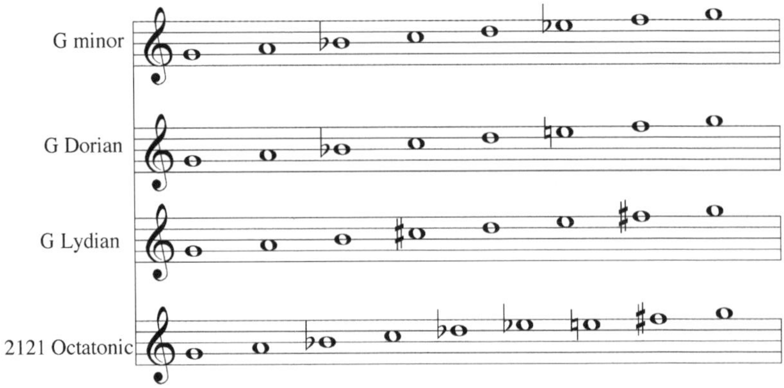

"Rondino" emphasizes one aspect of *la grande ligne*—formal clarity—thereby paying further tribute to Fauré and revealing the influence of Boulanger's classicism. Fauré valued conventional formal design. Copland uses a loosely modified sonata-rondo form, A–B–A–C–B–A–Coda (see table 2.3). Section C serves as the development, rendering Copland's "little rondo" a sonata-rondo (see table 2.4). In his earlier *Scherzo humoristique,* Copland's A–B–A′ form was essentially ternary (possibly reflecting his (mis)understanding of sonata form as a three-part form, rather than two-part; see table 1.2 in chapter 1), a form he would favor for the majority of his later works, both large- and small-scale. The conventional sonata-rondo of "Rondino" represents one of Copland's few retentions of a classical form. Additionally, the form demonstrates how Copland meets Ottenberg's sixth principle, formal clarity, economy, and technical mastery. The A sections serve as the refrains; the B sections serve as the episodes. The overall architectonic structure is i–♭v–V–♭vi–i–I.

TABLE 2.3 *Two Pieces for String Quartet,* II. "Rondino," Sonata-Rondo Form ABACBA

Section	A	B	A	C	B	A	Coda
Measures	1–10	11–25	26–34	35–89	90–96	97–117	118–25
Theme	T^1	T^2	T^1	"Dev"	T^2	T^1 & T^2	
Texture	CP	HP	CP	Varying	HP ostinato^1	CP & HP	HR, a & b motives octatonic
Harmony		i	i–iii♭	i–♭V^9–V	♭vi	i	i–I

Key: CP = contrapuntal; HP = homophonic; HR = homorhythmic; Dev = development

TABLE 2.4 *Two Pieces for String Quartet,* "Rondino," Section C, the "Development"

Subsection	a motive	Canon at the octave	a motive	a motive	a motive	a motive	Canon at the octave
Measures	35–38	39–48	49–57	58–67	68–71	72–81	82–89
Scale	G Dorian	g minor, G Lydian		2121 octatonic on G		G major	
Ostinato		Ostinato^3	Ostinato^4, ostinato^5, ostinato^6	Ostinato^6, ostinato^4 + ostinato^5, ostinato^6		Ostinato^6, ostinato^4	Ostinato^3
Texture		Counterpoint in violins 1 & 2	Interlocking polyrhythmic ostinati				
Harmony	i–iii♭	G-D/E-B dyads, i–vi	♭V^9	i–V	C♯-G♯ dyad, ♭V	A-E dyad, ii	C♯-D♯ dyad, ♭V

"Rondino" has other hallmarks of a Boulanger-influenced composition, namely, an *au courant* contrapuntal style (cf. Ottenberg's first principle). Influenced by Boulanger's emphasis on counterpoint from the sixteenth through the early twentieth century, Copland creates a work that is highly contrapuntal—a technique lacking in his earlier *Scherzo humoristique*. The first theme, found in refrain A and introduced by the first violin and viola (mm. 1–6), appears as a canon at the octave (see example 2.1). The secondary theme is introduced in the episode, B, initially presented by the first violin. In contrast to the canonic theme of A, the theme of B is treated homophonically.

Copland varies the texture from section to section, contrasting refrain with episode (Ottenberg's third principle of uncomplicated textures and textural variety). All refrains feature counterpoint, either as the canon or counterpoint between the two themes. In contrast, the B episodes are all homophonic. In m. 19, B features two-voice counterpoint supported by a double pedal in the cello. These contrasting textures help delimit the formal divisions. Furthermore, the technique of contrasting textures again recalls contrapuntal music of the late fifteenth and early eighteenth centuries, from Josquin's Renaissance masses to Bach's Baroque concerti grossi.

Copland borrows a technique from another French composer that cannot be attributed to Fauré. This time, he turns to an émigré, naturalized French composer, Stravinsky. Copland's development, section C, does not feature harmonic or motivic development and exploration. Instead he introduces six interlocking polyrhythmic ostinati (see table 2.5). Ostinato3 is related to the first measure and a half of the canon subject: it comprises successive perfect fifths rather than successive minor thirds; the rhythm of both melodic fragments is the same. The development begins imitatively, with ostinato 3 in the violins appearing above a sustained G-D double pedal in the violoncello. At m. 49 Copland presents three ostinati simultaneously, 4, 5, and 6 (see example 2.2). Each has a different

TABLE 2.5 *Two Pieces for String Quartet*, "Rondino," Ostinati 1, 2, 3, 4, 5, and 6

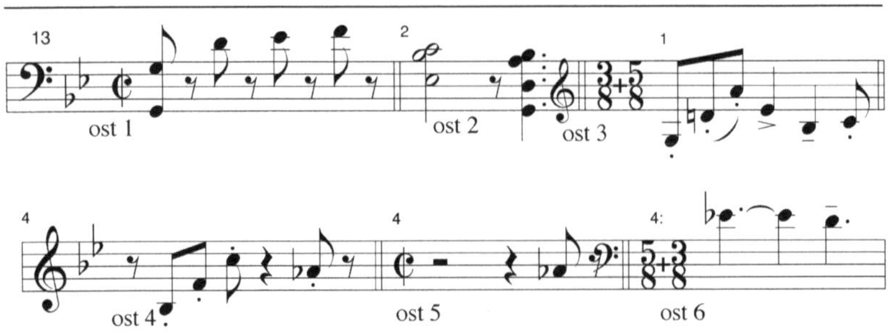

EXAMPLE 2.2 Copland, *Two Pieces for String Quartet,* II. Rondino, Interlocking Ostinati 4, 5, and 6

rhythm and melody. Individually, each ostinato is relatively simple; yet, when played simultaneously, their rhythms combine to produce a rich interlocking polyrhythmic texture as rhythmically complex and melodically intricate as the contrapuntal texture of the preceding section. These three interlocking polyrhythmic ostinati, after the arrival on ♭V⁹ (implied) at m. 49, suspends all sense of forward harmonic motion.

Copland briefly introduces the 2121 octatonic collection in the passage after the polyrhythmic ostinati, mm. 58–63. As in *Scherzo humoristique,* again, all forward harmonic motion halts (see example 2.3). Copland uses octatonicism to shape the harmonic flow. The entire development section is organized architectonically around the four important pitches of the octatonic collection, D♭, E-natural, G, and B♭. In "Problems of Pitch Organization in Stravinsky," Arthur Berger discusses the characteristics and harmonic implications of the octatonic scale, delimiting its potential for establishing four tonal centers and pointing out its lack of a single pitch hierarchy and leading tone. Composed of overlapping diminished seventh chords, the four half-steps of the collection create momentum and propel the scale toward the succeeding pitch. These half-steps thereby act as four separate leading tones, yet no single pitch acts as a tonic as understood in functional tonality. Thus, the octatonic collection contains four possible tonal centers. With respect to the 2121 collection, here the pitches C-natural, E♭, F♯, and A each serve as "leading tones" to D♭, E-natural, G, and B♭, respectively, and any of the latter can function as a tonal center, either as a larger organizing principle, or temporarily.

Copland applies this principle of octatonicism to the tonal flow in his development. At some point in this section, G, D♭, E-natural, and B♭ each briefly serves as a tonal center and point of arrival. The development begins with G as tonal center, followed by the establishment of E-natural at

EXAMPLE 2.3 Copland, *Two Pieces for String Quartet,* II. Rondino, Octatonicism, mm. 58–67

m. 45 and D♭ as the tonal center in m. 49. The tonal center of the passage mm. 58–63 is B♭. These four pitches correspond to the harmonic "progression" i–vi–♭V–iii. The double pedal involving D♭, functioning here as a harmonic pedal, suggests tritone substitution of the dominant. In this passage, Copland refines his use of the octatonic scale, using it as did Stravinsky throughout his career.

Copland's "Rondino" is, in short, eclectic. Ottenberg understands eclecticism (one characteristic that defines Boulanger) to encompass the use of seemingly disparate stylistic elements and techniques. Glenn Watkins expands upon the meaning of this eclecticism, defining the technique of collage:

> Collage: cut-and-paste, assemblage, re-contexting of images collected from both quotidian experience and our knowledge of the past. In the foreword to a recent study Kim Levin has spoken of collage as "the all-purpose twentieth-century device." Noting the capacity of the technique to support a variety of artistic movements from the first decade to the present, Levin traces its vitality to a dexterity in accommodating a series of emerging avant-gardes while simultaneously aiding in the definition of what was new in each of them.[31]

The use of Stravinskian layers of octatonic polyrhythmic ostinati with counterpoint *and* elements borrowed from the jazz idiom (for example, see *L'histoire du Soldat*) serve as one example of collage. Copland, then, clearly does not confine himself exclusively to modernist techniques, in this case alternating octatonicism with diatonicism. Instead, he juxtaposes the old and the new, recycling classical form, canon, Renaissance techniques, and contrapuntal texture of the past with the contemporary techniques of Stravinskian modernism.

Boulanger's pedagogical method stressed mastery of counterpoint (as did Goldmark) and counterpoint remained a part of Copland's style in later years, though not to the degree found in "Rondino" or *Movement.* His ideas about counterpoint are most fully presented in *What to Listen for in Music* (1939). Written in the spring of 1938, the book is essentially a collection of fifteen lectures for an eponymously titled course he offered at Manhattan's New School for Social Research in 1936 and 1937.[32] Listing melody as one of four basic elements of music (along with rhythm, harmony, and tone color), Copland proffers that the only texture that challenges the listener is polyphony, because of its "separate and independent melodic strands, which together form harmonies."[33] Polyphony demands one "listen in a more linear fashion" to hear the independent melodic lines and their interplay. Citing past masters such as Palestrina and J. S. Bach, Copland also mentions contemporary composers interested in polyphony, particularly Paul Hindemith. Copland sees this "renewal of interest in polyphonic writing" as "part of the general reaction against nineteenth-century music, which is basically homophonic in texture," as well as part of the neoclassical aesthetic, which looked back to the eighteenth century for models. The new counterpoint, Copland stresses, could also include dissonant counterpoint, which helps the listener to hear the separateness of the individual melodies because the lines cannot be lost in the overall harmony. Regardless of whether the polyphony is Bach or Hindemith, consonant or dissonant, Copland points out, it is listened to in the same way. He goes on to discuss the fugue and fugal techniques (e.g., invertible counterpoint, stretto, inversion, augmentation, and other contrapuntal techniques and genres).

In both Copland's discussion of counterpoint and "Rondino," Boulanger's influence comes shining through—particularly in his articulation of counterpoint as a linear procedure. Copland's model composition and Boulanger's influence extend beyond the use of techniques from the remote past seen in section C and the development. Copland supplements G minor by adopting various G modal scales: G Dorian in theme 2 (mm. 35–38); G Lydian (m. 45, formed by using B-natural and F♯). These modes appear only in this section, not in the refrain nor any other episode. Thus, Copland also borrows from the by-then conservative

French tradition of Boulanger's mentor, Fauré, who represented the recent past.

Symphony for Organ and Orchestra

Copland's professional emergence in modernist music circles of public performances, critical recognition, and publication began not in New York but in Paris. The French publisher Jacques Durand published Copland's *Scherzo humoristique* after hearing Copland perform the work on September 23 at the closing concert of the Fontainebleau summer session.[34] Through Boulanger Copland was fortunate enough at a crucial stage early in his career to form an association with an internationally recognized figure who promoted contemporary music, Serge Koussevitzky, then artistic director of Paris's Concerts Koussevitzky. Copland formed his association with what he noticed was relative ease. They remained friends after "Koussie" moved to the United States to lead the Boston Symphony Orchestra. Koussevitsky was the impetus behind the composition of Copland's first American success, Symphony for Organ and Orchestra. The conductor commissioned Copland to compose an orchestral work, with Boulanger intended as organ soloist. Copland began the work in May 1924, finishing the first movement in Paris and the remaining two in the United States.[35] The work's premiere was Copland's first American performance following his permanent return to the United States; it was his first large-scale orchestral work.

Symphony for Organ and Orchestra served as a conduit for the latest musical styles and techniques from Europe—specifically, from Paris—to New York and Boston audiences. On January 11, 1925, the work received its first performance at Aeolian Hall in Manhattan by the New York Symphony, Walter Damrosch conducting. It was reviewed in the *New York Times,* the *Herald-Tribune,* and in the arts journal *The Dial.*[36] The *Times* critic was of the opinion that it represented the best of the ultramodern school. Particularly impressed by its rhythms, he heralded Copland as an original and distinctive talent.[37] *Dial* critic Paul Rosenfeld commented on the shifts of moods and textures:

> One [mood is] a sensitive, contemplative, pastoral vein, whimsical and tranquil in turn, a musical idealogical early April with teglins from the ponds, chirps of a single bird, cool shadows [the vein of the Prelude and middle section of the Scherzo]; . . . the other a bold feeling for strident, breathless, obsessive rhythm as advanced as anything in Stravinsky [the vein of the Scherzo proper and passages of the Finale].[38]

For all New York critics (and presumably the audience), the Symphony for Organ and Orchestra epitomized ultramodernism. What the audience heard as a radical departure from Common Practice conventions stemmed from the work's tonal organization, its rhythmic techniques, and its textures.

The Symphony for Organ and Orchestra uses octatonicism and layers of interlocking polyrhythmic ostinati, things other scholars have overlooked. As Pollack has identified, Copland self-borrows the work's first theme from the closing slow section of his *Movement* for string quartet, and there is a connection between the symphony and Copland's ballet *Grohg*.[39] Pollack's analysis of this work focuses on rhythm, ostinato technique, and themes, and on the modified sonata form found in the last movement. Neil Butterworth's earlier analytical study of Copland's orchestral works, *The Music of Aaron Copland,* rather facilely focuses on the importance of the major and minor third found in the first theme introduced in the solo flute in the Prelude. Butterworth does offer useful comments:

> The Scherzo maintains a strong rhythmical drive from beginning to end with one brief interruption of slower music. There is no clear "theme" as such; all the melodic derives from the pervading ostinato set at the beginning of the movement. Many of these passages are built up from irregular groupings of notes with uneven accents which disregard the bar-lines.[40]

Butterworth accurately identifies the first theme of the work, introduced at the outset of the Prelude, but does not mention Stravinsky. Arthur Berger's discussion of this work is hardly more illuminating. Most scholars overlook the technical and stylistic elements and their provenance. Only Julia Smith draws minor attention to the influence of Stravinsky.

As in *Scherzo humoristique* and "Rondino," in Symphony for Organ and Orchestra Copland uses octatonicism harmonically and melodically. The Prelude's tonal material is based on the 1212 octatonic collection beginning on G♯ (G♯–A–B–C–D–D♯–F–F♯–G♯). The melody Butterworth identified as characterized by major and minor thirds is more accurately described as octatonic (see example 2.4), as are two ad-

EXAMPLE 2.4 Copland, *Symphony for Organ and Orchestra,* mm. 1–6, Theme 1, flute

ditional themes Copland introduces. A secondary theme, T^1 inv, first appears quasi-canonic in the organ at m. 10 (rehearsal number 1; see example 2.5). A third theme, T^2 appears at 3 – 4 (see example 2.6). All three themes, T^1, T^1 inv, and T^2, and two additional melodies used as ostinati, ostinato^1 (see example 2.5) and ostinato^2 (see example 2.6), are derived from this collection. In the first movement the themes and ostinati are organized as what will become Copland's customary ternary form (see table 2.6).

The large-scale architectonic tonal organization is also based on the same collection, as Copland uses octatonicism to unify the symphony. The second movement, Scherzo, is based on the 1212 octatonic collection beginning on C (here, C–C♯–D♯–E–F♯–G–A–A♯–C; the organ solo in section B uses the 2121 collection, here C–D–D♯–F–F♯–G♯–A–B–C). The intervals prevalent in the themes lie a third apart, organization Arthur Berger identified as a property of the octatonic scale and Stravinsky's use of octatonicism. The tonal centers lie a tritone apart, a harmonic relationship (along with the minor third) characteristic of octatonicism. The tonal scheme from movement to movement is also octatonic.

Critics remarked on the Symphony for Organ and Orchestra's rhythmic intensity and complexity. These rhythmic techniques, tonal organization, and textures pervade the entire work. It features dense polyrhythm, interlocking layers of rhythmic ostinati, and cross-rhythm. There are three contrasting ostinati (see example 2.6). This second ostinato is characterized by polyrhythm (the dotted quarter notes and the quarter-eight figure above comprise the first two polyrhythmic layers), and contrapuntal texture. The addition of T^2 (featuring perfect fifth pedals in the organ) adds a third polyrhythmic and contrapuntal layer. The second movement, Scherzo, also features interlocking polyrhythmic ostinati that tend to obscure the few themes (see example 2.7). Ostinato^3 has two distinct

EXAMPLE 2.5 Copland, *Symphony for Organ and Orchestra,* T^1 inv and ostinato^1

EXAMPLE 2.6 Copland, *Symphony for Organ and Orchestra,* Theme^2 and, ostinato^2

rhythms: two eighth-notes–quarter rest combinations that are one eighth note out of phase. The rhythms interlock, creating propulsive, seemingly perpetual motion. Of three hundred measures, ostinato^3 (or a rhythmically augmented variant) is absent for only sixty-two measures. Thus, this ostinato or a related form is present in nearly 80 percent of the movement. Returning to the thematic material, one can now view it in this new rhythmic context to uncover another Copland rhythmic technique. Above this interlocking polyrhythmic texture is a melody that is barely recognizable as a theme. It, too, is derived from ostinato^3 (see example 2.8). This theme allows some rhythmic flexibility; its freer, unmeasured rhythm, indicated by "senza misura," allows Copland to introduce cross-rhythms,

TABLE 2.6 Symphony for Organ and Orchestra, Form

Section	A	B	A′
Measures	1–28	29–61	62–91
Melody	T^1, T^1inv, ostinato^1, 1212 octatonic	T^2, ostinato^2, T^1 inv, T^1, 1212 octatonic	T^1, T^1inv, ostinato^1, 1212 octatonic
Tonal center G♯:	G♯, I–♮V	D♮,♮V–♮V	G♯, I

EXAMPLE 2.7 Copland, *Symphony for Organ and Orchestra,* "Scherzo," ostinato[3]

albeit briefly and limitedly. Thus, the primary focus of this theme is on rhythm, rather than melody.

Other techniques that would become hallmarks of Copland's mature Americanist style are also present, marking the first time that they appear in a fully realized orchestral work (Copland's earliest large-scale work was the unpublished and unperformed ballet *Grohg*). First, Copland establishes bitonal poles by two means. One is to oscillate between two harmonic pedal points (see example 2.9). The second is through ostinati. The opening ostinati are tonally ambiguous, suggesting C and A as tonal poles a minor third apart. Theme T^1 begins on G, suggesting the dominant and thereby giving C greater weight as the tonal center. At 21 – 4,

EXAMPLE 2.8 Copland, *Symphony for Organ and Orchestra,* "Scherzo," Theme^1

EXAMPLE 2.9 Copland, *Symphony for Organ and Orchestra,* "Scherzo," harmonic pedal points, 21 – 4

the bass ostinato reinforces C as the primary tonal center. However, the dyads E♭-B♭ and D♭-A♭ suggest D♭ as tonal center of the treble parts, creating the effect of bitonality. Second, the E♭-D♭ oscillation suggests the progression ♭III–♭II leading to I, the entire "progression" forming the lower trichord of the octatonic collection, E♭-D♭-C. Thus, once again, Copland uses a variant of the II–I progression identified by Taruskin as part of the harmonic motion of Stravinsky's *Petrushka*.

"Boulangerie"

Inspired both by the letters of his friend Aaron Schaffer and his own understanding that Paris was the epicenter of musical modernism, Copland left New York to study at Fontainebleau and stayed on past the summer. He arrived in Paris an advanced composition student, with his own distinct style and musical personality, bringing with him several works Goldmark had refused to critique. As seen in *Scherzo humoristique (Cat and Mouse)* (chap. 1), Copland had gained a basic understanding of ultramodern techniques involving the whole-tone and octatonic scales. In Boulanger Copland found a teacher far advanced beyond the conservatism of Goldmark. From her he received much the same training he would have gained had he studied at the Paris Conservatory. She nurtured his interest in Stravinsky, while providing him with a thorough grounding in basic compositional techniques and introducing him to her aesthetic of *la grande ligne*. Boulanger was also an important professional contact, providing him with an introduction to Koussevitsky, who was later responsible for the American premiere of his first major orchestral work.

Under Boulanger's guiding hand, Copland mastered counterpoint, among other compositional techniques, and further borrowed from his hero, Stravinsky. Copland refined his mastery of octatonicism and openly adopted Stravinsky's use of interlocking polyrhythmic ostinati and tonal organization based on the alternation of octatonicism and diatonicism. He advanced from short piano pieces to composing for string quartet, and large-scale works for orchestra and organ, one of the most difficult instruments for nonorganists to compose for. "Rondino," his first complete work for string quartet, stands as more than a pedagocial work, more than a student composition. In modified sonata-rondo form, it reflects Boulanger's ideas about clarity of form, *la grande ligne,* and respect for counterpoint. Copland also injected his own stylistic and aesthetic sensibilities, juxtaposing octatonicism with diatonicism. "Rondino" also shows Copland's highly developed rhythmic sense, with its interlocking polyrhythmic ostinati and syncopation (or additive rhythms of three plus two).

These techniques are retained in his first major orchestral work, Symphony for Organ and Orchestra. By this time he had advanced to using octatonicism both for large-scale organization within individual movements and to unify his symphony from one movement to the next. Clearly, Copland had mastered ultramodern melodic, rhythmic, and harmonic techniques and found his own ultramodern style by the early 1920s.

CHAPTER THREE

Popular Music and Jazz :: Authentic or Ersatz?

The same month Copland returned to the United States from Paris, Louis Gruenberg, one of the founders of League of Composers, wrote in the pages of *Modern Music:*

> The American composer can only achieve individual expression by developing his own resources, instead either of submitting to the prevailing tendencies of various countries, however vociferous they may be in their appeal and in their success, or of blindly following the traditions of classical form.
>
> These resources are vital and manifold, for we have at least three rich veins indigenous to America alone,—Jazz, Negro spiritual, and Indian themes. There is, besides, local color in California (Spanish), Louisiana (Creole French), Tennessee (English), and along the Canadian border (French Habitant). From these extraneous influences, an idiom must be evolved that will be tinged with the same quality that makes the foreign incomer, after a short period of habitation in the United States, decidedly an American, recognizable the world over as such. It seems to me that is the indefinable and at the same time unmistakable atmosphere in America that must be youthfully interpreted in a new idioms, not merely exploited in a characteristic melody.
>
> A new technique should be invented which will combine a knowledge of tradition and the modern experiment, if for no other reason than to avoid the pitfall of imitation. Music in Europe to day is suffering from over-sophistication and perhaps America's trouble is under-sophistication.[1]

In the mid-1920s Gruenberg would adopt jazz and spirituals in modernistic compositions *The Daniel Jazz* (1924), *Jazz Suite* for orchestra (1925), *Jazzettes* for violin, and *Jazzberries* for piano. Other American composers such as George Gershwin and John Alden Carpenter adopted jazz rhythms and melody. Independent of these composers, Copland had begun to borrow extensively from jazz and popular songs while he studied with Goldmark. Rather than quaintly combining these indigenous musical resources with nineteenth-century Romantic style, Copland ventured far beyond the American inflections of Goldmark and other so-called American nationalist composers. Copland took at least one of these works with him to Paris, "Jazzy," later incorporated into the multimovement short piano piece *Trois Equisses (Three Moods).*

In the past few years, the idea of musical nationalism has fallen out of favor among American music scholars (perhaps rightly so). Rather, a profound intellectual shift has taken place that situates developments in American art and popular music in the broader international stylistic context and intellectual framework of modernism (and rightly so). "Nationalism" has connotations of chauvinism and jingoism, and, to a certain extent, a parochialism that limits how one views the works of Copland, Gruenberg, and their peer composers who reached maturity during the 1920s or a little earlier. Unlike the previous generation, whose careers were largely confined to American shores, these younger composers endeavored in the broader field of international music. Yet even they grappled with issues of identity—in some cases, racial and ethnic identity (such as Copland and William Grant Still), regional or geographic identity (such as Henry Cowell, Roy Harris, and Charles Ives), and even sexual identity (such as Copland, Cowell, and Virgil Thomson). Thus, one can examine their works with a critical eye toward how they received past American musical traditions and ideas about American musical nationalism as they shaped their own aesthetics and styles. While American musical nationalism is a loaded term, from time to time it usefully expresses the idea that composers, however innovative and modern, were indeed concerned with expressing an American, racial, or ethnic identity. Yet, unlike Norwegian (Grieg), Bohemian (Dvořák), or Hungarian (Bartók) nationalism, in which composers sought to cast off the cultural dominance of a hegemonic or occupying power, America musical nationalism was, if you will, a kind of (over)compensation for a self-perceived sense of cultural inferiority of American art music when measured against European art music. While American art music came into its own during the early twentieth century, it would take several decades before American composers, critics, and academics truly felt confident enough to move beyond overt nationalism. Thus, during the 1920s and 1930s, the assertion of an American musical identity and the desire to improve the state of American music was very real to composers, critics, and music academics.

During his study with Boulanger and his European residence, Copland was made acutely aware that his style was somehow "American." While studying in Paris and traveling from musical center to musical center in Europe, Copland began to acknowledge nationalist sentiments that only an expatriate could express. Instead of turning from this growing sense of American identity, he became actively interested in composing music that could unquestionably be associated with the United States. Yet before Boulanger began to nurture these longings of Copland to participate in developing an American idiom, or national music, he had come already prepared to explore and develop his musical voice, not just as a modern composer, but specifically as an American one. The generation of Goldmark had been influenced by Dvořák and his interest in African-American and Native American folk music. Goldmark had composed works such as *Hiawatha Overture, Negro Rhapsody, The Call of the Plains,* and *Requiem.*[2] Copland also used African-American idioms, but rather than taking from the past, he borrowed the modern music of African-Americans, namely jazz and the blues. His ideas about jazz as a resource to create a recognizably American modern music were coherently and succinctly expressed in an article appearing in 1927 in *Modern Music,* ideas that he had already put into practice in works dating from the early 1920s.

Copland as a Jazz Musician?

The questions arise: to what extent was Copland interested in African-American culture? To what extent was Copland familiar with African-American music? He came to jazz as did many other white New Yorkers, from an outsider's perspective. Jazz and popular music pervaded New York and entered the Copland home *via* both amateur music making and a relative's phonograph. Music performed in his childhood household included ragtime and selections from popular shows and operas.[3] In 1917, the Original Dixieland Jass Band released the recording "Tiger Rag," popularizing the New Orleans style, bringing jazz to a national, white audience. Yet Copland had no experience as what we would recognize today as a jazz musician at the time he became interested in using the idiom in his concert works.

Copland had more than passing familiarity with popular music, having performed dance music and popular song as a freelance musician. He was familiar with ragtime as a teenager and encountered "sweet jazz" before leaving for Paris in 1921. After graduating from high school he took several jobs as a pianist to earn money, playing popular songs in dance bands.[4] In 1918 he played in a trio (violin, clarinet, and piano) for dances two nights a week at the Finnish Socialist Hall in Brooklyn. The summers of 1919 and 1920 he found similar jobs at resorts in the Catskill Mountains. In July 1919 he was employed at the White Sulphur Springs Hotel, and in August he worked at the Breezy Hill Hotel in Fleischmanns, New York. In summer of 1920 he worked at Schoharie Mansion in Elka Park, Green County, New York.[5] After returning from Paris in 1924, Copland initially tried to support himself by playing dinner and dance music, taking a job in an ensemble (violin, piano, and cello) at a resort hotel in Milford, Pennsylvania. When he wrote Boulanger in Paris informing her he had resigned his position because he could not find time to work on the

Symphony for Organ and Orchestra, he referred to his job as "jazz pianist." This Milford stint was the last time Copland would work directly in popular and dance music.[6] In later years Copland claimed never to have performed or had any extensive experience with popular music. In the late 1970s he discussed his lack of expertise with jazz. "No, I never had any talent that way."[7] He added, "No, I never knew how. I never learned."[8] Here, Copland's memory was not faltering, nor was he intentionally attempting to deny his popular music past. Rather, his understanding of jazz and popular music had deepened.[9] By the 1940s Copland realized that improvisation was central to the jazz tradition. By the 1970s he was aware that he had never performed "hot jazz" but a variety of syncopated music and fox-trots that was considered "authentic" jazz in the 1920s. When he referred to his lack of talent as a jazz musician, he referred not to musical invention but to improvisational skills. Yet his experiences as a dance-music pianist not only exposed Copland to light classics, but to a fair range of popular songs and what was then understood to be jazz, enough so that he self-consciously and overtly borrowed what he understood to be jazz and the blues for numerous compositions in the 1920s, from "Jazzy" to his Piano Concerto.

What Was Jazz to Copland?

What did Copland already know of jazz before meeting Boulanger? Many types of music passed for jazz during the 1920s. There were many styles of authentic African-American jazz, for example, that of New Orleans musicians such as King Oliver, Kid Ory, Jelly Roll Morton, and Louis Armstrong. There was also an early form of jazz closely related to ragtime performed in New York and the East, represented by James Reese Europe and the Clef Club Orchestras and Will Marion Cook's Southern Syncopated Orchestra. There was also the highly personal music of Duke Ellington. Additionally, various orchestras, black and white, played varieties of popular music used for social dancing in nightclubs, hotels, lounges, society soirees, ballrooms, and radio, such as those with which Copland himself played. There were also a number of white jazz musicians who successfully played hot jazz, like the Austin High Gang (Bud Freeman, Jimmy McPartland, Frank Teschemacher, Dave Tough), Benny Goodman, Bix Beiderbecke, and "Pee Wee" Russell. Additionally, there was another type of popular dance music known as "sweet jazz," which jazz and cultural historian Burton W. Peretti defines as

> the highly visible and popular dance music—a derivative of ragtime and popularized by Paul Whiteman, Ted Lewis, and Tin Pan Alley—that displaced more sedate popular music after 1919. This music syn-

> copated mildly, rarely used the blues of swing, and it almost never stressed improvisation, and it is rarely considered part of the great jazz tradition.[10]

The distinction was not merely a racial one, for various types of jazz crossed racial lines: hot jazz was played by white musicians such as the Austin High Gang and Goodman, and sweet jazz was played by black musicians such as the early ensemble of Fletcher Henderson. Paul Whiteman, who represented jazz to many white New Yorkers, billed and promoted as the "King of Jazz," was popular among thousands of white New Yorkers and, later, when he hosted a national radio show, millions of white Americans. His was variety of syncopated, heavily orchestrated dance music that millions of white Americans identified as jazz.

Three years following his return to the United States, Copland advocated jazz as a music that the American composer should explore. He was very much taken with certain aspects of jazz and attempted to analyze it in technical terms. He even began to lecture on jazz. Following a League of Composers concert in either November or December 1925, Copland went up to Rochester, New York, and gave a talk on this topic.[11] A year later, in late December 1926, Copland began work on what he believed would be the definitive article on jazz, "Jazz Structure and Influence," for the January–February 1927 issue of *Modern Music.* He sought to write an analytical article that went beyond description of the idiom as captive or expressive of the 1920s zeitgeist. In Copland's view, nothing had been written on jazz's "structure." Furthermore, although there had been much written about jazz as popular dance music expressive of the era and the art of jazz (or nonart by jazz's dissenters), no article had yet addressed the influence on jazz on "non-commercial composers."[12] Thus, Copland's purpose in writing his article was twofold: to provide a technical analysis of jazz and to outline its usefulness as a resource for the "serious" composer. But when Copland composed such early jazz-influenced works as "Jazzy" from *Trois Equisses* and later works such as *Four Piano Blues* and *Music for the Theatre,* and when he explored polyrhythms with Boulanger and spoke of "jazz," which type did he have in mind: hot jazz or sweet jazz?

In referring to jazz's structure in his 1927 article, Copland did not have in mind form as used by African-American jazz composers and musicians, for example, the twelve-bar blues, the thirty-two-bar song-form, sectionalized revue form, or sixteen-bar march/strain form. For Copland, jazz had one primary feature. "One point has been generally made and agreed upon: that the essential character of jazz is rhythm. Yet no one has carefully analyzed even this," he began.[13] He attempted to trace the origin of jazz's fascinating rhythms. Copland could only inexpertly assess to what extent its roots were in Africa. More clearly, he saw ragtime as jazz's direct precursor, finding, however, a profound difference between the rhythm of ragtime and that of jazz. In Copland's estimation, the "rhythmic foundation of ragtime" was based on a four-beat measure supplying the ground. The first and third beats of the measure were emphasized (see example 3.1). In the melody, a dotted eighth–sixteenth rhythm produced what Copland called "the characteristic ragtime jerk."[14] Copland saw an advance over ragtime in jazz, finding ragtime "much inferior to jazz and musically uninteresting; it consists of old formulas familiar in the classics which were discovered one day and overworked." Again, he focused on rhythm as jazz's most salient feature. For Copland, jazz rhythm differed significantly from ragtime rhythm in two important ways. Connecting the primary rhythm of jazz with popular dance, the fox-trot, Copland stated, "Modern jazz began with the fox trot." Like some ragtime, he reasoned, jazz was in 4/4, but had a slower tempo and emphasized the weakest beats of the measure, the second and fourth beats. This Copland referred to as the "fox-trot accent" (referred to in today's contemporary popular music as the backbeat; see table 3.1). Second, Copland pointed out that jazz used a new type of rhythm in the melody instead of the "characteristic ragtime jerk."

> With this [the "fox-trot accent"] was combined another rhythmic element, sometimes in the melody but by no means always there, which is generally supposed to be a kind of 1-2-3-4 and is always written: [musical example of three eighths, two tied eighths, three eighths].

This tied rhythm, Copland observed, could also be interpreted another way:

> It contains no syncopation; it is instead a rhythm of four quarters split into eight eighths and is arranged thus: 1-2-3-:1-2-3-4-5-, or even more precisely 1-2-3-:1-2-3-:1-2.

That is, it was played three eighths, quarter, eighth, two eighths (here Copland quotes Don Knowlton, who in his April 1926 *Harper's* article had pointed this out).[15] This rhythm, one in which a 4/4 measure is subdivided and the eighth notes grouped as 3 + 3 + 2 is now known as additive rhythm. Copland accepted this new rhythmic grouping as a major departure and one of jazz's great innovations. He did not see it as syncopation (in contrast to how he viewed the rhythm of ragtime). Furthermore, Copland noted that when the two rhythms of divisive 4/4 (simple subdivision, 1 & 2 & 3 & 4 &) and additive 4/4 (grouping eighths, 1-2-3-1-2-1-2) were combined, each maintained its own independent rhythmic character. The result produced polyrhythms. "Put this over the four-quarter bass: [musical example] and you have the play of

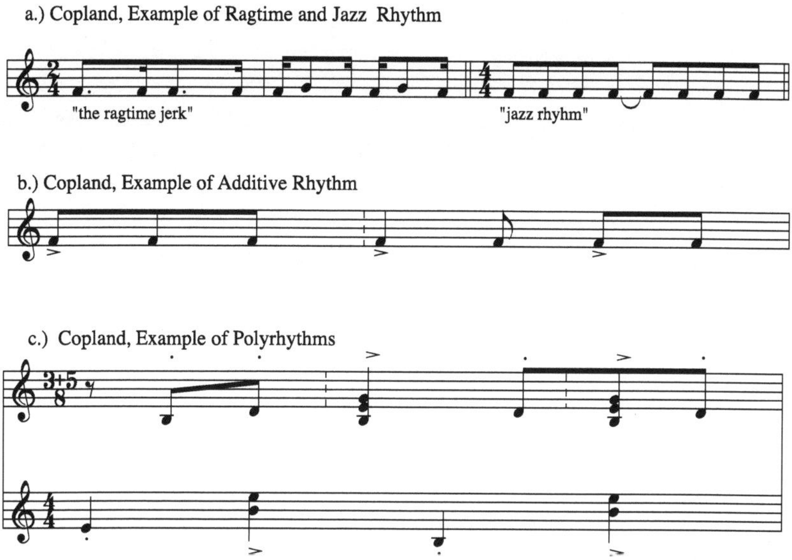

EXAMPLE 3.1 Copland, Example of Ragtime and Jazz Rhythm[1]

two independent rhythms within the space of one measure. It is the beginning, it is a molecule of jazz." Finally, Copland theorized that "whatever melody is subjected to this procedure [additive rhythm] comes out jazzed. . . . It is not the melody which determines this point, but the interplay of rhythms around, above and under it."

The rhythm of either the bass (the quarter-note ground) or the melody (the additive rhythms) alone did not produce the characteristic rhythmic vitality of jazz, nor did the two appearing together as polyrhythms. True jazz, according to Copland, resulted from the cross-rhythms and the interplay of one rhythm against the other. In other words, how one rhythm was related to another—the way in which they interlocked or produced cross-rhythms—produced jazz's characteristic rhythmic effects. "In employing two rhythms within one measure jazz after all merely did something that had been done before, if we remember, for instance, the use by older composers of 3/4 against 6/8. But the next era in the jazz age—typified by the song *Stumbling*—saw independent rhythms spread over more than one measure, over a series of measures."[16] Copland saw this type of polyrhythm in the music of several popular white composers. He mentioned Zez Confrey's "Kitten on the Keys" and George Gershwin's "Stumbling," "Fascinating Rhythm," and "Clap Yo' Hands."

TABLE 3.1 Ragtime versus Jazz Rhythm

Ragtime rhythm	1	2	3	4
Jazz rhythm	1	2	3	4

In Copland's view, then, simple polyrhythm was not the essential innovation in jazz. Polyrhythm had been present in other types of music, such as the Elizabethan madrigal, "primitive" music, and even some modern European music. However, the way in which jazz used these two techniques of polyrhythms and cross-rhythms was unprecedented: "The polyrhythms of jazz are different in quality and effect not only from those of the madrigals but from all others as well. The peculiar excitement they produce by clashing two definitely and regularly marked rhythms is unprecedented in occidental music. Its polyrhythm is the real contribution of jazz."[17] In Copland's estimation, jazz rhythmic technique depended on a *particular type* of polyrhythm, that of *cross-rhythm,* exploiting the interplay of contrasting rhythms. The excitement of jazz resulted from the rhythmic pull and tension generated when two or more rhythms conflicted.

Whites and the Harlem Renaissance

Copland's embrace of pentatonicism and octatonicism can be located in his exploration of the music of Debussy and Stravinsky. Similarly, his continued interest in jazz both before leaving for Paris and upon returning to the United States reflects a broader fascination white Americans had with developments in black culture during the 1920s commonly called the Harlem Renaissance. George Hutchinson, in *The Harlem Renaissance in Black and White,* investigates the involvement of white patrons, intellectuals, and artists in the movement and the influence of the culturally pluralistic philosophers William James, Thomas Dewey, and George Santayana and the anthropologists Franz Boas and Melville Herskovits on both black and white intellectuals and artists.[18] Whites were participants in the Harlem Renaissance to a limited extent because of their interest with African-American arts. Langston Hughes and James Weldon Johnson are reported to have described the Harlem Renaissance as the era "when the Negro was in vogue."[19] The account Hutchinson gives can be applied to Copland's appropriation of jazz during the late 1920s. Part of white involvement in the Harlem Renaissance included an interest in black theater: the 1921 production of the musical *Shuffle Along* sparked a major trend. White audiences also heard black concert artists such as Roland Hayes and Paul Robeson. And of course, black performers such as Bessie Smith, Ethel Waters, and Louis Armstrong performed for white patrons in nightclubs and on records. White Americans became obsessed with the nightlife of Harlem, which was transformed into a bohemia in the popular mind. It offered "excitement and entertainment to those whites daring enough to venture uptown."[20]

Some white Americans were involved in the Harlem Renaissance because of leftist, radical, or liberal politics. Several artists, intellectuals, and activists found that the Renaissance overlapped their own literary or political activities.[21] According to David Levering Lewis, "Some expected the great renewal in the form of a political revolution and, like McKay's friends Muriel Draper, Louise Bryant, and Max Eastman, anticipated that the Afro-American would somehow play a major role in destroying the old order." Some of those involved, less radical than those above, were not working for revolution, but were moderates, sympathetic to the African-American struggle for civil rights and equality. There were also writers who were sympathetic to the movement's cause, for example, Pearl Buck, Fannie Hurst, Dorothy Parker, T. S. Stribling, Clarence Darrow, and Sinclair Lewis. Members of the Lost Generation were also drawn to Harlem. Artists such as Van Wyck Brooks, Hart Crane, Zona Gale, and Waldo Frank made the neighborhood a stopping point on their way to Paris.[22]

Perhaps the most notorious white promoter of the Renaissance was the photographer, critic, and author Carl Van Vechten, who counted Langston Hughes, Bessie Smith, Alain Locke, and composer William Grant Still among his friends. Van Vechten has been credited with "almost singlehandedly generating the Negro vogue" with his *Vanity Fair* articles on African-American music and the publication of his roman à clef *Nigger Heaven,* and "then perpetuating [the vogue] with the infamous 'tours' of Harlem night spots that he conducted, always with a crowd of white celebrities in tow."[23] Among the white artists who visited Harlem with Van Vechten was Aaron Copland, who also attended many parties organized by Van Vechten.[24]

Links between American Modernist Composers and the Harlem Renaissance

Although jazz is most closely identified with the Harlem Renaissance, jazz was also connected to New York modernism. Carol Oja recognizes that white American composers were also, to a degree, participants and contributors to the music of the Harlem Renaissance, albeit in a lesser and indirect way. These white composers, as did their literary and entertainment counterparts, recognized the uniqueness of the jazz idiom and advocated the music as a distinct tradition with important implications for the development of modern American art music. On occasion, white composers set texts by African-American poets, as did Whithorne, who set Countee Cullen's *Saturday's Child,* combining modernist techniques with African-American idioms. But some went beyond the popular white versions of black culture represented by sweet jazz to study and use in more depth the actual black jazz idiom. Copland was among these.[25]

The League of Composers and Jazz

Modernist composers were further connected to the Harlem Renaissance through its institutions. David Metzer links the League of Composers to the Harlem Renaissance. The League's interest in jazz and African-American music reflected its interest in modernism. According to Metzer, it astutely sought to capitalize on the fascination with African-American culture that resulted from the Harlem Renaissance in order to promote its modernist agenda. The League sponsored a performance of Gruenberg's *The Creation,* which set James Weldon Johnson's *God's Trombones,* a literary stylization of an African-American sermon. The League sponsored a lecture on jazz by bandleader Vincent Lopez, Harvard composer-professor Edward Burlingame Hill, and *Dial* critic and former editor Gilbert Seldes just two days before the famous Aeolian Hall concert of Paul Whiteman. Vincent Lopez and His Orchestra, a Whiteman-like orchestra of "symphonic jazz," performed.[26] Furthermore, the rival International Composers' Guild programmed jazz-inflected works by William Grant Still.

Three Moods (Trois Esquisses)

As we saw in chapter 1, Copland took his earliest modernist pieces composed in New York with him to Paris, where they were first performed. *Three Moods (Trois Esquisses),* with movements originally titled "Amertune," "Pensif," and "Jazzy," spans two periods in Copland's development. Before he left New York Copland completed the first two movements on January 8, 1921 ("Wistful"), and November 14, 1920 ("Embittered"), respectively, during his Goldmark days. The third, "Jazzy," was sketched in the United States but finished in Paris in July 1921, during Copland's first summer at Fontainebleau.[27] "Jazzy" received its first performance at the Salle Gaveau on September 23, 1921, with Copland himself at the piano. It was this work that Copland auditioned for Boulanger, leading to her accepting him as a private composition student.[28]

Both Pollack and Tick recognize the importance of "Jazzy" among Copland's early works, as have earlier scholars such as Berger, Smith, and Butterworth. All see the links between this work and Copland's later interest in jazz, from 1925's *Music for the Theatre* through his Piano Concerto (1926), and the residual effects of jazz-inflected rhythms in Copland's work in later decades. As Pollack notes, "Jazzy's" irony is expressed through its dissonant harmonies, "formal asymmetries," and whole-tone clusters.[29] Tick has identified connections between "Jazzy" and Scriabin, particularly Copland's borrowing and adapting the elder composer's mystic chord.[30] "Jazzy," however, is a far more important and subtle work than scholars have previously thought. It shows Copland's early rhythmic technique and documents his earliest experiments with jazz. Close analytical study of this piece reveals the rhythmic techniques Copland explored on his own in New York and illuminates which compositional techniques and stylistic features intrigued Boulanger—that is, what Copland knew of jazz.

"Jazzy"

"Jazzy" represents Copland's first attempt at using jazz in a modernist work. As he described, this last movement of *Trois Esquisses* "is based on two jazz melodies and ought to make the old professors sit up and take notice."[31] This piece must be counted among those that prompted Boulanger to notice Copland's American rhythmic sense and his use of polyrhythms. In "Jazzy" Copland explored several rhythmic devices: syncopation, polyrhythm, the rhythmic feel of "swung" eighth notes, and cross-rhythm, all of which he would later describe in his *Modern Music* article. Copland also signaled his awareness of African-American piano music by alluding to a type of piano jazz that emerged during the Harlem Renaissance and one that French composer Darius Milhaud, one of Les Six, had no doubt heard in Harlem: stride piano.

Copland begins his piece by imitating jazz's rhythmic feel of "swung eighths," or what he characterized as the "ragtime jerk" (see example 3.2). Rather than notating the eighths as "straight" eighths or leaving it to the performer's judgment to interpret the rhythms correctly, Copland notates them as dotted eighths followed by sixteenth notes.[32] This latter rhythm pervades. Although the swung-eighth rhythm is the most prominent, Copland introduces syncopation in the first section of the piece, at mm. 2, 6, 9, 11, and 13–15 (see example 3.2). These syncopated rhythms break up the monotony of onbeat dotted rhythms, which could have become "singsongy." The irregularity of Copland's syncopation emphasizes the offbeat.

Copland also explores polyrhythms. In several measures steady onbeat bass quarter-notes accompany these dotted and syncopated rhythms (see example 3.2). Playing these two rhythms simultaneously produces cross-rhythms. Not only does Copland borrow the rhythms of African-

a) Copland, "Jazzy" from Trois Esquisses, mm.1-2 b) "Swung" versus "Straight" Eighths, after Andrew Jaffe, Jazz Theory

EXAMPLE 3.2 Copland, Example of Additive Rhythm

American jazz, but his textures signal his awareness of African-American piano music. One of the stylistic features of Harlem stride piano as practiced by 1920s jazz pianists such as Willie "The Lion" Smith, James P. Johnson, Earl "Fatha" Hines, and Thomas "Fats" Waller was the alternation of octaves with triads or sevenths. Against this steady rhythm, the stride pianists introduced cross-rhythms in the right-hand melody similar to the ones this movement displays. Copland confines the steady, regular onbeat quarters to the left-hand bass and the melody to the right-hand upper registers of the instrument. The bass alternates minor sixths, a moderately large interval. To emphasize certain beats of selected measures throughout the piece and on the final beat of the measure of each section of the ABA form, Copland introduces an octave in the left hand or an octave leap in the right hand.

Copland was interested to some extent in jazz and blues melody, specifically the blues base of the idiom. Judith Tick has shown that melodically, he borrowed heavily from Scriabin in adapting the mystic chord (consisting of augmented fourth–diminished fourth–augmented fourth–perfect fourth–perfect fourth) for melodic use, found in mm. 2–3. However, more pervasively, Copland works with blues-inflected melody in "Jazzy." The chief characteristic of the so-called blues scale, as Copland would have understood it, is the flatted third and the flatted seventh of the major diatonic scale, which represents an attempt to imitate the microtonal inflections of African-American vocal music. Blues and blues-inflected jazz contain an inherent tonal ambiguity that results from the tension between the minor third and minor seventh (the so-called blues scale) of the melody and the major third and major seventh (leading tone) of the supporting diatonic harmony. "Jazzy" contains both allusions to the "blues scale" and this harmonic ambiguity. In mm. 3–4 Copland introduces a melody in the right hand that contains A♭, the flatted third of F major (see example 3.3). This blues scale occurs against the backdrop of diatonic harmony. Copland exploits the harmonic ambiguity inherent in blues melody by introducing D♭ in the bass, creating a ♭VI and a seeming shift to minor. However, this harmony is illusory, for F major remains the tonic. This is confirmed by the I^7 that appears on the final beat of m. 3. This represents a somewhat limited use of the blues scale. Copland does not develop this idea or use it extensively. When the key signature changes to G major, one would expect that Copland would use the B♭ to retain the character of the blues; however, B-natural appears throughout this section. The blues element does return for section A′, however.

Copland also explores modernist harmonic techniques in "Jazzy." The movement's harmony in fact comes more from modern music than from jazz. Rather than functional tonality, Copland establishes his tonal center through the use of two techniques. First, he uses pedals. In the first four measures of sections A and A′ the pitch F appears in the left-hand

EXAMPLE 3.3 Copland, Example of Polyrhythms

bass part as the root in alternation with D♭. Similarly, in mm. 5–9 of section A and mm. 38–41 of section A′ he introduces B♭ as a pedal. The F pedal alludes to the tonic; the B♭ pedal alludes to the subdominant. In section B where G is tonicized, G is introduced as a pedal. As in *Scherzo humoristique,* Copland uses whole tones, however neither as extensively nor in such an accomplished fashion. He employs two whole-tone chords to close sections A and B here. Section A ends with all pitches of the C whole-tone scale in m. 16; section B also closes on the C whole-tone scale in m. 33 (see example 3.3). These whole-tone clusters replace the conventional V–I cadence and signal closure at the end of these sections. These are the only places where whole tone occurs in "Jazzy."

Copland uses other modernist harmonic techniques in the piece. In contrast to much popular 1920s music where the V–I cadence ends phrases as well as the major formal divisions, Copland does not use the authentic cadence to mark the end of a phrase. Instead, he uses rhythmic contrast. In mm. 2, 6, 15, 18, 20, and 22, syncopation contrasts the dotted eighth–sixteenth rhythms, marking the approaching end of the phrase. None of these rhythmic gestures is accompanied by any type of conventional tonal cadence. The authentic cadence—or one similar to it—occurs in only two instances. The first shows Copland's consideration of long-range tonal planning. By closing section A on the C whole-tone collection and section B on the F whole-tone collection, Copland sets up a V–I relationship. The other authentic cadence occurs in the final measure of the piece, where Copland concludes with a $V^{9}_{\sharp 5}$–I cadence. Despite this, the movement lacks true jazz or popular music harmonic style. Harmonically, "Jazzy" is more aligned with French Impressionism than with jazz.

All these disparate elements—the rhythm and harmony of jazz, Impressionism, the whole tones and pedals of ultramodernism—are organized into Copland's typical formal organization. "Jazzy" does not use any of the popular forms that appear in jazz works of the 1920s, such as the strain/march form, 12-bar or 8-bar blues, or the highly sectionalized forms of Ellington (whose forms come from a popular source as well, the revue). Instead, Copland uses a simple ternary form: A (mm. 1–16)–B (mm. 17–33)–A′ (mm. 34–42). Each section has its own rhythmic character (see table 3.2). The dotted eighth–sixteenth rhythm predominates sections A and A′. Section B contrasts: syncopated rhythms pervade. However, its rhythms relate to those of section A: the dotted eighth–sixteenth rhythms of A are augmented to become the dotted quarter–eighth of section B, creating a jazz, rather than ragtime, effect. In this section, Copland continues to produce polyrhythm by setting syncopated rhythms in the right hand against steady quarter-notes in the left. The overall shift from dotted to syncopated rhythms and back suggests that Copland is chiefly interested in rhythm in this movement and that he perceives that rhythm can be developed as much as melody in African-American jazz.[33]

TABLE 3.2 "Jazzy" from *Trois Esquisses,* Formal Organization

Section	A	B	A′
Style	Ragtime	Jazz-blues	Ragtime
Rhythmic character	dotted eighth–sixteenths	syncopation	dotted eighth–sixteenths
Pedal	F to B♭	G	F to B♭
Key	F	G	F
	I	II	I

Copland and Popular Song

As a teenager and young dance band musician, Copland gained exposure to American popular song, or Tin Pan Alley. Just as he used his understanding of jazz—syncopation, cross-rhythm, and swung eighths—in "Jazzy," Copland drew upon his knowledge of the popular song repertoire, quoting or paraphrasing two songs by Gus Kahn and Walter Donaldson, "Makin' Whoopee" and "My Buddy." The theme in section A resembles "Makin' Whoopee."[34] Copland directly borrows the opening motive (the sixteenth–dotted sixteenth–sixteenth rhythm), which fits neatly with his conception of jazz described in his *Modern Music* article. Copland also borrows the pitch and melodic contour for "Jazzy's" opening, which also features an upper neighbor note followed by the leap of a major sixth, which occurs in the pickup and m. 1 of section A, and the pickup to m. 34 and m. 33 in section A′. The second melodic motive of "Makin' Whoopee" consists of the upward leap of a minor seventh, occurring in m. 2, and 21; perfect fifth, minor sixth, and octave leaps are prominent in this song. Rather than quoting the song directly, Copland appropriates its motivic profile in "Jazzy," particularly the seventh leaps, transforming this motive into major sevenths as found in mm. 3, 4, 7, 8, 36, 37, and 40. The fifth leap motive occurs in the pickup to m. 6 and the pickup to m. 39. Rather than direct quotation, here Copland distills the characteristic melodic and rhythmic motives of "Makin' Whoopee."

Copland treats "My Buddy" differently by directly quoting a song that was popular during World War I, his own teenage years.[35] "My Buddy" melodic material appears in section B (see example 3.4). Copland alludes to the popular song's harmony, modified slightly in his version. He borrows the melody, presenting the rhythm in diminution.[36] Beneath these popular melodies, Copland uses harmonic pedals (F and B♭ in section A; F in section A′) and static parallel harmonies, such as F–E^{o7} (the diminished seventh being unprepared and unresolved) in mm. 1–3 to G-minor^{7}–F♯-minor^{7} in mm. 5–9. Copland closes this section not with a C major, or dominant chord, but with a C whole-tone cluster, which substitutes for V. This F pedal and static harmony, F–E^{o7} followed in this case by G minor^{7}–F♯ minor^{o7}, returns in section A′ when he uses "Makin' Whoopee." Harmonic motion increases in section B. This "My Buddy" passage oscillates G–E minor, closing on a C^{7}, which functions as a pivot chord to prepare for A′. Thus, even when borrowing popular song, Copland subjects his materials to modern harmonic treatment through the use of pedals and nonfunctional, dissonant harmonies, eschewing functional tonality (and certainly Tin Pan Alley or jazzlike "changes"), but nonetheless alluding to them.

The significance of the songs Copland chose are highly personal and encode the narrative of romance. "My Buddy" is a popular song about

a)

b)

EXAMPLE 3.4 a) Walter Donaldson with lyrics by Gus Kahn, "My Buddy," Chorus b) "My Buddy" quotation in "Jazzy"

lasting friendship, and—when considered in the context of its World War I—a song about pulling together for a common purpose to fight the "war to end all wars." It remained popular in 1921, when soldiers were still returning from war. Judith Tick also explores this song's meaning in the context of the era after World War I, arguing that Copland quoted "My Buddy" as "a way to encode personal feelings into a composition," which he had also done in "Wistful," the second movement of *Trois Equisses,* and another planned fourth movement, "Petit Portrait." She notes that "My Buddy" never refers to the specific sex of the narrator. Here we must turn to Pollack for more about "Petit Portrait." This unaffixed movement was intended as a portrait of Copland's friend, violinist Abe Ginsburg, described as a moody and unhappy person. Now we turn to "Makin' Whoopee," which optimistically encourages a young man that love, marriage, and children—a picture of domestic bliss—can indeed be part of his future. Tick asks, "Who was Copland's buddy—a friendly beloved or a beloved friend?"[37] Pollack notes that by the time he left Brooklyn, Copland had come to terms with his homosexuality but finds no evidence Copland was romantically involved with any of his Brooklyn friends. The pairing of "Makin' Whoopee" is striking, because "Jazzy," when considered with what is known of "Petit Portrait," becomes a work not only about the stylization of American dance rhythms and parody and satire of popular song, but a work evocative of personal relationships and romantic longings for that special "buddy"—whether for Ginsburg or Copland himself—with whom one can make a home.

Synthesis

Copland would again quote popular American song in 1925 in *Music for the Theatre,* Mexican folk songs in *El Salón México,* and American cowboy songs in *Billy the Kid* during the late 1930s after he had ceased to overtly use jazz. Yet the direction Copland would take for the remainder of the 1920s, both during his Paris sojourn and upon his return to New York in 1924, was clear. In addition to using Stravinskian ostinato techniques, he would also continue to draw upon American vernacular music. As shown in his article on jazz, Copland's knowledge of this music was limited. The incorporation of two Tin Pan Alley songs in "Jazzy" also corroborates what Judith Tick and other Copland scholars acknowledge: having little understanding of authentic jazz, including improvisation and performance practice, Copland conflated jazz with popular music. Nonetheless, he began to embrace what jazz had to offer the modern composer before Gershwin, Gruenberg, Carpenter, George Antheil, and many other young American art music composers. Copland's use of jazz during the later 1920s would prove controversial, as jazz itself had not gained acceptance and respect as an art; later scholars would critique his lack of true understanding of the idiom. His appropriation of jazz would also be seen as suspect among some African-American intellectuals and artists. Yet in 1921, Copland was not only well on his way to finding his own compositional voice and winning acceptance from Boulanger as a composition student, he was also on his way to finding a modern *American* music, expressive of contemporary American culture and zeitgeist that used *new* American technical resources. His earliest forays into jazz would be further encouraged by Boulanger and reinforced by a new aesthetic coming from Paris, neoclassicism.

CHAPTER FOUR

Paris and Jazz :: French Neoclassicism and the New Modern American Music

> Without really knowing it, I think that the North American and South American composers found themselves in Paris with what might be called, a similar need to assert a certain independence from Europe. That's rather ironical, isn't it, that men who were trying to break away from it. Perhaps it wasn't as conscious in their own minds at that time as it seems to us now. But at any rate it seems to me that the first world war may be part of the reason for this need to cut oneself off, so to speak from the apron, the creative apron strings of European art. The fact that the first world war was forcibly made the separation for us both in Latin and North America, I think was one of the contributing causes for our being able to conceive of an independent spirit free of the European spirit.
>
> —Copland, *Copland on Music*

While in Europe Copland began to acknowledge nationalist sentiments only an expatriate could express. Instead of turning from them he became actively interested in composing music that could unquestionably be associated with the United States. In Paris Copland and many of his fellow expatriates came under the multiple influences of Nadia Boulanger, Igor Stravinsky, and a new aesthetic and stylistic trend. Often grouped under the generic heading of Neoclassicism, this latter influence reflected the aesthetic ideals of Satie and Jean Cocteau and Les Six, a group of young French composers, especially Darius Milhaud, Francis Poulenc, and Georges Auric. The aesthetics of Cocteau, combined with the examples set by these three French composers, freed their American counterparts openly to embrace American popular and, later, folk culture.

Influenced by the neoclassicism of Satie and Milhaud, and the compositional techniques of Stravinsky, Copland began linking French Neoclassicism and American modernism with American "nationalism." Beginning in the mid-twenties and continuing through the end of the decade, Copland strove to combine his modernism with Americanisms drawn from African-American jazz and blues. African-American vernacular music—sacred and secular, rural and urban—could be used by American composers, black and white, as a musical resource for art music. While the embrace of American musical vernacularisms resonated with the aesthetics of Cocteau and Les Six, it also echoed the nationalism of earlier generations even as it simultaneously signaled a departure from the parochial Romantic nationalist style. In France Copland found a nationalism, if you will, that was anti-Romantic, that is, anti-German, but that embraced the vernacular of the composer's immediate cultural environment: the neoclassicism of Cocteau, Satie, and Les Six (particularly that of Milhaud) prized French popular and folk influences. Influenced by their aesthetic position and stylistic choices, Copland turned even more extensively toward using elements of jazz , blues, and other popular American idioms in composing his new American music.

Why Copland Was Drawn to Paris

Copland read the music criticism of *The Dial's* Paul Rosenfeld, which exposed him to ideas about the new music and gave him the impression that Paris was the most prominent center of musical modernism. The young composer was not drawn to study with a particular teacher, but to be in the midst of the latest musical trends of the early twentieth century, which ultimately led to him to seek out "popular" sources. As influential as his private lessons with Boulanger was the musical milieu to which Copland gained entrance. Though Boulanger was not then active as a composer, she moved in circles of composers who were shaping twentieth-century music. Copland analyzed their music, along with that of Palestrina and Monteverdi, in her Wednesday afternoon analysis and sight-singing classes. Boulanger also presented the music of Stravinsky, Schoenberg, Milhaud, and Honegger in these analysis classes. Among her personal friends were Stravinsky and Milhaud. Through Boulanger Copland came into contact with the leading French composers of new music in Paris. He met Ravel, Stravinsky, Roussel, Milhaud, Honegger, Poulenc, and Auric in Boulanger's salon teas. Copland found Paris outside the salon stimulating. He heard many of the works he encountered in class in concert performance, regularly attending premieres at the Concerts Koussevitzky, a series at the Paris Opera every spring and fall. In fact, the first evening he arrived in Paris, Copland attended a performance of the Suedois Ballet's collaborative work, *Les Mariées de la Tour Eiffel,* which included Milhaud's *Le boeuf sur le toit.* As he documented in his travelbook, that summer he also heard Debussy's *Pelléas et Mélisande,* Milhaud's *L'homme et son desir,* works by Schoenberg and Ravel at the Concerts Koussevitzky, and a performance of Stravinksy's *L'oiseau de feu* by the Pasdeloup Orchestra. Music by German, Hungarian, Italian, and Russian composers was also performed in Paris, and Copland heard works by Hindemith, Prokofiev, Szymanowski, Malipiero, Bartók, and Kodály.[1]

Copland's interest in new music extended beyond Paris to other international music centers. He traveled briefly to Berlin and Vienna; unfortunately, he arrived in Berlin mid-August 1922, after the concert season had ended. He did, however, have the opportunity to attend the opera, hearing Max Schilling's *Mona Lisa,* Hans Pfitzner's *Palestrina,* Busoni's *Arlecchino,* Franz Schreker's *Der Schatzgraber,* and Schoenberg's *Pierrot Lunaire.* Copland was also able to purchase many musical scores in Berlin that were not available in France. That summer he studied Schoenberg's *Pelleas und Melisande,* Richard Strauss's *Til Eulenspiegel,* and Alexander Scriabin's *Le Poeme de l'extase.* He noted that most "German" music was coming from Vienna: Schoenberg and his disciples, Alban Berg, Anton Webern, and Egon Wellesz. The following summer Copland traveled to Salzburg to attend the International Festival of Contemporary Music, where he heard the music of Bartók, Hindemith, Bliss, Prokofiev, Krenek, Janáček, and Habá. He admitted being most impressed with Habá. The extent of Copland's enthusiasm for and attraction to new European music is evident in a letter written to Boulanger on his way to Salzburg: "Six successive evenings of modern music should prove a big enough feast for even so insatiable a gourmand as myself."[2] The residual influence of the varied styles of Habá and Schoenberg can be heard in works from the late twenties and early thirties such as "poet's song," Piano Variations, and *Vitebsk* (discussed in chapter 6).

Modernism as Nationalism

During his stay in Paris, Copland's "ideas came of age" as he began to connect modernism and the use of American vernacular music in a way that could be described as an updated nationalism. Two issues confronted him at this stage: how to compose music that used American indigenous materials and at the same time was modern; and whether modern music could be American without overt references to "Americana" or trite Americanisms. Unlike Goldmark's use of American idioms, Copland's approach demanded that modern music composed in an international style represent for him and others *modern American* music, and thus be nationalistic, but not old-fashioned Americanist.

Copland's study with Boulanger and his experience in Paris profoundly influenced his further musical development, with respect to the formation of his modernist-nationalist aesthetic. When he arrived in

Paris, the neoclassicism movement was entering its second stage. Rather than Stravinsky and his *Pulcinella* or Octet, neoclassicism was now shaped by the writer Jean Cocteau, a group of six young French composers, and their musical godfather, Erik Satie. Cocteau had already published his booklet *Le coq et l'harlequin,* and Milhaud had composed works such as *La création du monde* and *Le boeuf sur le toit* that drew on popular French entertainments. Nancy Perloff's 1991 study, *Art and the Everyday: Popular Entertainment and the Circle of Erik Satie,* traces the influence of Satie's aesthetics and music on the ideas of Cocteau, Milhaud, Poulenc, and Auric, arguing that Cocteau was fascinated by popular entertainment and that the three young composers modeled their music on Parisian popular entertainments of the circus, the fair, the café concert, the cabaret, the music hall, and the merry-go-round in their efforts to establish a modern French national music.[3] In his famous pamphlet *Le coq et l'harlequin* and in the *Carte blanche* articles of 1919, Cocteau called for a new French modernism—for a French music free of the dense chromatic style of Wagner and the vagueness of Debussy's Impressionism. He thought that styles taken from French popular culture could serve as the basis for this new music. Les Six, the French avant-garde, so named by critic Henri Collet, consisted of Poulenc, Auric, Germaine Tailleferre, Louis Durey, Arthur Honegger, and Milhaud.[4]

In formulating their new aesthetic and new French modern style, Cocteau, Milhaud, and Auric ironically were inspired by *American* popular culture and music. American popular entertainments, music, and dance pervaded the cultural life of Paris during the second decade of the century. American popular music had been present in France since the 1880s when the John Philip Sousa band first visited and performed concerts that included ragtime, marches, and cakewalks. Later visits by Vernon and Irene Castle, whose musical director was African-American composer James Reese Europe, not only included the same genres of music as the Sousa band, but also introduced the French to Tin Pan Alley songs and syncopated dance tunes. Reese returned to France during World War I as leader of the famous band of the 369th Infantry (an African-American army unit). This visit introduced the French to early jazz. The French embraced African-American popular music and dance, drawn by its spontaneity. This wave of Parisian interest in early-twentieth-century American popular culture peaked at the end of World War I, though Parisians continued long after to be obsessed with American popular music.[5]

The connection between French modernism and American popular culture can be understood by considering Milhaud and Auric. Both borrowed directly from American popular music. As Cocteau expressed the idea, popular music served as a counterweight to nineteenth-century dense, chromatic German musical style. His ideas influenced Milhaud, Auric, and Poulenc, who turned to American jazz, ragtime, and popular culture in composing their modernist-nationalist French works of the 1920s. Fascinated by American jazz—black jazz particularly—Milhaud drew upon it in composing *Le boeuf sur le toit* (set in a nightclub) and *La création du monde*. Auric too was directly influenced musically by jazz. His *Huit poèmes de Cocteau* (summer 1918) stands as one of the first attempts by a European composer to use the lowered third and seventh scale degrees to capture blue notes. His well-known *Adieu, New York* (1919) also borrowed directly from American popular music: the dotted rhythms of the fox-trot, ragtime, and Tin Pan Alley songs, and the strain or sectional form of contemporary music.[6] Poulenc as well was inspired stylistically by French popular culture.

For Milhaud, jazz was an important new music and the United States' contribution to both the international modern music repertoire and to performance practice. He first met it in Europe, not America. (We have seen that Europeans realized the nationalist and modernist character and significance of jazz and its musicians before Americans.) Milhaud first heard jazz during a visit to London in 1920; when he visited the United States in 1922 he found New Orleans jazz in Harlem with the assistance of friends such as Yvonne George who were then living there. Staying in Columbia University's French House, Milhaud actively sought out more opportunities to visit Harlem to hear authentic African-American jazz (he may have seen *Shuffle Along*).[7] Living (rather symbolically) on the southern border of Harlem, the boundary between the uptown and the downtown intellectual worlds, Milhaud recognized something distinct and authentic in the music there—something he thought of as "racial."

> Harlem had not yet been discovered by the snobs and aesthetes: we were the only white folk there. The music I heard was absolutely different from anything I had ever heard before, and was a revelation to me. Against the beat of the drums the melodic lines criss-crossed in a breathless pattern of broken and twisted rhythms. A negress whose grating voice seemed to come from the depths of the centuries, sang in front of the various tables. With despairing pathos and dramatic feelings, she sang over and over again, to the point of exhaustion, the same refrain to which the constantly changing melodic pattern of the orchestra wove a kaleidoscopic background. This authentic music had its roots in the darkest corners of the negro soul, the vestigial traces of Africa no doubt. Its effect on me was so overwhelming that I could not tear myself away. From then on, I frequented other negro theatres and dancehalls. In some of their shows, the singers were accompanied by a flute, a clarinet, two trumpets, a trombone, a complicated percussion section played by one man, a piano and a string quintet.[8]

Milhaud continued his study of black music when he returned to Paris, having purchased several "Black Swan" records issued by the African-

American-owned Pace Phonograph Corporation in a Harlem record shop. Having resolved to use jazz in one of his own compositions, Milhaud ultimately went beyond mere enthusiasm for the music and used it in his ballet: "At last in *La Création du Monde,* I had the opportunity I had been waiting for to use those elements of jazz to which I had devoted so much study. I adopted the same orchestra as used in Harlem, seventeen solo instruments, and I made wholesale use of the jazz style to convey a purely classical feeling."[9] In this work Milhaud combined the jazz- and blues-inspired and blues-inflected melody with the formal clarity of French neoclassicism.

Copland and Les Six as Nationalists

Copland believed that the composers of Les Six represented "new attitudes in music and the spirit of the period." For Copland, this neoclassicism of the young French composers was both nationalist and modernist.[10] It was modernist because of what it had rejected. "They signified the absolute end of the Germanic Brahmsian and Wagnerian approach." It was nationalist because it asserted a distinctly French musical identity and profile. Most struck by Milhaud and his anti-German musical statements, Copland believed that Milhaud had a "program" or agenda for French music: it had to be "anti-German, anti-grandiose, anti-impressionist, and even anti-impressive."[11] This directly summarizes for Copland the Satie-Cocteau aesthetic that informed the musical styles of Satie, Poulenc, and Milhaud and to some extent set Copland's own agenda for use of American idioms.

For Copland, rejection of German Romanticism made Les Six *modern* composers. Defining modernism in 1942, assessing the later developments of the thirties, he moved beyond general references to "nineteenth-century Germanic ideals," and identification of Debussy and Ravel as the two chief composers who had inaugurated the move away from the styles and aesthetics of Wagner.[12] As Copland understood the term, "Modernism is generally taken to mean the Debussy-Ravel aesthetic." Their French nationality and their decided anti-Wagner/anti-German stance made Les Six not just modern, but also *nationalist* composers. The crux of Copland's consideration of their aesthetic was based on the contrast he saw with *German* Romanticism, that is, German music. Copland saw the nineteenth-century Romantic or conservative composer who attempted consciously to avoid imitating German musical style or succumbing to German musical aesthetics as a forerunner of modernism. This led to a certain identification of anti-German nationalism with modernism itself. Copland drew a parallel between the nineteenth-century Russian nationalists such as the Mighty Five and Glinka, whose break with German music was similar to the struggles of Americans, who, as he stated in the Chavez articles, sought "musical autonomy" from Europe. For Copland modernism subsumed an asserting of individual style, which would embrace the use of the American vernacular in a way that could be viewed by older or more conservative composers and critics as nationalist. For the younger composer modernism trumped nationalism, yet the two were inseparable. Ironically, Copland's definition of "German" music was such that even some contemporary Germans and Austrian composers could fit it—but specifically, he meant composers of the past. Although composers such as Schoenberg, Berg, Webern, Schreker, or Hindemith were Germanic and not French, their music did not continue German Romanticism as long as a stylistic line to their antecedents Wagner or Brahms had been broken.

Modernism and nationalism, if you will, were conjoined for Copland as they were for Milhaud and Les Six, although the latter were placed in the odd position of redefining French music in reaction to Debussy and the French Impressionists. They saw modernism for their generation as freedom from these seemingly overarching and overwhelming influences. They also sought a common international musical language for all post–World War I Europe.[13] Milhaud and his comperes Poulenc and Durey clearly saw themselves not only as young modernist composers, but as young French composers who would further the development of French music as Europe sought to recover and rebuild after the horrors of the Great War. Milhaud and Auric set modern French music in a new direction by drawing upon French urban, popular, and "folk" music, American jazz then popular in Paris, the music of the café concert, the fair, the circus, the cabaret, the dance hall—the music of the various popular entertainments. Like the German modernists who rebelled against Wagner's aesthetic and sought a new national style, the French modernists of the generation after Debussy redefined what it meant to be French. Similarly, Copland and his peers, both back home in the United States and expatriated, sought to define what it meant to be American.

"Our Own Far Country"

Thus, in Europe Copland began to think about American music in nationalist terms, in the sense of defining what it meant to be a modern American composer. But he was not immediately interested in developing an American school of music, as nineteenth-century pronationalist composer-critics had proposed. Copland was primarily interested in seeing American music represented internationally. In Paris he discovered the music of moderns such as Schoenberg, Stravinsky, Bartók, and de Falla and, at the beginning of August 1923 attended the first festival of the International Society for Contemporary Music (ISCM) in Salzburg. It was at this time that Copland began to desire to see American music represented among the European works:

> We were thrilled to be there with so many of the world's leading composers. It was a stimulating experience and one of the checkpoints in time when the place of my own country's music on the international scene became clear to me. I knew then that I wanted to see American music represented with more important offerings than the modest Emerson Whithorne piece that alone was American.[14]

The paucity of American musical works was brought into sharp relief against the backdrop of the latest in musical composition.

While abroad, Copland began to feel the need to find a style that would express or represent modern America. He began to associate jazz with Americanism, internationalism, and modernism. That Copland should have his first thoughts of American music nationalism while abroad rather than at home was so not unusual for those of his generation who found themselves abroad after World War I. Writer Malcolm Cowley, one of Copland's contemporaries and a fellow expatriate in Paris, described how expatriation served to awaken artistic *Heimweh*. From a distant perspective, Americans could look at the United States through a different lens: "We saw the America they wished us to see and admired it through their distant eyes. . . . We had come three thousand miles in search of Europe and had found America, in a vision half-remembered, half-falsified and romanced. Should we ever return to our own far country?"[15] According to Cowley, in Paris the artists also found art. From his European vantage point Copland too felt he could envision and realize a distinctly American music.

Had Copland stayed at home and not gone to Europe, perhaps popular music and ragtime would not have significantly influenced his musical development. However, hearing jazz in Europe shaped his musical thinking regarding modern *American* music as he became increasingly aware that the United States lacked an *art music* that *Europeans* could identify as typically American. As a consequence, Copland first fastened on the "stereotypically American" idiom of jazz. He did not hear jazz in the concert hall or in the French cabarets; the latter were too expensive and he could not afford to frequent them. He wrote of the summer of 1923, "In Vienna that summer I listened to jazz in bars and hearing it in a fresh context heightened my interest in its potential. I began to consider that jazz rhythms might be the way to make an American-sounding music."[16] The popular composers had developed a style of music that the whole world recognized as American; why could not the same be done for American art music?[17]

Copland's Jazz as Modern Music

Seeing the French adopt jazz awakened in Copland the idea that it could be the idiom of the modern American composer. Gradually and through his study with Boulanger, imitation of his models Milhaud and Stravinsky, and his travels, he was brought to the realization that Americans too could contribute distinctively and uniquely to the nationalist-modernist ferment. Copland's epiphany that jazz was dually a nationalist and modernist music was precipitated by several circumstances and conditions. First, his European counterparts understood the music's value. Americans were stunned to learn of the respect European composers such as Milhaud, for example, had for this music. During his 1922 visit to New York, Milhaud informed American reporters that he was inspired by jazz, and caused a minor sensation:

> When I arrived in New York, I had told the newspapermen interviewing me that European music was considerably influenced by American music. "But whose music?" they asked me, "Macdowell's or Carpenter's?" "Neither the one nor the other," I answered, "I mean jazz." They were filled with consternation, for at that time most American musicians had not realized the importance of jazz as an art-form, and relegated it to the dance-hall. The headlines given to my interviews prove the astonishment caused by my statements: "Milhaud admires Jazz," or "Jazz dictates the future of European music."[18]

Second, Copland's eyes, ears, and mind were open and receptive to the idea that the United States had something unique to offer, a receptivity that only came about because he was viewing his nation from distant shores. Once again, Boulanger in particular was important to Copland's sense of American musical identity and his sense of modernism. She did not overtly suggest that Copland compose in a distinctly American style, or—since his earliest pieces were jazz-influenced works—that he adopt the jazz idiom with the deliberate intent to be an "American composer." While avoiding the jingoism that excised any "foreign" influence from French music, she did subscribe to a sort of nationalist sentiment, believing that the culture and spirit of a nation could be captured and expressed in modern music, and that composers as diverse as Fauré, Debussy, and Stravinsky, among others, had done this for France (and Russia). Though she never prescribed any particular style of composition, she did encourage students to find their own voice within their respective national cultures. That is, she saw her students not only as individuals but as citizens of their respective nations.[19]

Copland, through Boulanger, first began to believe that the personal style he was refining was both modern and recognizably—though at first unintentionally—American. Studying with Boulanger particularly suited

Copland because "she was especially intrigued by new musical developments," and her interest in the new was not limited to art music. Jazz, particularly its rhythms, fascinated her. She had heard James Reese Europe's army band during World War I. Jazz was also found in Boulanger's salon, played by one of her American students, Mario Braggiotti.[20] She noticed Copland's unconscious use of jazz rhythm and called his attention to it.

> Boulanger was the first person who pointed out to me that I had a rhythmic sense which was very different from the Europeans. I was unaware of it, but she was fascinated with trying to play two independent rhythms herself, you know, one with the right hand and one with the left hand. And I remember our doing it together at the piano poking away at one rhythm while she was playing the other.[21]

Boulanger had noticed that this new rhythmic technique of Copland's was also a trait of Braggiotti and Europe and his band of African-American musicians. She heightened Copland's awareness of his own rhythmic sense, and suggested that it was an Americanism on his part. The sophisticated rhythms of jazz therefore further drew his attention.

> The idea of finding a music which was recognizably American in quality—although it didn't have its origin in the twenties—seemed to flower most importantly then. During the teens there had been a certain wave of interest in using specifically American folksongs—or what passed for such at that time. But not until jazz came along did we have a popular music that was completely expressible of our era and at the same time, had musical interest for composers.[22]

Copland apparently did not think his sense of rhythm was unique, but admits that Boulanger took special interest in it, intrigued by the polyrhythms and the cross-rhythms.

> I can still remember the eagerness of her curiosity concerning my jazz-derived rhythms of the early twenties, a corner of music that had somehow escaped her. Before long we were exploring polyrhythmic devices together—their cross-pulsations, their notation, and especially their difficulty of execution intrigued her.[23]

Boulanger convinced Copland that jazz rhythms could characterize new music.

> She made much of their appearance in my own work, and rather pointed them out to me as one of the new features of music in the 20s, different from what the typical young French student would be producing. She showed great interest in my rhythmic experiments, and made me more conscious of my own potentialities as a rhythmicist.[24]

Copland named Boulanger as the first to tell him that his sense of rhythm differed from that of Europeans—that his rhythmic sense was modern and American. She, along with other European composers, now recognized jazz as a distinctive American music, and connected it with modernism for Copland, validating his interest in its rhythms and confirming his ideas about its national flavor.[25]

Years later, in his 1927 *Modern Music* article on jazz, Copland would identify Milhaud and *La création du monde* as a masterpiece inspired by American jazz. He would also point out that for Europeans, the use of jazz in a modernist work had fallen out of fashion. Jazz had become "passé in Europe and not a young composer there is interested in it any longer."[26] However, Copland believed that the idiom still had much to offer the young *American* composer in the late 1920s.

> This is not so in America, nor is it going to be. Since jazz is not exotic here but indigenous, since it is the music an American has heard as a child, it will be traceable more and more frequently in his symphonies and concertos. Possibly the chief influence of jazz will be shown in the development of polyrhythm. This startling new synthesis has provided the American composer with an instrument he should appreciate and utilize. It should stir his imagination; he should see it freed of its present connotations. It may be the substance not only of his fox trots & Charlestons but of his lullabies and nocturnes. He may express through it not always gaiety but love, tragedy, remorse.[27]

He argued that jazz could serve as a resource for the young composer seeking a style that was both modern and *American.* Knowing that European composers were using jazz further validated and legitimized Copland's own use of the idiom, which (as we have seen) had begun as early as his study with Goldmark. Copland had heard the way Krenek, Milhaud, Stravinsky, Debussy, and Ravel used jazz. As he wrote in retrospect toward the end of his active composing:

> I think it was mostly the fact that the Europeans themselves seemed so interested in jazz, that Stravinsky and even Debussy and Ravel, Milhaud, were all using jazz materials that possibly gave some of us the notion that if they could do it, certainly Americans could do it better, since it was the music we were familiar with and had grown up with.[28]

It is crucial to point out that Copland saw jazz as a music that needed to be refined and further developed by the composer. Polyrhythms and cross-rhythms in his view made jazz what it was, music compositions to be combined with new harmonic techniques. Yet, in and of itself, the jazz idiom—the music created by jazz musicians such as Duke Ellington, the Fletcher Henderson Orchestra, or Louis Armstrong—was not suitable for direct use, was not suitable in its original state. Rather, Copland proposed that the composer utilize the idiom's rhythmic techniques. He used them to give music an immediately recognizable American quality in his large-scale works of the mid-1920s and first half of the 1930s, particularly in *Grohg, Dance Symphony, Music for the Theatre,* Symphonic Ode, and the Concerto for Piano and Orchestra. The first three works typify how Copland commingled jazz and European influences in Paris and in the years immediately following his return to his native country.

Grohg and *Dance Symphony* (1922–25)

Grohg and a work that incorporates parts of it, *Dance Symphony,* were the first large-scale orchestral works Copland composed. Originally titled *Le Nécromancien* and intended primarily as a study in orchestration and form, *Grohg* was inspired by the grotesquerie of the German horror film *Nosferatu.* Begun in Berlin in June 1922, Copland completed the ballet in Paris under the instruction of Boulanger. His Paris roommate, Harold Clurman, wrote the scenario. In Berlin Copland had seen *Nosferatu,* the story of a vampire magician with the power to make corpses come to life. At the time, he was contemplating writing a ballet and was searching for a story. Latching upon this story-line, he felt that the bizarreness of the plot, "the need for gruesome effects," gave him an excuse to use "'modern' rhythms and dissonances." The characters are the magician Grohg, an "adolescent," an opium-eater, a streetwalker, a "woman of the world," a young artist, and a "beautiful young girl."[29] *Grohg* was never published or performed during Copland's lifetime. To complete a commission he extracted three of the dances from the ballet and put them into the new work, *Dance Symphony.*

Although it premiered after his Symphony for Organ and Orchestra, *Dance Symphony* is, in a sense, Copland's first orchestral piece. The opening section of the original ballet, the Procession, became the separate work, *Cortège macabre.* The public performance and publication of *Cortège macabre* (in Howard Hanson's Rochester American Composers's Concerts concert series!) and *Dance Symphony* began to establish Copland's reputation after he returned to the United States. The three dances of *Dance Symphony,* which are actually those of *Grohg* reorganized, are "Dance of the Adolescent" (Allegro), "Dance of the Girl Who Moves in a Dream" (Slow Waltz), and "Dance of Mockery."[30] Stylistically coherent, *Dance Symphony* represents Copland's amalgam of the various stylistic, aesthetic, and technical elements assimilated while studying in Paris. *Dance Symphony* reflects what Cowell identified as French in his assessment of Copland's style in *American Composers on American Music,* but in reality the work shows the multiple

EXAMPLE 4.1 Copland, *Dance Symphony,* Movement I, [4] + 2–[6] – 3, Theme 2, Ostinato 1, 2, and 3

influences of American jazz and blues, Stravinskian ostinati, and Milhaudesque polytonality.

Upon his return to the United States in 1924, Copland was not only recognized for his modernist, dissonant, and unconventional harmonies, but also as a rhythmicist. Critics immediately attributed his idiosyncratic rhythms to American jazz. The third movement of *Dance Symphony,* the "Dance of Mockery" (the Finale), where the vampire Grohg is mocked by his victims and servants, features additive rhythm (often incorrectly referred to as syncopation), polyrhythm, and cross-rhythm. The first theme has two characteristic pervasive rhythms, divisive and additive, that Copland juxtaposes (see table 4.1). In part B, Copland introduces a second theme, one also borrowed from *Grohg.* It is adapted from a melody that originally appeared as the "Tender Regard Theme" (see example 4.1).[31]

Example 4.1 *(continued)*

The sections contrast rhythmically. Most of A is rhythmically straightforward—with onbeat rhythms. Section B and the Tender Regard theme feature displacement of the metrical accent, heard and felt as syncopations. *Dance Symphony* also marks Copland's first extensive use of jazz

Table 4.1 *Dance Symphony,* Movement I, "Dance of the Adolescent," Form

Section	A^1	B	A^2	C	A^3	D	A^4	Coda
Theme	T^1	T^2	T^1	T^2 var, T^3	T^1	T^3	T^1	
Ostinati	Ost^1	Ost^1, ost^2, ost^3	Ost^1	Ost^1 var	Ost^1	Ost^1		
Pedal	E-B dyad	F-D-D♭-B		F-D-B-A♭-D♭-F	F-D	D♭-G-D♭-D		
Tonal flow	i	ii–vii–♭VII–v		ii–vii–v–♭iv–♭vii–ii	ii–vii	♭VII–III–♭VII–vii	v–i	i
Pitch center	i	ii–v	i	ii	ii–vii	♭vii–vii	v–i	i

polyrhythms in a large-scale work, the first movement built on the principle of polyrhythms. To accompany the first theme Copland introduces four ostinati in section B (see example 4.1). The theme and each of the four ostinati have distinct rhythms that interlock, resulting in multiple, complex layers of rhythmic activity.

Copland imitates jazz melody. In the "Dance of the Adolescent," the first movement, the bassoon plays a jazzlike theme that recurs throughout this movement (see example 4.2). The contour, intervallic construction, and rhythm of the melody suggest jazz, specifically the falling minor third so common in the blues.[32] The tonal center is E; by consistently using D, Copland alludes to the lowered seventh and thereby further reproduces the tonal ambiguity of the blues scale.

EXAMPLE 4.2 Copland, *Dance Symphony,* Movement I, "Dance of the Adolescent," Theme 1, [3] + 1–[4] – 7

Several other musical parameters of *Dance Symphony* show the influence of Boulanger and French neoclassicism. The work displays the modernist techniques found in his earlier works *Scherzo humoristique,* "Rondino," and "Jazzy" (see chapters 1 and 3). But in *Dance Symphony* Copland uses ultramodern and neoclassical techniques such as octatonicism, counterpoint, and clearly definable eighteenth-century form, as well as the devices used in the earlier pieces. The "Dance of the Adolescent" betrays the influence of several composers whose music Copland certainly knew. First, the titles of both his original ballet and later symphony bear strong resemblance to those found in Stravinsky's *Rite of Spring* and *Petrushka.* For example, *Rite of Spring* bears titles such as "Dance of the Adolescent" and "Dance of Adoration," which refer to characters in the ballet and to the dramatic action and mood onstage. So do Copland's titles "Dance of the Adolescent," "Dance of the Street-Walker," and "Dance of the Opium Eater." However, these could be considered merely parallels, not necessarily a direct attempt to emulate the elder composer by the younger. There are stronger, concrete musical links between the two composers in tonal language, form, and compositional and rhythmic techniques. Previously, Copland had used octatonicism to organize *Scherzo humoristique* but had never applied it as a method of tonal organization to a large-scale work. Again following in the footsteps of Stravinsky (as we have seen), as Copland made the leap to larger works, he also used the technique of contrasting octatonicism with diatonicism as a means of architectonic organization. Themes T^1 and T^3 of

Dance Symphony are built on the 1212 and 2121 octatonic collections on E, respectively; the ostinati are diatonic. Copland avoids overt or direct reference to functional tonality: there is not one functional cadence in this first movement. In the absence of tonal themes, Copland had to rely on other means to establish a tonal center; he achieved this by repetition of ostinato^1. Emphasizing the first and fifth scale degree, this ostinato alludes to the tonic and dominant of E. The pitch centers for the various sections of the movement are all drawn from the same octatonic collection as the melody. Thus, as he did in *Scherzo humoristique,* Copland uses the octatonic scale for large-scale tonal organization.

Dance Symphony is a neoclassical work as it borrows from an eighteenth-century baroque form. Copland draws upon the rondo-reprise of the French baroque. The first movement begins with a slow introduction. The bassoon begins section A with the introduction of the first theme. This melody returns three more times, revealing the overall form, A^1–B–A^2–C–A^3–D–A^4–Coda (see table 4.2).[33] Section A acts as the refrain; B, C, and D are the episodes, each with contrasting themes. In Copland's rondo, harmonic relationships of the baroque French rondo are generally retained, albeit octatonically.

In keeping with the classical adaptation of rondo form, Copland uses the episodes as a kind of "development." The term is problematic when applied to a nontonal work: how can there be a development when there are no tonal relationships to explore? Copland develops his ideas in two ways. First, there are procedural and textural contrasts. Rather than continuing the use of ostinati and polyrhythms, he introduces complex counterpoint eighteen measures into section D at [11], midway through the episode. He creates a melody related to the Tender Regard theme (see example 4.3). This variation appears in canon at the octave in the winds and upper strings four measures after [11]. The lower violoncelli and bassoons introduce a countermelody below.

The voices remain completely independent, melodically and rhythmically, providing textural contrast to the preceding and succeeding polyrhythmic refrains. Harmonically, this passage "progresses" from C♯,

TABLE 4.2 Milhaud, *Le boeuf sur le toit,* Overall Tonal Scheme Outlining Interval Cycles

Sections	{A}	B	C	{A}	D	E	{A}	F	G	{A}	Transition
Key	C	c	E♭	**E♭**	e♭	G♭	**G♭**	g♭	A	A	A–G
Sections	{A}	H	I	{A}	J	K	{A}	L	M	{A}	Transition
Key	G	g	B♭	**B♭**	b♭	D♭	**D♭**	d♭	E	E	E–D
Sections	{A}	N	O	{A}	P	Q	{A}	R	S	{A}	Transition
Key	D	d	F	F	f	A♭	**A♭**	a♭	B	B	B–A
Sections	{A}	T	U	{A}	Coda						
Key	A	a	C	C							

EXAMPLE 4.3 Copland, *Dance Symphony,* Movement I, 11, counterpoint

or ♯VI, to G, or III. The overall harmonic direction mimics the tonic-dominant relationship of tonal harmony; however, G and C♯ lie a tritone apart. This tritonic relationship subverts the conventional functional progression.

Just as he borrows the technique of interlocking polyrhythmic layers from Stravinsky, Copland also borrows the technique of combining polyrhythms with shifting metrical accents. In his seminal study of Copland's music, composer-theorist Arthur Berger first discussed the extensive influence of Stravinsky in this work, particularly the irregular rhythms in the "Dance of Mockery." The following discussion of polymeter is based partly on Berger's work. The opening march and the "Three Dances" (especially the Tango) feature the innovative rhythmic techniques of polymeter and shifting metrical accents as seen in Stravinsky's *L'histoire du soldat,* for example. At [10] of "The Soldier's March" Stravinsky establishes a regular pulse in the bass. The alternating duplet, triplet, and quintuplet rhythms played variously by the clarinet or trumpet destroy any sense of regular meter as the unexpected accents make it seem as though the meter constantly shifts. The bass and winds also produce cross-rhythms, as the angular rhythms of the winds are heard against the regular bass pulse. Copland uses the identical technique (see example 4.4). The third movement begins with constantly changing

EXAMPLE 4.4 Copland, *Dance Symphony,* Movement III, "Dance of Mockery," [27] – 6, polymeter

meters, 5/4-3/8-3/4-3/8 in the first phrase, and irregular periods in the second, 5/4-3/8-3/4-2/4-3/4 (or, the addition of two extra beats).

At Meno Mosso, Copland introduces a third technique also reminiscent of Stravinsky (see example 4.5). He accents the eighths irregularly so that this 6/8 section can be rebarred as

3/8 + 4/8 + 2/8 + 6/8 + 4/8 +2/8 + 6/8 | 6/8 + 4/8 +2/8 + 2/8 + 2/8 + 2/8 + 3/8.

The 4 + 2 and 2 + 2 + 2 eighth-note patterns can also be reorganized as

3/8 +12/8 + 12/8 | 12/8 + 6/8 + 3/8.

Copland frames the phrase with 3/8, or half a measure of 6/8. The overall rhythmic structure results in irregular periodic phrase structure similar to that in Stravinsky's *The Rite of Spring.*[34]

EXAMPLE 4.5 Copland, *Dance Symphony,* Movement III, "Dance of Mockery," 29, Shifting metrical accents and Rebarring

It is no mere coincidence that in forging his own rhythmic voice, Copland directly borrowed techniques that were the hallmarks of Stravinsky's rhythmic style. At this stage in Copland's career, the Stravinsky influence now came from Boulanger rather than his own experimentation. Boulanger developed a student's rhythmic sense by teaching a passage from *L'histoire du soldat.*[35] The multiple interlocking polyrhythmic layers of orchestral ostinati and the octatonic collection in *Dance Symphony/Grohg* show the direct influence of Stravinsky, as does Copland's earlier *Scherzo humoristique.* But the use of syncopation in the melody against an onbeat accompaniment to produce cross-rhythms aligns with jazz as Copland understood the idiom.

The Influence of Boulanger

Copland's *Grohg* and *Dance Symphony* are then truly the first products of his study and experiences in Paris. They are in fact a "French" development of a set of earlier pieces, *Petites Valses.* Copland originally composed these three smaller works in New York, and they form the basis for both *Grohg* and therefore *Dance Symphony.* Roberta Lewise Lindsey discovered them and details their connection to *Grohg* and how the ballet was apportioned into the symphony, the *Cortège,* and *Hear Ye! Hear Ye!* The waltzes frequently use the intervals of the fourth and the fifth; they all use ternary form, ABA with a Coda. Boulanger encouraged Copland to develop these waltzes into the ballet.[36] It may be impossible to discover the exact suggestions that Boulanger made to the young composer, but her influence is present in the now-emphasized traces of Stravinsky. In *Scherzo humoristique* Copland emphasized pitch structures—octatonicism, pentatonicism, and whole-tone constructions—and explored tonic-supertonic harmonic relationships. Post-Boulanger, Copland stressed rhythmic interplay, as seen in the interlocking polyrhythmic ostinati and octatonicism, revealing (ironically) a heightened awareness of a uniquely American rhythmic sense.

Copland later developed several thematic and rhythmic ideas from the first waltz, which appears in example 4.6 as transcribed by Lindsey. The "Adolescent" theme is derived from this waltz. Instead of the A♭ minor triad, Copland transposes it a diminished fourth and arpeggiates an E minor triad. Lindsey sees no semblance of jazz rhythms or inflection.

EXAMPLE 4.6 Waltz from *Petites Valses,* later used as "Theme of the Adolescent" in *Dance Symphony*

Rhythmically, Copland retains the anacrusis, albeit shortening the durations to eighths rather than quarter notes. The rhythm is relatively straightforward, primarily onbeat. The only rhythmic intricacies are the anacrusis and the ties across the barline every other measure. When Copland converts this waltz to the first theme of "Dance of the Adolescent," these even rhythms are "jazzed": Copland diminishes the rhythms by using ♪. 𝅘𝅥𝅯 instead of ♩. ♪. The former is the rhythm Copland identified as the ragtime rhythm, a precursor to jazz. The ties across the barline invoke the syncopations that appears in the Tender Regard theme—syncopations Copland identified as among the hallmarks of modern jazz.

The Influence of Cocteau, Milhaud, and French Neoclassicism

Copland's *Grohg* and *Dance Symphony* also show the influence of Cocteau, Milhaud, and French neoclassicism—the French influence that Cowell remarked upon. But it is really Copland's decision to jazz his waltzes that shows how extensively he was shaped aesthetically and technically by his Parisian surroundings and comperes. It is clear that this piece imitates the rhythms of jazz as Copland understood jazz (as he elucidated in his 1927 article). As the original melodies show, Copland was not thinking in terms of jazz when he began them in the United States, but encouraged by Boulanger and French neoclassicism and the Satie-Cocteau-Milhaud aesthetic, he naturally turned to jazz. Just as he had emulated Stravinsky in technique, Copland emulated Cocteau, Milhaud, and other younger French composers aesthetically in turning to the urban twentieth-century vernacular music of his native land.

Dance Symphony bears a strong resemblance to Milhaud's *Le boeuf sur le toit* (1919). Both—though now accepted as concert pieces—began as ballets. The first movement of *Dance Symphony* closely resembles *Le boeuf* in form. Like Stravinsky, Milhaud returned to earlier forms, specifically those from the eighteenth century. The first movement of *Dance Symphony* (as we saw) drew upon the baroque rondo. Elliott Antokoletz analyzed the latter work's form and tonal scheme. Like Copland's ballet/symphony, Milhaud's ballet is organized into the refrains and episodes of a rondo. As Antokoletz points out, the melodies of section A consist of a syncopated, sharply accented opening Brazilian tune in the violins. This section is also bitonal, with C♯ against C, or the juxtaposition of pentatonicism and diatonicism. Section C, for example, in contrast, juxtaposes major and minor: C minor is followed by its relative major, E♭. This section also has polytonal minor-third and tritone relations.[37] However, these tritone and minor-third relations extend beyond section C, and, indeed, are the organizational principle underlying the entire work. These intervallic relationships reveal the work's octatonicism, used here not to organize the melodies but as a means by which to organize large sections. Although the primary source of Copland's octatonicism in *Grohg/Dance Symphony* was Stravinsky, the younger composer would have recognized the octatonic principle organizing the refrains and episodes of Milhaud's work. Copland certainly knew Milhaud's work: he attended a performance of *Les Mariés de la Tour Eiffel* on June 19, 1921, the day he arrived in Paris.[38] In Cocteau's ballet, different composers provided music for each of the different scenes, and consequently, Milhaud had supplied *Le boeuf sur le toit* for one scene of the ballet: Copland's introduction to Parisian neoclassicism came on his first day in Paris.

The Synthesis: A Collage

Neoclassicism shaped Copland's aesthetic position toward overtly incorporating jazz within an art music composition. *Grohg/Dance Symphony* is not a nationalistic piece in the sense that stylistically Copland did not strive self-consciously for Americanisms. It is an ultramodern neoclassical international work with Americanist sensibilities. By the time Copland had arrived in Paris, jazz had become an international music associated with the United States and was used frequently by European composers, particularly the Expressionists and the Neoclassicists. At the time Copland began composing *Grohg/Dance Symphony,* he had only a nascent sense of any Americanism. As a temporarily expatriated American, he was only beginning to notice the lack of American works at international modern music concerts and festivals. As an American tourist in Vienna, he was only beginning to notice that the dance music and jazz similar to that he himself had played as a teenager was different from the vernacular music of Europeans. But before Copland was fully cognizant of exactly how American jazz was, he understood jazz as an international modern, urban vernacular music.

Thus, *Dance Symphony* also displays the extent to which Copland absorbed the aesthetics of Cocteau and Les Six. Milhaud's French neoclassicism embraced the vernacular as an anti-impressionist stance. Cocteau, in *Le coq et l'harlequin,* in opposition to Romanticism, the "Russian" style of Stravinsky, the atonality of Schoenberg, and the Impressionism of Debussy, had prescribed that the young French composer eschew pretentiousness and academicism in music and be receptive toward the music of the café concert, the music hall, the circus, and African-American jazz.[39] Copland emulated Milhaud's *Le boeuf sur le toit* in a second manner: instead of Brazilian rhythms, Copland used jazz, which is the American's popular music—dance-hall music—in Copland's mind an exact parallel to the French vernacular that Cocteau demanded of French composers.

Copland combined the French traditional and the French modern via the neoclassicism of Stravinsky. His mix of disparate elements resulted in an eclectic style, a mélange—or, to borrow Glenn Watkin's term, a collage. While the harmonies of works such as *Dance Symphony* and Symphony for Organ and Orchestra were consistently recognized as modern, Copland's rhythms and rhythmic techniques came to be viewed as jazz, whether they were derived from sweet jazz or from Stravinsky. Whether accompanied by harsh, ultramodern harmonic technique and the exploration of new tonic and tonal possibilities or by conventional functional tonal harmony, jazz came to be viewed as the means by which the serious composer could create a new American music. Copland realized that a synthesis of modernist harmonic, tonal, and melodic techniques and jazz-derived and jazz-inflected rhythms could be the style and substance of a technically mature, modern, urban American art music that equaled that of Europe.

CHAPTER FIVE

Back in the United States :: Popular Music, Jazz, and the New American Music

> The League of Composers' first commissioned work was Aaron Copland's *Music for the Theatre.*
> —METZER, "The League of Composers"

On June 7, 1924, Copland boarded the ship *France* in Le Havre with Harold Clurman and departed France for the trip home, arriving in New York on June 13, 1924.[1] He returned to pursue his career and proceeded to establish himself as one of the United States' leading young composers. In those years immediately following his repatriation, he was recognized more as a modernist—as innovative and forward thinking—than as a composer whose music had a decidedly nationalist style. The first large-scale work to win him recognition as one of the country's promising young lions was Symphony for Organ and Orchestra. Upon the New York premiere conducted by Walter Damrosch, the harsh dissonances and intricate rhythms won Copland a reputation as a brash ultramodernist. Subsequent works reinforced this reputation, but critics and audiences also responded to another element in his "ultramodern" works: what they perceived as his nationalist tendencies. In *American Composers on American Music,* Cowell described Copland's style as European *and* American:

> A fifth group [out of eight broad categories devised by Cowell] may be made of Americans who do not attempt to develop original ideas or materials but who take those which they already find in America and adapt them to a European style. To this group belong: Aaron Copland, who uses jazz themes and rhythms in music which is otherwise modern French in conception. Such of his music as does not utilize jazz material is also French in style, and is of the type that is amusing and sounds well immediately.[2]

Copland's early works did reveal a nationalist aesthetic and intent in the guise of international modernism. Copland increasingly borrowed more overtly from jazz during the middle to late 1920s than he had during his Paris years. Copland's style of the twenties, by his own admission, had been colored by what he saw as the "notion that Americans needed a kind of music they could recognize as their own."[3] He saw that in quality Bartók's music was somehow Hungarian and that Stravinsky's was Russian, yet the music of both was considered modern. Copland's own music, as Cowell says, did assimilate European styles and techniques. In these first twelve years after his return from Paris, Copland's now-mature style, seen in *Music for the Theatre,* showed the influence of Stravinsky and Milhaud, and his fuller assimilation of the idiom of American jazz, adopted as the expression both of the twentieth century and of urban American life.

Music for the Theatre (1925) and Copland's Individual Voice

Upon returning to the United States Copland felt the need to shed elements of his international style. Although it still showed indelible traces of his European training, his first truly American work was *Music for the Theatre:* that is, he composed the work in the United States with the intention of embracing Americanism and moving beyond the European styles he assimilated. Commissioned in 1924 by the League of Composers, Copland retreated to relative seclusion during the summer of 1925 to the MacDowell Colony. There among the woods of New Hampshire, far away from the hustle and bustle of his native urban environment, Copland, supported financially by a Guggenheim Fellowship, worked to fill the commission. Forty-five years later he saw this as the beginning of his conscious Americanism.

> Now I was free to devote my entire energies to the composition of the new works for Koussevitzky's League concert. I was anxious to write a work that would immediately be recognized as American in character. This desire to be "American" was symptomatic of the period. It made me think of my Symphony [for Organ and Orchestra] as too European in inspiration. I had experimented a little with the rhythms of popular music in several earlier compositions, but now I wanted frankly to adopt the jazz idiom and see what I could do with it in a symphonic way. Rosenfeld suggested the MacDowell Colony as a good place to work during the summer months. It was there that I wrote my *Music for the Theatre,* a suite in five parts for small orchestra.[4]

The work did more than just suggest an American atmosphere: it self-consciously drew overtly and rather freely upon the style of jazz popular among white Americans during the mid-1920s.

Scholars have long recognized the influence of jazz in this composition. Smith, Berger, Butterworth, and recently Larry Starr all identify

Music for the Theatre as one of Copland's jazz works and point out that jazz rhythm is its salient feature. Berger sees this piece as a watershed: "Copland's style period came to the public's attention with *Music for the Theater* (1925). It is marked by a trend towards an indigenous idiom through incorporation of jazz."[5] Norman Kay states that in this work, Copland was "grappling with the problem of incorporating indigenous material such as jazz into his writing."[6] According to Butterworth, the jazz influence is seen first in the orchestration and the use of the instruments. He describes the ensemble for which Copland scores (single woodwinds, two trumpets, trombone, percussion piano, and reduced strings) as that of a theater orchestra. He considers Copland's writing for the trumpets (requiring extensive use of mutes) and for the percussion ("virtually a dance-band kit") as "very close to jazz."[7] Starr considers this the first work in which Copland found a mature voice.[8]

Copland does use jazz in this work, as well as in others. However, distinctions must be made between works in which he merely imitates the sound or style of jazz and those ways in which he attempts to apply specific techniques borrowed from the idiom. Here we turn to Copland's contemporaries. In 1919 composer and bandleader, war hero and former army lieutenant James Reese Europe explained jazz to a largely white readership in a short *New York Tribune* article (later reprinted in a slightly revised version in *Literary Digest*). He described jazz as a music originating about the turn of the twentieth century in New Orleans that featured wind instruments exploiting new timbres and performance techniques and improvisation.[9] Jelly Roll Morton proffered that "*Jazz* music is a style, not compositions, any kind of music may be played in *jazz,* if one has the knowledge."[10] He described melody, harmony, and rhythm as its central features. Stressing the importance of the riff as its foundation, he stated that the riff "gives an orchestra a great background and is the main idea in playing jazz."[11] An anonymous writer in *Current Opinion* described jazz as a music primarily of rhythm, but also featuring melody and "a certain modicum of contrapuntal inner voices."[12] Swiss conductor Ernst Ansermet discussed not only rhythm, but also timbre and microtonal inflections, or bent notes.[13]

One can discern a pattern among American and European white writers and black writers on jazz. The former (most of whom were not jazz musicians) tended to emphasize jazz's rhythm and syncopation and sometimes new instrumental techniques and timbre. Black American writers who were jazz musicians stressed that harmony, melody, and improvisation were as important as rhythm. African-Americans musicians and composers whose endeavors were strictly in concert music differed, too, in how they understood jazz. Copland's peer, African-American Harlem Renaissance composer William Grant Still, had worked as a jazz/dance band musician in Ohio and New York, and as an arranger and popular songwriter since 1916 (his concert works would debut under the auspices of Varèse's International Composers Guild). Still identified contributions jazz musicians had made to American music: new instrumental, rhythmic, and orchestration techniques; a unique scale; original forms; and, emotional expressiveness.[14] In contrast, in his article on jazz Copland identifies the idiom's primary contributions as rhythmic. Clearly, the two composers had different ideas of what jazz had to offer the art music composer, with Copland's being quite limited.

Music for the Theatre and Jazz

Music for the Theatre borrows from jazz, both "sweet" and "hot," further showing Copland's understanding (or limited understanding) of the idiom.[15] Jazz during the 1920s had distinct forms, such as the twelve-bar blues (showing blues as a major tributary), march-strain form (particularly showing the relationship between jazz and ragtime), and sectionalized forms as found in the music of composers such as Ellington and Fletcher Henderson. Copland ignores jazz's idiomatic forms, choosing to use his customary formal organization, A–B–A′. Many of Copland's borrowings are foreground elements, such as his orchestration. He scores prominently for trumpet and clarinet, creating "hot" sounding solos (see example 5.1). The Prologue begins with a trumpet imitating an improvised solo, suggesting the spontaneity of extemporaneously created African-American jazz. Copland allows the trumpet to play free of a predetermined meter in an attempt to reproduce improvised jazz's swing and rhythmic elasticity, treating m. 5 as a rhythmically free and unconstrained cadenza. He instructs the performer to play this passage "beginning slowly, senza mesura (faster and faster)." This opening trumpet solo also imitates jazz melody: it uses a quasi-pentatonic melody (A pentatonic). Copland suggests pentatonicism by presenting only the first, third, fourth, fifth, and lowered seventh scale degrees.[16] He also uses another instrumental effect borrowed from jazz: the flutter tonguing in the trumpet in m. 6.

Copland also scores for the clarinet in a manner that subtlely but directly imitates the New Orleans style of clarinet performance. First he

TABLE 5.1 *Music for the Theatre,* Prologue Overall Form

Section	Introduction	A	B	Transition	A′
Theme	Hot trumpet solo	Hot trumpet solo T^1 & T^2	T^3 & T^4	T^4 & $T^{2\prime}$ closing theme	
Measures		15–36	37–67	68–103	104–21
Key/tonal center	octatonic	b minor i	D major III	D major III	b minor i

EXAMPLE 5.1 Copland, *Music for the Theatre,* Prologue, Section A, mm. 1–5

chooses the E♭ sopranino clarinet (see example 5.2). The second movement, "Dance," features similar "hot" clarinet solos, as at 20. Copland could easily have scored for B♭ or A clarinet—ones conventionally found in a modern orchestra or chamber ensemble. Instead, he scores the entire piece for E♭ clarinet, an instrument rarely encountered in most orchestral and chamber music. Clarinetists often complain about the E♭ clarinet's poor intonation. Indeed, if a performer were to play this passage on the E♭ clarinet and then on either the B♭ or A clarinet (allowing for transpositions), he or she would notice a marked difference in intonation between the latter two and the former. Copland chose the E♭ clarinet for its timbre, which imitates the variable, microtonal speech-inflected intonation of New Orleans jazz clarinet players. Comparison of this passage with the recorded solos of clarinetists such as Sydney Bechet, Johnny Dodds, Omer Simeon, or Jimmy Noone, all important New Orleans jazz clarinetists (Bechet later switched to soprano saxophone), shows how closely the timbre and intonation of the E♭ clarinet resembles that of New Orleans clarinetists.[17]

Copland, then, clearly imitates jazz melody, instrumentation, and timbre. But the most important and influential techniques he borrowed from jazz were rhythmic. In *Music for the Theatre,* he made extensive and pervasive use of syncopation (additive rhythms), polyrhythms (and polymeter), and cross-rhythms. Almost as a cliché, Copland uses syncopation to suggest African-American jazz. If rhythmic elasticity is the device Copland used to suggest it at the beginning of section A, the "hot solo" he gives to the E♭ clarinet at the beginning of B at 5–6 contrasts, in that it is strictly metrical. Like the trumpet in the opening, the E♭ clarinet also features pervasive syncopation, further imitating improvised

EXAMPLE 5.2 Copland, *Music for the Theatre,* "Prologue," 5–6

jazz. Unlike the trumpet solo, however, this passage is plainly and clearly diatonic.

Music for the Theatre is built on polyrhythmic ostinati, which first appear in the Prologue. After a jazzy introduction and a stately chorale-like and homorhythmic A section, Copland begins the polyrhythmic B section at 5–8 (mm. 37–47). The E♭ clarinet "hot" solo is accompanied by two rhythmically interlocking ostinati (see example 5.2). The first (played by the contrabass, cello, left hand of the piano, and bassoon) emphasizes the first and third beats of the measure; the second (in the violins, viola, and piano) emphasizes the second beat. The overall effect is one of rhythmic propulsion. Copland introduces new ostinati in subsequent sections of B and the transition (Rehearsal 11 marks the beginning of a closing theme; here Copland returns to the homorhythmic texture). Similar interlocking polyrhythms are prevalent throughout the second movement, "Dance," and the third movement, "Interlude."

Copland also borrows the technique of cross-rhythm from the jazz band. In section B and the transition of the Prologue, the constantly shifting onbeat/syncopation of the melody creates subtle cross-rhythms against the ostinati in the strings and piano, reinforced by registral contrast (see example 5.2 above). The contrabass provides the lowest pitches, constantly playing a perfect fourth on the first beat of the measure, A–D, which suggests a V–I cadence. Copland begins the span 5–6 in 3/4. The rhythm of the bass and cello and left hand of the piano interlock with the viola, violins, and the right hand of the piano. The higher-pitched instruments subdivide the weakest part of the 3/4 measure, the second beat. Since all the instruments playing the ostinato are of similar timbre, one hears the first and third beats as the stronger ones. Above this steady, unvarying 1–2–**3** pulse, the clarinet plays syncopation. At 6 3/4 alternates with 7/8. Copland particularly exploits cross-rhythm in the second movement, "Dance." The introduction of the 7/8 measures in B offsets the regularity of the 3/4 measures. Irregular rhythms that unexpectedly accent the weak parts of the measure relieve the tedium of regular rhythms. In other words, with the 7/8 measures, Copland introduces rhythmic interest by shifting the metrical accents, a pattern that becomes even more perceptible as the transition progresses. Spanning 9 + 2–11, it alternates 3/4 with either 5/8 or 7/8. Copland effectively creates a triple meter with an eighth-note pulse, which he maintains with the return of a regular 3/4 meter at 10. Although the meter is 3/4, Copland does not notate the rhythm as divisive rhythm, that is, to be played as three pairs of eighth notes. Instead, he accents the downbeat and the second half of the second beat so that the 3/4 measure is now played as two groups of three eighth notes.

Copland also borrows from jazz in the third movement, "Interlude." However this time, instead of the up-tempo improvisation or dance number, the movement is lyrical and slow, "Lento moderato." Here Copland draws upon the blues, also used in jazz. His melody at the beginning of the movement is reminiscent of the blues: the syncopated English horn melody features the falling third (see example 5.3). It is not

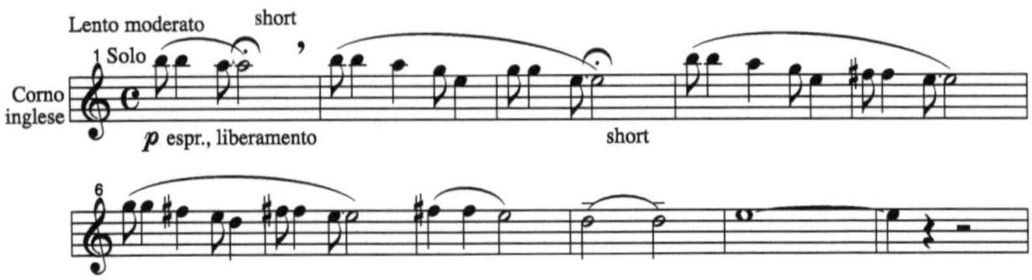

EXAMPLE 5.3 Copland, *Music for the Theatre,* "Interlude," mm. 1–11

a blues in the strictest sense—it lacks pentatonicism—nor is it in twelve-bar blues form. But it is a "blues" nonetheless in affect: emotive, melancholy, in a slow tempo and plaintive in character—a highly expressive stylized blues, rather than one meant for dancing (as in African-American cultural practice, either up-tempo or as a slow drag). Copland casts his melody in an apparent minor key: it hovers about the pitches C, A, and E, outlining an A minor triad. The minor key suggests the melancholy of the blues and evokes the blues scale. The melody recurs throughout the movement as a blueslike theme in several places: five measures before [33] (transposed a minor third higher) and three measures before [38] to bring the movement to a close. This melody recurs in other places as well, though not as a blues theme.

Copland also uses a blues theme in the fourth movement, "Burlesque." Here he introduces the theme in section B (see example 5.4). Instead of presenting the blues as a lyrical, sentimental, or tender theme as in the "Interlude," Copland casts it as provocative and risqué—salacious. With the appearance of this sexy "stripper" theme, furthermore, Copland introduces an element of the grotesque (the theme is marked as a "solo grotesco").[18] Rather than burlesque in the sense of parody, this theme hints that this movement is a burlesque in the sense of girlie show.

EXAMPLE 5.4 Copland, *Music for the Theatre,* "Burlesque," [47]–[48] – 2

In the passage [47]–[48] – 2, Copland retains the muted trumpet of jazz as well as the "blues scale" in the melody; however, these elements are played to broad effect. This "Molto meno mosso" section begins with a decrease in tempo and a broadening of the rhythm. Instead of having the strings play pizzicato throughout a measure, Copland has them alternate arco-pizzicato. The change in articulation contrasts with the preceding section and creates the comic grotesque effect. Similarly, Copland requires the trumpet to play this passage unmuted while the trombone inserts a mute. Rather than imitating a jazz band, at this point, the exaggerated rhythm and comically played melody, in keeping with the title of the movement, parodies the jazz band not of the Harlem or Paris nightclub, but of the more risqué vaudeville or burlesque theater.

Music for the Theatre as a Modernist Work

Contemporary critics and Copland scholars have noted the use of jazzy elements in this work, seeing it as a complete departure from the style of works such as *Cat and Mouse,* "Rondino," *Dance Symphony,* or Symphony for Organ and Orchestra. In doing so, they tend to overlook other influences that came to bear upon *Music for the Theatre.* Smith, for instance, wrote: "*Music for the Theatre* is an important work in the development of Copland's musical style because it marks a separation from the French, or European, manner of composing into a consciously American style, with its new jazz idiom."[19] Butterworth considered this Copland's first truly nationalist work, one completely devoid of European influences. "This was Copland's first wholly characteristic 'American' work; the melodic, harmonic and rhythmical features owe nothing to Europe. The piano writing is totally derived from jazz and the popular music of his own country."[20] Kay described technical procedures, stating that Copland's method of construction had now changed: "instead of placing themes over an ostinato, or continuous pattern accompaniments," he was now writing "short concentrated phrases."[21] Smith remarked to some extent about the work's harmony but was nonspecific. "The suite has style and bears the stamp of individuality. Again employing cyclic implications, it is completely twentieth century in technical craft, containing both polytonal and polyrhythmic elements, and is completely national, American, in expression."[22] The dichotomy of jazz/Americanism versus modernism is a false one. Berger, Smith, Kay, and Butterworth were accurate in pointing out that Copland was influenced by jazz. However, they all overlooked the pervasive ways in which Copland remained a modernist influenced by Stravinsky, Milhaud, and the French neoclassicists and how *Music for the Theatre,* like other works of the 1920s, shows the residual modernist techniques and stylistic and aesthetic influence of these composers. More accurately, *Music for the Theatre* features the same modern textures and rhythmic, harmonic, and melodic techniques Copland borrowed from Stravinsky and other French modern composers, and mastered while in Paris.

Copland uses the whole-tone collection and does so in two ways. First, after the opening trumpet cadenza of the Prologue, he introduces whole-tone-based harmony in a passage with five-part harmonies spanning [2]–[5]. Set in a style that resembles a Bach chorale, the slow-moving harmonies are decidedly not Bachian (see example 5.5). The key is B minor; the harmonies progress in inversions of ♯III–♯II$^{\flat 7}$–I$^{9\sharp}$, with D♯, C♯,

EXAMPLE 5.5 Copland, *Music for the Theatre,* "Prologue," reduction of [2]–[3]

and B as roots (here, rather than remain in B minor, Copland mixes the mode and builds his harmonies on the roots of B major). Repeating throughout the passage 2–3 − 2, this progression functions as a harmonic ostinato. A similar passage occurs in section B beginning at 5, where Copland transposes a minor third higher to D major, the relative major (this minor third is in keeping with the principle of third relations possible in octatonicism). As at the beginning, the harmonic ostinato is built on inversions of III, II, and I, this time involving F♯, E, and D as roots.

Copland's use of the whole-tone scale in these passages is not a fluke, for a telling example of conjunct whole-tone movement occurs in a crucial passage later during the Prologue. At 8 he presents a transposed and retrograde version of this fundamental progression (see example 5.6). This brief lead-in to the transition descends by whole tone (B♭–A♭–G♭–E–D–C) to effect the transition from the rhythmically complex preceding section to this rhythmically regular and straightforward one (i.e., it lacks polyrhythms, interlocking rhythms, and cross-rhythms and is subdivided, using divisive rhythms instead of additive rhythms). The preceding section ends on a C sonority, and the transition at 8 + 3 begins on the same sonority. The use of the whole-tone scale at 8 allows Copland to suggest harmonic motion (B♭–A♭–G–, etc.), yet remain harmonically static because this passage lacks the sense of forward motion or harmonic propulsion that diatonic descent would create. Indeed, this is confirmed at the end of each measure of this brief passage. Although the underlying motion is whole-step, in ending the first descent and starting a second descending scale, the sole half-steps involve C–B–B♭. The half steps here do not offer harmonic motion, but reinforce the arrival on the downbeat (B–B♭).

Just as the Copland scholars have been too hasty in commenting superficially upon this work's "jazz" features and have overlooked its

EXAMPLE 5.6 Copland, *Music for the Theatre,* "Prologue," 8–8 + 3

modernist elements, they have also overlooked its academic elements. For example, Butterworth sees some similarity between this piece and *Dance Symphony* in the avoidance of counterpoint. "Throughout the work Copland avoids counterpoint, concentrating upon melody and accompaniment as the principal features."[23] This simply is not so. Counterpoint is found throughout *Music for the Theatre.* As a student of Boulanger's, Copland never completely abandoned counterpoint, and it remained deeply ingrained in his musical personality. Although counterpoint may have been viewed as an academic and European technique, above all, Copland's primary concern was to create a music that showed technical mastery. In creating an American art music in *Music for the Theatre,* he did not avoid counterpoint, but merely bent it to his compositional will. This work has numerous contrapuntal passages: in these Copland, however, combines conventional counterpoint with modernist harmonic and African-American jazz rhythmic techniques, making the counterpoint less prominent and less apparent to scholars.

Copland uses three different types of counterpoint: note-against-note, imitation and canon, and free counterpoint. The chorale-like four-part style of the Prologue, the opening section A, is note-against-note counterpoint. Copland introduces imitation and a brief canon in the Prologue at [8], albeit somewhat buried by the dense polyrhythmic texture (example 5.6); a more extensive, prominent three-part canon at the octave involving the E♭ clarinet, violin, and piano, unobscured by dense rhythmic activity, occurs in the fourth movement, "Burlesque," in the span [44]–[44] + 6. The "Interlude" is the most contrapuntal movement, with imitation and canon between the piano and the glockenspiel at [30] − 2–[31]. The counterpoint is not independent of the polyrhythmic texture. Copland ingeniously integrates the two: the canon between the piano and glockenspiel forms an additional interlocking ostinato. He also introduces free counterpoint into this movement by composing countermelodies. From [33] + 2 to [35], Copland combines the English horn theme (now transferred to flute and violin) with a countermelody played by solo cello, adding another rhythm to the polyrhythmic texture. In the "Dance" Copland brings two melodies (the A melody of the bassoon, now in the oboe and bassoon) together with the hot clarinet solo at [20].

Music for the Theatre and the Influence of Stravinsky

Scholars have been too quick to identify characteristics and techniques found in this work as jazz-influenced, attributing all to the idiom, nothing to modernism, and sometimes misidentifying "jazz" elements. Much of what scholars attribute to jazz (sometimes wrongly) stems from Copland's rhythmic technique. They limit their observations to the rhythmic aspects of the piece, rather superficially attributing some complex rhythms in a single line or instrument or changing meters to jazz. Further, they have attributed certain melodic elements heard in the trumpet and clarinet to the idiom. Smith's comments about the third movement, the "Dance," serve as an example of how overeager Copland scholars have been to point out this work's jazz elements.

> Here, Copland frankly adopts the popular style of the jazz idiom in this brief, nervously rhythmical piece. Jazz polyrhythms are manipulated according to (1) the harmonic progression of a dominant seventh chords to its implied root in a 3-2 (5/8) application of the old 1 2 3 4 ragtime bass; and (2) by a modified canonic imitation of the same material in the melodic line above.[24]

Smith sees the use of 5/8 and 7/8 as evidence of Copland's using jazz rhythm and meter. Copland, however, saw this movement, with its varying meters and shifting accents, differently, stating, "I was thinking very much about the use of jazz. It was an attempt to make jazz even more exciting. The Dance movement is in 5/8 time, so it wasn't a literal use."[25] He did not consider irregular meters such as 5/8 (and 7/8) characteristic of jazz. Indeed, this type of rhythmic technique is more typical of Stravinsky.

Stravinsky's influence pervades *Music for the Theatre,* which is stylistically similar to *Dance Symphony* and the Symphony for Organ and Orchestra. First, Copland combines interlocking polyrhythmic ostinati with constantly shifting meters. Although ostinati can be found in African-American music, it is also a technique fundamental to Stravinsky's style, found in works such as *Rite of Spring* (cf. "The Augurs of Spring," [14] ff.). It is also the one Copland borrowed directly from the elder composer and modified for his own use. To find examples of constantly varying meter, shifting metrical accents, marked use of rhythmic interplay—in addition to interlocking polyrhythmic ostinati—one need only look to Stravinsky's *L'histoire du soldat* (*cf.,* "Marche du Soldat," especially [10] ff.; "Petits Airs Au Bord du Ruisseau"; the "Tango" and "Ragtime" of the *Trois Dances*).

Copland's transposition of the ostinati in the "Interlude" a minor third higher signals his use of octatonicism as architectonic poles. As if to show homage to Stravinsky, Copland incorporates a small amount of octatonicism in the Prologue, using two versions of the octatonic collection, Collection I and Collection III (see example 5.7). In m. 2, Copland partitions the collection into tetrachords and then selects the lower tetrachord, organizing its pitches into an E-minor$^{\flat 11}$, omitting the fifth and seventh. In m. 5, the pitches of the octatonic collection are organized as an A-minor$^{\substack{\flat 11\\ \flat 9\\ \flat 7}}$. The octatonic collection in m. 13 is organized as a C-minor$^{\flat 9}$. The overall harmonic sequence is E-minor$^{\flat 11}$–A-minor$^{\substack{\flat 11\\ \flat 9\\ \flat 7}}$–C-minor$^{\flat 9}$. Both

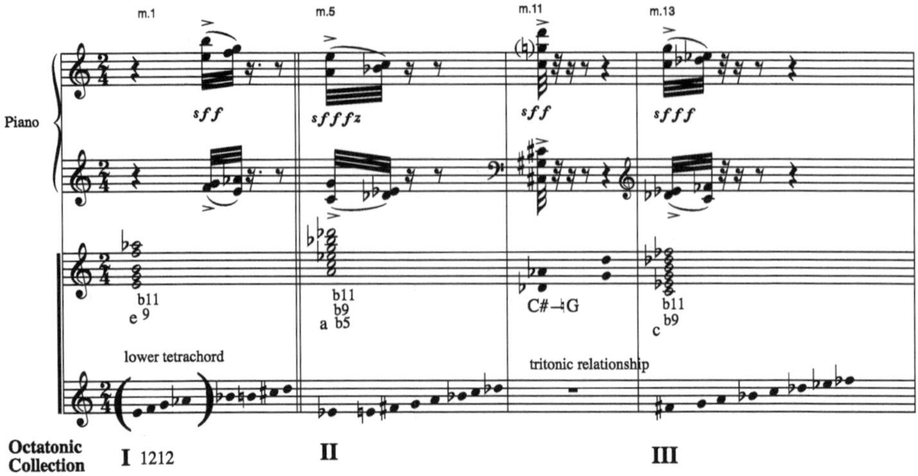

EXAMPLE 5.7 Copland, *Music for the Theatre,* "Prologue," m. 2, m. 5, m. 11, and 13, chords and the two versions of the octatonic

these techniques—partitioning the octatonic collection into its upper and lower tetrachords and third relations—are characteristic of Stravinsky's music.[26] With these chords sounded by the piano, Copland can suggest A minor, C minor, and E♭ minor as tonal centers that lie a third apart, a harmonic technique also used by Stravinsky (e.g., see *The Firebird*). Although Copland does use octatonicism other than in these introductory measures, the minor third continues to play a role throughout the piece: instead of fifth relations, Copland uses third relations in moving from one structural point to another. Although octatonicism never became a major feature of his harmonic style, third relations did, and—as he shows here at the beginning of the Prologue—Copland had now fully mastered octatonicism and its harmonic and melodic properties.

Music for the Theatre, French Neoclassicism, and the New American Folklore

Past scholars have been equally eager to equate Copland's use of jazz with "Americanness," seeing jazz as a kind of Americanism—a music symbolic of American culture, indigenous music, and life, especially of the 1920s. They identify characteristics and techniques found in this work as jazz-influenced even in the face of direct evidence to the contrary. Butterworth is typical: "Considered by many to be one of his most important compositions, *Music for the Theatre* is totally American."[27] However, jazz's identity during this decade—and even to the present day—was multidimensional, varying from one context to another. This tendency to focus so narrowly on "jazz rhythm" has led scholars astray, in that they have persistently overlooked how Copland combined those jazz elements with modernist harmonic, melodic, and textural techniques to produce a work that, like "Jazzy," was consistent with the French neoclassical aesthetic of Satie and Poulenc that he had begun to absorb in Paris.

Aesthetically, Copland's use of jazz had as much to do with international modernism as it did with American nationalism. By the 1920s jazz had a threefold identity. It was an urban, twentieth-century, African-American music in which popular song, the blues, marches, and dance music had come together. It was an American music that included the regional styles of black New Orleans jazz musicians such as King Oliver and Kid Ory. On the East Coast, performers such as James Reese Europe and his Clef Club Orchestra impressed white New Yorkers just as they had the French during World War I. Other styles emerged during the twenties with figures such as Duke Ellington and Fletcher Henderson. Though not truly a jazz musician but a germinal figure in popular music, Paul Whiteman played an important role in popularizing what he called symphonic jazz, a style of dance music known as "sweet" jazz that was palatable to white society New Yorkers. Whiteman's coast-to-coast radio show brought this popular music before a mass audience. Jazz was also an international music. When Auric, Weill, Krenek, and other Europeans wanted to suggest the United States, jazz offered them the means to do so. Additionally, jazz infused their melodic and rhythmic imaginations with freshness and new techniques.

Paris provided Copland with what he needed to evolve from a purely abstract modernism to a nationalism that did not use quaint Americanisms. He discovered he could compose with the intent he was creating uniquely American music free of the German past, one that also placed America in the midst of the latest international musical developments. Under the tutelage of Boulanger, Copland found himself exposed to the music of French neoclassical composer Darius Milhaud and to a new aesthetic propagated by Cocteau and Satie. The aesthetics of French neoclassicism, specifically that of Milhaud, Cocteau, and Poulenc, opened Copland to the possibilities of African-American jazz, then recognized by Europe as both a distinctly American music and as a modern music. It could be used to create a modern, American music, and hence, his "Americanism" was filtered through "international music." Stravinsky, Milhaud, and Auric had turned to, quoted, incorporated, or imitated urban Parisian popular music—the songs and dance music of the cabaret, music hall, café concert, circus, and similar urban popular entertainments. Copland called upon the urbane popular music of twentieth-century urban America. One need only look to the *Trois Dances* of Stravinsky's *L'histoire du soldat* or to Milhaud's *Le boeuf sur la toit* or *Saudades do Brasil* to see examples of the incorporation of popular dance music, jazz, and popular songs, respectively. The style of Les Six and the aesthetic of Cocteau allowed Copland to overtly adapt the contemporary vernacular idioms without apology and keep abreast of international developments simultaneously. His sojourn to France exposed him to neoclassical style and aesthetics. It was the United States and racial-ethnic African-Americans that provided Copland with an American vernacular, jazz.

The previous generation of American nationalist composer had turned to Native American and African-American folk music, quaintly quoting melodies and placing the source materials in a nineteenth-century Romantic frame. Rather than looking to these musical traditions for new harmonies, timbres, or textures, these older composers borrowed only melody. They looked backwards—to past folk traditions of a bygone era. The western frontier had been "closed" and the fight for westward expansion won, although the last of the Indian Wars ended the first few years of the 1900s and African-American spirituals were still a living tradition. These musics were seen as part of America's *past* musical heritage. Instead of turning to other types of musical Americana music such as Anglo-American, African-American, or Native American folk music of the past as his predecessors Goldmark, Arthur Farwell, Amy Beach, or George Chadwick had (Dvořák's name must be mentioned as well), Copland turned to the *urban* folk music of his present-day United States, just as the French composers Milhaud and Poulenc had turned to the urban folk music of their present-day France. In *Music for the Theatre* Copland also adopted as models Milhaud's *Le boeuf sur le toit* (1919) and *La création du monde* (1923), works in which the French composer overtly drew upon American jazz and imitated "hot" jazz. In adopting elements of the jazz idiom in this 1925 work, Copland also followed the lead that had been set in 1918 by Stravinsky's use of ragtime in *L'histoire du soldat* (as well as his Ragtime for Eleven Instruments and *Piano-rag-music*). This was not a coincidence but part of Copland's immediate musical milieu: he had met all these composers while he studied with Boulanger and he knew these works quite well, or at the very least, had more than passing familiarity with them.[28]

Copland and Pastiche: *Music for the Theatre* and Popular Music

Music for the Theatre not only represents the extensiveness of Copland's musical and cultural interest in jazz. It shows the conflux of several musical and cultural streams. The neoclassical aesthetic partly looked to eighteenth-century styles. Pollack draws a parallel between *Music for the Theatre*'s movements and French neoclassicism, calling it a "Baroque suite in modern terms." The title and character of the individual movements have their antecedents in the eighteenth century: the Prologue parallels the French overture; the "Burlesque" is a modern update of the "burlescas."[29] But *Music for the Theatre* has neoclassical elements other than jazz, academic counterpoint, and eighteenth-century dance allusions. Here we ask, was there a new folk music for the contemporary, modern, urban United States beyond jazz? Copland's interest in more than just sweet jazz places him in the context of the Harlem Renaissance and allows an opportunity for the study of one case of cultural interchange among blacks and whites. But jazz was not the only vernacular music Copland borrowed and incorporated in this work. He also showed a latent interest in musical theater and, relatedly, American popular song—Tin Pan Alley—and this serves as further evidence of French neoclassical aesthetic influence on the young American composer.

We have seen that Copland had more experience playing popular dance music than he had playing jazz. Likewise, he had minimal experience with another popular American music, popular song (or Tin Pan Alley) and musical theater. During the 1920s and 1930s, the period of this study, musical theater was closely tied to the popular music industry. Often, original songs were strung together to create a revue, or a book (the musical theater equivalent of an opera libretto) was constructed around a group of songs. Songs from a popular musical would be sold as sheet music to amateur musicians, recorded by popular or jazz musicians, or featured in Hollywood films. As a youth considering a career in composition, Copland understood that he faced the difficult challenge of earning enough money from his music-making to support himself, and at one point he seriously considered going into musical theater or popular music while he continued his studies. He was advised against this by his friend Aaron Schaffer, who counseled Copland that many young musicians had taken this route and had become trapped in a "deadening atmosphere" and ended up "musical wrecks."[30] Schaffer was concerned that although work as a songwriter might provide Copland with lucrative income (as for George Gershwin), it would be ruinous for the young composer. He wondered if there might be some other way for Copland to earn money. Perhaps as a direct consequence of this advice, Copland did not pursue this route. Having not entered the field of popular song composition at all, Copland's experience with Tin Pan Alley was similar in some ways to his experience with jazz: he kept it at arm's length instead of diving into it as a performer and composer. The important result is that his use of Tin Pan Alley remained just as abstract (and cerebral) as his use of jazz and his characterization of it just as academic.

Music for the Theatre also shows both the influence of Copland's interest in popular music and musical theater and the extent to which his French neoclassical counterparts influenced him in another way. This work is a pastiche—collage—of not only Stravinsky-like interlocking polyrhythmic ostinato techniques, octatonicism, and jazz, but also American popular song, or Tin Pan Alley. *Music for the Theatre* (obviously playing, from its titles, with the idea of popular theater) grew out of Copland's ideas for an earlier planned work, "Incidental Music for an Imaginary Drama."[31] He attended Broadway plays frequently during the late 1920s.[32] In his autobiography, he wrote at length about the genesis of the work and freely acknowledged the partial inspiration of popular theater music:

> *Music for the Theatre* was written with no specific play in mind. It had started with musical ideas that might have been combined as incidental music to a play were the right one at hand. The music seemed to suggest a certain theatrical atmosphere, so I chose the title after developing the ideas into five short movements: The "Prologue" has a certain brashness about it that was typical of my age and the times. It begins rather suddenly with a trumpet solo, followed by a tenderly lyrical passage leading into an allegro mid-section with obvious jazz influence before a return to the lyrical material. (I am told that this resembles the nursery tune "Three Blind Mice," but there was no conscious intention on my part of quoting it.) "Dance," short and jazzy, quotes the familiar popular tune "East Side, West Side"; "Interlude," a kind of song without words, is built on a lyric theme repeated three times with slight changes. "Burlesque," best described by its title, emphasizes another characteristic of the twenties—the love of grotesquerie achieved by a liberal use of harmonic dissonance. It was partly inspired by the popular comedienne Fanny Brice. The "Epilogue" incorporates material from the first and third movements and recaptures the quiet mood of the "Prologue."[33]

The movement "Burlesque" was inspired to an extent by Fanny Brice, a musical theater and burlesque star known for her use of Jewish dialect and portrayal of immigrant characters.[34] In addition to the numbers Copland mentions in his autobiography, he quoted the chorus of the popular song "The Sidewalks of New York," by Charles B. Lawlor and James W. Blake (see example 5.8). The tune Copland chose was not ob-

EXAMPLE 5.8 Charles B. Lawlor and James W. Blake, "The Sidewalks of New York," Chorus

scure: copyrighted in 1894, it was a verified "hit," successfully selling over a million copies.[35] Though composed in the mid-1890s, it was one of many early Tin Pan Alley songs that remained popular years after their initial publication. Copland borrows the first four measures of the tune, the portion that accompanies the catchphrase, "East Side, West Side" (see example 5.9). He quotes the melody directly, combining it with interlocking polyrhythmic ostinati. Popular music also appears in "Burlesque" 40–41. Here, rather than quoting the melody literally, Copland abstracts from the original chorus a motive comprised of an oscillating minor-third that appears in the violins.

EXAMPLE 5.9 Copland, *Music for the Theatre,* "Dance," 25–26

A Portrait of Copland's New York: Race, Ethnicity, and Sexuality

Although the proper title of the song was "The Sidewalks of New York," it was also known as "East Side, West Side," sections of Manhattan with large immigrant communities. The significance of Copland's use of this particular tune should not be overlooked: he chose both a genre and a song that were overwhelmingly and unequivocally urban. Smith first recognized that Copland borrowed from a popular song and suggested a connection between it and Copland's own life.[36] The lyrics of "The Sidewalks of New York" deal with childhood in the City. As Charles Hamm writes in *Yesterdays: Popular Song in America,* this song presents a "[portrait] of happy childhood" (see table 5.2).[37] A sentimental reminiscence of Manhattan, the song is of special interest because it presents several ethnic groups in turn-of-the-century New York. In other verses the speaker goes on to list among his or her playmates Johnny Casey, Jimmy Crowe, Jakey Krause, and Nellie Shannon, and in the first verse, as quoted, there is "Ginnie" the organ grinder. These names refer to Irish-, African-, German-Jewish-, and Italian-American personages, respectively. Although the speaker remembers all these groups with fondness

TABLE 5.2 "The Sidewalks of New York," Verse 1 and Chorus

Verse	Down in front of Casey's Old brown wooden stoop, On a summer's evening, We formed a merry group; Boys and girls together, We would sing and waltz, While the "Ginnie" played the organ On the sidewalks of New York.
Chorus	East side, West side, All around the town, The tots sang "ring a rosie," "London Bridge is falling down"; Boys and girls together, Me and Mamie Rorke, Tripped the light fantastic, On the sidewalks of New York.

(presumably, judging from the lilting and melodious tune), he or she nonetheless uses pejoratives and stereotypical images. "Jimmy Crowe" is the son, presumably, of Jim Crow, the stereotype of the plantation slave who first entered American popular culture as one of the characters of the minstrel show. The line referring to the Krause boy contains a double entendre: "Jakey Krause / Who always had the dough." Like the reference to Jimmy Crowe, at first glance the line seems fairly innocuous. However, when one considers the second meaning of the word "dough"—money—the derogatory and offensive stereotype of the Jewish moneylender becomes apparent. The "Ginnie" is a mispronunciation of *Guinea,* an offensive term applied to Italian-Americans at that time. Although the speaker remembers childhood with fondness, he or she, nonetheless, as a child has learned prejudice.

Though the song contains now-offensive stereotypes, it shows the diversity of nineteenth-century New York in what its author intended to be a good light. It does not do so in an enlightened way from our perspective (pernicious stereotypes pervade), but it does present a vernacular portrait of New York life in which many American ethnic groups come together as equals in the urban environment's public spaces (in the streets, playgrounds, etc.). This is treated in the song as part of American culture and identity: the democratic ideal that in America all are created equal. It also paints a picture of an urban childhood in which an American identity is forged. The speaker learned how to dance "like an American." He or she "first picked up the waltz step on the sidewalks of New York." Note that he or she learned a middle-class formal, "refined" dance signifying upward mobility, not an ethnic, vernacular, popular, or "vulgar" dance. Regardless of the speaker's ethnic group, though "things have changed since those times, / Some are up in 'G, / Others they are wand'rers / They all feel just like me," that is, the speaker views them not as only his or her equal even as an adult, but as fellow Americans—*E pluribus unum.*[38]

It has not been ascertained where Copland learned this song. He may have heard it in his home as a child, since the song was also featured in the 1911 musical *Pink Lady* and the Copland children regularly played music together:[39] "I clearly recall ragtime and selections from popular shows of the day being played in the evenings at home."[40] However, the song's content can certainly be linked directly to Copland's own life. In his article "Composer from Brooklyn: An Autobiographical Sketch," Copland characterized his childhood neighborhood as ethnically mixed.[41]

> It probably resembled most one of the outer districts of lower-middle-class London, except that it was peopled largely by Italians, Irish, and Negroes. I mention it because it was there that I spent the first twenty years of my life. Also, because I am filled with mild wonder each time I realize that a musician was born on that street.[42]

The ethnic variety listed in the song reflects the neighborhood that Copland describes. Ostensibly he was drawn to the song, at least in part, because it recalled his own Washington Avenue neighborhood in Brooklyn and his experience as one of the upwardly mobile second generation, the son of Eastern European Jewish immigrants.[43]

In choosing to quote this particular tune in one of his first post-Paris works, Copland reveals the extent to which he was influenced by Milhaud, Poulenc, and Cocteau—an influence that extended beyond the use of jazz. This can be further understood by considering Copland's first quotation of popular song and comparing it with the song he chose for *Music for the Theatre.* He used "My Buddy" in section B of "Jazzy" from *Trois Equisses* (see chapter 3, example 3.9). Copland also borrowed the song's harmony—modified somewhat in his version—melody, and rhythm (in diminution). Although the compositional technique remains similar to "Jazzy," in *Music for the Theatre*'s "Dance" and "Burlesque" Copland goes beyond what he does in "Jazzy." His usage of the songs' melodies is similar—direct quotation and modernist harmonic support, complex rhythms and textures, and tripartite form—but the significance of the songs he chooses varies greatly. "My Buddy" is a popular song about lasting friendship, about possible homoeroticism, and, when considered in the context of its World War I popularity, a song about pulling together for a common purpose to fight a "war to end all wars." "The Sidewalks of New York (East Side/West Side)" is a song about a multiracial, multiethnic city with what was by then an international reputation, the destination for millions of immigrants. Furthermore, at this time in American history, immigration was politically controversial. Anti-immigration laws enacted during the 1920s limited the number of immigrants from eastern and southern European countries.

Music for the Theatre and New York's Gay Subculture

The use of "The Sidewalks of New York" had topical, social, and personal relevance for Copland. In choosing to quote this song directly in "Dance" and the derivation of the minor-third motive used in T^2 in "Burlesque," Copland also alludes to New York gay subculture. Recent scholars have begun to address issues of Copland's sexuality in his life and music as gay and lesbian studies scholars question and theorize about music, gender, and sexuality. Pollack devotes an entire chapter, "Personal Affairs," to this question. Gay and lesbian studies scholars seek not just to identify gay composers but to ask questions about how sexuality and sexual identity affect compositional choices, musical intent, aesthetic positions, and reception of the works of not only homosexual composers, but also heterosexual ones (witness recent Ives scholarship and the exploration of modernism as masculinity in Ives's music).[44] Copland scholars, too, can ask questions about whether and how being a gay male influenced the style, aesthetics, and reception of his music. Methodology and theory from gay and lesbian studies can be applied to *Music for the Theatre.* In one movement particularly, "Burlesque," one can discern a gay subtext and sensibility that would have been read by gay (and lesbian) members of his audiences on one level and by heterosexual males on another.

The choice to incorporate a "Burlesque" as one of the movements of *Music for the Theatre* signifies New York's gay subculture. Pollack was the first to draw this connection. "Burlesque," he writes, features "the sexually suggestive dancers" of the burlesque stage, depicted by the "hilariously vulgar theme for trumpets . . . marked 'grotesco'" as the cornerstone of this connection. For Pollack, the reappearance of this trumpet theme at the end of the "Burlesque" movement "evokes the final moments (often the baring of breasts) of a burlesque striptease." Contrary to popular opinion about "burlesque" being an entertainment that appealed to heterosexual males, some gay men in New York were attracted to burlesque theater. In linking the movement "Burlesque" to this subculture, Pollack relies on further external evidence and describes the burlesque theaters on Forty-second Street as an attraction for homosexuals, who were drawn to them because they flouted "traditional sexual mores."[45] Pollack is corroborated by historian George Chauncy, who documents a link between gay men and vaudeville and burlesque houses in New York dating back to the 1890s, first near East Fourteenth Street, between the Third Avenue and Union Square area, before the gay street culture migrated to the Times Square area by the 1920s and 1930s.[46]

Certainly by the time Copland composed *Music for the Theatre*, he had accepted his sexuality. As a teen Copland had read Havelock Ellis's groundbreaking study of homosexuality, *Sexual Inversion* (1897), which he found in the Brooklyn Public Library. Pollack concedes that it is not known if Copland was involved sexually with any of his close friends (male or female) before he left for Paris. He does state that the composer "came to terms with his homosexuality before leaving Brooklyn for Paris." Copland was passionate about the writings of André Gide, a gay writer who explored sexuality in his work. Copland lived in Montparnasse, Gertrude Stein's *arrondissement* (he would be introduced to her in 1931 by Paul Bowles). Upon his return to New York, Copland stayed only briefly in Brooklyn, taking an apartment at West Seventy-fourth Street on Manhattan's Upper West Side, where he resided from October 1926 to 1929. This area was popular with artists and intellectuals and close to Broadway theaters, midtown jazz clubs, the Metropolitan Opera (then on W. Thirty-ninth St.), and Town Hall (W. Forty-third St.).[47] In traveling between his apartment and the theater, opera, concert halls, and other downtown and Brooklyn destinations, Copland traversed the theater district regularly, and thus would have been aware of the burlesque houses. Harlem had its own African-American gay and lesbian community, which also attracted white homosexuals. As Chauncey describes, with its gay speakeasies, clubs, buffet flats, private parties, and drag balls, Harlem was a gay mecca.[48] Copland is known to have visited Harlem with Carl Van Vechten, who, though married to actress Fania Marinoff, was homosexual. It is not known whether Copland went to one of these Harlem locales. Throughout his life, though he was relatively open about his sexuality and had many relationships with men, Copland was discreet and not promiscuous. As Pollack states, he did not "seek out sailors and other 'trade' as did a number of his friends."[49]

The various sources Copland draws upon in *Music for the Theatre* lead one to consider that this work—and Copland's daring—is multivalent. On one level, with its waltzing quotation of "The Sidewalks of New York" in "Dance," it is a picture of a happy childhood. On another, with its use of jazz and blues, it is bold: during the 1920s white Americans associated jazz with a liberated sexuality and freewheeling rejection of traditional Victorian values. Roy Harris once described the "Burlesque" as "whorehouse music."[50] In quoting "East Side, West Side," combined with jazzy rhythm in "Dance" and the East Side minor-third motive in "Burlesque," Copland refers to New York's gay subculture by camping it up. Burlesque theater and New York's gay male subculture (as well as the Roy Harris quotation!) were full camp. As Jack Babuscio defines:

> The term *camp* describes those elements in a person, situation, or activity that express, or are created by, a gay sensibility. Camp is never a thing or person per se, but, rather, a relationship between activities, individuals, situations, *and* gayness. People who have camp, e.g. screen "personalities" such as Tallulah Bankhead or Edward Everett Horton, or who are in some way responsible for camp—Busby Berkeley or Josef Sternberg—need not be gay. The link with gayness is established when the camp aspect of an individual or thing is identified as such by a gay sensibility. This is not to say that all gays respond in equal measure to camp, or, even that an absolute consensus could easily be reached within our community about what to include or emphasize. Yet though camp resides largely in the eye of the beholder, there remains an underlying unity of perspective among gays that gives to someone or something its characteristic camp flavor. Four features are basic to camp: irony, aestheticism, theatricality, and humor.[51]

For Babuscio, "irony is the subject matter of camp" and is "any highly incongruous contrast between an individual or things and its context or association." Camp "relies largely upon arrangement, timing, and tone." He identifies ways in which camp is aesthetic: "as a view of art; as a view of life; and as a practical tendency in things or persons." As a liberating aesthetic it is "an assertion of one's self-integrity—a temporary means of accommodation with society in which art becomes, at one and the same, an intense mode of individualism and a form of spirited protest." Camp simultaneously allows the gay person to challenge moral rules and to plead for another morality, one based on "sympathy" (here, one might append "tolerance" to Babuscio's term "sympathy"). In defining camp as "theatricality," Babuscio refers not to the stage but to the notion that life *is* "role and theater, appearance and impersonation." Babuscio's camp humor results "from an identification of a strong incongruity between an object, person, or situation and its context," and he relates this to irony. Humor, which can take several forms, is essential to camp as a strategy of survival, "a means of dealing with a hostile environment and, in the process, of defining a positive identity."[52]

"Burlesque" is campy music. Copland himself admitted that there was an element of the grotesque, or exaggeration and theatricality, in this movement. "'Burlesque,' best described by its title, emphasizes another characteristic of the twenties—the love of grotesquerie achieved by a liberal use of harmonic dissonance."[53] Its irony turns on the presentation of jazz rhythms, festive, blaring trumpets, and slightly out-of-tune clarinets, dancingly juxtaposed with sedate Bachian interludes. More incongruous is the brash invocation of a low-brow, risqué—some would say, vulgar—entertainment of burlesque in a social space serving in 1920s America as a bastion—nay, temple—of high culture, the concert hall. And, what could be more incongruous and humorous than asking conservatory-trained classical Boston Symphony Orchestra musicians to strip down their pretenses of high art? Audiences at the Boston premiere experienced even more incongruity: Koussevitzky placed *Music for the Theatre* after two works, the overture to Mozart's *The Magic Flute* and Beethoven's Fourth Symphony and before the Prelude to Wagner's *Tristan und Isolde.* But the most daring aesthetic and social strategy is Copland's double entendre and how he introduced to an audience in Boston—a city so known for it conservatism that "banned in Boston" became a common expression—a coded reference to New York's gay male scene. Heterosexual and homosexual members of the audience would have perceived his intentions in "Burlesque" quite differently. Straight members of the audience would have recognized the reference to the "girlie" show and perhaps would have smiled as one would at a naughty but charming schoolboy; gay male members of the audience who understood the code, and especially those who had indeed visited New York, would have smiled and winked knowingly that Copland was "a member of the choir," to borrow a term from the pre-Stonewall era used in the twentieth century by closeted gay men to refer to each other.[54]

Pastiche and Neoclassical Resonances

In his autobiography, Copland says that this work has a certain theatrical quality. His works using Tin Pan Alley songs do not evoke the legitimate stage but the atmosphere of vaudeville.[55] Burlesque (the successor of the girlie show) and the vaudeville show both succeeded minstrelsy. Like Poulenc, Milhaud, Auric, and Cocteau, Copland turned to the popular institutions of his native country. Rather than the café concert, circus, music hall, or fair of the Parisians, Copland turned to the burlesque or vaudeville—the variety show, America's second form of popular theatrical entertainment, which began during the 1880s (one of its successors was in turn film, a medium for which Copland would later compose). Rather than the dramatic unity of a stage play, opera, or book musical, a vaudeville show offered a variety of acts, ranging from classical music, singing, juggling, and dancing to animal acts, paralleling the change in mood and character from movement to movement in *Music for the Theatre.* "Burlesque" also alludes to Stravinsky's *Petrushka:* ostinati in the fast sections of the Prologue recall parts of the ballet. The parallels between Copland's "Burlesque" and Stravinsky's ballet are stronger. *Petrushka* contains two forms of popular entertainments: (1) the opening and closing tableau take place at the fair; and (2) the ballet is based upon the popular entertainment of the Petrushka puppet play, and indeed, the puppet is incorporated into the ballet.[56] *Music for the Theatre* contains two kinds of popular entertainments as well: (1) the burlesque and

(2) American popular song. Both are Americanisms. As Pollack writes, "Many young artists and intellectuals saw in burlesque, as in the equally controversial jazz, a vital American art form, comparable and yet different from the Parisian dance hall and the German cabaret."[57] *Music for the Theatre* would not have been appropriate for Broadway, radio, the nightclub, musical theater, or the vaudeville stage. It was not meant to be played in any of the typical places in which jazz and Tin Pan Alley songs would have been heard in the mid-1920s. It is modern concert music. Rather than bringing a concert work into the nightclub, Copland has brought the music of the dance halls and nightclubs to the concert hall and in this fashion transmogrifies his own vernacular idiom, the popular song, placing it in a modernist context.

Just as the speaker in his song had become an American by learning to dance the fancy, upper-middle-class, but popular waltz, Copland proposed that the American composer could create his own musical idiom from the American vernacular of popular music, both jazz and Tin Pan Alley. But as in the song, Copland's preference for the "fancier" European tradition in music always came into play. In quoting from "The Sidewalks of New York," Copland shows the influence of Poulenc and his aesthetic. Poulenc saw French popular songs and French popular culture as a kind of modern, twentieth-century urban folklore. Copland, after returning to the United States, posited that popular songs were the folklore of the modern composer. He "used" jazz, but actually defined white popular songs as the real indigenous material he had imbibed in his childhood. As he explained during the 1950s:

> If we haven't a folksong foundation, we must invent one. I began by thinking—what is a folksong after all? And I came to the conclusions that in my case it was the songs I heard when I was a child—rather commonplace jazz tunes and music of the "Old Black Joe" variety. These, then, are my material, and I must accept them for what they are. If we have only these elements as essentially American, our music must make the best of it and do the work so well that something worth while will come from the effort.[58]

Copland's reference to jazz is clear; however, his reference to the song "Old Black Joe" is not. One might think that this song is an American folk tune. On the contrary, it is a nineteenth-century popular minstrel song composed by Stephen Foster. Copland's "folk" music during the late 1920s was not folk music of the British-American variety; nor was it rural at all. His "folk" music was "manufactured," in a sense, from the urban songs and dances of musical theater, Tin Pan Alley, and sweet jazz. He belonged to a generation whose first taste of music was filtered through popular entertainments—the vernacular music of his own background. His identification of this music as "folk" music is not so much inaccurate as revelatory of the state of "popular" music in the early twentieth century: Tin Pan Alley songs were so pervasive in the shared culture—and factual knowledge of authentic folk music traditions so obscured for many urban Americans—that popular songs and jazz were indeed an urban, American folk music.

Disavowing the Use of Jazz as an Americanism

Copland continued to draw upon jazz in works he composed during the late 1920s and into the 1930s. However, he soon found the idiom limited for his purposes.

> The jazz element in *Music for the Theatre* was further developed in my next work, a *Concerto for Piano and Orchestra,* which I played as soloist with the Boston Symphony in Boston and New York. This proved to be the last of my "experiments" with symphonic jazz. With the Concerto I felt I had done all I could with the idiom, considering its limited emotional scope. True, it was an easy way to be American in musical terms, but all American music could not possibly be confined to two dominant jazz moods—the blues and the snappy number. The characteristic rhythmic element of jazz, being independent of mood, yet purely indigenous, will undoubtedly continue to be used in serious native music.[59]

It is clear from this, however, that the "limitations" he saw in jazz as an idiom were due also to his own limited experiences with jazz. His own lack of improvisational skill led him to caricature jazz because he did not fundamentally understand the music. Copland was not aware of the range of jazz in terms of the idiom's emotional power, but he did feel he could use the part most analytically available to a composer with French neoclassical training: its rhythm, instrumentation, and ostinati. Copland ceased to quote jazz directly or to explore the harmonic ambiguity that is part of blues and blues-based music. By the end of the 1930s, Copland thought that the vogue and international interest in jazz had run its course.

> Jazz played a big role in the twenties. But I had been observing the scene around me and sensed it was about to change. Moreover, I realized that jazz might have had its best treatment from those who had a talent for improvisation. I sensed its limitations, intended to make a change, and made no secret of the fact.[60]

He ultimately abandoned direct imitation or emulation of jazz, in part because he felt frustrated by its dependence on improvisation. Although in the mid-1920s he had been enthusiastic about jazz as an easy way to make his music sound American and acknowledged that it represented a resource for the composer, Copland drew upon this music only briefly, essentially moving beyond it after his Piano Concerto (1926) and Symphonic Ode (1927–29).

> After writing several works based on the jazz idiom I came to the conclusion that the general spirit of jazz was much too limited to be used as a basis for a fully rounded music. The rhythmic element, on the other hand, is important, I think, because it is typically American in quality, and yet may be used quite apart from a jazz context.[61]

Nevertheless, although he ceased to imitate jazz directly, his style remained forever influenced by at least one element of the idiom.

Synthesis

Nearly sixty years after composing *Music for the Theatre* Copland stated in his autobiography:

> Perhaps jazz was, as Virgil put it, "Copland's one wild oat," but *Music for the Theatre* and the *Piano Concerto* were characteristic of my musical thinking at the time. And long after the fad of concert jazz faded, the influence of jazz would be felt in the development of polyrhythms. In a 1927 article, "Jazz Structure and Influence," I addressed these issues, concluding: "It [jazz] may be the substance not only of the American composer's fox trots and Charlestons, but of his lullabies and nocturnes."[62]

In the 1920s jazz was an international music expressive for the modern age. Thus, with jazz, Copland had an international music, a modern music, and an American one. For Copland the idiom was both American folklore and modern, urban folklore. The lessons learned from the use of jazzy syncopations, polyrhythms, and cross-rhythms were never lost on Copland. Jazz remained part of his style, fused with the interlocking polyrhythmic ostinati and shifting meters and metrical accents that he had learned from Stravinsky's music. Ironically, Copland absorbed an aesthetic position that permitted him to view jazz as a modern American music in France. African music had crossed the Atlantic westward. Copland had gone east to find his African-derived American music. There is still more irony: he had virtually no experience beyond his teens performing or composing for the kinds of popular entertainments—the revue, the dance hall, the nightclub—that Cocteau, Satie, Auric, Poulenc, and Milhaud saw as the source of a French modernism free of Wagnerian or Romantic influences. The use of jazz and quotation of popular song once again point to the influence of French neoclassical aesthetics on Copland. The goal of Cocteau's aesthetic was to create a new French music that was at once non-Wagnerian and non-Debussyesque. Cocteau urged younger French composers not to emulate Wagner's Romanticism nor Debussy's Impressionism and proposed that they adopt the styles of popular music found in the cafés, circus, cinema, music halls, cabarets, and use jazz. Copland's use of jazz directly paralleled Poulenc's suggestion that a modernist composer draw upon his or her own popular music in creating a national art music. During the late twenties Copland did thoroughly assimilate all the modernist styles of Paris and mixed them with American jazz and popular music. Copland drew upon his own variety of urban folk music: a mélange of jazz and the songs of Tin Pan Alley.

CHAPTER SIX

European Influence beyond Stravinsky and Les Six :: Hába and Schoenberg

> The basic premise of Schoenberg's harmonic revolution was his abandonment of our hitherto unquestioned need for the sense of a central tonality.
> —Copland, *Our New Music*

As Copland adopted and modified Stravinskian techniques for his own use, explored the possibilities of jazz, and embraced the aesthetic of Les Six, he did not limit his style to these approaches. He also familiarized himself with the music of other modern European composers, particularly those in Germany, Austria, and eastern Europe. Some of these works he encountered through studies with Boulanger and in her Wednesday afternoon analysis class, but a large amount of this music Copland explored on his own. In the summers 1922 and 1923 he traveled to various music centers in Europe—Berlin, Vienna, Salzburg, Rome, London—especially to attend the annual music festivals of the newly founded International Society for Contemporary Music. At these weeklong events he was exposed to the music of Schoenberg and his pupils, Béla Bartók, Ernst Krenek, Paul Hindemith, Alois Hába, and Eastern European composers Sergei Prokofiev and Leoš Janáček, among others. Copland responded by composing a handful of works that reflect the influence of Schoenberg and, especially, of Anton Webern. Although Copland did not write a strictly twelve-tone work prior to the 1940s, he did experiment with his own version of the method in works such as "poet's song," "Pastorale," "Vieux Poeme," and the later *Piano Variations.*

Copland's exploration of Eastern European music raises the issue of his own Eastern European Jewish ethnicity. He did not visit the countries from which his parents had emigrated (Lithuania and Russia) during these Paris years. Nor did he put the use or quotation of Jewish liturgical, sacred, or secular music at the forefront of his musical style. Yet, just as his jazz-flavored works show the influence of European modernism and appropriate modernist techniques, so too did *Vitebsk.* While evocative of his own religious and cultural heritage as well as his family's origin, this work combines a traditional Jewish melody with modernist techniques, borrowed this time not from Stravinsky or Les Six, but from Alois Hába.

Copland and the Second Viennese School

While Boulanger exposed her students to all the latest trends, Austro-German as well as French, she herself was not drawn to the music of Arnold Schoenberg and his pupils, an aesthetic Copland came to share. Yet Copland was exposed to a range of new Germanic music outside of Boulanger's classes and salons. He identified two centers of music: "Most German musical activity seems to be centered in Vienna around Schoenberg and his pupils such as Egon Wellesz and Anton Webern. Whatever happens of any importance in Berlin seem to emanate from Shrecker and his pupils."[1] During summers of 1922 and 1923 he and Clurman traveled to Vienna, Berlin, and Salzburg, where the young composer delighted in new music performances as he continued work on his ballet *Grohg* for Boulanger. Copland wrote her from Berlin and Vienna, chronicling the concerts he attended and the works he heard. His letter of August 1922 from Berlin, where he had spent July, reveals how extensively he had embraced French neoclassicism and Boulanger's teaching. He joked, "I'm afraid that my year spent in France, my view point has become so Gallic that I can't understand the Germans." While he continued composing *Grohg,* he attended concerts, hearing Max Schilling's *Mona Lisa,* Hans Pfitzner's *Palestrina,* and Busoni's one-act opera *Arlecchino,* none of which he found very interesting. One benefit of the trip, it seems, is that he was able to purchase a large number of scores, though he did not list the specific compositions in his letter. Copland spent the following summer in Vienna, a city he enjoyed far more than Berlin (he found Berliners rather bourgeois). On July 23, 1923, he excitedly wrote Boulanger of his plans to attend the first festival of the International Society for Contemporary Music: "Six successive evenings of modern music should prove a big enough feast for ever so insatiable a gourmand as myself."[2] He especially looked forward to hearing Bartók's second violin sonata. Copland wrote to his teacher again in mid-August after returning to Vienna and reported hearing more Bartók, as well as works by Schoenberg and others. "I was most impressed by the works of Hindemith, Krenek, and Hába," he wrote.[3] The latter's system of quarter tones and one work in particular struck Copland. "Alois Hába is the least daring despite his system of quarter tones. But his string quartet also made a very favorable impression on me."[4] Copland also heard Krenek's Third String Quartet. Thus, just as he had independently sought out modern music when he studied with Goldmark, he continued this practice as a student of Boulanger and actively sought out the music of German, Austrian, and Eastern European composers.

Copland's statement about having a Gallic viewpoint is telling, for even after his return to the United States, new Germanic music never greatly influenced him during the interwar years. While he had been exposed to Schoenberg's atonality and twelve-tone method, he remained somewhat aesthetically distanced, even as he experimented with it. Primarily he saw Schoenberg's style and aesthetic (especially his early music) and reverence for past German masters from Bach to Brahms as indissolubly linked to German Romanticism carried over to the twentieth century. Copland had heard Schoenberg's *Pierrot Lunaire* in Paris and viewed it as a landmark in modern music composition. For years after his return to the United States, Copland continued to travel to Europe for the annual music festivals of the International Society for Contemporary Music, writing reviews for *Modern Music.* His reviews for 1926 and 1927 reveal that he was never fully convinced of the vitality and promise of Schoenberg's dodecaphonic method. In his review of the fourth annual festival held at Zurich in June 1926, he found the festival less successful than the ones in 1923 and 1924 and many of the works presented there less adventuresome—no single work stood out. He harshly condemned Schoenberg's *Quintet for Wind Instruments:*

> Of equal significance is the fact that no one work proved an outstanding success this year; but there was, so to speak, an outstanding failure—the Arnold Schoenberg *Quintet for Wind Instruments.* Seldom has a new work from the pen of a composer of wide repute suffered such universal condemnation. Except for the certain parts of the scherzo and the final rondo, there seemed to be nothing but principles and theories of composition leading to complete aridity. The Schoenberg disciples, however, are undismayed.[5]

Yet he praised Anton Webern's *Five Orchestral Pieces.* "One listens breathlessly: each piece lasts but a few seconds and each separate note seems filled with meaning. Most striking of all is Webern's orchestration—a subtle mingling of single timbres producing a magical result."[6] Copland would continue to view Schoenberg with disdain even as he embraced the music of Webern and Alban Berg. In his review of the festival of Deutsche Kammermusik held the following year at Baden-Baden, Copland reported that Berg's *Lyric Suite* for string quartet had been well received (he would favorably review it in a 1937 *Modern Music* column).[7] While there, Copland also had a chance to hear Bartók perform his own *Piano Sonata* (1926). The performance of four operas—Milhaud's *The Abduction of Europa,* Weill's *Mahagonny,* Hindemith's *Hin und Zuruck,* and Toch's *The Princess on the Pea*—marked the highlight of the festival.[8] Copland's fascination with the music of Webern and Berg continued into the 1930s. Again reviewing an International Society for Contemporary Music Festival held in July 1931 at Oxford, England, Copland praised the *Symphony for Small Orchestra.* "There are certain things that can be said of von Webern. His music has a wonderful poignancy, and a sensitivity which is related in some way to Debussy's; he can compress his emotional activity into a single moment, and he has absolute mastery over the means he employs."[9] Yet he had reservations about this work and Webern's style: it was anemic, of limited emotional scale. When he inaugurated his review column in *Modern Music* where he critiqued new scores and recordings, Copland had further opportunities to assess the music of the Second Viennese School.

Copland did not limit his engagement (or disengagement) with the Second Viennese School composers to reviews of recordings or attending performances. He disseminated his view of their method and works to an audience outside modern music circles. When he began teaching courses on modern music at the New School for Social Research, he included these composers in his lectures. An announcement for his music appreciation course "The Forms of Modern Music," printed in the *New York Times* in 1929, reveals that Copland introduced his students to Berg's *Wozzeck* as well as Bartók's piano music. Conspicuously absent from the works to be taught as announced in this article were those by Webern and Schoenberg and other of the latter's pupils.[10] In the book that grew out of those lectures, Copland discussed the music of Schoenberg. The first mention of Schoenberg occurred in the passage where he discussed Mahler's orchestration technique. Schoenberg's orchestration technique, in Copland's view, was derived from Mahler. Devoting several pages to Schoenberg in the fourth chapter, "The Middle Ground—Before 1914," he wrote about Schoenberg's expressionist period. Copland viewed Schoenberg in succession of a long line of German composers. The Austrian struggled to break free of this tradition but without much success.

> Schoenberg inherited the full weight of the German tradition; he was the spiritual son of Bruckner, Strauss, and Mahler. He paid them homage in early works like the first songs, the string sextet *Verklärte Nacht,* or the choral symphony *Gurre-Lieder.* But an inner voice surely must have whispered that German romanticism was dead. For when Schoenberg reached the age of thirty-five or thereabouts he made frantic and desperate attempts to dodge the implications of his heritage. From our present perspective we can see that there was something inherently tragic in this struggle. Because the more Schoenberg tried to escape his romantic background the more deeply enmeshed he became. His music, instead of becoming less intense in feeling, became even more so. This resulted in a kind of exaggerated and exasperated romanticism, which has since been commonly referred to as expressionism in music.[11]

Even Schoenberg's atonality was just another extension of German Romanticism. While Copland acknowledged that the Austrian's free atonality was "the most important new experimental harmonic principle in modern times," it still "stem[med] directly from Wagner's continual use of chromatic progressions."[12] Schoenberg's twelve-tone method, too, was just another continuation of a Germanic aesthetic. "From the standpoint of the orderly German mind, atonality had one serious drawback. It lacked a unifying principle, particularly in the construction of any work on large lines."[13] Inherent in Schoenberg's development of the twelve-tone method was a German aesthetic that valued unity, internal logic, and organicism as well as the preference for large-scale orchestral works, particularly the symphony. Copland's most pointed criticism of Schoenberg's method was that it was cerebral, overly technical, and thus, not accessible to the nonspecialist: "A full explanation of the twelve-tone system can be of interest only to professional students of composition."[14] Copland went on to explain in layman's terms the basics of the twelve-tone method. He continued to praise *Pierrot Lunaire,* particularly the *Sprechstimme* and *Sprechgesang* techniques and Schoenberg's sonorities and exploration of instrumental timbre.

Copland also discussed the music of Berg in *Our New Music.* Again, Copland saw Berg's music, like Schoenberg's, as a continuation of Germanic principles. "Berg managed to normalize the Schoenberg idiom by relating it more frankly to its Tristanesque origins." But Berg's music seemed "warm and sweetly human." Particularly outstanding were his operas *Wozzeck* and *Lulu,* the Violin Concerto, and his *Lyric Suite,* which contained passages that were "of a magical inspiration—sensuously lyrical, violently dramatic, and profoundly erotic by turns." Yet in Copland's final assessment:

> This does not change the essential truth that Berg's music belongs to the German past. It is that fact that makes it less exciting than it would otherwise be. For it is music that, despite the modern means employed, sends us back to an emotional experience the essence of which we have thoroughly lived through. In that sense, it must reluctantly be admitted, it is music without a future.

Schoenberg's expressionist "tendency" had also manifested itself in the music of Webern, whose condensed style still owed its origin to German Romanticism.

> We see this tendency in its most extravagant form in the work of Schoenberg's pupil Anton von Webern. The new aesthetic of an extreme intensity of expression brought with it a contraction of the musical line. All the former expansiveness of German romantic feeling was now concentrated in one single supersensitive phrase. Thus, logi-

cally, we find von Webern writing a three-movement symphony lasting, in all, but a few minutes.[15]

Thus, while Copland fully understood the technical innovations of Schoenberg's atonality and the twelve-tone method used by him, Berg, and Webern, he viewed these techniques as a continuation of the German Romantic tradition from an aesthetic and, to an extent, stylistic point of view.

Influence of the Second Viennese School on Copland

Copland did not confine himself to attending performances of works by Schoenberg, Berg, and Webern or reviewing recordings and scores. He himself experimented with atonality à la Schoenberg and his own modification of the twelve-tone method. He composed his earliest twelve-tone work, "poet's song," in August 1927 while in Königstein, Germany. A setting of a text by e. e. cummings, it is highly condensed, lean, and spare, like Webern's works. Julia Smith first identified Copland's tone row, B–D–F–G–C–C♯–A♭–F♯–B♭–A–E–E♭.[16] Copland uses the method freely: he repeats pitches before all twelve tones are exhausted. Furthermore, as Pollack asserts, Copland manages to create an atonal work that combines "bluesy harmonies" in the piano accompaniment with an "expressive melody."[17]

Further analysis reveals how loosely Copland adapted the twelve-tone method. He does repeat pitches, and the prevalent use of minor sevenths in the piano accompaniment and the minor thirds in the voice do lend "poet's song" that "bluesy" feel. Rather than exploiting the method to the fullest through use of retrograde, inversion, and retrograde-inversion forms of the row, Copland presents the row only in prime form, albeit at different transposition levels. After presenting the row P^{11} (C = 0) in mm. 1–5, he presents only two more versions, all in prime form: P^{10} (mm. 6–9) and P^{0} (mm. 10–13). Copland closes the short song with two statements of P^{11} in mm. 14–18. For the span mm. 14–16, the row is incomplete, lacking A; in the final measure, this A occurs in the right hand of the piano, bringing the piece to a climax. Schoenberg disseminated a rigorous method of segmenting the row into hexachords to produce "harmonies" and counterpoint and rigorously avoided tonal implications (although Berg, in contrast to his teacher, managed to use twelve-tone techniques with tonal implications). Copland departs from Schoenberg's technique, choosing to use four- and eight-note motives. In the opening, he repeats the eight notes of the row in mm. 1, 2, and 3, creating a sense of pitch centeredness in using P^{11} (C = 0) (see example 6.1). Furthermore, he uses bass ostinati that consistently present major fifths,

EXAMPLE 6.1 Copland, "Poet's Song," mm. 1–5, Row and bass ostinato

thereby alluding to a V–I cadence. The bass ostinati are carryovers from techniques seen in earlier works, *Cat and Mouse, Dance Symphony, Symphony for Organ and Orchestra,* and *Music for the Theatre,* where Stravinsky's influence is most prevalent. Thus, while Copland adopts the serial technique from Webern, he also combines it with a Stravinskian ostinato, bluesy melody and sevenths, to create his unique synthesis of dodecaphony, Stravinsky, and jazz.

Copland did not abandon twelve-tone and its implications completely during the 1920s and 1930s, although he would wait until after World War II before he would more fully adopt serialism. Vestiges of twelve-tone techniques can be seen in his *Piano Variations.* Copland scholars generally agree that this is one of the first *major* works in which Copland applies his own brand of serial procedures. As in "poet's song," he was more influenced by Webern's pointillism and economy than by Schoenberg's cerebral approach and Berg's romantic inflections. *Piano Variations,* composed in 1930 after *Symphonic Ode,* is Copland with all the fat trimmed. A four-note octatonic motive is presented at the outset, E–C–D♯–C♯. This motive at once invokes the German classical (especially the keyboard literature) tradition, from Bach's Fugue 4 from *The Well-Tempered Klavier,* Book I (where this same four-note motive occurs) and the B–A–C–H motive in Bach's B Minor Mass, to Schumann's *Abegg* Variations, op. 1 (1830) and Schoenberg's signature S–B–E–R–G motive. The keyboard, choral, and instrumental literatures have a rich tradition of composers using short motives as acrostics, musical monograms, short codes, or musical puzzles embedded in a given work. So while, stylistically, the work owes much to Webern, it also invokes the whole German music tradition from Bach to Beethoven, from Schumann to Schoenberg.

Stylistically, in *Piano Variations* Copland did not apply strict serial procedures. In contrast to "poet's song," however, where his handling of the row was rather free, Copland confines himself to rigorously working out this short motive. The most useful analysis of this work remains that of Julia Smith. She identifies a complete tone row that occurs in the seventh variation of the twenty total (plus coda): E–C–D♯–C♯–A–D–F♯–G♯–

B–G–B♭–F, of which the first four pitches function as the motive from which Copland generates the entire theme, subsequent variations, and coda. Pollack relates this motive to the octatonic scale, as well as to Stravinsky's Octet and, tangentially, to Shostakovich's D–S–C–H motive.[18] Copland transposes this motive to different pitch levels in variations 6, 7, 8, 10, and 11, returning to the original motive in variation 12. The resulting tonal poles are E–G–B–F–F♯–E. More significant than Smith or Pollack observes is Copland's counterpoint. As Smith noted, the first variation presents the motive in a canon at the unison. Further analysis by this author reveals that in variation 2, Copland presents his own version of invertible counterpoint: this variation features three-voice counterpoint (with the original motive, E–C–D♯–C♯, occurring in the right hand of the piano) and a permutation of the motive, D♯–C♯–E–C. Variation 3 features four-voice counterpoint involving both the original motive and the first permutation. Variation 4 contrasts in texture in that it is chordal/homorhythmic. In subsequent variations, Copland places the pitches of the motives octaves apart, often with octave doublings. He strikingly exploits different timbres, contrasting the lugubrious and sinister lowest two octaves of the piano with the extreme shrill and piercing high treble registers. Coupled with this registral contrast are abrupt shifts in rhythm and meter. In this work, according to Antokoletz, Copland has "infused serial elements of the Vienna Schoenberg circles as well as techniques from other European composers into his Stravinskian neoclassicism."[19] True, Copland has appropriated aspects of Schoenberg's serial technique, but he looks to Webern in creating a pointillist work that is spare, and exploits the piano's registral and timbral contrast by distributing the motive and theme throughout different octaves. Vestiges of Stravinsky can be seen in the metrical changes and frequently shifting rhythms.

Alois Hába, Copland's Ethnicity, and *Vitebsk* (1928)

Copland was also briefly influenced by a composer little known today whose string quartet had particularly impressed him in late summer of 1923 in Salzburg: Alois Hába and his system of quarter tones. The first opportunity for Copland to compose a major work using quarter tones came five years later, two years after he had attended a production of the S. Ansky play *The Dybbuk,* where he heard what he later referred to as a Jewish folk song. In discussing this work in his autobiography, Copland raised the issue of his ethnicity and whether and how it influenced him stylistically. In the trio *Vitebsk,* we can see the convergence of both Hába's influence and Copland's ethnicity in the way he combined quarter tones with Jewish folk song.

In his autobiography, Copland pondered why *Vitebsk* was considered his only "Jewish work." As a youth he had quoted Jewish liturgical chant in early compositions and made arrangements of Jewish folk songs. He mentioned to two well-known critics' references to Jewish elements in his music, the critics being Roger Sessions and Virgil Thomson. Copland likened his use of Jewish themes to his use of jazz:

> It seems to me that my use of Jewish themes was similar to my use of jazz—Jewish influences were present in my music, even when I did not refer to them overtly. I have often been asked why I wrote "cowboy" music rather than "Jewish" music. I never thought about these things at the time, but it must have been partly because I grew up in the Eastern European tradition and there was no novelty to it.[20]

He went on to write that he had never given much thought to using Jewish folk music until he attended the play *The Dybbuk* and heard a Jewish folk song used as incidental music. As an adult, he appears to have directly quoted from a Jewish music source only once in a mature work, *Vitebsk* (1929). This work, as Copland wrote, depicts the harshness of Jewish life in White Russia. Although it invokes Jewish history in czarist Russia, Copland's own family history, and uses a Jewish folk song, Copland rarely publicly discussed his Jewish identity or drew upon it as a musical, cultural, or stylistic resource outside of this work.

In his published writings Copland rarely referred to Jewish culture or the history of Judaism. His most extensive writing on Jewish music came in the form of a book review, "What is Jewish Music?" Copland reviewed Peter Gradenwitz's *The Music of Israel* for the *New York Herald-Tribune* four years after the end of World War II. "A new book on the subject of Jewish music is especially welcome these days," he wrote. Copland approached his topic not from the standpoint of an established author of books and articles (which by this time he certainly was), nor from the standpoint of a "Jewish composer," but from the position of a modern American composer who was also the descendant of Eastern European Jewish immigrants. Gradenwitz had attempted to chronicle Jewish music from antiquity to the present day. Copland acknowledged the author's expertise: "Peter Gradenwitz—both a musicologist and composer, with a central European musical background; [*sic*] resides in Tel Aviv. He has published in this country a steady stream of information concerning musical events in Palestine."[21] Copland praised Gradenwitz, particularly for his treatment of the Middle Ages. Although the book filled a void, Copland judged it flawed, detecting three major errors. The first problem for Copland was that the author attempted to cover the entire history of Jewish music from antiquity to the present. This was monumental and too broad a topic:

> If the book is somewhat disappointing, that is not the author's fault, for it is inherent in the nature of the available knowledge of the subject itself. No one can write a satisfactory history of the rise and growth through 5,000 years of the music of Israel (as this book promises to do) because so much of the story must remain sheer guesswork. The early part of the story—the first few thousand years—are only beginning to be laboriously pieced together by students in the field of comparative musicology [i.e., ethnomusicology]. Noone really knows what the music of the ancient Hebrews actually sounded like. Mr. Gradenwitz understands his predicament. He solves it by filling out the early chapters of his book with considerable amounts of Jewish history that is not specifically musical.[22]

It was an impossible task to write a history of Jewish music because the important sources—the music itself—were often lacking. A second chief problem stemmed from the question, "What is a Jewish composer?" How did one determine whether or not a composer was Jewish or a *Jewish composer?* Copland found it problematic that someone should try to write a history of Jewish music that included European Jews of various nationalities such as Mendelssohn, Meyerbeer, Offenbach, and Mahler.

> From all these lacunae and conjectures it is a relief to turn to the sure values of Mendelssohn, Meyerbeer, Offenbach, and Mahler. But these men bring with them their own problem for the historian—an old one and a tough one—namely, the problem of the assimilated Jewish artist and how he is to be considered. Gradenwitz is of the opinion that their works cannot be claimed for a specifically Jewish history, "though the Jewishness of these masters does offer an explanation for some characteristics of their life, their artistic growth and their esthetics."[23]

Although these composers were Jewish, they were also German, French, or Austrian in nationality and culture. In Copland's opinion Gradenwitz had faced the problem of what determined Jewishness and had failed to answer it adequately. Copland posed a counterquestion: were not these composers more representative of their respective nationalities than of their religious and ethnic history and culture? If Gradenwitz offered the caveat that it was true that these composers were central European rather than Jewish, then he defeated his own purpose in researching and writing the book, Copland reasoned. Therefore, Gradenwitz simply failed to identify the ways in which these composers' *music* could be considered Jewish.

Copland disagreed with the author, who took the Swiss-American composer Ernest Bloch as the best example of a twentieth-century Jewish composer.

> In our own day Gradenwitz believes that the Swiss-American composer Ernest Bloch best exemplifies the incorporation of Jewish characteristics in a music of European inspiration. That is, of course, the usual opinion. As I see it the author slights an equally and perhaps more eloquent case by devoting a mere paragraph to the French composer Darius Milhaud. In Milhaud's compositions we have proof that a composer can remain profoundly national and at the same time profoundly Jewish.[24]

Copland did not take issue with Bloch's use of Jewish themes in his works but with his overall style. As was typical, Copland was more interested in and more committed to twentieth-century modernist music than to ethnicity.

Copland did not find any topic that the author handled successfully; but "the most absorbing feature to this reader was the comprehensive chapter on composers now resident in Israel who are building the foundations for an indigenous art of the future." Reviewing this book after World War II and the creation of the modern state of Israel, Copland was interested in the formation of a new, modern Jewish music in the same terms as a new American music. In other words, the modernist possibilities of Jewish music intrigued him in a way that the ethnic "raw" material and a nationalist approach did not. Copland saw the modern music of his own ethnicity as in the process of formation, of becoming. "The settlement of Jewish composers in the new state of Israel, and the first signs of music created there by native born composers is satisfying to one's sense of form, for it rounds off the long history of Jewish music and presages the beginning of a new era."[25]

Copland's Ethnic Identity

Although Copland never systematically or consistently explored his ethnicity in his music and rarely wrote or spoke about Jewish identity, culture, or history, others did. Copland's contemporaries and fellows at Fontainebleau, Virgil Thomson and Roger Sessions, noted certain "Jewish" stylistic elements in his music, and Copland acknowledged their opinions. "In 1926 and 1932 respectively, Roger Sessions and Virgil Thomson wrote about the Jewish elements in my music."[26] Sessions "reviewed" Copland's *Nocturne, Serenade,* and *As It Fell Upon a Day,* presented in Paris in May 1926 as part of the Societé Musique Indépendante (Sessions misidentifies the organization as the Societé Musicale Indépendante). Sessions, however, did not actually review Copland's music but took the opportunity to comment upon his ethnicity. He chose not to evaluate the success of these works as art because Copland was an established composer whose talent had already been recognized, Sessions speciously wrote. Instead he referred to the music's supposedly ethnic character: "In passing, it was interesting to note the occasional Jewish character of Copland's music, approaching in this respect the spirit of Bloch and even of Mahler, though with his own idiom and feeling."[27] Sessions never identified exactly what recalled the spirit of Bloch or Mahler in these or other works. Virgil Thomson also perceived a "Jewishness" in Copland's music, but he was more explicit:

> Aaron Copland's music is American in rhythm, Jewish in melody, eclectic in all the rest. . . . His melodic material is of a markedly Hebrew cast. Its tendency to return on itself is penitential. It is predominantly minor. Its chromaticism is ornamental and expressive rather than modulatory. When he sings, it is as wailing before the wall. More commonly his material is used as a framework for a purely coloristic compilation.[28]

Thomson went on to characterize his music as limited in subject but "deeply felt."

> Its emotional origin is seldom gay, rarely amorous, almost invariably religious. Occasionally excitation of a purely nervous and cerebral kind is the origin of a *scherzo*.[29]

Thomson further described Copland's music as nervous, strained, strident—drawing on anti-Semitic stereotypes. Thomson accurately perceived a minor quality in Copland's melodies; however he misattributed it to Copland's ethnicity, rather than to its actual origin in the African-American blues scale or Stravinsky's octatonicism. Thomson's references to Copland's music as singing before the Wailing Wall and its being religious, alluding to one of Judaism's holiest shrines, the Temple, crossed the line from appropriate criticism to crude offensiveness. Thomson's "criticism" had no relationship to Copland's music. That these critics stereotyped Copland is borne out by the fact that none of the works Sessions and Thomson described as Jewish was actually influenced by specific Jewish folk songs, genres, or tradition.

In 1939 Copland wrote a short autobiographical article for *Magazine of Art* (reprinted in 1968 in *ASCAP Today*) about his childhood and Paris years. This is the source of the now-famous quote, "I was born on a street in Brooklyn which can only be described as drab." He described his neighborhood as populated by "largely Italians, Irish, and Negroes."[30] He did not mention that his old neighborhood also had a large Jewish population. His middle-class Bedford/Crown Heights neighborhood was largely immigrant, populated by older German and Irish immigrants, with small communities of British, African-American, Finnish, and Italian residents and a large, long-established community of West Indian immigrants. The Jewish inhabitants were mostly German-Jewish, with Eastern European Jewish residents later moving into the neighborhood from Manhattan's Lower East Side after the 1903 opening of the Williamsburg Bridge. Despite this influx into Brooklyn, Crown Heights, including Copland's Washington Avenue, remained largely Irish. The Coplands were one of the few Jewish families in their neighborhood around 1900 when he was born. With such a large and diverse immigrant and second-generation American population, there were ethnic tensions, mostly among the Irish, German, Italian, and Jewish residents, which Copland experienced when he entered public school. In his autobiography he describes how he had to make a "tough school trip" and pass through "dangerous territory," a few blocks near St. Patrick's Catholic School on Dean Street. "A Jewish boy had to watch out for himself."[31] This he apparently did not recall with fondness, having "blotted out the eight years of grammar school attendance—teachers, fellow pupils, and all." Copland acknowledged feeling different in high school (which Pollack attributes to both his homosexuality and his being Jewish). Yet Copland made friends with other boys his own age, regardless of ethnicity—Jewish, Italian, Irish, African-American.[32]

Of all the Copland scholars, Howard Pollack has given the most attention to Copland's involvement in Judaism as both child and adult. Copland's family was Orthodox and observed major holidays; Yiddish was spoken in the home and by his paternal grandparents, who never mastered English. Both his father and brother were quite active in their neighborhood synagogue, Congregation Baith Israel, the second oldest synagogue in the borough. His father, Harris, was treasurer and chairman (later president, 1907–09) of the Talmud Torah; his brother Ralph briefly served as superintendent of the Sunday school. In accordance with Jewish tradition, Copland had his bar mitzvah at the age of thirteen. Yet Copland described his family as "more traditional than religious, but observant."[33] Like many other middle-class city kids, he was sent to camp in the summers, attending a Jewish camp (Camp Carey) in the Poconos during the summers of 1910–13. The following summer he was sent to a camp run by the Young Men's Hebrew Association. These camps were important not just because they gave children and adolescents a chance to vacation outside the city (and their parents a break!). As Karen Mittelman writes, they played an important role in "shaping what it meant to be an American and Jewish. That's something beyond nostalgia. It's about the meaning of a Jewish-American identity."[34]

Copland's parents and childhood provided him with religious education, and his experiences during these years further shaped his sense of his Jewish identity and heritage. Particularly important is the summer he spent at the Fairmont Hotel, a "gathering place for well-known Jewish literary people."[35] Here he met what he described as his first intellectual friend, Aaron Schaffer (son of a Baltimore rabbi), along with Martha ("Marty") Dreiblatt. Copland and Schaffer shared a passion for literature and music. Schaffer was also a Zionist and a supporter of Judah ha-Levi. The extent of Schaffer's Zionism is seen in his activities at Johns Hopkins: letterhead from an epistle he wrote Copland in July 1918 indicates that he served as president of the Intercollegiate Zionist Association of America.[36] Schaffer told Copland of his plans to emigrate to Palestine and suggested that they emigrate together.[37] Pollack considers "My Heart Is in the East," composed May 1918, a setting of a Zionist text by Schaffer, as Copland's first overtly "Jewish" work.[38] At this early stage, Copland's style was in a modernist cast, as Schaffer's critique reveals: "The sudden changes of key and the occasional discords, à la Debussy and Ravel have won their way into our heart, as you prophesied, and I find that you have admirably translated into music the emotions I desired to arouse with my words."[39] Schaffer's musical tastes were more conservative than Copland's, but he supported his friend's venturesome musical language. After receiving Copland's setting of his poem, Schaffer offered Copland some of his "longer things" that might be suitable as programs for a symphony or perhaps even an opera.[40]

During his early teens Jewish music served as a resource for Copland. Pollack asserts that Schaffer "may have brought Copland closer to his Jewish roots." The same month Copland completed "My Heart Is in the East," he also composed *Lament* for cello and piano on the hymn "Adon Olom." Even before Copland met Schaffer, he had attempted to draw upon Jewish musical traditions in his juvenilia. "Lola!" a scene from Copland's abandoned setting of Turiddù's libretto of *Cavalleria Rusticana,* has stylistic elements of Jewish melody. Its prominent use of augmented seconds, Pollack writes, "bears the obvious imprint of Russian-Jewish melody."[41] Another early work from 1916, the *Capriccio* for piano and violin, combines Italian opera, Russian-Jewish dance music, and American popular music. Copland also outlined a biblical oratorio about Exodus (a book of the Torah), planning to write sections "With a Mighty Hand and an Outstretched Arm," "Song of Miriam," and "Burial of Moses." The following fall Copland began study with Goldmark. Thus, from his earliest attempts at composition until his earliest formal composition training, Copland drew upon the music from everyday life that was closest to him—music he heard in his home, at synagogue, at camp, and in his piano lessons—a mélange of Jewish sacred and secular music, popular music, and the standard classical repertoire.

As an adult Copland was not inclined to draw overtly upon traditional Jewish sacred or secular music. In the late 1930s he made a single arrangement of a Jewish folk dance, the hora, "Banu (We've Come)." This was included in a collection edited by Hans Nathan, *Folk Songs of the New Palestine,* published by the HECHALUTZ Organization and

MASADA, a branch of the Youth Zionist Organization of America. Among the list of contributing composers were Milhaud, Stefan Wolpe, Ernst Toch, Kurt Weill, and Arthur Honegger. Accompanying Copland's entry were explanations of the *banu* type of hora tunes and a short history of the hora's origins. With its blend of Hassidic, Eastern, and Western elements,the *banu* genre was of special significance; it "mark[ed] the beginning of an original style of Palestinian *hora* tunes."[42] Copland, who was given a melody to arrange, did not provide a tonal harmonic accompaniment. Once again he turned to bass ostinati, as seen in the F–A♭ alternation supporting a melody that is clearly in G minor in mm. 6–8. His arrangement of this Jewish folk song was dissonant and self-consciously modernist (see example 6.2)

> Poor and needy came we here,
> Paupers of Yesterday;
> Yet the future has in store
> Millions for us by the score.
> Dance the Hora, brethren; rout
> Shades that girdle us about.
> Dance the Hora, do not tire,
> Hearts aflame and breasts afire.
> Join the circle, dance along,
> Sing about the pauper's song.
> Lo, the children of distressed
> Dance and shout with mirthfulness.

Here, Copland contributes to a political cause, this time the Jewish settlement of Palestine before World War II and the subsequent establishment of the modern state of Israel. Pollack links "We've Come" to Copland's involvement in the Popular Front. After the emergence of the Popular Front in 1935, the American Communist Party adopted a pro-Zionist policy. Pollack writes, "This helps explain the participation of Copland and other left-wing composers in this project, entitled *Folk Songs of the New Palestine* and edited by Hans Nathan."[43]

Although as an adult Copland was not especially observant, in setting this hora, vestiges of Copland's and Schaffer's youthful dreams of emigrating to Palestine reemerge. Copland did visit Israel much later, in 1951 (he lectured in Jerusalem on Jewish composers), which stirred further support of Israel in him, and again in 1968.[44] Yet, though he identified strongly as Jewish, he did not consider himself a "Jewish composer." One statement reveals much of Copland's sense of his ethnic identity as it relates to his music:

> A man doesn't create Art because he is a Jew, but because he is a Man. His creative Nature is influenced by his temperament and his environ-

EXAMPLE 6.2 Copland's arrangement of folk song "Banu (We've Come)"

> ment. If by temperament he is deeply racial, [his] art will come out Jewish. If his environment [is] non-Jewish, that will mix with [his] temperament.[45]

This view also suggests how he might have perceived anti-Semitism during this and earlier stages of his career.

Sessions and Thomson did not hesitate to characterize his music as "Jewish." Far more damaging than their stereotypes were views such as those of Daniel Gregory Mason (whose anti-Semitic views concerning music recall Wagner's). Mason stated: "The speciousness, the superficial charm and persuasiveness of Hebrew art, its brilliance, its violently juxtaposed extremes of passion, its poignant eroticism and pessimism" could not possibly be authentically American in character. "Legitimate" American music possessed "the poignant beauty of Anglo-Saxon sobriety and restraint . . . the fine reserve so polar to the garrulous self-confessions, the almost indecent stripping of the soul."[46] Others such as Cowell and Lazar Saminsky remarked upon Copland's Jewishness, as did critic Paul Rosenfeld. Both those who were Jewish and those who were not were quick to project upon his music traits that stemmed not from his style or techniques, but traits based on his identity and ethnic heritage. Non-Jews such as Mason and Cowell repeatedly invoked "Anglo-Saxon" as a marker of true Americanism, and since Copland was Jewish, he was considered a racialized Other. Those who were Jewish, such as Saminsky, lambasted Copland for only dabbling in his Jewishness in *Vitebsk* and in other works that drew upon jazz or Anglo-American folk song. He compared Copland to Mahler, painting the former as a mere assembler of music from various vernacular sources but lacking true depth and commitment. Moreover, Saminsky branded Copland as something of an opportunist who calculatedly composed works to win popular success with audiences. Copland's Americana works were really warmed-over echoes of Eastern European or Russian music. For Saminsky, also Jewish, Copland was a sellout who possibly used his Jewish identity when it suited him, and thus was not authentically Jewish. In contrast, Paul Rosenfeld and Leonard Bernstein, both also Jewish, saw Copland as a kind a prophet (an idea first applied to Copland by Thomson), or a patriarch (Bernstein, being Copland's younger contemporary). Given these three perspectives by his contemporaries, Copland simply was in a no-win situation. He would always be viewed as a Jewish composer, whether or not he used specifically Jewish secular or sacred music in his work. His supporters criticized him for not being Jewish enough. Non-Jewish composers tended to ascribe to him special status because of his ethnic identity. His anti-Semitic detractors, whose racialized views deemed American music as primarily Anglo-Saxon, thus saw Copland as an interloper from an immigrant culture that could never be fully and truly assimilated into the greater American cultural fabric.

Vitebsk

Regardless of how his friends, supporters, and detractors might have viewed him and his ethnicity, Copland did compose a work that treated a Jewish theme and used a Jewish folk song and went far beyond his juvenilia. As a mature composer Copland addressed the issue of ethnicity or religion, in *Vitebsk* (Study on a Jewish Theme), a trio for violin, cello, and piano. Inspired by the S. Ansky play *The Dybbuk,* this is the sole mature work Copland identified as being especially Jewish.[47]

> Based on a Jewish folk song, the trio has often been cited as my only "Jewish" work. But when I was younger, I had set traditional Hebrew melodies for cello and piano, and in the thirties I made arrangements of some Jewish folk songs that were published.[48]

The connections between *Vitebsk* and his ethnic identity are extensive. S. Ansky (nom de plume of Shloyme Zanvl Rappoport) himself both collected Jewish folktales and had grown up in Vitebsk, Belarus, where he first heard the folk song. The Yiddish-language play is based on a Hasidic folktale and set in a shtetl in an area on the Russian border, the Pale of Settlement.[49]

Copland himself admitted that this was his first ethnically Jewish piece. The place of ethnicity and religion in his music does legitimately deserve further study, if only to correct the errors and missteps of earlier scholars. Pollack's biography lays important groundwork in doing this. When earlier scholars noted an Eastern or non-Western influence in *Vitebsk,* they have only obliquely identified it with a specific culture or hemisphere. Berger notes: "Quarter-tones, suggesting somewhat the portamento of oriental vocal style, have an incidental role in this work, but never recur in his music."[50] Stylistically, Smith places it with Copland's modernist works that have no programmatic or nationalist overtones, nearer the works of the abstract period.[51] She describes *Vitebsk* as blending "austerity and acid dissonance." Butterworth appropriates Smith's category and also places this work in Copland's abstract music period (1928–35). Pollack finds that *Vitebsk* exhibits "a new mood, a tragic sense that goes beyond the bittersweet sadness of the earlier jazz pieces" and relates it to the later works *Symphonic Ode* and *Piano Variations.*[52] Butterworth's and Pollack's observations about *Vitebsk* are quite extensive. Butterworth argues that Copland intentionally set out to compose a work reflecting his own ethnic identity. He invokes the issue of ethnicity in his remarks about the outer sections; however, he contradicts himself:

> The succeeding semiquavers in violin and piano suggest wild gypsy fiddle music. The middle part of the dance fragments the music into three- and-four-note patterns derived from the principal theme exchanged between the three players.[53]

The comment "wild gypsy fiddle music" refers to a different ethnic group entirely, the Roma. Butterworth does place the work more accurately in some geographical and ethnic context: a Russian one. The texture, melody, and harmony recall klezmer, a violin-based tradition of Eastern European Jews. He describes the third and final part as a "recapitulation of the complete theme in grand style on the violin and cello with Russian bell-like sonorities for the piano."[54] Pollack provides extensive background information about the play that inspired Copland, and a brief analysis.

Vitebsk is Copland's first original mature composition that draws upon folk song, antedating *Billy the Kid.* Copland first heard the folk song in 1925 while attending *The Dybbuk,* but it would take two years before he began working on the trio. Copland worked on this piece along with a composition for large orchestra, *Symphonic Ode,* while he was in Königstein in Taunus, Germany, in 1927. He brought it with him to Santa Fe, New Mexico, and to the MacDowell artists colony in 1928.[55] Pollack has identified this melody as the Hasidic folk song "Mipnei Mah" ("Wherefore, O Wherefore") used by Joel Engel, the composer of *The Dybbuk*'s original incidental music (Engel collaborated with Ansky from the play's early stages).[56] The folk tune Copland heard is shown in example 6.3. Somewhat incongruously with a folk song, Copland treats his melody very academically: as a canon.

With this tune, Copland borrows a folk style and folk genre: the *parlando rubato* and the genres of the *hora* and *lange Gesang.* Copland organizes and integrates his original and preexisting material following the formal schemata of these genres. He identified his trio as having three parts, two slow outer sections and a fast inner section, or ternary form. The ternary form is also found in the *lange Gesang.*[57] *Vitebsk's* first section begins with extreme dissonance produced by quarter tones, a technique borrowed directly from Hába. Here, form follows function,

EXAMPLE 6.3 Copland, *Vitebsk,* D, folk song treated as a canon

that is, the sections of the work correspond to the divisions of the *lange Gesang* folk genre. The *parlando rubato* is slow in tempo, emotionally intense, and declamatory in style. Copland's *parlando rubato,* section A, spans mm. 1–63 and can be subdivided into three subsections x (mm. 1–12), y (mm. 14–20), and z (mm. 21–26). The outer x and z subsections feature quarter tones. Section y is triadic, its theme an abstraction of the folk tune rather than a literal quotation. Its pentatonic melody and quartal harmony are reminiscent of Bartók. Pollock links the intonation of this *parlando rubato* to specific Jewish liturgical practices. The quarter tones and dotted rhythms of the opening measures parallel the microtonal inflections and rhythms of the shofar (ram's horn) used for High Holiday services (a period of atonement beginning with Rosh Hashanah, the New Year, through Yom Kippur, the Day of Atonement; Pollack also sees some resemblance to the exorcism scene from *The Dybbuk*). *Vitebsk's* slow section hovers around C, used here as an intonation or reciting tone (see example 6.4). Copland also uses this intonation in the middle of this first framing section that begins at Rehearsal B of section A (see example 6.5). This passage corresponds to the floridly ornamented middle section of the genre. The recitative-like second subsection corresponds to the *parlando rubato* of Eastern European folk music (see example 6.3). Here, Copland hovers around the pitch B, tonal center C's lower neighbor, thereby implying I–vii–I motion. At C Copland returns to the quarter-tone passage.

Copland introduces the "Mipnei Mah" folk song at D. Rather than present it in unison as a folk singer would have performed it, Copland treats it as a canon. It is accompanied by filigreed sixteenth- and thirty-second-note flourishes in the piano that first appeared in section B. There are three statements of the folk tune, first as a canon at D, then by the

EXAMPLE 6.4 Copland, *Vitebsk*, mm. 1–5, intonation

EXAMPLE 6.5 Copland, *Vitebsk*, B

cello solo at E, followed by another canon at F. A codetta based on A material closes this part of section B. At section B, the tempo changes from Lento molto marcato to Meno Mosso-Grave. This tempo further evokes the *lange Gesang* genre. Five measures before H the tempo nearly doubles to Subito Allegro Vivace, marking the second subdivision of B. Copland introduces another folk element at m. 64, the Jewish folk dance, the hora (see example 6.6). This hora continues until m. 178, when "Mipnei Mah" returns, this time stated by the strings in octaves. This hora corresponds to the scene in the play where the main character, Leah, dances with blind and crippled villagers. Pollack also sees stylistic similarities here between Engel's original incidental music and Copland's hora.[58]

Copland expressly wanted to depict Jewish life in the homeland of his father, mother, and grandparents.

EXAMPLE 6.6 Copland, *Vitebsk*, H

> The full title of the trio is *Vitebsk (Study on a Jewish Theme)*, and it was my intention to reflect the harshness and drama of Jewish life in White Russia. So it did not surprise me when the work was described as "hard," "dry," and "dissonant." Performers and audiences have told me that they find *Vitebsk* a strangely moving work. Musically, I knew I had found something that I intended to explore further as soon as I finished the orchestral piece, which would be titled *Symphonic Ode*.[59]

These works notwithstanding, he did not systematically, regularly, or consistently explore Jewish identity in the greater body of his work. When he did, Copland claimed that the idea of exploring national or ethnic identity came first from the music itself.

> It was always a musical stimulus that got me started, as when I heard the folk theme that the Polish-Jewish author S. Ansky used in his play *The Dybbuk*. It appealed to me just as it had to him. Vitebsk, a small Russian village, was the playwright's home; it was there he had heard and transcribed the tune. It seemed an appropriate title for my trio based on the same tune. Years later when I traveled in the Soviet Union, the Russians were amazed that any composer would name a piece of music after the city of Vitebsk, a large industrial complex resembling Pittsburgh or Cleveland![60]

The idea to explore a Russian theme might also have come from another source. Pollack further links *Vitebsk* work to the Popular Front: the Russian Revolution inspired American Communists and Socialists. Furthermore, in dealing with the harshness of Jewish life in the shtetl, *Vitebsk* shows Copland's sympathy for the Russian Revolution. *The Dybbuk* was first performed by a theatrical company that was popular during the beginning of the Russian Revolution and remained popular in both Moscow and New York, due to its themes of poverty, violence, and oppression. As the son of Russian immigrants immersed in Jewish culture as a child and adolescent, the adult Copland would easily have been drawn to the play, perceiving its political overtones while responding to it as a second-generation American of Russian-Jewish heritage. Copland would return to the Russian Revolution theme in 1943 in his score for the anti-German/pro-Soviet film *The North Star*, about the 1941 German invasion of the Soviet Union.[61]

Alois Hába

Copland's exploration of Eastern European folk music also had modernist intent. Two of his European contemporaries were closely identified with Eastern European folk music traditions, Hungarian Béla Bartók and

Czech Alois Hába. Hába learned folk songs from his mother and played violin and double bass in his father's folk band. After study with Schreker, he developed a way of composing with quarter- and sixth-tone music that was influenced by his own ethnic Moravian music. Similarly, Bartók's study of folk music led the composer to discover ways to free himself from conventional tonality. Copland was familiar with the music of both composers.[62] The Bartók influence is present in Copland's choice of the *parlando rubato* genre. In the second section of the work the residual influence of Hába can be heard: here Copland experiments with quarter tones, as did Hába in the Second String Quartet.

As discussed previously, Copland first heard Hába's Second String Quartet, op. 7 in concert in Salzburg in 1923, where it was presented on August 6, along with Honegger's *Sonata for Violin and Piano,* Ravel's *Sonata for Violin and Cello,* and a two-piano version of Ferruccio Busoni's *Fantasia contrappuntistica* (modeled after Bach's *Kunst der Fuge*).[63] Copland did not merely encounter the work in concert: he heard the musicians rehearsing it in the room adjoining his at the hotel where he lodged. Inspired, he incorporated quarter tones in the composition he was working on at the time, *Grohg,* where a quarter-tone passage in the viola solo links the slow movement to the Finale. The passage in *Grohg* at 90 closely resembles the opening of Hába's Second String Quartet (Copland also used quarter tones in his *Ukelele Serenade,* 1928).[64]

Synthesis

As his letters to Boulanger document, Copland followed all new stylistic trends with keen interest and enthusiasm during his stay in Europe. He continued to do so when he returned to the United States. Throughout his career he traveled extensively, maintaining ties to composers in Europe, Britain, and Mexico, as well as throughout the United States. Consistently throughout his career he would experiment with a new compositional technique if it piqued his interest. For example, he explored strict serial procedures in works of the 1960s, *Connotations* (1962) and *Inscapes* (1967).

Given his interest in new music, Copland came to "Jewish" music—his own folk tradition—mainly through modernism, which was coupled with a desire to explore his ethnicity. Rather than drawing upon music remembered from his youth or own background, he related more to music suggestive of his ethnicity after hearing the works of Eastern European modernists and was influenced by their integration of folk songs, folk performance practices, and genres in their works. Copland was not alone in drawing upon Jewish musical sources and combining them with modernist compositional techniques. Almost ten years later, Schoenberg would return to tonality in setting the liturgical chant for Yom Kippur, *Kol nidre,* op. 39 (1938). Working with Jewish folk songs for Copland, however, was not an expression of faith; it was like working with jazz, and later, cowboy songs and Anglo-American ballads and hymns: "In any case, I never gave much thought to including or excluding *any* kind of influence from my work."[65] The world's folk music traditions were his musical oysters.

CHAPTER SEVEN

Toward a New National Music during the 1930s :: Copland's Populism, Accessible Style, and Folk and Popular Music

Copland could not have been more prophetic in 1933 when he signaled the end of a period of experimentation in the pages of *Modern Music.*

> Modern music during the next ten years will have entered in a new phase. The day of the "pathfinder" and the "experimenter" is over. We are in a period of "cashing in" on their discoveries. The struggle which was begun by Varèse and his associates of the International Composers' Guild must be carried on, but on a wider front. By that I mean that new music in future should no longer be confined to the sphere of the special society. Now it must interest the general public through the usual concert channels and usual interpreters; pianists, singers, chamber organizations, choral societies, etc. Their interest in the contemporary music field must be awakened, for it no longer contains elements of which they need be frightened.[1]

In retrospect, Copland saw the decade 1920–30 as having been an "especially alive" period for music. A period of experimentation and avant-gardism had been inevitable: now he saw a period of retrenchment in the offing.

During the 1930s Copland himself entered a new phase. The decade saw a marked change in his musical style and ideas about the development of modern American music. His focus shifted: he found that he was composing for a different audience. No longer was he content to write for the small concert hall audience. Wanting to reach a broad audience, he no longer saw direct imitation and American importation of European styles as a solution to the problems American composers faced.

His change in attitude and musical style can be attributed partly to the social and economic crises that developed as the 1920s ended. The Great Depression began in 1929 and did not fully abate until the nation became involved in World War II. As the "Jazz Age" ended and the economy plummeted, the changing conditions affected music: in modern music circles, audience tastes began to change, and attendance declined; patronage began to drift away and became scarcer. The severity of the crisis and depressing climate demanded a new style. Experimental and dissonant new music was considered out of step with the social and economic conditions. Composers were suffering financially and realized that if they were to continue creating music, they would have to court a new audience.

Copland increasingly questioned the relation of music to modern American life. The most pressing problem, in his assessment, concerned the audience, whom had been "left behind."

> Music, it is true, passed through a very critical period of change during the first thirty years of this century. During this change, the audience, the "lay-listener" had gotten left behind so to speak. Audiences were still accustomed to the sounds of the nineteenth-century. When the advances of twentieth century music occurred, the audiences were left behind. A larger and larger gap separated the composer and his audience, until, by the end of the twenties, there seemed no way of bridging it again.[2]

Composers' musical language had advanced far beyond audience's understanding, the latter's tastes still being rooted in nineteenth-century Romanticism. In an article written at the start of the 1940s, "The Musical Scene Changes," in *Twice a Year*,[3] Copland noted that the audiences during the 1930s were significantly different from those of the 1920s:

> Since the Depression, roughly speaking, the musical picture has changed. The old special audiences, their curiosity satisfied, have melted away no one knows where. The symphony concert subscribers, year in and year out, listen for the most part to the same old "classic" music. The individual recitalist seldom attempts anything not already sanctioned by the headline performer. Composers would be dull indeed, not to realize that they were losing all contact with any real audience, and that this lack of contact was placing them in a critical situation.[4]

As he wrote in 1935, listeners had been willing to stretch themselves in the 1920s; now they only wished to hear standard repertoire. Audiences no longer expected to find a new genius with each new composer, to be shocked by a daring work, no longer looked forward to a succès de scandale. More than a matter of musical taste or listening preference, this problem reached far beyond matters of style or aesthetics, for the composer depended upon the audience and other musical institutions to earn a living. Despite the efforts of organizations such as the League of Composers, International Composers' Guild, Pro Musica, the New Music Society, the Pan-American Association, and others, modern music still reached a small audience.[5] How, then was the composer to bridge this gap?

Copland had always questioned the role of the composer in society. Influenced by the ideas of progressivism he read in the pages of the *New Republic,* the *Nation,* and the *Dial,* throughout his career he had a sincere desire to connect with his listeners.[6] Concern about expanding the audience for modern music led to his involvement with the League of Composers, the Copland-Sessions concert series, and Yaddo beginning in 1928.[7] The crisis of the Great Depression intensified his aesthetic belief that music should reach as large an audience as possible, and strengthened his social and political convictions. Copland had met with young American composers and saw how they reacted to the new conditions they faced. In 1935, in the pages of *Music Vanguard,* Copland queried composers, "Whom are you writing your music for?"[8] Was it for himself or herself? Was it for a specific audience? Or was it for the general public? Copland saw that composers influenced by Schoenberg found dodecaphony or expressionism no longer suited them. The weltschmerz with which they had previously filled their pieces was merely their own discontent. They realized that the small audience for Schoenberg's music could never comprise their own. Those influenced by Stravinsky were unable to follow his foray into neoclassicism; furthermore, it was unlikely that they could re-create masterworks such as *Petrushka* and *Les Noces.* In contrast to the freewheeling creative atmosphere of the 1920s, in 1935 a different zeitgeist challenged Copland and his fellow composers. The new conditions intensified the mood of the young composer. The pessimistic composer asked, "Why bother?" The optimistic composer tried to align his or her work with social problems.

For whom *did* the composer create? And *how* should the composer respond to the Depression? As Copland observed, the younger composers faced a problem that the composers of the 1920s did not have to face. The audiences previously eager to hear new music were now gone, and the composer had to find an audience beyond the small one that followed new American music or the one typically found in the 1920s concert hall.[9] The Depression-era audience needed an accessible music, and the composer had to change his or her style. A declining audience for art music had serious repercussions. The economic crisis severely hindered the American composer and threatened to be the death knell for the development of modern American music. Yet Copland did not see the situation as hopeless; the composer should not give in to despair or pursue commercial or popular music. The composer was not just to sit back and wait for the audiences to return, nor "cater" to low tastes by writing popular-sounding concert music. Instead, a composer must "discover" an audience.

Copland saw that modern music "in future will no longer be confined to the sphere of the special society. Now it must interest the general public." While he proposed that the performers, orchestras, and other music institutions had a duty to present modern music before this public, he also proposed that composers must change their musical language, "for it [contemporary music] no longer contains elements at which [audiences] need be frightened."[10] Yet Copland saw more value in standing one's modernist ground. While he never abandoned art music to compose vernacular music, he did view vernacular music favorably: it offered him and other composers a chance to become more accessible yet remain modern.

Copland attempted to reach out and connect again with the audience in a musical language it could understand. Feeling he had exhausted jazz, Copland turned away from its overt use toward a style that was simpler and leaner in texture, yet melodically, harmonically, and rhythmically consistent with his music from the mid-1920s. He greatly reduced the density of his textures, the dissonance of his harmonies, and the complexity of his rhythms. He did not necessarily embrace functional tonality but returned to triadic harmony as a foundation, albeit used in novel ways. Copland incorporated vernacular idioms in this streamlined style, not, however, the vernacular music of contemporary American culture. This deliberate turn toward an accessible modern style may be called populism. Copland's populism led him away from urban music toward abstractions of folk music of the past, drawing on regional, national, and ethnic folk music in creating nationalist modern American music. Copland called on the pioneer and frontier past, particularly the West and Southwest. Populism means more than writing accessible music for the concert hall; it also subsumes writing for other outlets such as the school group and the amateur musician. Accordingly Copland also wrote in more accessible genres such as the ballet and opera.

Copland scholars all acknowledge a change in Copland's style in works from the 1930s and 1940s, from the Depression through World War II. In consensus they link this change both to his desire to reach out to his audience and to his political views. The latter issue, politics and his aesthetic ideology, will be discussed in the following chapter. This chapter discusses Copland's populism, which came partly from a European source, as did his jazz of the mid-1920s. In compositions of the 1930s and 1940s Copland turned to vernacular resources, just as he had in earlier works. In this case, however, he embraced foreground elements that would have been familiar to many of his listeners: Copland quoted folk music. He also directly cultivated students and young people by composing pieces that would expose then to modernist styles and techniques in a systematic, nonintimidating, and uncomplicated manner. Copland's turn toward folk music—the use of Mexican folk tunes in *El Salón México*—represents such an attempt, as do *The Second Hurricane* and his piano pieces for teaching.

Accessibility, Modernism, and the New American Music of the Depression Era

Was it necessary for composers of the 1930s to abandon the new directions in which they had gone during the 1920s and return to more conservative styles in the changing climate of the Depression years? Or would it be possible to remain modern, yet find a style that was accessible to an audience broader than the one that had been receptive toward experimentalism and avant-gardism of the 1920s? Once again, we return to Cowell's 1933 book on modern American composers. Copland and Cowell had linked modern music not only with exploration of new styles and techniques but also with the desire to break from German Romanticism and imitation of past conventions. Cowell defined modernism along aesthetic and stylistic lines, emphasizing harmonic innovation and renunciation of functional tonality. Roy Harris, whose harmonic style Cowell considered conventional, was difficult to categorize: though harmonically conservative, his music was, paradoxically, modern in style. Cowell considered Harris's music modern because of the originality of his musical ideas and handling of other musical parameters such as form, rhythm, and phrase length. Harris was not imitative of past musical styles. In reconciling the apparent conflict between modern and conservative, the determinant was *originality* in how harmony, melody, form, and the like were treated. Music could *sound* conventional harmonically but could exhibit innovative traits in other areas and still be deemed modern. Thus, it *was* possible to compose accessible music with conventional sounding harmony, yet remain modern in style.

Copland's "Music for Use"

Scholars sometimes insinuate that Copland's new style of the 1930s is of lesser substance and value than his "abstract" and "serious" works. P. Garvie remarks that during 1934–41 Copland did not compose any "serious" music for the concert hall, but rather composed lighter works, listing his ballets, incidental music for theater, film scores, an opera for high school performers, an overture for high school orchestra, and *El Salón México,* a work based on popular Mexican dance-hall tunes.[11] Berger attributes Copland's change in style to the realization that orchestral composers were forced to court a broader audience. Like Garvie, Berger does not consider this music serious; rather, he places it in the context of *Gebrauchsmusik,* or music for use, to which composers such as Hindemith, Virgil Thomson, Shostakovich, and Marc Blitzstein also turned in order to appeal to a wider audience.[12] Similarly, Smith sees the thirties as a period when Copland simplified his style and wrote, not "serious" music, but music with "popular" appeal. Thus, these scholars view Copland's turn toward populism and accessibility as incompatible with serious music.

Just as he had gone to Europe to study composition, Copland still looked to Europe, now for models and inspiration to the question of how to reach a broad audience. He saw himself as part of a larger trend. Composers who perhaps had written ultramodern works during the 1920s now were simplifying their styles. Quoting W. H. Auden, Copland wrote:

> Without a secure place in society, without an intimate relation between himself and his audience, . . . the poet [or, as Copland has in mind, musician] finds it difficult to grow beyond a certain point. Isolation breeds an ingrown quality, an overcomplexity, an over-refinement, both of technique and of sentiment.[13]

In his *Twice a Year* article of 1941, Copland took up the issue of *Gebrauchsmusik,* just as Blitzstein had done in *Modern Music.* Copland identified Germany as the country where modernist composers first noticed the gap between themselves and their audiences. They first grappled with the issue of audience dissatisfaction and decline, especially Hindemith.[14] Hindemith's solution was to write *Gebrauchsmusik*—music "especially designed to familiarize nonprofessional performers with musical devices different from those in the classics they knew so well."[15] Beginning in 1918 Hindemith moved toward a more accessible style and in the early 1930s began to address political and social issues in his music, including the question of the composer in society. Barbara Zuck finds it difficult to make a direct link between Hindemith's (and the German) concept and American composers' understanding of the term. Instead she sees that there is a similarity between composers of both nations reacting to (1) changes in music as a result of modernism; and (2) the use of folk music or popular idioms. Copland noted that some German composers had begun to write opera that showed "popular appeal" without compromising musical ideals: *Zeitoper.*

> This time it was the opera public that was sought after. Kurt Weill and Ernest Krenek, two highly trained composers, deliberately went in for "popular appeal" in their stage works. The post-war [World War I] opera-goer in Germany was not the comparatively erudite listener of the preceding epoch. He was completely unprepared to appreciate the atonal complexities of Berg and Schoenberg. By introducing songs in a pseudo-jazz manner in place of the old-fashioned aria, Weill gave his public something they could easily comprehend. His best work to date, the *Three Penny Opera,* was written during that period.[16]

Works such as Hindemith's *Mathis der Maler* (about painter Mathias Grünewald and Germany's Peasants' War), Krenek's *Jonny spielt auf,* and the Weill-Brecht collaborations directly addressed political issues in contemporary German society. Americans had emulated Weill. Marc Blitzstein's *The Cradle Will Rock* borrowed the Brecht-Weill style of popular musical theater and social commentary. Hindemith began composing *Schulmusik,* works for performance by children, such as *Wir bauen eine Stadt* (1920); the teaching piece, *Lehrstuck* (1929); and *Kammermusik,* music for performance by amateurs.

Finally, for Copland, another method of reaching a wider audience came from the East. Soviet composers created music for the broadest audience possible.

> The third, and possibly, most significant sign of the new tendency came by way of Russia, principally through the works of the young Dmitri Schostakovitch. It is easy to see how a young composer in the Soviet Union, living in the midst of social revolution, would have uppermost in his mind the problem of his relationship to his audience. Obviously, the new, untutored mass public was totally unprepared to cope with musical subtleties. And yet, the Soviet composer must have known that his works could be addressed only to that same mass public. We see the challenge met most clearly in the music of Schostakovitch. Whatever its weaknesses,—and it seems unnecessarily trite and conventional at times,—the fact remains that it is couched in a musical language that the majority of listeners can grasp.[17]

Copland's reaction was guarded, agreeing only with some of the Soviet composers' aims: they tried to write for a *mass,* untutored audience, rather than for an elite that followed the latest trends; and they took into consideration what this audience could or could not understand and modified their styles accordingly.

Copland understood that some would consider inadequate the solutions Weill, Krenek, Hindemith, and Shostakovich had found.

> These three unconnected phenomena all point in the direction of the main tendency in music today: namely, a simplification of style for the sake of once more making contact with the large mass of listeners. No doubt the tendency will shock those who hold that it is the duty of the creative artist to ignore every outward influence, and to work from inner necessity alone. But do composers really work like that?[18]

While appreciating what Hindemith had done, Copland was dubious about composing this type of "popularizing" music. While it may have given amateurs a twentieth-century repertoire to perform, it did not necessarily result in the creation of good music. When composing for amateurs, Copland argued, the composer did not offer his or her best ideas.

"But the value of this first step was purely tactical, for the actual musical content of most *Gebrauchsmusik* was weak. Composers continued to reserve their best thoughts for development in their 'serious' music."[19] Copland also suggested that publishers supported *Gebrauchsmusik* because it meant increased sales of sheet music. Sympathizing with the directions these Europeans had chosen, he recognized nonetheless that new types of music were now in demand. "Suddenly, at the end of the 1930s, functional music was in demand as never before, certainly as never before in the experience of our serious composers."[20] Two new industries born during the 1920s that had come into their own during the 1930s, radio and film, supplied part of the new audience.[21]

> Motion-picture and ballet companies, radio stations and schools, film and theater producers discovered us. The music appropriate for the different kinds of cooperative ventures undertaken by these people had to be simpler and more direct. There was a "market" especially for music evocative of the American scene—industrial backgrounds, landscapes of the Far West, and so forth.[22]

Copland saw himself as responding to the "new" mass audience's needs. In "Composer from Brooklyn" he identified precisely which of his works reflected this new aesthetic of the masses:

> My most recent works, in their separate ways, embody this tendency toward an imposed simplicity. *El Salón México* is an orchestral work based on Mexican tunes; *The Second Hurricane* is an opera for school children of high-school age to perform; *Music for Radio* was written on a commission from the Columbia Broadcasting Company especially for performance on the air, *Billy the Kid,* a ballet written for the Ballet Caravan, utilizes simple cowboy songs as melodic material; *The City, Of Mice and Men,* and *Our Town* are scores for the films. The reception accorded these works in the last two or three years encourages me to believe that the American composer is destined to play a more commanding role in the musical future of his own country.[23]

Copland also composed incidental music for several plays: *Miracle at Verdun* (1931), *The Five Kings* (1939), and *Quiet City* (1939). He composed music for a puppet show in the Hall of Pharmacy at the 1939 World's Fair, *From Sorcery to Science.* He also completed three works for radio: *John Henry, Music for Radio,* and *Letter from Home.* Although these were intended as background or incidental music, they ultimately had a longer life than the typical film or ballet score: Copland revised film works into concert suites. All his ballets except *Hear Ye! Hear Ye!* also exist as suites. Excerpts from Copland's major film scores were compiled as *Music for Movies.* That Copland would easily convert film or ballet music into a concert work suggests that he maintained the same quality and inventiveness in creating the purely functional work as he did for the absolute or programmatic concert work. It also suggests that Copland drew no stylistic or aesthetic difference between these venues—if the technical rigor of the music remained constant.

For his final exemplars of "music for use," Copland again turned to Europe. At an Oxford music festival in 1931 he heard Hindemith's *Wir bauen eine Stadt*. His review in *Modern Music* interestingly claimed that this small work's appeal depended on its presentation by the children (i.e., not its musical virtues).[24] Yet Hindemith's work did impress him. Ten years later Copland wrote:

> There is, finally, that enormous unexploited field known as school music: Why should our young people be brought up exclusively on the musical triumphs of a past era? Why can we not supply them with a music directly related to their technical abilities and on a level with their emotional age? There are literally thousands of school orchestras, bands, choruses, and ensembles of every variety spread all over the land. Here we can supply our immediate need and at the same time build future audiences for our music.[25]

Copland, too, would compose music for use throughout the remainder of his career: songs, orchestral, and band works suitable for performance by accomplished amateurs. His *Gebrauchsmusik* differs from that of his German counterparts in two key ways. First, he did not necessarily attach political or ideological issues to these works that can be classified as such. Second, Copland thought that the composer should compose music in a genre and style that was relevant to his or her culture and time, even if it was for amateurs or those not counted among the modern music cognoscenti. Above all else, the composer was not to give in to self-indulgence, nor create in isolation solely to please himself or herself.

What Do We Plant? (1935)

During the 1930s Copland would write several pieces of school music (the American English equivalent of the German term *Schulmusik*)—music intended for performance by schoolchildren. These include the choral work *What Do We Plant?* (1935); the teaching pieces *Two Children's Pieces [for Piano]:* "Sunday Afternoon Music" and "The Young Pioneers" (1936); an opera, *The Second Hurricane* (1937); and a work for band, *An Outdoor Overture* (1938). In composing works for students and musical amateurs, Copland by no means wrote condescendingly. As he stated later in his career, he always sought to provide them with good music that communicated something to performer and listener:

I don't believe in writing "music for amateurs," but I do believe in writing plenty of music which is within the capacity of amateur performers. In other words, I detest "writing down" in any shape or form, but I am firmly convinced that communication is an essential part of the process of creation, and that a composer should write music of some immediate service to his contemporaries.[26]

Composed for the Henry Street Settlement Music School's Girl's Glee Club, *What Do We Plant?* features simple, diatonic melody accompanied by mostly diatonic harmony. Despite its diatonicism, Copland continues what had become a signature of his tonal style: rather than retaining functional, triadic tonality, he establishes tonal centers through ostinati. He introduces a recurring bass ostinato (E^2–G^2–E^3–G^2) in mm. 24–31. As in earlier works where he uses tonic and dominant pedals, here he introduces rhythmic subdominant pedals at the end of major sections, for example, in mm. 34–36, mm. 72–74, mm. 86–88, and in the codetta, mm. 112 to the end. The A–E double pedal marks formal divisions; it is accompanied by the rhythmic motive comprised of three eighth notes.

Copland also introduces new scales to his young performers and listeners. The rhythmic motive-pedal complex appears above a simple progression of triads built on the whole-tone scale. The choruses end with the combination of rhythmic motive, whole tone, ostinato, and A–E pedal (see example 7.1). Since the scoring is so sparse and the harmony so simple and straightforward, Copland had to find one parameter in which to create musical rather than didactic interest. He varies the texture to delineate the rondo form, which alternates verse and chorus. The first chorus begins, "What do we plant / When do we plant" with unison singing followed by simple imitation between the soprano and the alto. This texture is used in all repetitions of the chorus. Each verse is contrapuntal; the latter two feature simple note-against-note counterpoint (verses 2 and 3).

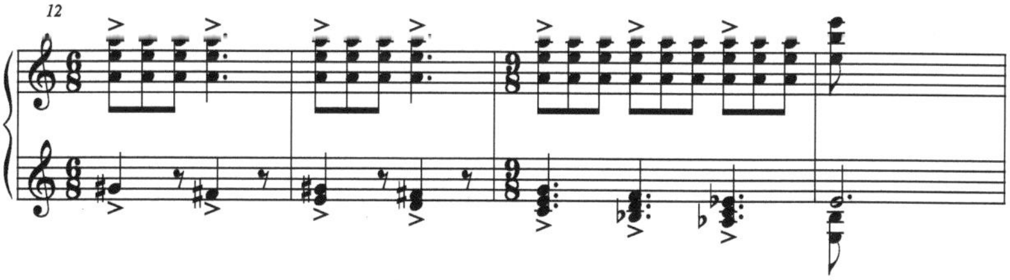

EXAMPLE 7.1 Copland, "What Do We Plant," Whole-Tone Scale, mm. 12–14

Two Children's Pieces: "Sunday Afternoon Music" and "The Young Pioneers" (1936)

Lazar Saminsky and Isadore Freed invited Copland to compose two piano pieces for inclusion in a collection of works by contemporary composers.[27] The teaching pieces, "Sunday Afternoon Music" and "The

Young Pioneers" (1936), introduce "the young ear to the contemporary idiom."[28] In "Sunday Afternoon" Copland acquaints the young pianist with polytonality through the progression in example 7.2, which oscillates about B♭ and A♭. The progression is far simpler than it appears. The harmonic motion involves a $V^{\flat 9}$ moving to I^{7sus4}, voiced to appear polytonal. The piece also introduces the young pianist to ostinati, here the pitches A–B♭–C–D moving in quarter notes above a whole note F♯. Ten measures of the twenty-two-measure piece consist of a single bass ostinato. "The Young Pioneers" teaches additive rhythm. In an inset box Copland indicates that the 7/8 should be performed as 3/8 + 4/8 measures, which alternates with 4/8 + 3/8 (see example 7.3a & b). Composing for schoolchildren was (predictably) for Copland an exercise in creating music that was free of extraneous material. In these works he simplified his ostinati, thinned his texture by writing in octaves and unisons, and placed more emphasis and importance on diatonic melody.

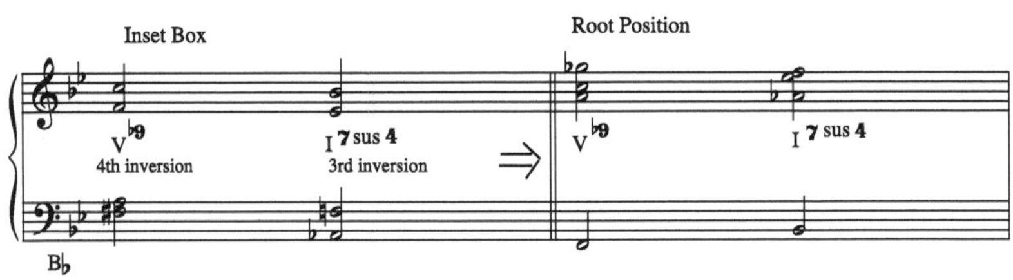

EXAMPLE 7.2 Copland, "Sunday Afternoon Music," the progression in the inset box

a)

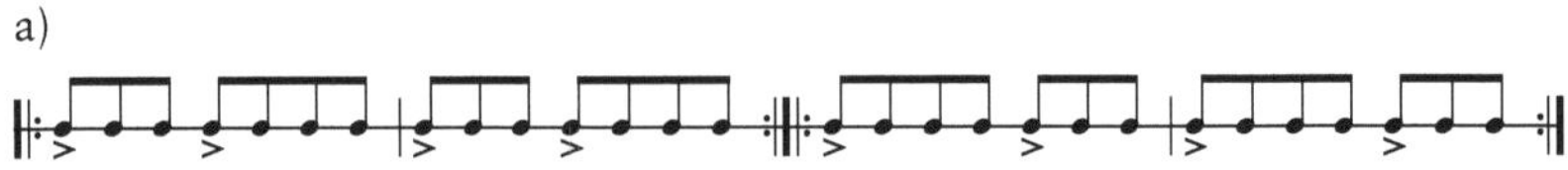

b)

EXAMPLE 7.3 Copland, "The Young Pioneers"; a) Inset box explaining rhythm; b) mm. 1; m. 17

Beyond Diatonicism

Teaching pieces, music for amateurs, and school music were, but in a sense, side paths for the composer to follow during the Depression. Aesthetically, they permitted the composer to reach an audience outside regular modern music circles and outside the concert hall, and thus were indeed populist. Furthermore, these works could be instrumental in inculcating a taste for new techniques in the untutored or more conservative musician and listener. Yet Copland was first and foremost a composer of orchestral music and large-scale works, and his *Gebrauchsmusik* represented just one small niche. In the next chapter we shall see how Copland courted a broader audience in embracing an aesthetic that went beyond simplicity and accessibility.

CHAPTER EIGHT

Copland's Journey Left

Repatriating to the United States five years, four months, and five days after his departure, Copland, along with millions of other Americans, faced the most severe economic catastrophe of the twentieth century: the stock market crash of October 1929. For a period Copland had yet to feel the immediate effects of the ensuing Great Depression. Following his fall 1929 return from a trip to France, he was getting by on commissions, performances of his works, and lectures at the New School (in 1927 he assumed critic Paul Rosenfeld's teaching responsibilities). As an artist he was used to a life of frugality; moreover, he had the assistance of relatives who could ease the burden of living expenses by providing him with an apartment in Lexington Avenue's Montclair Hotel. By the time he moved into a rented house outside of Manhattan in Bedford, New York, in early January 1930, his out-of-town lecture-recitals became more limited. By 1931 Copland felt the economic squeeze.

> The Depression was affecting the general quality of life in New York. From the carefree twenties, we had plunged into a grim and difficult period. The artist is always the first to suffer, particularly in America, where he does not have the respect enjoyed by creative artists abroad.[1]

After a trip to London for the final Copland-Sessions concert in December 1931, Copland returned to New York in January 1932 and house-sat Harold Clurman and Stella Adler's vacant apartment at 52 W. Fifty-eighth Street. By 1933 Copland was in low spirits.[2]

Moving to the Fifty-eighth Street neighborhood placed Copland in the midst of New York's leading intellectuals and artists who, like him, were beginning to question the position of the artist in society. Many were influenced by leftist politics and aesthetic ideology, and Copland saw them often. Writer Edmund Wilson lived in the same building, and several members of the Stieglitz circle lived in the neighborhood.[3] Since his teens Copland had been interested in politics, both socialism and mainstream electoral politics (the latter stemming from his father's involvement in the Democratic Party). Shaped by newspapers and magazines such as *The*

Nation and *The Dial,* the youth developed his own independent political ideas. These were further radicalized during the Depression, spurred by his aesthetic concern over the role of music and the arts in American society. As he wrote in 1941:

> The need to communicate one's music to the widest possible audience is no mere opportunism. It comes from the healthy desire in every artist to find his deepest feelings reflected in his fellow-man. It is not without its political implications also, for it takes its source partly from that same need to reaffirm the democratic ideal that already fills our literature and our stage. It is not a time for poignantly subjective lieder, but a time for large mass choral singing. It is the composer who must embody new communal ideals in a new communal music.[4]

During the 1930s he moved to embrace leftist political and aesthetic ideologies. Throughout the decade and into the 1940s Copland would seek to bridge that gap between the modernist composer and audience that widened during the Depression.

The American Left during the 1930s

Copland's aesthetic and style changes were shaped by his own sociopolitical views and those of other artists and intellectuals, who during the crisis of the Depression years embraced leftist politics and its cultural and aesthetic ideology. Today Roosevelt's New Deal rather than leftist politics is associated with the Depression years. During the 1930s, however, the Left was a significant political and cultural force in American life.[5] The "Left" was not monolithic, with a single ideology or party dominant. Indeed, the Left was particularly factious, perhaps even more so than mainstream American politics. John Patrick Diggins identifies three leftist movements, the "Lyrical Left," of the World War I era; the Old Left, active during the Depression years; and, the New Left, which arose during the Cold War and was active throughout the Vietnam era.[6] The movement pertinent to this present study is what he terms the Old Left.

Even when one speaks of the Old Left, one still refers to several different political movements and parties, for no single party or ideology characterized the Old Left of the 1930s. Old Left radicals varied in "ideology, social background, cultural sensibility, life-style, and political commitment," with at least three distinct groups. The first comprises those from the "Literary Left" of the 1920s. The second clusters around a group of younger writers associated with *Partisan Review.* The third comprises "cultural refugees" from the 1920s, many of whom had been "lost generation" expatriates, such as John Dos Passos and Malcolm Cowley. Thus, the "Left" was a conglomeration of a wide range of groups and individuals: a small group of members of the American Communist Left; a liberal center; so-called fellow-travelers who supported the idea of communism but did not join the party; and sympathizers with the Soviet Union who supported the Soviet-style economy and what the Soviet Union had achieved economically but who "rejected communist ideology."[7] A myriad of organized political parties falls under the umbrella of the Left. There were the Socialist Party (formed in 1901 and led by Eugene Debs); the American Communist Party; the Communist Party USA; the American Workers Party (founded in 1934 and led by A. J. Muste); the Socialist Labor Party; the Socialist Workers Party; and other Socialist and Trotskyist groups. The Old Left also had its own class division between (ironically) the intellectuals and the working class.[8] While the Left attempted to create a single political force from these two groups, their interests and motivations, political action and engagement, and goals were not always the same. Nor were the ideologies and tactics of the various parties.

The radical parties never entered the mainstream of American politics, but did exert significant political influence. As Alexander Bloom chronicles, "American radicalism flowered for one of the few times in American history during the Depression decade."[9] The Left had been active in union organizing in the country since World War I. The Socialist Party had been at its height during 1902–19, when its ranks swelled from 10,000 in 1902 to 118,000 in 1912, garnering nearly 900,000 votes for Debs in the 1912 presidential election. At this time the Socialist Party had elected one congressman, fifty-six mayors, 160 councilmen, and 145 aldermen to office in the United States. Its ethnic pluralism attracted many European immigrants—Italians, Jews, Germans, and Eastern Europeans—many of whom would had been familiar with the socialist party in their native homelands. The Red Scare of 1919 forced many party members underground, and as a result, the Socialist Party was in decline by 1921. The Communist Party USA (CPUSA) dominated the Left during the 1930s and 1940s until the Cold War and McCarthyism, when infighting brought about its decline.[10] The CPUSA's main policies concerned organizing workers into unions to combat the conservatism of the American Federation of Labor; organizing the jobless; confronting racism and racial issues; and, relatedly, addressing the problems faced by blacks and the Scottsboro Boys. The CPUSA also supported Roosevelt and the New Deal and Civil Rights. During the Depression, conditions were ripe for the Communist parties in the United States to rebound. With 25 percent of the population out of work and workers laboring for a pittance, the Socialist and the American Communist parties gained strength, vying with the established parties to become a part of America's political mainstream. In 1930 the Communist Party had only 7,500 members; by 1938 its membership had swelled to 75,000. In the 1932 election Norman Thomas, the Socialist Party candidate, received almost 900,000 votes, although the Socialist Party had only 17,000 members. The Communist Party candidate, William Z. Foster, received 100,000 votes. By 1939, the CPUSA had 80,000–90,000 members and exerted influence in government, labor, black youth, cultural, and other organizations. Although it began the decade with a strong show of support among the American people, after the election of Franklin D. Roosevelt and the implementation of his New Deal policies, the revelation of the Hitler-Stalin Non-Aggression Pact, and the beginning of World War II, the party declined in both membership and influence.[11]

An offshoot of the labor movement and Communist Party was the Popular Front. As Michael Denning writes in *The Cultural Front: The Laboring of American Culture in the Twentieth Century,* this was a social and *cultural* movement that grew out of the birth of the Congress of Industrial Organizations (CIO) (a rival to the more conservative AFL), union organizing, antifascism, and the struggle against lynching. The Popular Front united "industrial unionists, Communist, independent socialist, community activists, and émigré anti-fascists around laborist social democracy, anti-fascism, and anti-lynching." It engaged in three types of political activity: electoral politics, antifascist and anti-imperialist solidarity, and a prolabor and antilynching campaign. The Popular Front also gave rise to an attendant radical cultural movement that, as Denning writes, "triggered a real and lasting transformation of American modernism and mass culture, what I will call the *laboring* of American culture." By "laboring" Denning refers to "the pervasive use of 'labor' and its synonyms in the rhetoric of the period," identifying terms such as *proletarian, work, industry,* and *toil* as rhetorical terms used by both the political and the cultural movements. He also includes as part of his definition "the 'proletarianization' of American culture, the increased influence on and participation of working-class Americans in the world of culture and the arts," due partly to the growth of mass culture, education, and the entertainment and amusement industries. As he notes, "There was a laboring of American culture as children from working-class families grew up to become artists in the culture industries, and American workers became the primary audience for those industries." The third aspect of the laboring of American culture Denning lists is that culture had become an industry, and "artists, musicians, and writers were laborers in that industry," some of whom organized themselves into unions. As Denning argues, "The laboring of American culture connotes a birthing of a new American culture, a second American Renaissance."[12] This new renaissance had at its core artists not too far removed from their working-class backgrounds; they sought patronage from the larger working-class masses rather than the monied elite.

Copland and the American Left

Copland's change in style in the 1930s came about as part of an aesthetic shift tied to his sociopolitical views. Copland was drawn into the American Left's orbit, becoming involved in the Communist Party's Popular Front. The Popular Front and its political ideology influenced Copland, his friend Clurman and others associated with the Group Theatre, and the Stieglitz circle. For many years, his involvement in the Left has been obscured, as many scholars have shied away from the issue. Writing in 1953, his friend and former student Arthur Berger attributed Copland's change in musical style not to any particular political involvement but to the critical response to his *Short Symphony* and *Symphonic Ode;* the decline of the modern music audience; and a general international trend toward simplicity as found in the works of Shostakovich and Hindemith's *Gebrauchsmusik*. Berger skirts the issue of Copland's political involvements, never mentioning socialism or communism, but rather states that Copland began to write ballets and film music. Berger goes on to mention Copland's association with Clurman and the Group Theatre and a coterie of young musicians, the Young Composers' Group. Mentioning that the group discussed "ideologies of the time," he continues that these "bore some distant relationship to the sort of thing Copland encouraged informally in the Young Composers' Group about the same time." Berger connects Copland's politics to "liberal thinking," placing his views in a sweeping historical context of the link between music and politics dating back to the classical era.

> Liberal thinking has often been accompanied by the humanism and the idealistic outlook of creative individuals, as we may observe without any difficulty if we look back upon the history of the masters in all artistic fields. The directions in which their aspirations turned did not always prove, in the end, to be conducive to the realization of these hopes—for example, Beethoven and his shattered expectations with regard to Napoleon. But an artist looks for something on which to fasten these aspirations, and for Copland's generation, in the 'thirties, the New Deal provided it.[13]

Berger, however, must not be faulted in attributing Copland's change in style and political views to international modern music, "liberal thinking," or the New Deal: he was writing in the early 1950s, during Wisconsin senator Joseph McCarthy's rise to power and the anti-Communist witchhunts. He wrote with care, concern, and caution, for he had been a former Copland student and a member of the Young Composers' Group. Berger himself leaned far left.[14] Even in the midst of the American Left's ascendancy, Berger did not fully acknowledge to the general public that political ideology generated a shift in the aesthetics and style of Copland

and those of the Young Composers' Group. Earlier he attributed "their hope to contribute artistically to American culture" to international neoclassicism in a 1933 article announcing a January 15 concert as the group's public debut. By 2001 Berger could freely reveal, "Like many of us in the arts in the thirties, Copland felt pressured by leftist sympathies to communicate to the masses."[15] Julia Smith, writing two years later than Berger, completely avoids the issue of Copland's politics, also placing his change of style in the context of an international trend toward simplicity and *Gebrauchsmusik*. By the 1980s, scholars were finally able to look at Copland's music in a broader social, political, and cultural context. At that time Vivian Perlis wrote:

> Copland was not by nature a political person; he joined neither Socialist nor Communist Party, but for a time in the early thirties he was what might be called a fellow traveler. When questioned about his leftist activities, his answer is simply, "It seemed the thing to do at the time." In fact, so many artists were caught up in the strong wave of sympathy for socialism that it *was* the thing to do. The Party slogan, "Communism is twentieth-century Americanism," took full advantage of the "affirm America" movement.[16]

Fortunately, subsequent Copland scholars have been able to build upon Perlis's work. Recently, the post–Cold War era has brought about a revaluation of the American Left and its influence on American politics and culture. Pollack, Elizabeth Crist, Jennifer De Lapp, and Sally Bick have begun to situate Copland's politics and music of the 1930s and 1940s in the context of the Popular Front without the fear of recrimination that Berger and Smith undoubtedly felt. Crist focuses on the interwar years; De Lapp investigates the 1950s McCarthy years, having gained access to FBI and other government files on Copland under the Freedom of Information Act. It is undeniable that Copland was politically engaged and that his politics resulted in a change in his musical style, the change earlier remarked upon by Berger, Smith, Perlis, and Butterworth, and others who evaded the issue of the historico-political context.

Copland was an active participant in the Left. Though they themselves may not have been members of the Communist Party, many intellectuals and artists became involved in the leftist movement, their sense of purpose galvanized by the Depression, especially at the beginning of the 1930s. Alexander Bloom draws a profile of the 1930s-era radical intellectuals, a group he terms the "Young Radicals." He particularly studies the lives and careers of a group of self-made writers first associated with leftist publications and later with the *Partisan Review* after it broke with the Left. European immigrants filled the ranks of radical organizations. In 1928 over half the members of the Socialist Party were also members of "foreign-language-affiliated" organizations, and of these, the vast majority were European. Many individuals and families of the European Jewish immigrant community in New York's impoverished neighborhoods (especially those working in the garment industry) supported leftist causes. Typically, the young 1930s radical was the child of Jewish immigrants, working-class parents, lived in Brooklyn or the Bronx (rather than Manhattan), and felt himself or herself neither part of the Old World nor part of America. The public schools provided the arena where the assimilation process began. Study and intellectual pursuits as part of Jewish culture were thought to grow out of the Talmudic tradition. As the Young Radicals went through the American acculturation process, these young men and women excelled in the public schools and made their way to prominent eastern, especially New York, universities, where they confronted anti-Semitism and discrimination in many forms.[17] Although Copland was not associated with the *Partisan Review* and moved in different circles, he indeed shares many things in common with Bloom's "Prodigal Sons." He, too, was the son of Eastern European Jewish immigrants and went through the assimilation process in Brooklyn's public schools. His father was active in his local synagogue and the local Democratic Party as well; the father and son could intellectually debate politics and current world events. And, as discussed in chapter 6, Copland faced ethnic stereotypes and anti-Semitism.

Copland can be best situated in the context of the Popular Front. Denning distinguishes between cultural politics and aesthetic ideologies. As he defines the former, cultural politics consists of the artist's outward political engagement in terms of "the politics of letterheads and petitions, the stances taken by artist and intellectuals, the pledges of allegiance and declarations of dissent . . . the history of the institutions and apparatuses in which artists and intellectuals work."[18] Denning defines "aesthetic ideologies" as a politics of form; the term can be applied to the works of art created by Popular Front artists, for these used "a repertoire of forms and styles, genres and conventions; the critical controversies and debates that surrounded them established ways of seeing and judging, canons of value." Crist applies Denning, interpreting this as "the intrinsic political sensibility embedded in a text."[19]

Copland was part of the Popular Front. Yet, like many other intellectuals and artists who embraced Leftist ideology and engaged in its politics and strategies, he never joined the Communist or Socialist Party. He can be considered, then, what is known as a "fellow traveller," one interested in the Left or sympathetic to its causes but who never formally joined either party. In *Copland 1900 through 1942* he described his political sentiments as "rather liberal, but not leftist."[20] Copland actually never joined *any* political party. Perlis attributes this partly to his own personality and nature, describing him as "cautious about politics, but he was not a loner and would not have gone underground."[21] Party policy may not have permitted him to join, as—according to Harry Hay, actor-singer, socialist, gay activist, and Copland's contemporary—homosexuals were not allowed to become members.[22] Denning briefly explores the link between homosexual communities and the Popular Front. The struggle for gay and lesbian rights never became part of the Popular Front's politics. He points out, however, that the founders of the Mattachine Society (the first U.S. gay political organization, formed in 1950) were Popular Front activists who had been a part of the People's Educational Center, a labor school where Hay, one of the Society's early leaders, had taught courses in music.[23] Thus, while concerned primarily with labor and union issues, the Popular Front did attract many gays and lesbians.

Copland's interest in leftist politics did not suddenly develop during the 1930s. Interested in politics and world events, he read the paper daily and various public affairs publications regularly. As a young man he had an interest in leftist politics. During his teens he had discussed socialism and socialist ideas, particularly those of Eugene V. Debs, with clarinetist Arne Vainio while playing for dances at the Finnish Socialist Hall in 1918. Here Copland made his first contact with what he called "radical politics."[24] Vainio introduced him to the socialist newspaper *The Call.* This job placed Copland in the midst of an immigrant leftist environment where he could not help but be exposed to socialist ideology. He could not have voted for Debs in 1919, as the voting age had not yet been lowered to eighteen, but the ideas he discussed with Vainio left an impression. As he himself wrote, "Coming as I did from a thoroughly bourgeois environment, I found Vainio and his contact with Finnish socialism fascinating." Although in his autobiography he admits that he thought of himself as a "young radical," Copland does not seem to have had particularly strong political leanings at this young age: he did not join any organizations.[25] He remained fascinated by socialism, but had no strong communist convictions or adherence to party ideology. His own father offered a model for political engagement in party politics. Harris Copland had long been a member of the local Democratic Club and was a staunch Democrat.[26] Copland did engage in political discussions with his father, defending the 1917 Russian Revolution, apparently without much success. His zeal, no doubt, was tempered by his father's own experience: "My father had too vivid a memory of Russian oppression to believe that any theory of socialistic government could possibly establish itself in so backward a country as Russia."[27] Yet, more than a decade later, Copland would come to admire the Soviet Union, attempting to arrange visits there, as did many other leftist artist and intellectuals during the 1930s.

Copland's most decisive and extensive ties to the Left began in the wake of the Depression. Many of his friends, associates, and peers were involved in leftist politics. Circulating among composers, musicians, writers, and actors and directors placed him in the midst of a politically charged community. As Pollack writes, whether his friends were members of a party or not, they regularly engaged in political discussions and activities and embraced parts of its ideology: identification with the masses and proletariat and a rhetoric of revolution and anticapitalism. They also read seminal leftist works by Marx and Lenin, as well as the leftist press, the *Daily Worker,* and the *New Masses.* Actively engaged, they participated in May Day parades, supported communist candidates, and defended Stalin until news of the Hitler-Stalin Pact was revealed.[28] Copland's longtime companion, Victor Kraft, was a Communist. His old friend who had accompanied him to Paris, Harold Clurman—like other members of the Group Theatre—was strongly interested and involved in the American Left, though he too never joined the American Communist Party. The Group had its own seven-member communist cell (most Group members never joined the Party) comprising both member and nonmembers of the party. Increasingly throughout the 1930s, its stagings evolved from topical theater in its first 1930–31 season to overtly political theater. Copland was closely affiliated with the Group Theatre from its beginning, becoming an associate and advising it on matters regarding music. Its founders, Stella Adler, Lee Strasberg, and Harold Clurman, embraced leftist politics and ideology, as did Elia Kazan (a member from late 1933 to early 1935) and Clifford Odets (a member for most of 1935). Pollack marks 1932 as a watershed, a year in which one-third of the American workforce found itself unemployed. In May 1932 Clurman wrote Copland about reading Marx, Engels, Lenin, and Trotsky and about other political matters. Clurman began to publish theater reviews under the pseudonym Harold Edgar in the leftist newspaper *Daily Worker.* By the mid-1930s the Group began to present plays dealing specifically with labor issues, unemployment, and fascism. In keeping with party ideology the Group began to express Communist rhetoric, an interest in Marxist writings, and belief in the imminence of revolution and a new world order. As the Group and its members became increasingly politically involved, they lent support to communist political candidates.[29]

Copland met many writers and intellectuals who openly advocated leftist ideologies and were associated with publications such as *The Nation* and *New Republic,* for example Van Wyck Brooks, Lewis Mumford, Edmund Wilson, and photographer Alfred Stieglitz (Copland himself subscribed to the left-leaning publications *New Republic* and the *Nation*). Copland's friends in the Stieglitz circle included Waldo Frank, photographer Paul Strand, and Wilson. He maintained close friendships with Frank and Strand. These associations and friendships were especially important and influential for Copland because, as Crist argues, "in this particular circle of artists and intellectuals as well as in the progressive tradition more generally, Copland discovered a community pursuing socially responsive forms of *modernist* expression" (emphasis added). He saw in their ideas and works ways in which the artist could bridge the gap between modernism and audience during the economic crisis of the Depression. Many writers whom he admired, including Frank Norris, Theodore Dreiser, and Upton Sinclair, were socialist, and their novels addressed social and labor issues. Cowley, Frank, and Wilson, whom Crist terms "radical progressives," were in the vanguard of social change, in that, as Denning shows, they "pioneered the major themes of the Popular Front social movement before the Communist Party itself adopted them." They stressed "American exceptionalism and . . . 'Americanizing' Marxism; the appeal to radicalized white-collar workers; and the turn from a rhetoric of a 'proletarian culture' to a notion of a 'cultural front.'"[30]

A number of Copland's fellow American composers such as Marc Blitzstein were interested in leftist causes during the 1930s, and many of his younger associates were affiliated with the Left, including Leonard Bernstein and David Diamond. Copland was also a close associate of well-known leftist composers Elie Siegmeister and Charles Seeger. Both members of the Communist Party, as the 1930s wore on they became increasingly militant. Copland's affiliation with the Left continued into the early 1940s, during the height of Stalinism. He also associated with the radical German composer Hanns Eisler during the war when the United States was allied with Stalin against Nazi Germany. Copland, in supporting the war effort, rallied and (like contemporaries such as Lillian Hellmann and Langston Hughes) became involved in groups that sought to strengthen cultural and musical ties with the Soviet Union as well as provide wartime relief. He supported the Friends for Russian Freedom and the Koussevitzky-organized music committee of the National Council of American-Soviet Friendship (the parent body formed in 1941 and was led by writer Corliss Lamont), which grew out of the earlier Friends of Soviet Russia (formed in 1921). In 1943 Copland joined the music committee of the National Council; by 1944 he was vice-chairman. In 1946 the music committee was reorganized (along with the theater and literature committee) and the council renamed the American-Soviet Music Society, with Koussevitzky as chairman and Copland along with Bernstein and Siegmeister as vice-chairmen. In 1947 Koussevitzky would sever his ties with the organization, and Copland became chairman. Copland's interest in Russian-Soviet organizations was natural, since both his parents were born in Russia.[31]

Copland wrote three articles that appeared in leftist publications. In 1935 the *American Mercury* published "The American Composer Gets a Break." The same year, "A Note on Young Composers" appeared in the *Music Vanguard,* a short-lived publication that brought together leftist politics and modern American music. Copland also reviewed the *Workers*

Song Book (1934) for the prominent and influential leftist publication *New Masses*.[32] There is one documented case of Copland directly participating in a leftist political demonstration. While retreating to a cabin near Bemidji, Minnesota, lent him by his cousin to complete *El Salón México,* Copland made what Perlis calls his "one and only political speech." He and Kraft went to a picnic/campaign meeting held by local farmers and the Communist Party. The Communist candidate for governor, S. K. Davis, spoke, and Copland, at the urging of the farmers, addressed the group, the occasion giving him the opportunity to move beyond theorizing about revolution to "preach it from the streets—OUT LOUD." As he wrote Israel Citkowitz, "Well, I made my speech . . . and I'll probably never be the same!"[33] Afterwards, when Copland went into town, he was greeted warmly by other Bemidjians, who offered "friendly nods from sympathizers, and farmers come up and talk as one red to another. One feels very much at home and not at all like a mere summer boarder. I'll be sorry to leave here with the thought of probably never seeing them again."[34] This experience gave Copland one of his few real grassroots experiences and feelings of solidarity with the workers about whom he theorized with New York intellectuals and artists.

During the early 1930s Copland's opinion about the purpose of music reflected the Left's position on the social function of music. "A Note on Young Composers" addressed some of the problems "perennially with us," including the question, "For whom did the composer create?" The article revealed an inchoate concern for the composer's struggle that aligned with the ideology of the Left. The main problem facing modern European composers was how to continue the sense of excitement and brilliance following the successes of Milhaud, Honegger, and Auric. The American composer faced a similar problem:

> We in America have our own special problem of seeing to it that the sense of new life that came into American music soon after the War [World War I] be continued in a fresh batch of younger "lights."[35]

Copland advised younger composers that first they should "see themselves clearly" and realize that the problems they faced and the course of their training differed from those of composers active during the 1920s. Indeed, there had been many improvements in the composer's lot. The American composer of the 1920s of necessity had gone to Europe to complete studies; the composer of the 1930s could now complete training in the United States. Yet composers reaching maturity during the 1930s faced a musical zeitgeist different from that known by composers such as Copland who had begun their careers in the 1920s. During the 1920s, Copland pointed out, the modernist watchword was experimentation, and modernist music found its niche among elite audiences, patrons (especially philanthropic women), and music critics.[36] By the 1930s composers such as Copland, Tomson, Cowell, and others were well established, having garnered performances, publication, the financial support of both private patrons and fellowships, and teaching positions in universities. They had begun their career in an era of optimism after World War I and extending into the 1920s. Composers of the 1920s had societies such as the International Composers' Guild or the League of Composers to perform and promote their music (though both remained active into the 1930s). Copland's own career had been aided by associations he had formed both in Paris and New York during the 1920s. Koussevitzky, whom he had met in Paris while studying with Boulanger, proved an important friend and associate, performing many of Copland's works with the Boston Symphony Orchestra throughout his career and eventually inviting Copland to teach at Tanglewood, which the conductor was instrumental in founding. Copland had met the composer Marion Bauer in Paris, and she recommended Copland for membership in the League of Composers; Copland joined during its second season. It was through the League that Copland had his first New York performance, the *Passacaglia* and *The Cat and the Mouse* at the League's first "Young Composers' Concert."[37]

There had been steps backward. Younger composers who began their careers during the 1930s struggled during a time when financial support declined as patrons lost their wealth and could no longer provide extensive support. Two important modern music publishers, Cos Cob Press (founded 1929 by Alma Wertheim) and Cowell's *New Music: A Quarterly of Modern Compositions* (founded 1927), barely survived the Depression. Copland believed that these young composers were a different group with different needs. The older societies had become difficult for the younger composer to enter, and thus composers of the 1930s did not have any single organization devoted *exclusively* to their needs, as had the older generation.

The composer of the 1930s faced the additional burden of coming to terms with the modernism of the 1920s, the audience's changing tastes, and the current (supposed) lack of interest in modern music. Copland wrote, "The whole field of modern music no longer carries with it a sense of novelty or even of experimentation."[38] The changing time demanded that music change. Copland advised young composers to "[throw] in their lot with that of the working class."[39] This alignment would answer the question of for whom they composed. But what would be the style and content of their music? What sort of music would align with the working class? What kind of music would young composers create? How should they address practical matters concerning performance of their works? Invoking the language of the Left with a reference to class struggle, Copland thought these were problems the composer in the "ordinary bourgeois field of music did not have to face." He saw a puzzling dearth of new talent addressing the issue:

> Still, I look about me and wonder why I see no young composer in America with a "First Symphony" under his arm. Inevitably, one wonders where the fault lies. Does our young composer lack the necessary craftsmanship, or the sense or economic stability, or an ideological basis for his work, or what?[40]

The young composer's merely committing to the working class would not solve all problems of audience:

> The young composer who allies himself with the proletarian movement must do so not with the feeling that he has found an easy solution, but with a full realization of what such a step means, if his work is to be of permanent value to the workers and their cause.[41]

Copland advocated an accessible music that could easily be understood and enjoyed by everyone, regardless of musical sophistication, literacy, or training. But was he really advocating a shift of American art music from the complexity found in the European tradition toward a simpler style? Could this simpler style be found through the use of popular music? Would this comprise the new American music? Pondering these questions, Copland concluded that it was important for his music to be liked "by the people"; but there were limits to his willingness to "cater" to popular taste.

Young Composers' Group

Copland acted to assist younger composers emerging during the 1930s. He participated in the Young Composers' Group, which largely embraced Marxism. Membership included Arthur Berger, Henry Brant, Israel Citkowitz, Lehman Engel, Vivian Fine, Irwin Heilner, Bernard Herrmann, Jerome Moross, and Elie Siegmeister, among others, and the occasional visitor. The group met informally every few weeks during 1932. As Perlis writes, "The role of the arts in society was a favorite topic for debate at the Group Theatre, the Young Composers' Group, and the conferences at Yadoo. If a time in history can be located and defined by catch words and phrases, 'the masses,' the 'Proletariat,' 'workers' causes,' and 'comrade' would henceforth identify the thirties."[42] Copland served as an adviser to the group and close friend and father figure to several members.

Music and the American Left

Copland's concerns were already being addressed by those within the American Left. Various organizations and individuals were concerned with issues affecting musicians and others in the music industry. Invoking the rhetoric of Marxism, on February 5, 1935, Ashley Pettis, prominent leftist music critic, announced, "The cultural front in the class struggle is showing extraordinary signs of life."[43] He went on to list various leftist music activities such as instrumental and choral ensembles, and classical and modern music concerts. The music profession had been particularly hard hit by the Depression; this was compounded by the arrival of the sound motion picture, which put mass numbers of theater musicians out of work. Covering the activities of the New York Musicians Union, Local 802, Pettis addressed the issue of how the Depression had affected musicians, leaving many destitute. Despite its fifteen thousand dues-paying members, Local 802 found itself without funds to assist its unemployed musicians. A series of concerts in Madison Square Garden serving as fund-raisers for the Musicians Emergency Aid of New York was held in 1936.[44] The Left was also concerned with unions affecting others in the music industry and the exploitation of musicians. In his March 1936 column "Music: New Recordings" Henry Johnson mentioned the exploitation of blacks by record companies.[45] In April Johnson reported further labor activities as he wrote about the union's attempts to organize the copyists, arrangers, and proofreaders employed by music publishers.[46]

The American Communist Party had its own branch and many organizations devoted to music. The Workers' Music League was an umbrella organization that included workers' choruses, a symphony, and a folk orchestra of instruments such as mandolin or balalaika. Seeking to keep the social function of music in mind, professional musicians organized their own branch of the League, the Pierre Degeyter Club.[47] The club, with a membership of about fifty, met weekly and supported musical ensembles. It had both an orchestra and a chorus; it also offered organized courses, lectures, and concerts to members of the general public. The club was also concerned with music education.[48]

The *New Masses* devoted many of its pages to revolution and the arts. It regularly featured reviews of performances by ensembles associated with various leftist musical organizations. It also publicized upcoming events, especially in New York. The various musical organization associated with the American Left were by no means idle, and actively presented concerts. Concerts, recitals, radio programs, recordings, and other music venues were regularly reported and reviewed in the pages of *New Masses*. In keeping with the revolutionary nature of the publication, the magazine particularly covered events in New York's leftist music community. Pettis reviewed the Second Workers' Music Olympiad, held in New York on April 29, 1934, and organized by the Workers' Music League.[49] The concert included performances by the Pierre Degeyter Symphonietta, the Workers' International Relief Band, F.S.U. Balalaika Orchestra, Freiheit Mandolin Orchestra, Italian Workers' Chorus, Workers' Mixed Chorus, Freiheit Gezang Farein, Ukranian Workers' Mixed Chorus, Brooklyn Finnish Workers Mixed Chorus, Lithuanian Aido Chorus, and the Daily Worker Chorus. Choruses from the Eastern European New York community were well represented. The same issue also contained an advertisement for a "Joint Concert," with performances by the Daily Workers and Italian Worker Choruses in New Music and Old Favorites, G. Giovanny, conductor, assisted by the Pierre Degeyter Symphony at the New School.[50] *New Masses* also covered events of the larger international workers movement. In the March 6, 1934, issue Pettis announced the upcoming International Music Week, which would be partly a demonstration against fascism and war and partly a defense of the Soviet Union. He listed several leftist musical organizations participating in the week's events: the Workers' Music League; a federation of workers' choruses; bands, a string sinfonietta; mandolin, balalaika, and other orchestras; and the Pierre Degeyter Club. The event was to be observed in the United States, England, France, Austria, China, and Japan.[51] *New Masses* also printed articles on international music matters, particularly those in the Soviet Union. Siegmeister served as a foreign correspondent, reporting on music he observed during a visit to the Soviet Union in the summer of 1934.[52] Pettis also kept abreast of what was happening in Nazi Germany, reporting the resignation of Wilhelm Fürtwangler, who had defended composers and musicians who were out of favor with the Nazis, namely the modernists and the Jews.[53]

The Left even formed a Workers' Music School. An advertisement announcing the spring term (which ran from April 1 to July 1, 1935) of the Downtown Music School appeared.[54] In his music column publicizing it, Pettis charged that most music schools exploited students, which the Workers' Music School would not do. It would offer classes in theory, music appreciation, choral singing, and instruction in piano, violin, and other instruments. It would also offer music criticism from a Marxist point of view. "The classes have been planned with a view to practical work in the revolutionary movement."[55] An article written by Tony Clark on Eisler, published in conjunction with two courses he was teaching at the New school, also appeared that year in *New Masses*.[56]

Copland was involved in several of the Left's concerts and other musical events. In 1938 appeared an advertisement "We've Got the Tune, Have You Got the Name?" It promoted an as-yet unnamed musical event featuring Blitzstein, Paul Bowles, Count Basie and his band,

Chavez, Elliott Carter, Copland, Alex North, Wallingford Riegger, Earl Robinson, and Thomson.[57] The advertisement announced that the composers would play and conduct their own works. It included a performance of Copland's *Schuloper, The Second Hurricane.*

The Composers' Collective

Copland became involved in one of the Communist Party's music organizations, the Composers' Collective, an offshoot of the Pierre Degeyter Club. The same year the Young Composers' Group formed, Cowell and Seeger, along with Jacob Schaefer and Leon Charles, started the Composers' Collective after leading a seminar on composing songs for the masses.[58] An organization for composers that grew out of a desire among its members for more independence from the parent organization and a broad membership, the Composers' Collective never completely broke from the Degeyter Club. Headquartered at 47 E. Twelfth Street, seven blocks from the Degeyter Club (on E. Nineteenth Street), Collective members met Saturday afternoons in a loft at 5430 Sixth Avenue.[59] Concerned with the role of music in American culture during the desperate years of the Depression, the collective was active for four years, 1932–36, attracting many of the leading young composers then working in New York. Membership grew to about two dozen,[60] including many academically trained art music composers who had studied at elite eastern schools or with Boulanger. In addition to Copland, Cowell, Schaefer, and Seeger, members included Ruth Crawford Seeger, Riegger, Blitzstein, Siegmeister, Earl Robinson, Herbert Haufrecht, Henry Leland Clarke, Robert Grass, Norman Cazden, and Alex North.[61] Most of the collective's members were not members of the American Communist Party, Robbie Lieberman writes, "but as in other fields of cultural activity, they had turned to the party for leadership in response to the chaos of the Depression."[62] Some composers, including Seeger and Blitzstein, remained active throughout the life of the organization; others, such as Cowell and Copland, were active only at the beginning.[63] Seeger, himself prominent in political causes and the Left, described Copland, along with Eisler and George Antheil, as an intermittent member.[64] Though he wrote articles and songs, Copland seems to have attended meetings irregularly, as did Eisler and Antheil.[65] Among his collective activities, Copland organized benefit concerts, such as the first Festival of the American Music, held May 17, 1936. This concert featured seventeen different organizations such as the German, Italian, and Lithuanian choruses, the Fur Workers' Chorus singing in Yiddish, and the Freiheit Mandolin Orchestra, along with many individuals. Copland himself participated by performing his *Two Children's Pieces for Piano.*[66]

Aesthetics and the Composers' Collective

One of the weapons in the class struggle was proletarian art, that is, art created by, for, and about the working class. In a broader sense, it was art created from a proletarian point of view, expressing a class-conscious radicalism.[67] The main cultural focus of the Communist Party was on literature, drama, and film. But as we have seen, music soon became a part of the Left's movement culture,[68] especially songs and choral singing.[69] In *New Masses* Pettis described the Composers' Collective and the Workers' Music League working to change the "base of musical development in this country."[70] At the collective's weekly meetings, composers discussed each other's works, which were judged on the basis of both their accessibility for the masses and their technique. The composers of the collective were interested in raising both the political consciousness and the musical tastes of the proletariat.[71] "The collective set out to provide musical direction for workers' choruses in New York City and to produce and perform revolutionary music. Its work illustrates some of the problems inherent in creating proletarian culture."[72] The collective's views about the use of music reflected both the New York Communist movement's ideology and modernist aesthetics. American modernist composers were expected to use their training to create mass song, to improve upon "The Internationale" for revolutionary causes. They sought to create a new proletarian music—a modern music for the masses or workers, the nonelite.[73]

The members of the Composers' Collective as a group developed ideas about the role of the composer in society, music as a weapon in the class struggle, what style of music was suitable for the masses, and how to make *good* revolutionary music that was accessible. These were all important concerns for Copland, as we have seen. Specifically, at its inception, the Composers' Collective was interested in mass song style, growing from several members' work with ethnic workers' choruses. Seeger, who adopted the pseudonym Carl Sands, believed that proletarian music should be "militant in text and tune, associated with the working class, revolutionary in content, and nationalist in form." Proletarian music would be "one of the cultural forms through which the work of humanizing people and preparing the proletariat for its historic task operates."[74] The group modeled its music after that of Eisler, who insisted that his mass songs be both politically and musically progressive.[75] It is precisely these views that Copland expressed in his *Music Vanguard* article.

New Masses reviewed the concerts of the Composers' Collective. Max Margulis wrote of its first concert, "For the first time in American musical history, a concert audience experienced the palpable fact of a revolutionary content in music, a content that was infinitely rich, complex and varied."[76] The concert included Siegmeister's *Strange Funeral in*

Braddock and workers' rounds by Siegmeister and Sands. Margulis reported that the audience cheered the compositions. Copland himself offered an all-Copland concert on March 16, 1934, at the Degeyter Club, with Seeger providing a talk beforehand. Copland made a less than successful attempt to present his Paris-era works before an audience of workers and others who followed the Degeyter Club's musical offerings. Seeger, writing as Carl Sands, reviewed the recital in *The Daily Worker:*

> He brought still one more affirmation of the belief that contemporary art music has lost contact with the vital trends in present-day life and that the only hope for it lies in its frank identification with the great masses of the proletariat.[77]

The pieces performed at this recital were not Copland's more accessible works, but ones clearly intended for the modernist audience, such as the *Passacaglia.* These modernist works failed to reach the proletariat audience. Even Copland himself must have been apprehensive that his audience would respond negatively, for Sands reported that at the beginning of the concert the composer issued a disclaimer, informing his audience that the style of the works to be performed did not reflect his current musical thinking. Although Copland now called for the composer to create music for the masses, his own works up to this point had little to do with this particular audience. He had had to warn his audience "against viewing his compositions from a revolutionary angle. As Copland said with charming naiveté, he had not, at the time of their composition, any ideas of that sort in his head." Months later, in May 1934, the Degeyter Club sponsored a symposium, "The Problems of the Composer in Modern Society," featuring Copland, Seeger, Siegmeister, and Roy Harris.[78]

The Composers' Collective and Mass Song

The revolutionary chorus was the principal form of proletarian musical activity during the early years of the Composers' Collective. The collective's chief aim was to supply songs intended to be sung by the working class that would inspire them to leftist and social causes—music for the numerous workers' choruses and other proletarian choral groups. Throughout the life of the collective, its inspiration and models for mass song came from many sources. Members followed the IWW (Industrial Workers of the World—the "Wobblies") tradition of parodying hymns and popular songs, adopted the New Theatre movement's use of popular music in political drama, imitated the style of "hillbilly" music just beginning to be heard nationally on the radio, and drew upon Russian and European folk music. At the outset composers used classically derived musical forms to create mass songs and other choral and symphonic works, viewing this as the best means of combining proletarian content with the "forward-looking technic of bourgeois art music" in which they had been formally trained. They explicitly rejected native forms of American music. They did this not because they thought American music inferior, but because they were following the practice and conventions of leftist organizations throughout the world.[79]

Copland and the *Workers Song Books*

The collective first sought to compose its own music to be used in the workers' struggle. It published the *Workers Song Book 1* (1934) and *Workers Song Book 2* (1935). The first *Song Book* included music by L. E. Swift (Siegmeister), Lahn Adohmyan, Janet Barnes, Carl Sands (Seeger), and Jacob Schaeffer. The follow-up publication included music by Copland, Eisler, Stefan Wolpe, J. Fairbanks (Henry Leland Clarke), and J. C. Richards (Wallingford Riegger).[80] Copland reviewed the first *Workers Song Book* in the June 5, 1934, issue of the *New Masses*. Echoing party propaganda, he stated that mass songs were "a powerful weapon in the class struggle" and that "the song the masses itself sings is a cultural symbol which helps to give continuity to the day-to-day struggle of the proletariat." But aware, perhaps, of his elite training in composition, Copland thought that there was an inherent chasm between the composer and the worker. He sought, however, to bridge it without condescension or elitism: "Composers will want to raise the musical level of the masses, but they must also be ready to learn from them what species of songs is most apposite to the revolutionary task." The crux of the matter was that the composer listened to mass song as music, while the "workers who sing them will in the first instance decide how they apply to the actualities of the daily struggle."[81]

In the same review of the *Workers Song Book,* Copland recognized Swift's "The Scottsboro Boys Will Not Die" as a good example of a mass song that had proved popular with workers. This success, however, could not be attributed to musical reasons, Copland thought, because he did not judge Swift's song among the best in the volume. The poetry was poor and the music unimaginative. Copland praised Swift's other mass songs as better constructed musically; yet they had not become popular among the workers. Copland solved this seeming paradox by attributing this song's popularity to its topical nature: it was about the famous Scottsboro Boys case. This slightly critical stance on "movement music" was in fact Copland's usual one. For example, when he critiqued the songs of Adohmyan, Sands, and Schaeffer, he judged Sands's "Mount the Barricades" the best, suggesting that it could "serve as a model for future proletarian composers." In this song, Sands had managed to combine a simple melody with unconventional harmonies dear to Copland. Most of these songs fell short of the mark. On the one hand, Copland judged Adohmayan's songs, "Red Soldiers Singing" and "Song to the Soldier," popular failures because of their dissonant harmony and disjunct melodic lines. Schaeffer's three songs, "Hunger March," "Strife Song," and "Lenin, Our Leader," failed musically partly because of their conservative style. Copland queried, "Can a composer use the musical speech of the nineteenth century to express revolutionary sentiments?" He concluded the answer was no—in this case, however, not because of the older style itself (Schaeffer was an older composer) but because the songs were simply of "poor quality." Specifically, Copland meant their lyrics were poor because Schaeffer had relied on inadequate translations of Yiddish texts. Nonetheless, Copland also had a poor opinion of conservative or conventional music in general. In closing, he concluded that of the fourteen songs in the anthology, only four were truly mass songs. The remainder were "revolutionary choral compositions written for performance by trained workers' choruses and solo songs intended for concert performance."[82] The collective's guidelines for the creation of workers' music advised composers to create music that could be used in the class struggle, was "revolutionary in content and form, aimed toward redirecting and refining the workers' musical tastes."[83] These traits were described by Copland in both his *New Masses* review of the *Workers Song Book* and his *Music Vanguard* article. Copland saw himself as trying to promote high musical standards even while bowing to the needs of a mass audience. Yet, despite his attempt at nonelitism, Copland did indeed want to redirect and refine mass taste. He concluded that "a first rate mass song must be satisfying in text and music to *both* worker and musician."[84]

"Into the Streets May First"

Copland was not content to be a silent member of the collective or to write articles for leftist publications. He was an active member who himself tried to contribute to the store of proletarian music by composing mass songs for the workers. The collective and *New Masses* sponsored a contest to see who could provide the best setting of the text "Into the Streets May First" by Alfred Hayes. Copland submitted a song, as did others, including Siegmeister and Seeger. Copland's song was voted unanimously the winner. The entire song was published in the May 1, 1934, issue of *New Masses* and later reprinted in *Workers Song Book 2* (1935).[85]

Though it was a call to revolution (something not typically part of Americans' daily lives in 1934 in the midst of the implementation of Roosevelt's first New Deal relief measures), the text Copland was given to set was not very far from Americans' memories of riots and protests against the terrible economic conditions, particularly during the Red Scare of 1919. No doubt the text suited his criteria for one relevant to the daily lives of the workers. Wedding only the first twelve lines of the poem to rousing music, Copland provided a setting that reflected the poem's prosody, with the rhythms and pitch inflections reflecting those of American speech (see example 8.1). The octaves, heavy and pendulous, sound on every beat, suggesting the marching feet of the masses. The melody is fittingly stirring, despite its mostly conjunct motion. At dramatic points in the text Copland introduces large vocal leaps, such as those that accompany the lines "Red flag," or "Up with the sickle and hammer, / Comrades, these are our tools / A song and a banner," when the voice leaps a perfect fifth; or the words "Red flag," when the voice leaps an octave. Rhythmically, the voice sings mostly in quarter notes, reinforcing the "mass's" marching of the bass.

Copland carefully avoided all the stylistic traits with which he had found fault in his review of the *Workers Song Book* (1934). In his mass song he tried to combine simplicity of melody with a mildly adventurous modulation in order to meet his own criterion for a good mass song. Copland ventured beyond conventional nineteenth century harmonic practice, yet avoided harsh dissonance, which he had criticized in others in his review. The harmony, overwhelmingly diatonic and in the key of C major, consists of tonic, dominant, and dominant preparation (in this case, supertonic and subdominant). Copland rests on a tonic pedal throughout much of the piece, beginning in mm. 7–9.[86] This pedal technique occurs again at mm. 15–16. In m. 13 he modulates to B major (the triad built on the seventh scale degree) before cadencing in C. While in B, Copland moves to its neighboring A major, suggesting a modal inflection allusive of folk music with its Dorian, Phrygian, and Mixolydian melodies (i.e., these modes all have lowered seventh scale degrees).

Copland's "Into the Streets May First" was first performed by the Daily Worker Chorus on April 29, 1934, at the Workers' Music Olympiad at the City College auditorium. Pettis, who would later work for the WPA (Works Projects Administration) and the Federal Music Project in New York, reviewed the song's performance by the three-hundred-member Freiheit Gezang Farein at the Brooklyn Academy of Music. Pettis thought it was a bad performance, one that did not do justice to Copland's song.[87]

The Use of American Folk Music

During its first years, the Composers' Collective was concerned primarily with creating mass song style and building a mass song repertoire. At the

Example 8.1 Copland, "Into the Streets, May 1st"

outset the members of the collective did not view American folk music as a useful model for creating revolutionary songs. They ignored American folk and popular music, arguing that "revolutionary" music demanded a revolutionary style. Seeger initially described folk songs as complacent, "melancholy, and defeatist."[88] The only attention the collective paid to folk music in its early years stemmed from its concentration on foreign models, particularly the "Mighty Five" Russian composers (Mussorgsky, Balakirev, Borodin, Cui, Rimsky-Korsakov). At one point, the American composers even attempted to contrafact Russian folk tunes into American revolutionary songs. Only in the mid-1930s did the Composers' Collective become more interested in American folk music.[89] As Lieberman states, "The seeds of a new aesthetic were sown during this period, an aesthetic that was broader in many ways than the rigid art music standards of the Composers' Collective."[90]

The collective's new interest in folk music resulted from a confluence of several different trends. The turning point came in 1937, when the Popular Front began to use American folk culture to advance its cause.[91] Folk music officially became part of the movement. American composers at the time believed that their efforts until then to create a revolutionary mass song revolutionary in style and content had failed to appeal to its sought-after mass audience. With the realization that their own music was too "revolutionary" for the worker, and seeing the Communist Party's new interest in American folk culture, the composers turned with the party to (native) American folk music.

Ironically, published commercial editions of American folk songs played a pivotal role in raising the Composers' Collective members' awareness of American folk music. One influential collection was Sandburg's *The American Song Bag* (1927). This collection introduced many composers to American folk song, including Earl Robinson. Ruth Crawford Seeger was introduced to folk music by the Sandburgs when she made several arrangements for voice and piano for this collection.[92] Charles and Ruth were drawn to an earlier and less eclectic collection, George Pullen Jackson's *White Spirituals in the Southern Uplands* (1933). Seeger was also a reviewer for Macmillan when it was deciding whether or not to publish John Lomax's collection, *American Ballads and Folk Songs*.[93] These collections consist of transcribed versions of folk songs, some with piano arrangements playable by an amateur.

The Seegers were not alone in recognizing and perceiving that a change in approach was needed. During the late 1930s other Composers' Collective members were exposed to authentic performances of folk songs, having opportunities to hear folksingers perform their own music. Legendary Kentucky ballad singer-songwriter and union organizer Aunt Molly Jackson performed on one occasion before the group.[94] Charles Seeger recalled:

> I was trying to write music for protest marches and union gatherings. An old woman named Aunt Mollie Jackson had come to one of the meetings of the Composers' Collective, and I learned her songs and discovered that they were folk songs simply dolled up, with new words and perhaps a few touches of her own, and that the people could sing their songs and they couldn't sing our songs. So went up to her and I said, Mollie, you're on the right track and we're on the wrong track and I gave up the Collective. We were all on the wrong track—it was professionals trying to write music for the people and not in the people's idiom.[95]

Seeger's opinion was a radical one! The efforts of the professionals—of the Composers' Collective—had failed in creating a mass song style, a fact that hearing Aunt Molly Jackson and her songs reinforced. The masses were singing folk songs and those in the folk song style of musicians such as Jackson, Leadbelly, Josh White, and Woody Guthrie. Remarkably, Seeger was willing to give up "art music" altogether in favor of this popular folk song, but not every member of the collective followed suit.

Like the Popular Front and its promotion of indigenous culture, several New Deal policies addressed the issue of folk music and led the Composers' Collective further into folk music. Under various relief programs—beginning with a branch of the WPA and later the Federal Music Project—folklorists and collectors traveled throughout the country, assembling and recording music sung by the people themselves.[96] Three prominent members of the collective conducted this type of research: Earl Robinson, and Herbert Haufrecht, and Seeger, who became director of the WPA Music Project and oversaw its large-scale collection and recording of folk music. Among the results of this renewed interest in folk music were the large-scale dissemination and popularization of folk music via various venues (live performance, sound recordings, radio). In this context Copland began to turn his attention to folk music.

Folk music began to occupy a larger position in both the style and the aesthetic of various members of the collective as they attempted to appropriate or assimilate this idiom. Seeger relates how he performed folk songs at a room dedication at the New School during the 1930s. Robinson performed folk songs live and wrote his own "folk songs," that is, original songs created in simple, folk style. Others—not necessarily art music composers—such as Woody Guthrie did the same. Even the content of the *Workers Song Books* changed from the first volume to the third. The 1934 volume contained original songs by art composers and lacked folk songs. The second contained two folk songs, both taken from Lawrence Gellert's collection *Negro Songs of Protest*. The third, *Songs of the People* (1935), contained half folk and popular songs that were contrafacta, with leftist labor lyrics fitted to well-known tunes.[97]

By the middle of the decade the collective had ceased to use German and Russian folk music in their compositions altogether. As Robbie Lieberman points out:

> By the late 1930s, then, folk music began to be promoted as indigenous, progressive "peoples music." In contrast to proletarian music, created by professional composers for the working class, folk music was created by "the people" themselves. Folk music demonstrated that people were active participants in creating their own culture. It was accessible to people and did not require the training and sophistication that art music demanded.[98]

This new fashion was not received without controversy or hesitation. Siegmeister recalled in a late-1980s interview that the collective's composers remained divided on this issue. "One group felt that the music should be extremely simple in the so-called mass song; another wanted the music to be revolutionary because the movement was revolutionary." Nonetheless, many art music composers (as we have seen) abandoned the notion that a mass music style had to be "revolutionary"; those who did not completely give up art music, like Seeger, turned their attention toward finding ways in which to assimilate or absorb folk song into their compositions, whether arrangements or quotations.[99]

One member of the collective in particular had an opportunity to observe directly folk music's power, efficacy, and potential as a social tool. Seeger was tapped to head the Special Skills Division of the Resettlement Administration in 1935, a New Deal federal agency created by Roosevelt to meet the needs of the rural and urban poor.[100] Its director, Rexford Tugwell, established settlements, ethnically mixed communities of farmers, laborers, and industrial workers. The RA collective members were taught improved farming and agricultural management methods. However, ethnic and racial tensions developed. To defuse tensions and foster unity in striving toward common goals, artists and artisans—painters, actors, a weaver, furniture designers, woodworkers, and so on—were brought in. Seeger was tapped to develop and implement the program's music arm. The music bureau's goal was to put thirty-three musicians in three hundred communities. Ann M. Pescatello quotes at length the foreword of Margaret Valiant's published diary, *Journal of a Field Representative,* in which Seeger "outlined the principles by which he organized the Special Skills Division music program—principles that reflect his larger conception of the function of music in American society." Seeger wrote:

> 1. Music, like any art, is not an end in itself, but is a means for achieving larger social and economic ends;
> 2. To make music is the essential thing—listening is only accessory;
> 3. Music as a group activity is vastly more important than music as an individual accomplishment;

4. Every person is inherently musical, and music can be associated with any human activity;
5. The nation's musical culture is to be evaluated as to the extent of the participation of the whole population, rather than the virtuosity of a fraction of it;
6. The basis for musical culture is the vernacular of the broad mass of the people—its traditional, often called *folk,* idiom; popular music, such as jazz, and professional, high art music are elaborated superstructures built upon the common base;
7. There is no ground for quarreling between various idioms and styles, provided a proper relationship between them is maintained—jazz need not be scorned, nor professional art music artificially stimulated, nor folk music stamped out or sentimentalized;
8. The point of departure for any worker new to a community should be the tastes and capacities of the group; and activities introduced should be directed toward developing local leadership rather than encouraging dependence on outside help;
9. The main question is not be [*sic*] whether music is good, but what music is good for; and if it can help people become more independent, capable, and democratic, it must be approved;
10. Workers should combine music making with whatever other activities and arts that help make music serve a well-rounded function in the community.[101]

These "guidelines" issued to fieldworkers also served as what could be termed a People's Music aesthetic. Copland's aesthetic and musical style of the late 1930s resonates particularly with the first, fifth, sixth, and seventh principles. Although he continued to value art music more highly than popular music, Copland extended his knowledge of vernacular music in general to include folk music and agreed with Seeger that the ultimate goal of music is social—and turned to the development of what he saw as American folk music in his compositions.

The Left and African-American Music

Jazz and blues were of special use for the Popular Front, powerful tools in its fight against racism and fascism. One of the most often written about New York sites is Barney Josephson's Café Society, which featured performers such as Billie Holiday, Teddy Wilson, Josh White, Mary Lou Williams, Hazel Scott, and Lena Horne performing before an integrated audience (Café Society was the first integrated midtown jazz club).[102] Members of the Left such as Alan Lomax and Robinson frequently pointed out during this period the contributions blacks had made to American music and folk song,[103] and *New Masses* regularly reviewed recordings of African-American blues, jazz, and spirituals during the

Popular Front years (see below). The music critics who wrote for the *New Masses* saw African-American music as a great folk tradition, though for different reasons. The Left's primary interest in this folk music stemmed from its "revolutionary nature." Indeed, it was often viewed as *the* true music expressive of the class struggle. Richard Frank's 1934 article on African-American music addressed the relationship of the Communist Party to the Negro question—the issue of racial prejudice and discrimination—and claimed that African-American music had made its great contribution to revolutionary music because it was truly the music of an oppressed people.

> In the south, the ideology of the international working-class movement is beginning to be expressed in native Negro music. The importance of this cannot be overemphasized. The emergence of the music means that Marxism-Leninism is being expressed in native cultural media, for if the Negroes of America do not form a basic section of the native toiling masses of America, there are no such sections.[104]

Similarly, it was seen as a potent weapon in the struggle against class and race oppression. Frank again pointed out the potential the songs had for recruiting African-Americans to the movement. "Among the Negroes, it will be to a great extent through singing that recruiting will be done, for masses of Negro workers are held at illiteracy. Leaflets cannot appeal to them. But singing is their great form of artistic expression. In order to win the Negro people most effectively, the revolutionary movement will have to make use of this instrument."[105] Frank, as had members of the Composers' Collective, held Russian folk music as a model for American Communist music. Seeing parallels between the conditions of African-American bondage and those of Russian feudalism, he declared, "All through the days of slavery, they expressed their suffering, their despair, their hopes, their dreams of a false deliverance through religion, in their spirituals and work-songs, thus creating the most sublime folk-music, with the possible exception of the Russian, of any people on earth."[106] Frank announced that "a new stage in the creation of Negro music has commenced," the creation of Negro revolutionary folk music throughout the South.[107] African-Americans were now creating their own revolutionary music, "first, by the singing of new revolutionary words to the music of the old spirituals and work-songs; second, by the creation of entirely new revolutionary songs."[108] These new revolutionary songs, like many Anglo-American songs and hymns, were contrafacta of well-known songs. The spiritual "In Dat Great Gittin'-up Mornin'" became "In Dat Great Revolutionary Mornin.'" As the prototypical leftist music of the oppressed masses, African-American folk music could be the music of *all* the American masses. "When the American revolutionary movement finds expression in Negro music, therefore, it is expressing itself in a medium capable of arousing not only the twelve or fifteen million Negroes of America, but also the toiling masses of America who for generations in one form or another have made Negro music their own."[109]

Reviews appearing in *New Masses* during this period included collections of African-American folk music, some of which were made by African-Americans. R. D. Darrell, a regular columnist, reviewed J. Rosamond Johnson's *Rolling Along in Song*.[110] This eclectic eighty-seven-song collection included spirituals, ring shouts, jubilees, work songs, plantation and minstrel ballads, levee songs, jailhouse songs, street cries, ragtime, and blues that surpassed the leftist classic, Carl Sandburg's larger *American Song Bag:* Johnson's collection had higher musical standards. An article by Gellert promoting his new collection of songs gathered in the Carolinas and Georgia, *Negro Songs of Protest* (New York: American Music League, 1936), appeared in *New Masses* [from these "protest songs"]. Gellert printed selections of lyrics telling of oppressive conditions for blacks in the South.[111] Lan Adomian (Lahn Adohmyan) reviewed his collection in *New Masses:*

> The songs in this collection, it is true, do not express the "loftier-religious feelings," but sound an indictment against conditions which perpetrated the slander that a nation of thirteen million people, reduced to peonage, is nothing more than a grand minstrel show—and if those thirteen million people dare to be so "uppity" as to try to do something about this state of affairs, they are immediately labelled as "bad Niggers" with all the consequences of lynch justice.[112]

The songs were even good music, he ventured: "The book contains some of the finest examples in Negro folk music." He praised the arrangements, suggesting they could be useful for the American composer:

> Elie Siegmeister's very interesting piano accompaniments should be only one of the many ways of treating his new-found treasure of song. There should be others—more simple-versions available with guitar or banjo accompaniments added. . . . And American composers, especially those of the left, can learn a valuable lesson. For this is intelligible music—it is appealing without being "spiritual." These songs should be studied by composers.[113]

Jazz and the blues generally received enthusiastic reviews in *New Masses* during the late 1930s because they were considered "progressive" or "revolutionary" music.[114] Even swing was looked upon as a music with revolutionary significance because it brought together black and white musicians, thereby promoting integration.[115] *New Masses* critic Henry Johnson regularly reviewed jazz and blues recordings on an equal par with classical recordings. But if the blues and jazz could be used as mass music by the movement, the spirituals—or rather, concert arrangements of them, were antithetical to the movement. Johnson tended to be extremely critical of the spirituals when sung in any form except their authentic folk manner. He quite harshly reviewed Marian Anderson's 1936 Victor recordings of "City Called Heaven," "Lord I Can't Stay Away," and "Heaven, Heaven":

> There is probably no form of native music that has suffered so much in the concert hall as the Negro spiritual. Devitalized by arrangements with tinkling piano accompaniments, the music has been sentimentalized for the benefit of overstuffed concert artists with a patronizing interest in the plight of the Negro. Paul Robeson, Roland Hayes and the various choirs of the Southern Uncle Tom colleges are all guilty of robbing them of some of their earthy forceful quality.[116]

These recorded concert arrangements for Johnson were but "castrated replicas of the original."[117]

French Influence, Leftist Folk Music, and Copland's New American Music

The received history has been that Copland turned to folk music as a means by which to create a nationalist music, since Copland scholars have tended to de-emphasize his involvement in leftist politics of the 1930s. But even though the general consensus is that he never joined a leftist political party, Copland had an enduring interest in leftist politics dating back to his high school years. This interest blossomed during the crisis of the Depression years as Copland, like many artists and intellectuals, was drawn to overtly leftist causes, and his involvement in the Composers' Collective and the Pierre Degeyter Club reflected and helped to shape his aesthetic concerning the use and treatment of folk music in his compositions. During the 1920s, in works such as *Music for the Theatre* and articles such as the one that appeared in *Musical America,* Copland seemed to see the United States as lacking an indigenous folk music. Like Poulenc, he had considered American popular music (Tin Pan Alley songs and jazz) the American vernacular—the modern, urban American "folk" music that an American composer *should* draw upon in creating modernist American works. Lacking any direct experience performing authentic jazz, however, Copland came to view it as limited in emotional range; he left it behind as a music predicated primarily upon rhythm. During the 1930s, as his associates collected folk music, Copland came to understand that the United States did indeed have indigenous folk music he could use—some of it even African-American, the roots from which jazz had sprung. His relationship to folk music, however, would remain somewhat distant and far removed from his subject: he had not grown up singing or performing or hearing Anglo-American folk music, or cowboy songs for that matter. Nor would Copland use tunes he had collected himself by conducting his own field research. Instead of relying upon cultural memory that he either did not think he had or did not trust to give him "good music," Copland, rather would turn to published collections. He would use tunes (some of which were favorites with members of the Composers' Collective) from books—cultural reconstructions, in a sense—of folk music to create his version of populist music that sprouted from the aesthetic ideology shaped by his engagement with the cultural politics of the Popular Front.

CHAPTER NINE

"Folk" Music and the Popular Front :: *El Salón México*

> If you have ever been to Mexico you probably know why a composer should want to write a piece of music about it. Nevertheless, I must admit that it came as something of a surprise when I left Mexico in 1932, after a first visit, to find myself with exactly that idea firmly implanted in my mind.
> —Copland, "The Story Behind *El Salón México*"

We saw in the last chapter that Copland was first drawn to American folk music in the context of a folk music revival that got under way during the late 1930s.[1] As we have also seen, Copland's interest in and appropriation of folk music is contemporary with the collecting by the Lomaxes and others. It also reflects how he was influenced by leftist ideology and aesthetics during the years of the Popular Front. After having failed to win over his audience at a Pierre Degeyter Club with modernist works such as *Passacaglia,* he had come to the realization that if he were to reach a broader audience as he desired, a new style was demanded for proletarian or workers' music. He remained committed to modernism and modern music techniques, but the experience with the Degeyter Club and Composers' Collective had demonstrated that dense, overly complex textures and harsh dissonance had limited appeal to the very audience and Popular Front ideology with which Copland identified politically. He never again explored agitprop music so explicitly as he had with "Into the Streets May First."

Copland and other composers of the Popular Front began to realize that folk song could assist them in creating a modern music that could appeal to the masses. The cultural politics of the Popular Front, coupled with the work of the federal agencies, the WPA and Federal Music Project, had made them and others aware that the United States did indeed have a rich, diverse, and very old folk music tradition. Published folk song collections and the occasional performance of traditional singers such as Aunt Molly Jackson and Leadbelly (Huddie Ledbetter) at hootenannies, union organizing meetings, and other gatherings further raised awareness of the nation's folk music heritage. Copland could no longer ignore folk music: he had begun to believe, too, that rather than look to popular music and adhere to the Les Six and Satie-Cocteau aesthetic, he could find inspiration in indigenous folk music. He expanded his interest in proletarian culture beyond agitprop like "Into the Streets May First" and developed a new style that reflected this newfound interest, with, however, roots still in his training with Boulanger. Copland began to quote folk music in his works, especially Anglo-American folk music. He accompanied these folk melodies, however, not with folk-style accompaniments, but subjected them to the same harmonic, rhythmic, and formal treatment as his own original melodies, hoping perhaps to find a middle path between "modernist" art music and the radical turn of Seeger.

Former Composers' Collective member Henry Leland Clarke claimed that "without the Composers Collective there would have been no *Abe Lincoln Song* by Earl Robinson, and without his *Lincoln Song* there would have been no *Lincoln Portrait* by Aaron Copland."[2] Clarke overstates his case, for Lincoln was a favorite topos for the Popular Front. Numerous works (which Pollack dubs "Lincolniana") were inspired by this figure: Robert Russell Bennett's *Abraham Lincoln* Symphony (1929), Daniel Gregory Mason's *Symphony no. 3, A Lincoln Symphony,* op. 35 (1935–36), Siegmeister's *Abraham Lincoln Walks at Midnight* (1937), Polish-born émigré Jerome Weinberger's *Lincoln Symphony* (1941), Robinson's song "Abe Lincoln" (text by A. Hayes, 1936) and his later cantata *The Lonesome Train* (text by Millard Lampell, 1942), Morton Gould's *Lincoln Legend* (1942), and Robert Palmer's choral work *Abraham Lincoln Walks at Midnight* (text by Vachel Lindsay, 1948). But before Copland composed *Lincoln Portrait, Billy the Kid,* or *Appalachian Spring,* he composed *El Salón México,* and in his later years, he saw this work as the real beginning of his populist-accessible period.

El Salón México is the first large orchestral work in which Copland quotes actual folk song. By the time he composed this work an important shift in his aesthetic ideology had already occurred. The first chamber piece (apparently) in which he had used preexisting folk music was *Vitebsk* (1929). However, as discussed above, this trio owes more to Hába and Bartók and international and European modernism than it does to American ideas. *El Salón México* marks a turn toward conscious populism. Here, populism is used as a designation for those works Copland composed with the intent of reaching a broad, untutored audience beyond the modern music audience he had courted in the 1920s. Berger acknowledges that *El Salón México* was the work that brought Copland widespread popularity with both concert hall and radio audiences and established Copland as a major "successful" composer. The reception of this work in London at a festival of the International Society for Contemporary Music was particularly brilliant and in some ways a turning point for Copland. It was after this occasion that Boosey and Hawkes gave him a long-term contract, assuring the publication of each new work soon after its completion. Berger notes that although this work does not belong to Copland's group of *Gebrauchsmusik,* it has similar aims: "to refer beyond the realm of absolute music and thus provide some bridge to the music itself for listeners with limited capacity for formal or technical perception."[3] Thus, since Copland realized he could reach a wider audience by quoting folk music and simplifying his style, works composed with this intent can be referred to as populist-accessible—or, singularly, populist or accessible.

El Salón México and the Popular Front

As shown in the previous chapter, Copland's aesthetic ideology was shaped by the cultural politics of the Popular Front, which can still be seen quite readily in *El Salón México.* Copland (accompanied by his companion Kraft) first visited Mexico in August 1932, dividing his four months between Mexico City and Tlalpam. While in Mexico City he attended an all-Copland concert conducted by his friend, Mexican composer Carlós Chávez, and worked on *Elegies for Violin and Viola.*[4] Copland was profoundly moved by his first visit to Mexico. As he wrote to Virgil Thomson in somewhat romantic terms, "Mexico has turned out even grander than I expected . . . and I expected pretty grand things. The best is the people—there's nothing remotely like them in Europe. They are really the 'people'—nothing in them is striving to be bourgeois. In their overalls and bare feet they are not only poetic but positively 'émouvant.'"[5] He returned the summer of 1936 and again in 1937 to visit Tlaxcala; Copland visited Tepoztlán in 1946, and there worked on his *Third Symphony.*

Copland was drawn to Mexico not as an ordinary tourist, nor just because of his friendship with Chávez. His visit to Mexico also reflects his political engagement. Perlis was the first to connect Mexico with Copland's leftist politics. "Several influences nudged Copland towards the Left: Mexico and the 'people'; the Depression (now affecting Copland's own family); the Marxist concept of 'art for society's sake' espoused by Hanns Eisler and Marc Blitzstein; the lack of an audience for Copland's most recent compositions; and the political idealism of Clurman and the Group Theatre."[6] Pollack also notes the political environment Copland entered when he crossed the border by train from San Antonio (he and Kraft had driven from New York to Texas, where they garaged the car). The Mexican economy was part socialist, part capitalist and its government anti-Fascist, one of few countries to support the Spanish Loyalists.[7] The Partido Nacional Revolucionario (PNR) government instituted land and education reform, and freedom of the press. It also implemented economic policies supportive of workers by raising wages and nationalizing some industries. Its Ministry of Education began an art program aimed at the masses, realized by commissioning visual artists to create murals on walls in public spaces. Copland's friend Chávez was appointed director of both the leading Mexican orchestra, the Mexico Symphony Orchestra, in 1928, and the leading conservatory, the National Conservatory of Music. Chávez himself, as a participant in the Aztec Renaissance movement, drew upon Mexican folk music for his own modernist works. Chávez also composed several works about the Mexican Revolution.[8] As Crist has shown, Copland's visit to Mexico was more than a vacation destination, as the country and its history and culture stirred the imaginations of many Popular Front writers: "Mexico represented a uniquely American sensibility and offered a means to critique liberal capitalism. Mexican folk culture was construed as an alternative to contemporary industrial society by such liberal progressive authors as Carleton Beals and Stuart Chase."[9] Mexico was a potent symbol for Copland and other progressives. Mexican society was seen as harmonious, in contrast to life in the modern United States. Numerous writers idealized Mexican folk culture and the country's rural landscape. In his 1931 *Mexico: A Study of Two Americas,* first serialized in the *New Republic* (one of the periodicals Copland read), Stuart Chase contrasted the village Tepoztlán with Middletown, U.S.A., the subject of a major 1929 sociological study by Robert and Helen Lynd still read today. Tepoztlán had also been the subject of a 1930 study by anthropologist Robert Redfield. Mexico offered a model for those seeking reform of American society. Even Copland's view of the impoverished Mexican people he met and with whom he interacted was more than personal, it was political. Crist writes: "Copland's curious romanticization of poverty reveals a somewhat awkward attempt to align himself with the antibourgeois perspective of the landless farmers in rural villages and the working-class clientele of the urban dance hall. Encompassing both a mythical folk culture and a modern proletariat, the Mexican people served for Copland as an idol in the veneration of a pre-capitalist naiveté, constructed in opposition to the modern industrial social order."[10] Thus, Copland's visit to Mexico in 1932 was, as she writes, "just one example of the pilgrimages across the border made in the 1930s by so many progressive intellectuals, including Dewey, Frank and Chase."[11]

The Music of *El Salón México*

While in Mexico, Copland actively sought out Mexican folk music, taking particular interest in mariachi bands. Chávez took Copland to a Mexico City night spot, El Salón México, in November 1932. *El Salón México* is the first work in the style Copland later called his "imposed simplicity," a style earlier Copland scholars (Berger and Smith, for example) have also remarked upon.[12] *El Salón México* places a new emphasis on melody. Rather than his usual A–B–A′ form, Crist describes a rhapsodic form, which relies on what she terms "rhetorical coherence," seen in Copland's use of juxtaposition of trumpet fanfares, harmonies, and fragmented folk tunes. The way in which Copland uses these folk songs, she argues, constitutes a critique of capitalist society: "The fragmentation and deformation of the tunes mirror the distortion of the modern, capitalist social order, but *El Salón México* simultaneously projects a vision of utopian solidarity. The heterogeneous surface of the music suggests a discontinuity between pre-capitalist folk culture and industrial modernism while anticipating a symbolic reconciliation of that disconnect within the musical whole."[13] Focusing her analysis on the opening minutes of the work, she overlooks an important fact, neglecting Copland's own intent and source of his "people's music." While Copland may have been taken by the landscape and charmed by the people whose poverty he romanticized, in choosing his source material he did not conduct fieldwork by interviewing informants as would an anthropologist or ethnomusicologist. He did not follow the model set by his compere Charles Seeger, who sent FMP employees into the field throughout the United States to collect songs directly from the folk who produced them. Rather, in collecting his melodies, Copland had little engagement with the people he so idealized: he turned to published folk song collections.

Copland was *inspired* by the people and particularly by his visit to the eponymous nightclub, El Salón México. While Chávez might have led him to the nightclub, Copland first encountered the locale in a tour book in 1939: "I remember reading about it for the very first time in Anita Brenner's guide book. Under 'Entertainment' she had this entry: 'Harlem type night-club for the peepul, grand Cuban orchestra, *Salón México*.'"[14] Copland knew he could only limitedly represent Mexico and Mexican culture in a musical work. "I realized that it would be foolish for me to attempt to translate some of the more profound sides of Mexico into musical sounds—the ancient civilizations or the revolutionary Mexico of our own time—for that, one really had to know a country well."[15] So he sought to convey the convivial atmosphere of the dance hall, a site of recreation for the ordinary citizen.

> It wasn't the music that I heard there, or the dances that attracted me, so much as the spirit of the place. In some inexplicable way, while milling about in those crowded halls, one felt a really live contact with the Mexican *people*—the electric sense one sometimes gets in far-off places, of suddenly knowing the essence of a people—their humanity, their separate shyness, their dignity and unique charms. I remember quite well that it was at just such a moment that I conceived the idea of composing a piece about Mexico and naming it *El Salón México*.[16]

To suggest the ambiance of the dance hall and the people, Copland did not invent original themes; he turned to preexisting Mexican folk tunes:

> It was only natural that I should have thought of using popular Mexican melodies for my thematic material. Chabrier and Debussy didn't hesitate to help themselves to the melodic riches of Spain (in *España* and *Iberia*) so Americans like Robert McBride and myself have plenty of precedent for using the tunes of the hispanic land on our southern doorstep. It's an easy method composers have for translating the flavor of a foreign people into musical terms. At any rate, I found myself looking about for suitable folk material as the basis for *El Salón México*.[17]

After returning to the United States, he worked concurrently on *Statements for Orchestra* and *El Salón México* throughout 1933–34. In late August 1934, he received a commission from Ruth Page in Chicago to compose music for a ballet, *Hear Ye! Hear Ye!* Copland interrupted work on the other compositions and did not complete *El Salón México* until his residency at the MacDowell Colony in the summer of 1935. The orchestration was completed in July 1936; the work premiered in Mexico City in August 1937.[18]

Copland freely acknowledged his sources and his approach toward the Mexican folk tunes. He turned to two published collections for melodies, explaining his method: "I followed no general rule in the use of the themes that I treated. Almost all of them come from the *Cancionero Mexicano* by Frances Toor, or from the erudite work of Ruben M. Campos, *El Folklore y la Música Mexicana*. To both authors I owe thanks."[19] The quality, scope, purpose, and intended audience of these volumes differed.[20] Toor's *Cancionero Méxicano* did not aim to be comprehensive or to present all styles of Mexican songs but to make available a sampling of the variety of Mexican folk song genres.[21] The collection contained eighteen songs: six *corridos* (the equivalent of ballads, i.e., narrative strophic songs), four *canciones de amor* (lyrical love songs), four *sones* (music used for dancing), and four *canciones revolucionarias* (revolutionary songs).[22] From this collection, Copland chose the *son* "El Palo Verde" and the *canción revolucionaria* "La Jesusita." The Campos collection was more scholarly in scope, intended to give a history of Mexican music over four hundred years, 1525–1925. From this collection, Copland borrowed "El Mosca." He never quotes these songs verbatim, but approaches them in a manner similar to the way in which Stravinsky uses his folk songs: he segments the melodies.[23] Tullia Magrini cautions against crediting him with having fully assimilated Mexican folk music. Rather she suggests that Copland is more of a musical tourist, not truly bilingual.

But this is precisely all that Copland claimed. From the outset, he recognized that using Mexican popular tunes in a symphonic piece presented some problems and realized that he had several artistic and compositional decisions to make. Should he quote literally, providing new arrangements and interesting accompaniments? Or could he use the songs in another way? First, he assessed his sources, finding them (as usual) lacking in complexity.

> The use of folk material in a symphonic composition always brings with it a formal problem. Composers have found that there is little that can be done with a folk tune except repeat it. Inevitably there is the danger of producing a mere string of unrelated "melodic gems." In the end I adopted a form which is a kind of modified potpourri, in which the Mexican themes and their extension are sometimes inextricably mixed for the sake of conciseness and coherence.[24]

He rejected the technique of theme and variation and that of merely providing a new arrangement or accompaniment for a preexisting folk tune. "There is nothing very remarkable about a Mexican popular melody. My purpose was not merely to quote them literally, but to heighten without in any way falsifying their natural simplicity."[25] Copland abstracted the most salient features of these melodies, distilled their melodic structure in order to create several ostinati, and put the ostinati and fragments of the original melodies together in a pastiche.

The most basic and typical way in which Copland treats his three melodies is to segment the original folk melodies and use the fragments as melodic-rhythmic motives. The first part of *El Salón México,* a lengthy five-part Introduction spanning mm. 1–103, presents the four primary motives that recur both in their original form and with modification throughout the piece. The work opens with segments taken from the *son* "El Palo Verde." Copland generates two motives by segmenting this *son* (see example 9.1). At [2], the second section of the Introduction, Copland introduces the second melody, an almost complete quotation of "La Jesusita" (see example 9.2). This serves as the third motive. Copland has given this melody special treatment: the brief direct quotations are interrupted by recurring trumpet and clarinet cadenzas. At [4] the third part of the Introduction begins. At this point, Copland presents the second strain of "El Mosca" (from Campos; see example 9.3), which he acknowledges as the most extensive quotation. It is the only song that Copland presents in its entirety. He presents it "twice, immediately after the introductory measures (in which may be found fragments of *El Palo Verde* and of *La Jesusita*)."[26] *El Mosca* begins at [4] + 6, transposed up a whole step from the original F major to G major (see example 9.3). In section 4, beginning at [7], Copland presents the first strain of "El Palo Verde." At four after [8] the second strain of "El Mosca" returns to begin section 5 and to close the Introduction. Copland further depicts Mexico by suggesting typical

a)

b)

EXAMPLE 9.1 a) Complete *son* "El Palo Verde"; b) Copland, *El Salón México,* Motives a, m. 2–3; motive, b, m. 3–4

Mexican musical ensembles used in folk and popular music genres. In section 2, he imitates one type of the folk ensemble, the *irchuestra típica.* At [4], beginning of the third part of the Introduction, Copland presents the "El Mosca" melody in thirds, in imitation of the *canción ranchera,* a folk song genre characterized by parallel thirds.

Copland's folk borrowings are largely limited to melodies, folk-flavored orchestrations, and folklike textures. His harmonic treatment, melodic development, form, and handling of rhythm are consistent with his earlier modernist style. Conventional triads are characteristic of his harmony, but he applies them unconventionally. They first appear ambiguously, for Copland does not introduce actual vertical harmonies until [2], where he presents the third G–B, which suggests the G major tonic triad; the perfect fifth, G–D, arrives in the third measure after [2]. The B–B♭ in the bassoon and trombone introduces a Stravinsky-like coloring of triads, a tension between major and minor (see example 9.2b). At [8], section 5 of the Introduction, Copland presents full triads for the first time (see example 9.4). Rather than presenting the tonic and the dominant, he presents the tonic and the subdominant in full triads that are unambiguously major or minor. Beginning five measures before [10], Copland introduces a C major triad, which serves as a subdominant harmonic pedal. Rather than presenting this in root position as he had the tonic pedal, Copland presents the C major as a "Copland" triad,[27] in this

a)

b)

Example 9.2 a) Complete "La Jesusita"; b) Copland, *El Salón México*, [2] + 4, "La Jesusita" as it appears in the trumpet and clarinet

b) *(continued)*

EXAMPLE 9.2 *Continued*

a)

b)

EXAMPLE 9.3 "El Mosca" as it appears [4] + 6

a)

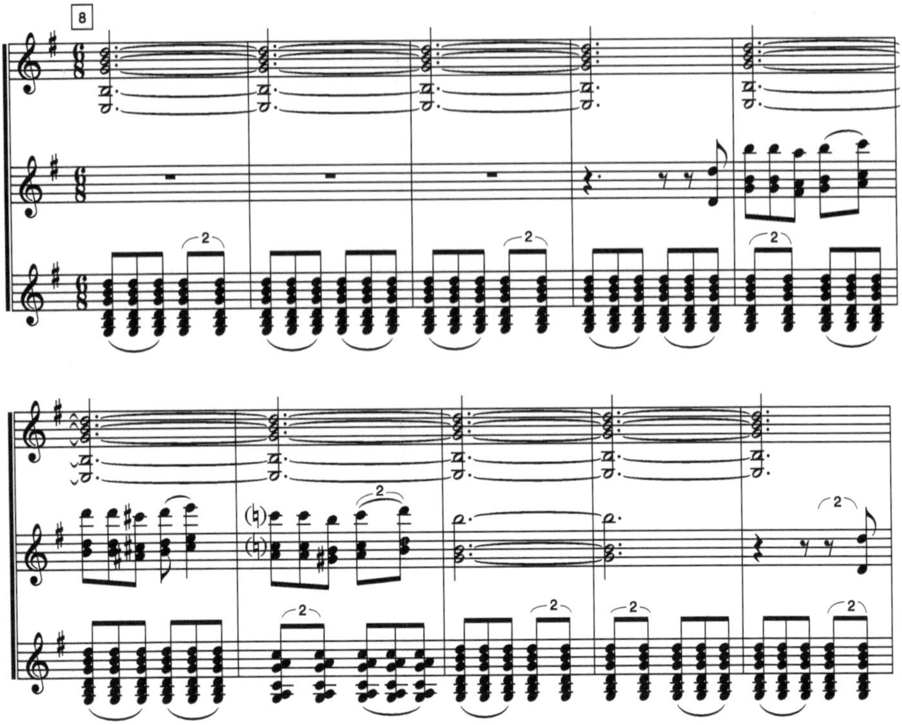

b)

Example 9.4 a) Copland, *El Salón México,* [8], Section five of the Introduction

case, a second-inversion triad, a technique that has become by now a mark of his tonal triadic style. As in earlier pieces, the second inversion allows Copland to be doubly referential, that is, to refer to both the tonic and dominant simultaneously. However, the C major triad introduced here functions as an upper neighbor to the G major triad.

Copland also exploits pedals, though not as extensively as in *Music for the Theatre* or as he would later in *Music for Radio*. The first pedal occurs at four measures before [8], where he introduces a G tonic pedal in the first violins. In the span [8]–[9] + 5 this single-note tonic pedal becomes a harmonic pedal, the perfect fifth formed by G and D appearing in the flutes, with the horn and B♭ clarinet doubling the tonic G; the third of the triad is supplied by the second horn.

Although Copland has retained the harmonic structure of the Mexican tune (mostly tonic and dominant), he avoids clichés and injects some original harmonic thinking by using ostinati and harmonic pedals to suggest multiple tonal centers. At [22] the piece moves from A♭ to F♯ (see example 9.5). While an ostinato beginning on the tonic F♯ appears in the celli, the violins sustain a C♯. The C♯/D♭ enharmonic retains this function throughout the first five measures of [23]. At this point, the C♯ now appears in violas and in the celli as part of a second inversion C♯ triad. An A♭ (enharmonically G♯) appears in the bass clarinet. Copland reinterprets the C♯: it has now become the root of a dominant triad instead of the dominant of a suggested F♯ tonic triad. This dominant harmonic pedal accompanies the appearance of the complete refrain of "La

EXAMPLE 9.5 Copland, *El Salón México*, [22]–[22] + 4 and [23]–[23] + 4

Jesusita," albeit somewhat modified. The original refrain was also in the dominant.

In place of functional triads, ostinati suggest the tonic-dominant relationship. At [22] Copland presents one consisting of the alternation of the tonic and dominant scale degrees to a "La Jesusita"–derived melody in the clarinet. When the second strain of "La Jesusita" begins at [23], an altered version of the ostinato appears in the dominant. Unlike the rhythmically intricate previous section, the ostinati in these passages are primarily onbeat accompaniments, very much like the onbeat bass of a march.

El Salón México also displays other characteristics of Copland's overtly modernist works, such as *Symphony for Organ and Orchestra* and Piano Concerto. Much of *El Salón México's* first section, A, is free of pedals, since Copland's purpose is to explore rhythmically propulsive ostinati derived from the folk songs, many of which originally accompanied folk dances. As he did in his symphony, in *El Salón México* Copland prefers melo-rhythmic ostinati to vertical harmonies, as can be seen two measures after [4], where a G (tonic) alternates with D (dominant).

Copland borrows more from "El Mosca" than melody and a melodic motive. The most characteristic ostinati are derived from its rhythm (see example 9.4). The pitches of the "El Mosca" tune are removed so that only the abstracted rhythm remains. This especially interests Copland: 6/8 alternates with 3/4 at least once per phrase in the original tune. In section 5 of *El Salón México,* four measures after [8], Copland borrows this characteristic rhythm of Mexican music, to which Latin American folk music scholar Gerard Béhague applies the term *sesquialtera,* or hemiola (borrowed from fourteenth- and fifteenth-century music).[28] At [8] Copland changes the meter, presenting the melody in 6/8 only, but still takes advantage of the three plus two, and the triple-duple, 6/8-3/4 alternation present throughout the close of the Introduction by introducing duplets. This *sesquialtera* or 6/8-3/4 alternation is modified at [12], where the triple-duple alternation continues, this time as the alternation of 4/4 and 3/8. This rhythmic ostinato continues throughout [12] and [13] (see example 9.6.) At [14]–[15], Copland presents an ostinato derived from "El Mosca" (see example 9.7). At [15] and at [36], an extended passage is devoted to the alternation of these two meters (see example 9.8). He changes the indicated meter to $\frac{6}{8} + \frac{3}{4}$. Rather than once a phrase, as in the original tune and the Introduction, the meters alternate so that 3/4 occurs every other measure throughout this passage. Similarly, at [31], the rhythm of the ostinato alternates $\frac{3 + 3 + 2}{8}$. In alternating duple and triple rhythms in this manner, Copland also imitates other genres of Mexican songs and dances. Songs used for dances such as *huapango,* the *huasteco,* and the *jarabe* features rhythms such as these, as does the *son.*[29] No doubt, Copland was attracted to Mexican folk music partly because of

EXAMPLE 9.6 Copland, *El Salón México,* 12 and 12 + 6

EXAMPLE 9.7 Copland, *El Salón México,* 14 + 3

EXAMPLE 9.8 Copland, *El Salón México,* 15 and 36

these rhythms, which strongly resemble the additive rhythms of jazz and the shifting meters of Stravinsky.

"La Jesusita"–derived melodies also have rhythmic ostinati, as did "El Palo Verde" and "El Mosca" in the first section of the piece. At 25–27, 28–30, and at 30 + 5–31, Copland presents an ostinato that results from telescoping the first three measures of "La Jesusita" (see example 9.9). He presents several ostinati simultaneously, as at 31 (see example 9.10). Through this technique Copland alludes to tonal function. The bass and celli suggest the dominant by alternating the perfect fifth dyad G and D with A (the A suggests the secondary dominant). Simultaneously, the violins and the violas suggest the tonic C major. A similar bitonal passage occurs toward the end of the piece at 36. By this time, the piece has shifted to A major, the key in which the "El Palo Verde" motive now appears. At 37 Copland shifts briefly to E major, the dominant. At 38 Copland presents the tonic A and the dominant E simultaneously (see example 9.11). The multiple ostinati technique permits Copland to introduce bitonality, D versus E. He wrote about this technique:

> For example, before the final climax I present the folk tunes simultaneously in their original keys and rhythms. The result is a kind of polytonality that achieves the frenetic whirl I had in mind before the end, when all is resolved with a plain unadorned triad.[30]

Copland presents three keys simultaneously. The flutes, piccolo, oboe, clarinet, horns, and viola play ostinati on A (dominant). The trumpet, first and second violins play a melody that arpeggiates a D-major seventh. The bass clarinet, tuba, violoncello, and bass play an ostinato in E major.

Rather than borrowing his formal organization from folk songs, marches, or any other folk genre, Copland organizes *El Salón México* as A–B–A′. The folk melodies mark the ternary form. Section A features motives derived from "El Palo Verde." Beginning at 22, several measures into the B section, Copland presents a melody derived from measures 3 and 4 of "La Jesusita." The final section, A′, is based upon motives and melodic material derived, as in the beginning, from "El Palo Verde."

Critics and scholars have recognized *El Salón México* as a landmark. Berger considers this work, along with *The Second Hurricane,* as heralding Copland's simpler style and his return to absolute music.[31] Geoffrey

EXAMPLE 9.9 Copland, *El Salón México,* mm. 1–4 of "La Jesusita," reduction showing thirds G-B and A-C; 25

EXAMPLE 9.10 Copland, *El Salón México,* 31

EXAMPLE 9.11 Copland, *El Salón México,* 38

Crankshaw offers the most useful criticism, noting "a jazz-sharpened technique to add point and urgency to what would otherwise have been a simple essay in the exotic. If we compare the original native melodies on which this brilliant piece is founded, with the variants of them which Copland fashioned, we can discover a good deal about the balance between sophistication and naturalness which is the essence of Copland's art."[32] *El Salón México* is deceptive, as Crankshaw sees. The use of folk melodies lends it a superficial air of simplicity. The structure, harmony, rhythmic, and motivic ideas, however, are as sophisticated and technically accomplished as are what Smith deems Copland's most difficult "austere" works.

El Salón México is also an Americanist work. As we have seen in previous chapters, while abroad Copland wished to see American music represented internationally in modern music concerts in Europe. The use of jazz had provided him with a music immediately recognizable to both Americans and Europeans as *American.* The use of American folk song provided Copland with additional musical material he could use to express or affirm America, in this case another North American country, Mexico. Works in which Copland self-consciously strove for their style to be recognized as such fit squarely with Barbara Zuck's definition of Americanist, that is, either compositional Americanism, "the music use of native elements," or conceptual Americanism, a "pro-American-music stance expressed in lectures and writings or through activities in behalf of American music."[33] Crist's study of Copland and the Popular Front adds another dimension to Copland's Americanism, or nationalism. Mexico served the Popular Front because the country and its culture offered a "pan-ethnic Americanism."[34] As Denning shows, the Popular Front was decidedly antifascist, both abroad and at home. One of its three bases in New York was comprised of the garment workers unions, which were multiethnic. Its second base was Harlem, and two popular causes were organizing the Brotherhood of the Sleeping Car

Porters and legally representing the Scottsboro Nine. On the West Coast the California Popular Front worked to unionize Asian and Mexican workers in the state's agricultural industries. In Southern California the Mexican-American branch had its own Popular Front organization, El Congreso del Pueblo de Habla Española. In cities throughout the United States, the Popular Front often met in ethnic lodges, such as the Slovene National Benefit Society, the Polonia Society, the Hungarian Brotherhood, the Slovak Workers' Society, the Croatian Benevolent Fraternity, the Serbian-American Fraternal Society, and other fraternal organizations that worked closely with the union-organizing activities of the CIO. Thus, in its unionizing efforts, the Popular Front worked to forge solidarity along class lines and strove to be pan-ethnic and to fight against racism. As Denning writes, "Under the sign of the 'people,' this Popular Front public culture sought to forge ethnic and racial alliances, mediating between American culture, in part by reclaiming the figure of 'America' itself, imagining an Americanism that would provide a usable past for ethnic workers, who were thought of as foreigners, in terms of a series of ethnic slurs."[35] In 1939 Copland wrote an article as a tie-in to the release of Koussevitzky's Boston Symphony Orchestra recording of this work in which he described his visit south. Mexico—to which parts of the southwest of the United States had once belonged—offered Copland the "peepul," both the usable past with its "ancient Mayan and Aztec Civilizations—those incredible pyramids at Teotihuacan or Chichen-Itzá; or places like Tlaxcala, the picturesque old town which Cortez passed through on his first journey to the capital" and its present, "with its heartening message of land and a fuller life for the impoverished peon—an aspect which is not without its musical implications."[36] Copland's "peepul" are not Anglo-Saxon but a racialized Other. As a musical act, *El Salón México* offered Copland a way to fuse modernist techniques and folk song in a simplified style. An article Copland wrote about Chávez and Revueltas that appeared in the May 9, 1937, issue of the *New York Times* is revelatory:

> They understand that in order to create a purely indigenous movement in music they must find a musical background in their own country, just as the painters have found their roots in the Mexican landscape. In a sense, this is easier for Mexicans than for artists in our own country, because Mexico possesses a very strong folk art derived from its own Indian civilization, which provides the artist with a rich source material.[37]

In *El Salón México* Copland fused music and politics by juxtaposing folk songs and two American narratives: (1) that of Mexico, with its ancient past and a future promise of social change; and (2) that of music in the

United States. In so doing he could express something of a country's past, present, and future through the use of folk song.

Synthesis

The genesis and musical style of this work clearly reflects Copland's aesthetic ideology that developed as the Depression deepened and he began to wed his desire to reach a broader audience to leftist politics. Intended for the concert hall, *El Salón México* stands, then, as Copland's first mature populist large-scale work that moved beyond *Gebrauchsmusik*. He composed this work, like *Vitebsk,* to depict a specific place and people. But unlike the earlier trio, Copland attempted here to construct in music a distinct memory of a place he himself had visited, one that was overtly linked to his political views. Musically, the tone poem shows a refined method of handling folk music. Rather than developing new techniques, Copland merely adapted ones he had learned in Paris and refined during the late 1920s: pedals, multiple ostinati, bitonality, the establishing of tonal centers and tonal poles rather than functional tonality, and the exploration of complex rhythms. Melodically, he chose to work with segments of the original folk melodies rather than inject lyricism or ensure the singability of the original tunes. *El Salón México* also shows the means by which he acquired his folk songs—namely from published folk music collections. In this era when his contemporaries, both European and American, conducted fieldwork, collecting folk songs in their original cultural settings. Copland—despite his political identification with the people and the working class—saw fit to draw upon folk songs from the shared culture, that of the popularized folk song collection.

Into the 1940s, as the United States entered World War II, Copland, like many other artists and intellectuals formerly overtly proposing social change, supported the war effort. While Copland never abandoned the issue of reaching a broad audience, he moved further and further away from the overt politics of the Left. Thus, even though there are residual traces of Popular Front cultural politics in works such as *Billy the Kid, Rodeo,* and *Appalachian Spring,* with their themes on American subjects and quotation of popular folk song, foremost is Copland's effort to reach as wide an audience as possible as he continued to compose in this populist-accessible style. His later works of the 1940s, in which he developed a way to quote preexisting folk tunes and transform this familiar material into music that was at once familiar and freshly modern, are the progeny of *El Salón México.*

CHAPTER TEN

Billy the Kid

Billy the Kid is Copland's first folkloristic ballet and his first work that makes extensive use of American folk music (rather than jazz or popular song). In *El Salón México,* Copland used folk music to translate "the flavor of a foreign people into musical terms." In this ballet his focus is on the United States, and the people are not "foreign" but his fellow citizens. The prototype of his so-called Americana concert works, *Billy the Kid* began as a work intended for an audience outside the concert hall.[1] Despite this, it does not relinquish its ties to modern music and attendant techniques and styles. After figuring out in *El Salón México* how to use preexisting folk material in combination with modernist techniques, in *Billy the Kid* Copland truly found a way to create a modern American music accessible to the average listener that retained both the technical and the stylistic developments he had mastered in the 1920s and refined during the early 1930s. In it, things Copland learned in Paris—Stravinsky-derived neoclassicism and ostinati, the inclination learned from Milhaud and Poulenc (as well as Stravinsky) to absorb and use popular urban music, and the rhythms of jazz—converged with his political ideology and concern for the American music-loving public.

Copland did not set out with the intention of creating an *American* ballet; rather, *Billy the Kid* reflects the vision and ideas about American modern dance of the ballet's commissioner, an influential choreographer and impresario. Lincoln Kirstein believed that modern ballet was dominated by Diaghilev and his Ballets Russes, which, in Kirstein's view, had ceased to be Russian and had become the dominant style of international ballet after Diaghilev left Russia in 1909. Russian dancers and choreographers dominated American ballet, and the majority of works performed were to Russian music, for example, Tchaikovsky or Stravinsky. Kirstein sought to move modern dance away from this hegemonic influence. His 1938 booklet, *Blast at Ballet,* described what was wrong with ballet in America and urged Americans to create their own style of modern dance. Kirstein called for many of the same things as did American composers: the promotion of American ballet by various institutions, the patronage of American ballet, and open-minded, kindred critics.[2]

Kirstein first called for the creation of a repertory of inventive and imaginative American works that would appeal to the public. The ideas for these ballets would surpass those of the Russians in inventiveness and creativity.[3] American choreographers and dancers should look to their own "character-dancing" traditions. By this Kirstein did not mean the dances of the Native Americans or Appalachian Anglo-Americans. He meant contemporary dance forms such as those that had grown out of social dancing and the stage. Kirstein's manifesto is quoted at length.

> It is only recently that Americans have discovered we also have our own character-dancing which can serve us theatrically better than any Russian or Spanish. And this is not the dance of the Sioux, or the Hopi, or the Navaho, nor the square-dance of the Tennessee Mountaineers. Our character dancing is a vital contemporary manifestation, not an exotic left-over. Since the tradition of "eccentric" dancing descending from the days of buck-wing minstrel shows vanished with four-a-day vaudeville, we have not been very aware of dancers employing "popular" dance-forms consciously. American character-dancing has stemmed from a double strain, one from vaudeville or musical-comedy, the other from social-dances in ball-rooms, barns, barracks, gyms or dance-halls. Buster West's American sailor number, Buddy Ebsen's hick fast flat feet, and of course such fine Negro teams as Buck and Bubbles have been continually paralleled by a "smoother" tradition stemming from Irene and Vernon Castle, Moss and Fontana, Veloz and Yolanda, and above all, Fred Astaire and Ginger Rogers. These "social dancers," even though they frequently dance on ball-room floors instead of on a stage, take over from annual popular dance fads numerous new forms and tricky steps, and theatricalize them by adding spectacular lifts, or free fantasies on jazz steps with astonishing tap cadenzas, as Paul Draper does. The recent wide-spread interest in Charleston, Black-Bottom, Suzy-Q, Lindy-Hop, Shag and Big Apple testifies to our inherent love for popular music and dancing on an intimate, or at least on a familiar basis. The ancestors of the Big Apple trace themselves back in an unbroken lineage to Bunny Hug, Turkey Trot and the Negro Cake-Walk. The complexity and ingenuity of "swing" band-music is equalled by the variety and invention of steps which the dancers create to accompany it. The Big Apple is a communal expression, recalling square-dancers of the mid–nineteenth century which from the *contredanse* later developed into the *German* and *Cotillon.* The Big Apple is a kinetic *dance,* which the static, ordinary two-step of the 'twenties hardly ever was. Elements of rhumba and tango, fragments of negro, Mexican, Cuban and Argentine gesture and movement are embroidered into a consistent fabric of motion whose spontaneous flow fits the personal mood of the improviser.
>
> This material offers an American ballet-choreographer as rich material as *go pak, saltarello* or *bolero,* with the added advantage that our dancers have enjoyed these dances as part of their own experience

> from their earliest school days. They are able to perform stage versions of them with conviction, not as an imitation of a form they have seen done by Russians or Spaniards, but rather because the quality of their jazz and gesture is as familiar to them as the kids with whom they first danced at high-school prom, Saturday night socials, or in the summer-dances on the Mall in Central Park. These social-dances must necessarily be redesigned for the stage, and can be hung on a structure of classic technique for their greatest stage effect.
>
> We are all of us familiar with the splendid stance, the proud spinal carriage of the Spanish gypsy. We easily recognized the jack-knife spring and release of Cossack knees. We have known the brilliant play of pantomimic flirtation in Italian peasant-dances. Let us also recognize our own native detachable snake-hips, our rangy legs, our educated feet. Our arms and fingers wave and snap in a special way. Our shoulders hang as no other people's shoulders hang. Our classic theatrical style will find an added authority and flavor from the essential qualities of American national dances.[4]

Kirstein founded the Ballet Caravan[5] as part of his program in 1933. He had been a member of George Balanchine's American Ballet Company, but he and Balanchine had had a parting of the ways. Upon leaving, he took with him dancers from the school with the express purpose of founding a company that would perform the sort of work Kirstein described. He chose American subjects and themes and enlisted American composers, many of whom had been schooled by Boulanger in French Neoclassicism.[6]

> For the second season we mounted our first American works successfully, and appeared with the Philadelphia Symphony orchestra. Our musicians, while they are all native-born Americans, had everyone of them been exposed to the School of Paris, directly or indirectly, through Nadia Boulanger, the heirs of Erik Satie, *Les Six,* and the principles of *musiquette;* or else they had refused to be affected by the Franco-Russians and were hence influenced in reverse. Each of them used American folk-material. Robert McBride had long played and arranged for a jazz band; Paul Bowles knew Kentucky and Mexican folk-songs from first-hand; Virgil Thomson, the composer of *Four Saints in Three Acts,* had just finished music for the United States Government film, *The Plough That Broke the Plains,* and would soon start on *The River;* Elliott Carter, Jr. had studied with Loeffler, Piston and Gustav Holst, and had conducted a workers' chorus all over France. All of them were in the lively traditions of *Les Jeunes.* They knew and loved Russian ballet as much as I did, shared my opinion of its uses and abuses, wanted to collaborate on American subjects.[7]

Among those Kirstein commissioned were Elliott Carter, *Pocahontas* (1936); David Diamond, *Tom* (1936, unproduced); Bowles, *Yankee Clipper* (1937); Thomson, *Filling Station* (1937); and, of course, Copland's

Billy the Kid.[8] Future plans included ballets based on the works of American literary figures: Herman Melville, Nathaniel Hawthorne, Mark Twain, Walt Whitman, Henry James, Stephen Crane, Hart Crane, Thomas Beer, and James Farrell, as well as "folk or popular material that is comprehensible to all of us whether we've read these particular writers, or have ourselves had experiences on this continent which they have already recognized."[9]

At the time Kirstein wrote his manifesto, the Ballet Caravan was working on *Billy the Kid,* based on the novel by Walter Noble Burns, *The Saga of Bill the Kid.* As a collaborative effort, it owes much to its originators, Kirstein and Eugene Loring (who wrote the outline), with respect to both the scenario and the music.[10] The initial idea to use American folk songs came from Kirstein: "The cowboy tunes—yes—I gave them to Aaron and the original idea for the Processional at the beginning of *Billy* somehow came from Martha [Graham]."[11] Initially hesitant at writing a Western ballet, Copland needed persuading. Kirstein convinced him that if he could use folk tunes in *El Salón México,* he could do the same with American folk tunes. Kirstein gave Copland three collections of American folk songs—cowboy songs, to be specific—from which he eventually would select those that appear in the final version of the ballet (and concert suite). Copland accepted: "It had been several years since my last trip abroad. I went first to London for the ISCM Festival, where *El Salon Mexico* was performed, and then to Paris. I carried with me two collections of 'cowboy' tunes given me before I left New York by Lincoln Kirstein."[12] Kirstein sent a third collection to him in Paris.

A New Chronology for *Billy the Kid*

Billy the Kid marks Copland's first use of Anglo-American folk music and is thus a watershed work looking forward to the "Americana" works of the 1940s and beyond. But as his first overtly popular *American* work, it has ties to his earlier "ultramodern," Stravinsky-influenced works, both stylistically and chronologically. There are preliminary questions surrounding the composition of *Billy the Kid.* The sources that document the germinal material Copland used for the Prologue and Epilogue and on which the discussion below is based are the sketches, now in the Copland Collection at the Music Division of the Library of Congress (the relevant pages are 55, 56, and 58–62) first discovered by Wayne Shirley. According to his autobiography, Copland worked on the ballet during the summer and fall of 1938. A chronology constructed from the quotations taken from the autobiography appears in table 10.1. As these sketches show, Copland began parts of the work years earlier. The Introduction/Prologue and Epilogue of *Billy the Kid* were begun in 1935, rather than in 1938.

TABLE 10.1 *Billy the Kid* Chronology Based on Autobiographical Accounts

July–August 1937	Copland in Mexico City.
Fall 1937	Copland back in New York, teaching.
Spring 1938	Copland living at Roy Harris's house in Princeton, revising his New School lectures into a book.
Summer 1938	Copland in Paris and briefly in London; receives printed cowboy song collection from Lincoln Kirstein; begins composing *Billy the Kid.*
June 1938	Copland receives letter from Elliott Carter, music director of Ballet Caravan, informing him of the instrumentation and enclosing the scenario, and several pages of "Notes on Billy the Kid's Character"; Kirstein sends him a third collection of tunes.
July 10, 1938	Copland begins work on the ballet in Paris, July 10–21.
August 9–23, 1938	Copland returns to Brooklyn and continues composing.
September 2–10, 1938	Copland at MacDowell Colony; finishes the orchestration of *Billy the Kid;* also works on choral work "Lark."
October 1938	Premier in Chicago.

Page 55 of the *Billy the Kid* sketches documents that the ballet's earliest material dates from August 5, 1935, when Copland started working on "Violin Piece." During the summer of 1935, while he was at the MacDowell Colony, he worked on *El Salón México;* the *Gebrauchsmusik* pieces, *What Do We Plant?;* and the teaching pieces for piano, "Sunday Afternoon Music" and "The Young Pioneers."[13] During that summer, Copland continued to develop ideas for the "Violin Piece." At the end of August he left the colony, returning to New York in September.

By August he had composed a violin theme, bass ostinato, and accompanying harmony (see example 10.1). The harmony found in the treble of the piano accompaniment is quintal, rather than triadic (see example 10.2). In the sketch, Copland indicates a treble chord comprising F, E♭, and G and moving to one made of A♭, F, and G. If these pitches are rearranged so that they lie a fifth apart, E♭ appears as the root of a quintal chord (minus the B♭, which occurs in m. 3 as part of the melody and C). This harmony seems simultaneously to suggest and oscillate between E♭ major and C minor. Copland uses most of this material in *Billy the Kid.* The violin theme first appears in the Prologue at [2],[14] first in the flute, then the oboe (see example 10.3). The harmonic ostinato does not appear in the score exactly as it does in the sketch. Rather than nonfunctional chords built on fifths, Copland returns to third-based chords (see example 10.4). This opening passage retains the tonal ambiguity, the oscillation between C minor (the harmonic ostinato) and E♭ (the melody).

a)

EXAMPLE 10.1 a) Copland, "Violin Piece," *Billy the Kid* sketches, p. 55; b) E♭ Quintal Chord (F, E♭, G, B♭ moving to A♭, F, G)

EXAMPLE 10.2 Copland, *Billy the Kid,* mm. 14–26 melody in flute and oboe

EXAMPLE 10.3 Copland, *Billy the Kid,* mm. 1–8, harmonic progression

These sketches for this never-completed violin piece closely link *Billy the Kid* to *El Salón México.* Copland first conceived of what would become the Prologue and Epilogue—the framing sections of the ballet—as he worked on the orchestral piece. Also, during this period Copland addressed in print the aesthetic question of for whom the composer created. The "Violin Piece" and the Epilogue and Prologue of the ballet can be viewed as Copland's answer to this question: the piece presents the listener with an abstract work with modern quintal harmony, straightforward melody instead of multiple ostinati, and harmonic pedals. Thus, parts of *Billy the Kid* were composed at the same time Copland figured out a way in which to incorporate folk music in a style that was both modern and accessible for the ordinary listener.[15]

Copland's Use of Folk Music in *Billy the Kid*

In composing *El Salón México* Copland tried to represent the spirit of a particular locale through the use of indigenous folk music, that is, by borrowing folk songs for use as more than mere melodies, as we saw. In that work he orchestrated to suggest folk ensembles and explored rhythmic complexities and interplay suggested by the folk rhythms themselves. In *Billy the Kid,* for the first time Copland sought to represent the American West, and more broadly, American culture itself, through the use of American folk song, in this case, a kind that was quickly becoming popularized as part of the shared American culture.

The idea of using cowboy songs came initially not from Copland but from Kirstein: "To use or not to use cowboy songs as the basis for my ballet score was a decision left up to me. So said Lincoln as he slipped two tune books under my arm."[16] As he had in *El Salón México,* Copland worked from published folk music collections, *The Lonesome Cowboy: Songs of the Plains and Hills,* compiled by John White and George Shackley, *Songs of the Open Range,* edited by Ina Sires, and Carl Sandburg's *The American Song Bag,* as well as sheet music edited by John Lomax and Oscar J. Fox. These anthologies both preserved the songs and brought them before a broad American public. That summer of 1938 Copland selected six folk songs taken from these sources for the main part of the ballet.[17]

> An introductory prelude, "The Open Prairie," presents a pastoral theme harmonized in open fifths that gives the impression of space and isolation. The second section, "Street in a Frontier Town," is lively and full of action; for western flavor I used quotations from "Great Grand-Dad," "The Old Chisholm Trail," and "Git Along Little Dogies" (but not in traditional harmonies and rhythms), a Mexi-

can dance featuring a theme in 5/8, and "Goodbye, Old Paint" introduced by an unusual 7/8 rhythm. The third section, "Card Game at Night," has a sinister sound achieved by strings built on thirds and segments of "Bury Me Not on the Lone Prairie." "Gun Battle," the fourth movement, makes generous use of percussion. The fifth, "Celebration After Billy's Capture," depicts the townspeople rejoicing in the saloon, where an out-of-tune player piano sets the scene. "Billy's Demise," the final section of the Suite, makes use of material from the introduction, but with different coloration to convey the idea of a new dawn breaking over the prairie.[18]

Over the years scholars have been able to identify the folk tunes he quotes in *Billy the Kid*. Recently, Crist discovered the Lomax-Fox in Copland's copy of *The Lonesome Cowboy;* Jessica Burr found Copland's copy of *Songs of the Open Range* in the Copland Collection.[19] The songs and their sources are listed in table 10.2. The Introduction and Epilogue Open Prairie theme does not appear to be an actual folk tune, though it is folklike with its straightforward, onbeat rhythms and primarily conjunct diatonic melody.

Copland also chose how to treat the pre-existing material. His style in *Billy the Kid* is one of simplicity. Sensitively recognizing that as a theatrical work, it was more important to tell the story of the ballet than to try for personal expression, he chose this style partly because it suited the dramatic action and partly because of his aesthetic that had emerged through his involvement in the Popular Front.

It is a delicate operation to put fresh and unconventional harmonies to well-known melodies without spoiling their naturalness; moreover, for an orchestral score, one must expand, contract, rearrange, and

TABLE 10.2 Cowboy Songs Used in *Billy the Kid* and Their Sources

Song	Source
"The Dying Cowboy (Bury Me Not on the Lonesome Prairie)"	Sires; White-Shackley
"Great Grandad"	White-Shackley
"Whoopee Ti Yi Yo, Git Along Little Dogies"	Lomax-Fox, Sires (also collected in White-Shackley)
"The Old Chis[h]olm Trail"	Collected by Lomax, arranged by Fox; Sires (also collected in White-Shackley)
"Trouble for the Range Cook (Come Wrangle Yer Broncho)"	White-Shackley
"Old Paint"	Collected by Lomax; arranged by Fox (also collected in White-Shackley)

> superimpose the bare tunes themselves, giving them something of one's own touch. That is what I tried to do, always keeping in mind my resolve to write plainly—not only because I had become convinced that simplicity was the way out of isolation for the contemporary composer, but because I have never liked music to get in the way of the thing it is supposedly aiding. If it is a question of expressing the deepest ideas of ones own soul, then you write a symphony. But if you are involved in a stage presentation, the eye is the thing, and music must play a more modest role. There was another reason for being in *Billy the Kid.* Our hero, Billy, may have been a complex character from a psychological standpoint but as a stage figure in a ballet, he is a simple figure—a boy bandit who brags that he had killed twenty-one men, not counting Indians.[20]

Unlike in *El Salón México,* where he never presented the complete folk melody in its original form, Copland worked with complete tunes in *Billy the Kid,* using all six tunes nearly equally. In both works, Copland uses the same harmonic techniques for originally composed and preexisting folk material. In this manner, he performs his "delicate operation" to "put fresh and unconventional harmonies" to these diatonic folk melodies, thereby giving them "something of [his] own touch."

Copland's own touch seems to have been to apply the same techniques in this ballet we found in *El Salón México* and throughout his works of the 1920s and 1930s: multiple, often interlocking ostinati, polyrhythms, bitonality, and fragmenting and varying melodies. In other words, Copland applies the same techniques he mastered by emulating Stravinsky in working with the folk songs in *Billy the Kid.* He first introduces folk songs at [6], scene Ia, or "Street in a Frontier Town," where he presents "Old Grandad" and "Git Along Little Dogies," both taken from *The Lonesome Cowboy.* The first song is shown in example 10.4. As Copland indicated in his autobiography, he expanded and contracted the original melodies, remaining very close to the original in instances in which he did not borrow the melody verbatim. Typically he changes the key of the original folk song. During the span [15]–[17], he presents "The Old Chisolm Trail." He changes the key from the original E minor (the tune is somewhat ambiguous, at times suggesting G major, at times suggesting E minor). Copland heavily relies on a technique particularly associated with Stravinsky: he segments the melodies as in *El Salón México.* When "Great Grandad" appears for the first time at [6], Copland presents the entire tune, changing it from F major, as it originally appears in the songbook, to F minor. After its initial appearance Copland does not present the entire tune, but uses only the first half (e.g., at [7]). The second half appears at [7] + 10. The third time it appears, at [9] (see example 10.5), Copland repeats the entire tune, as he does the fourth time the tune appears, at [10].

a)

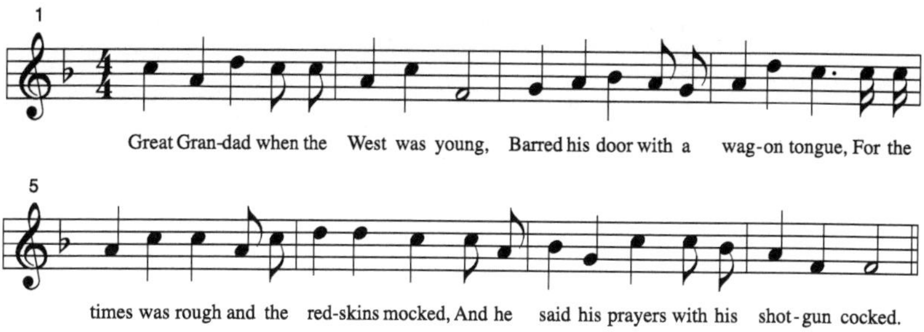

b)

EXAMPLE 10.4 a) "Great Grandad," from *The Lonesome Cowboy;* b) "Great Grandad" as it appears in *Billy the Kid*

Copland also combines melodic segments of one song with those of another. This second technique did not appear extensively in *El Salón México* but is reminiscent of Stravinsky. At 7 + 4, Copland briefly interrupts "Great Grandad," halving it and interpolating four measures of "Git Along Little Dogies." At 10 + 4, the chorus of this song (played by the trombones, which provide timbral contrast) is interpolated between two segments of "Great Grandad." Instead of quoting verbatim the complete chorus of "Git Along Little Dogies," Copland modifies it. He applies this technique in other places. "Old Paint" occurs throughout the passage 24 + 2–27a, with interpolations of "Git Along Little Dogies" at 26 − 4 and 26 + 10.

As he indicated in his autobiography, Copland this time around did apply fresh and unconventional harmonies to the cowboy songs, ones more triadic than those in *El Salón México*. But essentially, he continued to use the same Stravinsky-derived techniques that he had in works as varied

a)

b)

EXAMPLE 10.5 a) "Whoopee Ti, Yi Yo, Git Along Little Dogies" from *The Lonesome Cowboy;* b) Copland, *Billy the Kid,* "Old Grandad," 2nd statement, [9]

as *Dance Symphony, Symphony for Organ and Orchestra, Music for the Theatre,* and *El Salón México.* The original melodies feature primarily tonic, dominant, and subdominant harmonies. Pedals remain prominent, allowing Copland to suggest triadic harmonies without explicitly stating them. He does this through the use of single pitches, for example, using the fifth scale degree, E♭, to suggest the dominant and the first scale degree, A♭, as a tonic to accompany an unadulterated version of "Old Grandad" that begins at [6]. For the first variation of "Old Grandad" that begins at [9], Copland presents the cowboy song in a not-unadorned yet still simple fashion: the harmonic accompaniment uses pedals and multiple, interlocking ostinati (see example 10.7). Copland introduces an offbeat F pedal in the first and second violins; the violoncelli provide an on-beat F tonic pedal. These interlock to form an oscillating F-G minor ninth dyad that functions as an ostinato and accompanies the flute, piccolo, and piano melodies. Copland has not abandoned modernist tonal innovations: he uses pedals and ostinati to suggest bi- and polytonality in what will become his signature in later so-called Americana works. "The Dying Cowboy" returns at 40–49. At 40–45, Copland presents the song with a bitonal accompaniment, C and C♯ (see example 10.6). At 45, he

a)

b)

EXAMPLE 10.6 a) Copland, *Billy the Kid,* 40; b) Copland, *Billy the Kid,* 45

shifts the tonal procedure from bitonality to bimodality and presents the tune simultaneously in A major and A minor (parallel major and minor; see example 10.9). Copland moves to E♭, which is a tritonic dominant substitute at 46. The prevalence of minor thirds, combined with the prominence of the tritone, alludes to octatonicism, although this is not used systematically in this work.

Copland had previously associated intricate and complex jazzlike rhythms with Americanness. Jazz rhythms—the syncopations and fox-trot—embodied the spirit of America. They were to be the substance of the American composer's nocturnes, Copland had written in *Modern Music*. During his visit to Mexico he had discovered that folk traditions could also be rhythmically complex and intricate, just as much as jazz. *Billy the Kid*'s greatly simplified texture allows Copland to devote more attention to this parameter. In his treatment of the themes, his rhythmic devices—polyrhythm, polymeter, and shifting metrical accents—resemble those from his jazz period. The same rhythmic complexities of the Mexican *jarabe* found in *El Salón México* are seen in *Billy the Kid*. Copland presents "Git Along Little Dogies" as a waltz. He presents it in 4/4 but notates the accompaniment in 3/4, as a typical waltz; the harmonic accompaniment consists of the root tonic D♭ followed by two D♭ triads. The resultant effect is one of polymeter, as the 3/4 waltz of the accompaniment is heard against the 4/4 of the melody. This polymetrical section also recalls the *jarabe,* a Mexican song/dance genre and rhythm that Copland also used, as we saw, in *El Salón México*. In his treatment of "Git Along Little Dogies" Copland retains the hemiola; however, rather than alternate duple and the triple rhythms, he presents them simultaneously. He also uses the *jarabe* and hemiola principle in his treatment of "The Dying Cowboy (Oh Bury Me Not on the Lonesome Prairie)," and "Trouble for the Range Cook." At 29 Copland uses "Oh Bury Me Not," changing the original rhythms from triple to duple, although the indicated meter is 12/8. Copland presents "Trouble for the Range Cook" and "The Old Chisolm Trail" at 20–24 + 1 in a Mexican-*jarabe* version in D major. Copland keeps the original key of B♭ as his tonal center, changes the original 3/4 meter to 5/8. The use of 5/8 makes a double allusion: first, it alludes to the earlier appearance of "Git Along Little Dogies" at 10 in 3/4 (while the accompaniment continues in 4/4). In this passage Copland explores polymeter and the use of conflicting meters, duple and triple, and divides the meters among different instruments. Here at 20, Copland presents the 5/8 in the entire ensemble, using a single meter (that occasionally alternates with 4/8 at the cadence), eliminating the polyrhythmic aspects of simultaneous 3/4 and 4/4. However, he retains the idea of polymeter, of constantly shifting duple and triple meters of alternating 2/8 and 3/8 by notating the meter as 5/8 rather than using hemiolas. This time, rather than presenting a harmonic variation, Copland has presented

EXAMPLE 10.7 a) "The Dying Cowboy (Oh Bury Me Not on the Lonesome Prairie)," *The Lonesome Cowboy;* b) "The Dying Cowboy (Oh Bury Me Not on the Lonesome Prairie)," as it appears in *Billy the Kid*

rhythmic contrast and variation of the folk tune, exploring the rhythmic interplay of triple and duple meters, polyrhythms, and polymeter in much the same ways he had in his jazz-influenced works. The second allusion is to jazz: again, the alternating triple and duple rhythms recall additive rhythm, cross-rhythms, and polyrhythms that are prime characteristics of African-American jazz.

Billy the Kid's Western theme resonates with Copland's own interest in Mexico and Hispanic culture. As we saw, Copland maintained a close friendship with Chávez and visited Mexico several times. Geographically the West is quite distant from the urban jazz centers of New York, Chicago, St. Louis, and New Orleans. There are connections between the West and Mexico. Much of the territory—western Arkansas, Texas, New Mexico, Arizona, Colorado, and California—belonged at one point to Mexico or was a colony of Spain. The southwestern part of the United States (Texas, New Mexico, Arizona, and California) remains heavily influenced by Spanish and Mexican culture—food, clothing, music, architecture, art—and the landscapes of northern Mexico and the Southwest are similar. Indeed, the cowboy has his Mexican counterpart in the *vaquero*.

We have seen that the Popular Front encompassed the West Coast as well. No doubt Copland recognized the cultural similarities between Mexico and the American West, though political boundaries divided the region. In recasting American cowboy songs in Mexican folk rhythms derived from folk dance genres, he signified his knowledge that much American folk music was regional and ethnic in origin. If American folk music were comprised of ethnic, racial, regional, religious, and occupational repertoires, by implication, an American national art music could draw upon its ethnic, racial, regional, and religious heritages, as Copland demonstrates in his application of typical Mexican rhythms to his cowboy songs.

In working with these specific folk song collections and published sheet music, Copland confronted an issue he did not face in using the collections he consulted for *El Salón México:* how to handle variants. As ethnomusicologists and folklorists well know, a single folk song may have numerous variants. As seen in table 10.2, five of the six songs appear in more than one published source, and the tunes collected in these vary from one source to the next. The appearance of "Git Along Little Dogies" illustrates how Copland handled this problem. *The Lonesome Cowboy* presents two "authentic" versions of the chorus. The first version is in D♭ and is nearly an octave higher than the verse; it closely resembles a yodel. The second version (in E♭) is lyrical, intended for singing rather than yodeling. One of the popular published folk song collections did print yodels in connection with this song. The Lomax collection, *American Ballads & Folksongs,* reprinted two versions of the tune from an earlier Lomax collection, *Cowboy Songs*. It also presented three yodels to be sung *ad libitum* between the verses proper.[21] Copland chose the D♭ yodel chorus. He selects the rise and fall, or contour, of the yodel, retaining most of the intervals of the original song, but contracting the tune. Copland changes the key of the original verse to D♭; he also changes the rhythm by augmenting the note values. The key change in fact signals which variant Copland chose. (The second version is the one with which most people are familiar, not the one Copland chose.)

Why did Copland choose the yodel? In using the cowboy songs and the yodel, Copland moved away from his earlier vernacular music idioms of jazz and Tin Pan Alley, which were the music of 1920s and 1930s America. His preference for the yodel comes not so much from a folk musical tradition, but from American popular culture, which Copland had turned to in *Music for the Theatre*. The yodel, as Copland would have encountered it, came from three sources. First, as discussed above, it was presented in published song collections and the publications of Mississippi-born and Texas-reared John Lomax (who also wrote about southern African-American folklore).[22] Second, the subject and folk music of *Billy the Kid* also come from a performance practice, folk yodeling. Ironically, the Alpine yodel was first introduced to American popular culture not by the cowboy, but by a touring vaudeville troupe from Tyrol in the nineteenth century. It was further popularized by Emmett Miller in the mid-1920s, who included the blue yodel in his minstrel act.[23]

Copland's choice to use the yodel suggests that he also drew upon the Hollywood film Western and American popular music, more specifically country and western. The cowboy is a long-standing American icon popularized and romanticized in novels in the nineteenth century and onscreen in the twenties. Since the earliest feature Western, *The Great Train Robbery* (1903) the cowboy had remained a popular screen icon through the 1930s.[24] Magrini was the first to draw the connection between Copland's Americana works, American popular culture, and Hollywood films:

> The approach to themes dear to mass culture continues in the immediately following works of Copland—the ballets "Billy the Kid" (1938) and "Rodeo" (1942), which take place in the world of the prairie and which, particularly "Billy the Kid," refer to the success of western films of those days. The western films, in fact, use as background music the same tunes used by Copland in his works: in John Ford's "Ombre rosse" [*Stagecoach*] (1939) one hears "Bury Me Not on the Lone Prairie," which constitutes the principal theme of "Billy the Kid."[25]

Cowboy songs were thought of as American, though they are often contrafacta of British-American ballads.[26] A musical tradition that is occupation specific (such as stevedore songs, railroad songs, and river songs), they are not a distinct ethnic musical tradition, like African-American or Yiddish folk song, for example. Rather, according to country music historian Bill C. Malone, they are a blend of several ethnic and regional musical traditions. Cowboy music and western music are blends of Anglo-American balladry and its survivals brought west, Mexican, Cajun, African-American, and German and Czech music.

By the mid-1930s the yodel was associated with a well-known cultural symbol: the movie cowboy and his music. The yodel was popularized in the Western films of singing cowboys. Copland's audience would have been familiar with the cowboy's yodel from Hollywood films if not from records and radio. Malone provides an extensive list of popular singing cowboys: Carl Sprague, a Texan, and Jules Verne Allen, had both worked on the range and were thus authentic cowboys. Among the more popular singing cowboys was Hank Snow, promoted as the Yodeling Ranger. In the 1930s, the blue yodel was most closely associated with country and western music star Jimmie Rodgers, who wedded Western music with country and the blues in his recordings "Blue Yodel No. 1" and "Blue Yodel No. 4." Harry McClintock, a former cowboy and hobo who was also a member of the IWW, performed labor songs as well as cowboy songs (McClintock demonstrates a link between Copland's political interests and this music in ways the Kirstein anecdote does not). Of course, there were the singing and yodeling cowboys of the Hollywood films such as Gene Autry, Roy Rogers, and Tex Ritter, seen in serials and B movies as well as feature films that poured from the Hollywood studios.[27] Given a choice between a variant with which his audience might have been familiar and an unfamiliar one, Copland chose the well-known variant. If he did not choose the *melody* whose pitches and rhythms an audience would have recognized, he chose a *performance style*—and performance practice—that his audience would have known from folk or popular culture sources.

In choosing a folk and popular culture performance practice, the yodel, Copland reflected Kirstein's ideals. The *idea* for this peculiarly American ballet based on the life and death of an American folk antihero and the mythology of the American Wild West came initially from Kirstein. In creating an American ballet—one with choreography by Americans and reflecting American culture—Kirstein "made" an American art dance from American vernacular dance. But the enterprise was not foreign to Copland's own ideals. As did the numerous Westerns produced from 1903 through the 1930s, Copland and Kirstein's *Billy the Kid* looks not to contemporary American culture (its appropriation of the film cowboy notwithstanding) but nostalgically to a romanticized, idealized American past, as did the film Westerns. Copland and Kirstein turned to the usable past rather than the contemporary urban or rural folk sources, as can be seen in the titles of the ballets Kirstein commissioned and Copland's decision to follow his suggestion to use cowboy songs.

It is tempting to link Kirstein's choice of the figure of Billy the Kid, whom he saw as a Robin Hood figure, and Copland's of the cowboy tunes solely to Popular Front cultural politics. As we saw in the previous chapter, the Left became interested in American folk song. Benjamin Filene links the folk song collecting activities of John Lomax, an early collector of cowboy songs, and his son Alan to the Left: "The Lomaxes' work was in tune with the left wing's agenda."[28] But the use of cowboy songs reflects another cultural trend. While the cowboy was seen as a nostalgic figure of a bygone era, he was also seen as preindustrial and in contrast to modern industrial capitalism. John A. Lomax was committed to a pastoral ideal, a romanticized past he feared was threatened by modernity (he also used African-American folklore as his own protest against Victorianism and bourgeois life).[29] In offering cowboy songs and African-American folk song, Lomax challenged two paradoxical assumptions: (1) that the United States lacked a true indigenous folk music; and (2) the received history that its true folk music heritage came from either Native American (viewed in the nineteenth-century as unassimilable and in the twentieth century as a music of the past after the Western frontier closed) or Anglo-American sources. As Jerrold Hirsch writes, "Lomax helped redefine the canon of American folksong to include more than traditional ballads from the British Isles."[30] As the Western frontier closed around the turn of the twentieth century, the cowboy and his music came to symbolize not just a romanticized American past, but one from which racial Others—Native Americans, African-Americans, and Asian-Americans—had been erased, or marginalized. In the case of the Native American, the narrative of conquest and subjugation remained explicit in both the literary and the film Western. Thus, presented in these genres were the narratives of Americanization and of whiteness.[31]

A contemporary popular culture Western narrative even reinforced this process of constructing the West's myth of whiteness. John Steinbeck presented a different, gritty, nonnostalgic view of the West in his novel *The Grapes of Wrath,* as did the subsequent film starring Henry Fonda. Both depict the plight of Oklahoma farmers who, fleeing the Dustbowl of the 1930s, migrated westward to work in California's agriculture industries. Like the works of Upton Sinclair and Theodore Dreiser, Steinbeck's novel drew attention to the suffering of those who were working class and impoverished. Denning asserts that while Steinbeck's novel is "not a true exemplar of the cultural politics and aesthetic ideologies of the Popular Front," nonetheless, it is "only one part of the artistic and social formation by which the migrant workers in California's factories in the fields were represented *and* came to represent themselves."[32] This novel was just one of many "representation[s] of them in film and photographs, story and song" to the broader American public.[33] The plight of the Okies was chronicled in newspapers, in books such as Carey McWiliams's *Factories in the Field,* and Dorothea Lange and Paul Taylor's photodocumentary *American Exodus,* as well as in the film version of Steinbeck's novel directed by Darryl Zanuck. All these served to build public support for the farmworkers' unionizing, but ultimately doomed, effort.

There are racial implications to what Denning terms this "grapes of wrath" narrative, as it told the "story of white Protestant 'plain people.'" Mexican and Filipino farmworkers who had tried to unionize in 1933 and 1934 had been deported. Denning buttresses his racial divide argument in a discussion of Steinbeck's *In Dubious Battle.* In fact, 75 percent of the strikers in the unionizing effort on which Steinbeck's novel is based were Mexican; in Steinbeck's novel all the workers are white. In the pamphlet *Their Blood is Strong,* Steinbeck played the race card, writing that "future farm workers are to be white and American."[34] As we have seen, the Popular Front endeavored to build a pan-ethnic movement and eliminate racial barriers. Gellert had appropriated African-American blues as a vehicle of protest, as did Alan Lomax in his association with Leadbelly. Country and western music, although not viewed seriously by the Popular Front, was closely associated with the southern and midwestern working-class migrants moving from rural to urban areas. During the 1930s, as we saw, Western music became very popular, both on record and in Hollywood films. While former cowboy-hobo McClintock belonged to the IWW and included cowboy songs alongside his repertoire of labor songs, it was not the folk music of the cowboy and West that became the white folk music of the Popular Front. The Popular Front (as discussed in chapter 8) embraced southern folk music, black and white, especially the music of Appalachia with respect to the latter, associating this music with landmark strikes and workers' unionizing efforts in such locales as Gastonia, North Carolina, and Harlan County, Kentucky.

Copland's use of cowboy tunes thus has racial and political overtones. While historically, the West was multiracial and ethnically diverse, with African-American and Mexican cowboys, and conscripted Asian laborers who built the railroads, the cowboy as presented to American readers and moviegoers was white, usually of Anglo-American stock. Beth Levy further explores issues of race and sexuality in her study of the use of the West by American composers in the early twentieth century. She puts forth another implication for Copland's use of cowboy songs. As she documents in her study of Arthur Farwell, Charles Wakefield Cadman, Roy Harris, and Copland, many American composers in the first half of the twentieth century found inspiration in the West, including Thomson and the African-American William Grant Still. While Farwell and Cadman chose Native American melodies (and Still, Spanish and Mexican traditions) for use in their compositions, Harris and Copland turned to cowboy songs. Oklahoma-born and reared in San Gabriel Valley, California, and the son of a farmer, Harris could perhaps lay legitimate claim that cowboy songs were part of his cultural milieu as a westerner. For some critics, Harris music and its "Western, cowboy" character projected authenticity masculinity and virility.[35] Brooklyn-born and reared, Copland's connections to the West were more tenuous. His mother had grown up in Illinois and Texas before moving to New York. But like millions of other Americans who consumed pulp novels and films about the West, he was thoroughly urban. His first visit to California and Santa Fe, New Mexico, in 1928 had resulted in culture shock. He found the landscape barren, reminding him of "war-scarred battlefields I saw in France," as he wrote to his friend Gerald Sykes.[36] Despite his visceral reaction to the aridity of the West, the use of cowboy materials brought him popularity and increased his stock as an "American" composer. As Levy writes, for this son of Russian-Jewish immigrants, "Copland's westerness replaced his more contentious leftism, overshadowed his overt engagement with African American musical materials, and won nationwide popularity for a composer who might otherwise have been marginalized on the basis of his Russian-Jewish heritage or his homosexuality. The conjunction of whiteness, masculinity, and the West that was so significant a part of Harris's appeal had different, but still powerful implications for Copland's career."[37] Copland's appropriation of the virile icon of the cowboy and rugged Wild West helped deflect from his homosexuality, an open secret. Furthermore, as Levy writes, "Western Americana helped recuperate the international and suspiciously left-wing overtones of his 'pioneer' populism by channeling them into domestic settings more acceptable to the conservative establishment and the listening public."[38] In an 1893 essay, "The Significance of the Frontier in American History," historian Frederick Jackson Turner had viewed the westward expansion as "the line of the most rapid and effective Americanization," drawing people from various classes and nationalities who abandoned Old World ways in this new unsettled territory.[39] As Peter Stanfield writes, Turner expounded upon the frontier myth, that westward migration was the defining principle of an American exceptionalism. This westward expansion defined American history.[40] Copland, through use of Western materials, could appeal to a broader audience, rehabilitate his reputation as a radical, both politically and musically, and deflect any criticism, derision, or slurs about his sexuality or ethnicity and cast his music as virile, and 100 percent pure, red-blooded American.

Synthesis

Copland scholars have recognized some important stylistic and aesthetic connections between *El Salón México* and *Billy the Kid*. The links between the two are far stronger than previously realized, however, and more extensive than heretofore thought. Copland himself says:

> I feel that this ballet "Billy the Kid" is in the same vein [as *Fantasia Mexicana, El Salón México,* and *The Second Hurricane*]. I've tried to express what I wanted to say in terms as simple as I could find. Many of its melodies are derived from cowboy tunes, but I've not made any literal quotations from them.[41]

Combining modernist harmonies and textures with folk music caused the traditional music to lose its character. But the benefits far outweighed the risk: using the American folk music for Americans in a novel, imaginative, and original way that would win over a new unsophisticated, broad-based audience. After figuring out in *El Salón México* ways in which to use preexisting folk material and combine it with modernist techniques, in *Billy the Kid* Copland truly found a way to create a modern American music that both retains the technical and stylistic developments he had worked so hard to master and remains accessible to the average listener. When *El Salón México* was performed before American audiences, few people would have recognized the Mexican folk and popular tunes. When *Billy the Kid* and other works that used American popularized folk songs were performed for an American audience, the audience was familiar with their tunes. This had both positive and negative results. On the positive side, the audience was not put off by unfamiliar, dissonant, harsh, or aphoristic music. On the other hand, the composer ran the risk of appearing trite, clichéd, or unprincipled.

Copland was quite distanced from his subject and the musical tradition of Anglo-American and cowboy songs. He was not seeking to reveal to the world the inherent beauty of his own ethnic folk music heritage. He did not have a strong connection to cowboy songs or a strong affinity for them. As he stated, "I have never been particularly impressed with the musical beauties of the cowboy song as such. The words are usually delightful, and the manner of singing needs no praise from me. But neither the words nor the delivery are of much use in a purely orchestral ballet score, so I was left with the tunes themselves, which, I repeat, are often less than exciting."[42] Copland drew on America's shared culture of the cowboy, yet cowboy songs were remote from his urban New York experience and his heritage as the son of immigrants. It was Kirstein who led Copland to one of his great discoveries. Copland acknowledged, "When I suggested that, as a composer born in Brooklyn, I knew nothing about the Wild West, Lincoln informed me that Loring's scenario for *Billy the Kid* was based on the real life story of William Bonney, a notorious cowboy who had been born in New York! Lincoln was persuasive, and it did not take long to convince me that if I could work with Mexican tunes in *El Salon Mexico,* I might try home-grown ones for a ballet. Thus during the summer of 1938 I found myself writing a cowboy ballet in Paris."[43] The songs that he selected were chosen and tested in Europe, not in the United States, and Copland presumably had little idea which songs would appeal to a broad base of Americans.

> Whatever the reasons, it was not long before I found myself hopelessly involved with "Great Grand-Dad," "Git Along Little Dogies," "The Old Chisholm Trail," "Goodbye, Old Paint," and "The Dying Cowboy." David [Diamond] looked on in wonder as I played "Trouble for the Range Cook." I assured him that I would not use "Home on the Range," I decided to draw the line someplace![44]

While the cowboy songs themselves may have come from a regional American culture—that of the West and Southwest—the icon of the cowboy came from American popular culture, the Western being one of the major film genres of early Hollywood (e.g., *The Great Train Robbery*). Indeed, the same year in which Copland completed *Billy the Kid,* John Ford completed his classic film *Stagecoach* (1938). The cowboy and the

Wild West were completely identified with the United States and with no other nation or culture by both Americans and foreigners alike.

Again, as he had discovered America and American jazz while in Paris during the 1920s, it was in Paris that Copland partly discovered the Wild West. In 1939 he left to attend the ICSM Festival in London and from there went on to Paris, where he received another collection of cowboy songs. He recalled, "Lincoln sent a third collection of tunes to me in Paris. There in a studio on the rue de Rennes next door to David Diamond, I began to compose *Billy the Kid.* Perhaps there is something different about a cowboy song in Paris."[45] He had composed *El Salón México* in Mexico, where he was directly inspired by the local color and atmosphere of an actual dance hall that he had experienced directly. From it, perhaps, he discovered that folk music was an easy route to being nationalistic. "I was moved by that gesture, and the reviews that appeared in the newspapers after the premiere were no less kind. They seemed to agree that *El Salón México* might well be taken for Mexican music—'as Mexican as the music of Revueltas,' which was like saying at that time, as American as the music of Gershwin."[46] He had observed that his friend Chávez had used folk music and that his music was nonetheless decidedly modern.[47] In *Billy the Kid* Copland had now moved beyond appropriating the folk songs of another culture to appropriating that of his own America. He would continue to do so in works through the 1930s, 1940s, and 1950s in *Rodeo, Appalachian Spring, The Second Hurricane, John Henry, Lincoln Portrait,* and *Old American Songs.*

Conclusion :: A Vision for American Music . . .

In "Composer From Brooklyn," Copland reflected on how odd it seemed that a composer of his stature would rise from his old neighborhood. Nearly seventy years after leaving southern Bedford (now part of Crown Heights) Copland died in 1990 after a long period of declining health. Although he had retreated from public life during his last fifteen years, he was never far from modern American music. His orchestral works continue to be performed by professional, student, and amateur musicians, attesting not just to his compositional skill, but also to his visionary aesthetic: to create a modern music expressive of the United States and modern American culture, not just of himself as individual composer. Not long after his death, Copland's music could be heard as background for television commercials ranging from AT&T's use of the Shaker tune passage from *Appalachian Spring* to the use of "Hoedown" from *Rodeo* underscoring Sam Elliott's voice in the National Cattlemen's Beef Association's advertising campaign. Fittingly for a pioneer in film scoring, Copland's music was used in African-American *auteur* Spike Lee's film *He Got Game*. Copland's *Lincoln Portrait* first comforted the nation after the bombing of Pearl Harbor and sixty years later after the tragedy of September 11. Copland and his collaborators, from the ballet years of *Billy the Kid, Rodeo,* and *Appalachian Spring,* mythologized the American West. In his theater music, *Quiet City* and *Our Town,* Copland evoked the complex emotions of urban and small-town American life. In the public mind works such as these confirmed Copland as an *American* composer.

Though the public increasingly in the 1940s and 1950s saw Copland as the quintessential American composer, Copland understood his music and his work as critic, educator, and conductor as a *modern American* composer—the two being inseparable. Early on he mastered compositional techniques associated with Impressionism and the Russian modernists through independent study. As a youth he fell under the spell of modernists Debussy, Scriabin, and Stravinsky, whose music shaped his early style. His earliest works especially bear the marks of Stravinsky, Copland's sine qua non of modernism. From these composers Copland learned how to apply pentatonicism, the whole-tone scale, Scriabin's "Mystic chord," and octatonicism as new ways of handling melody and harmony and avoiding functional tonality.

Though known since the second half of the twentieth century as a composer of Americana, Copland matured as a French-influenced and French–inspired composer. Possessing the technical ability to complete short piano works after his time with instructors in harmony in New York, Copland sought further study. He charted a course for himself that led to Paris, drawn by his understanding that the city was then the leading center of musical modernism. First at Fontainebleau and later as a private student of Nadia Boulanger, Copland mastered her regime. He progressed to composing large-scale works for orchestra. While in Paris Copland embraced the aesthetic of Les Six. Noting how they had used jazz as the music of twentieth-century urban life, Copland—who had already experimented with it in "Jazzy" from *Trois Equisses*—explored its rhythms. Jazz rhythms, Boulanger's concept of *la grande ligne,* clarity of form and counterpoint, and Stravinskian ostinato and other rhythmic techniques became hallmarks of Copland's new, mature style that his compere, Henry Cowell, characterized as French-derived. In Paris he launched his professional career, securing the publication of *Scherzo humoristique* and making the acquaintance of Serge Koussevitsky, who would perform his works in the coming decades.

Though he came to be identified as the "dean of American composers," Copland was truly an international figure. He took advantage of his stay and traveled throughout Europe to hear new music. When he returned home, Copland established himself as one of the United States' brash, young modernists, his harmonies full of dissonance and octatonicism, his rhythms vigorous, with a new conception of handling of tonal materials deeply indebted to Stravinsky and French neoclassicism. Copland's orchestral music was first introduced to American audiences through his Stravinsky-cum-jazz Symphony for Organ and Orchestra, commissioned by Koussevitzky with Boulanger as organ soloist. Now combining Stravinskian interlocking polyrhythmic ostinati with jazz rhythm and melody in works such as *Music for the Theatre,* Copland further solidified his ties to neoclassicism by drawing upon the popular theatrical entertainments of the dance hall and burlesque theater, just as Cocteau and Les Six had drawn upon the Parisian entertainments of the cabaret and café concert.

Copland did not intentionally seek to become an *Americanist* composer, but by the mid-1920s, he developed a style that was considered so by audiences and music critics—first through his use of the jazz and Tin Pan Alley popular song, and, later, Anglo-American folk music. His Americana style, as it were, is also a by-product of his European training, one could certainly argue. The Depression years tempered but did not completely silence his dissonance as he sought a way to reach an audience beyond the small, modern music elite. A politically engaged citizen (initially interested in politics as a teen) as well as a composer, Copland's political views shaped both his aesthetic and his musical style during these years. Influenced by the Popular Front in the 1930s, he questioned modern music's relevance to contemporary American life. As the old modern music audience and sources of patronage declined, Copland deliberately courted a broad, mass audience. His music took on a new immediacy, first as he tried his hand at composing mass song, albeit applying the same techniques as in works such as *Scherzo humoristique* and Symphony for Organ and Orchestra, though simplified. Copland quickly realized that harmonic dissonances and dense, polyrhythmic ostinati could not be the music of the proletariat. Yet, his turn toward Anglo-American folk song would have to wait. Leaving behind mass song as he embraced the aesthetics of the Popular Front, Copland simplified his style to create a populist music for the American masses. He replaced his jazz-inflected speech of the 1920s first with Mexican folk song. His political interests had led him to Mexico, where during a brief sojourn he discovered the music of its people and promptly turned to published folk song collections for *El Salón México.*

We now have a new framework in which to view Copland as a composer of Americana—his use of American folk tunes in works of the late 1930s and 1940s that secured his place in the American soundscape. His use of folk music—cowboy songs in the 1930s and Anglo-American ballads in the 1940s—sprang less from a deep connection to those traditions than from Popular Front aesthetic ideology. As folklorists and WPA fieldworkers collected, recorded, and published American folk songs during the 1930s, the Popular Front turned to traditional folksingers in its unionizing and other movement activities. Copland (and many of his peers) realized the potential this music held. Understanding that folk music, not mass song style, was the music of the *American* people, Copland appropriated it during the 1930s and 1940s, beginning with *Billy the Kid,* turning to published collections rather than to the people themselves. He re-visioned the American pioneer in works such as *Billy the Kid* and, later, those enduringly familiar works *Rodeo* and *Appalachian Spring.* In these ballet collaborations with Kirstein, Martha Graham, and Agnes DeMille, Copland wedded modern American music to modern American dance.

By the end of the Second World War, Copland, now in middle age and midcareer, had become the quintessence of musical Americana. During these two decades, however, Copland never completely abandoned modern music, returning to the dissonant harmonic and polyrhythmic and jazz-rhythmic style of 1920s works throughout the 1930s and 1940s with works such as Piano Variations and Piano Sonata. It was this populist Stravinsky-cum-jazz neoclassical style that he introduced to film audiences in scores for *The Heiress* and *Of Mice and Men*. His approach to film scoring reflected his definition of modernism as the pull away from nineteenth-century German romanticism. In film scores from the 1940s Copland would lead Hollywood away from the Wagnerian leitmotiv and lush harmonies to a twentieth-century musical language now wedded to a twentieth-century mass medium, as he would for radio, with his *Music for Radio*. The late 1940s and 1950s would see Copland beset with difficulties stemming from his political involvements of the 1930s. The 1960s would see him compose his first rigorously serial works. By the early 1970s, he would effectively cease composing, turning to a conducting career.

There are many facets to Copland's music and aesthetic beyond Stravinskian modernism, French neoclassicism, and American modernism—his embrace of *Gebrauchsmusik* and *Schulmusik* (compositions for amateur and student musicians); his compositions that reflected his Jewish identity and his identity as a gay man living pre-Stonewall. The tendency to compartmentalize his work into neat little boxes is strong. Early Copland scholars Smith and Berger grouped his oeuvre into style periods, the modern works of the 1920s, the accessible works of the 1930s and 1940s, and the serial works of his later career, arguing that Copland changed styles every ten to fifteen years. Copland's biographer, Howard Pollack, argues (and rightly so) that this is a simplistic view. Yet the fact remains that certain works differ significantly in style from others, and one *can* see a shift in both his style and his aesthetics during the fifty-year span during which he produced his most enduring works.

These seemingly two competing viewpoints can be reconciled: there are stylistic consistencies, *pace* Pollack, from decade to decade, and aesthetic ones as well. Stylistically, throughout his career Copland retained the use of ostinato technique; segmented his melodic material; exploited the rhythmic techniques of polyrhythm, cross-rhythm, and shifting meters and metrical accents; and avoided functional tonality through the use of octatonicism, pentatonicism, modes, ostinati, or harmonic pedals, whether in the ultramodern *Scherzo humoristique* or the Americana of *Billy the Kid*. These were all hallmarks of modern music of the first half of the twentieth century. While his political ideology shaped his compositional choices, aesthetically Copland remained committed to modern music, seeking not to abandon the fundaments of his musical language, but to bring them first to the proletariat and then to the masses. A staunch modernist, Copland finally had found a way to make Stravinsky-derived ostinati, polyrhythm, nonfunctional harmony, and shifting meters palatable and approachable to the most untutored listener. Even his later turn toward serialism reflects Copland's genuine aesthetic and musical interest in *all* new international developments in art music. Thus, while foreground elements of his music or the source of his borrowed melodies and rhythms—jazz, Tin Pan Alley popular song, Mexican and American folk song—might have changed from one work to the next, consistently through the years Copland applied the same basic compositional techniques, whether composing for the small modern music audience, the electronic media of radio and film, the balletic stage, or amateur and school musicians.

Copland was dubbed the "dean of American Composers." While he founded no school of composers in the traditional sense, he emerged as a composer with a unique voice. Throughout his career, he taught hundreds of music appreciation students and scores of composers at various institutions and at the summer home of the Boston Symphony founded by his friend Koussevitsky. Copland also informally guided the careers of numerous young composers. *Rodeo* and *Appalachian Spring* particularly reached new audiences in the new millennium, thanks to the media of radio—which Copland so enthusiastically greeted—and television, hocking products from beef to telecommunications. Whether lecturing, writing music criticism, or critiquing the works of younger composers (sometimes too quickly dismissing the work of composers he thought too conservative, aesthetically and stylistically), Copland disseminated the "new music." He never abandoned his unshaken commitment to modern music and ceaselessly championed new developments in art music to the end of his active compositional and conducting career.

Notes

INTRODUCTION

1. As quoted in Aaron Copland and Vivian Perlis, *Copland: 1900 Through 1942* (New York: St. Martin's/Marek, 1984), 103–4.

2. *Bulletin of the Eleventh Annual Eastman School Festival of American Music* (Rochester, N.Y.: Eastman School of Music of the University of Rochester, 1941).

3. Paul Griffiths, *The Thames and Hudson Encyclopaedia of 20th-Century Music* (New York: Thames and Hudson, 1986), 122.

4. *The Harvard Dictionary of Music,* 1st ed., s.v. "Modern music."

5. Nicholas Slonimsky, *Music Since 1900* (New York: Schirmer Books, 1994), s.v. "Modern Music" and "Ultra-Modern Music."

6. Katherine Ruth Heyman, *The Relation of Ultramodern to Archaic Music* (Boston: Small, Maynard, 1921).

7. Ernst Krenek, *Music Here and Now,* trans. Barthold Fies (New York: W. W. Norton, 1939), 63–64.

8. Henry Cowell, "New Terms for New Music," *Modern Music,* May–June 1928, 21–28.

9. Elliott Antokoletz, *Twentieth-Century Music* (Englewood Cliffs, N.J.: Prentice Hall, 1992), 521.

10. David Joel Metzer, "The Ascendancy of Musical Modernism in New York City, 1915–1929," Ph.D. diss., Yale University, 1993, 4 and 17–18.

11. Henry Cowell, ed., *American Composers on American Music: A Symposium* (Stanford: Stanford University Press, 1933), v.

12. Cowell, *American Composers,* 3ff.

13. Cowell, *American Composers,* 8.

CHAPTER ONE

1. Carol J. Oja, *Making Music Modern: New York in the 1920s* (New York: Oxford University Press, 2000), 3–4, 14–18, 24–27, 47–48, 50–52.

2. Oja, *Making Music Modern,* 27, 48–50.

3. Copland and Perlis, *Copland,* 20, 22, and 28; Aaron Copland, "Composer from Brooklyn: Autobiography," *Magazine of Art,* September 1939, 522; Howard Pollack, *Aaron Copland: The Life and Work of an Uncommon Man* (Urbana: University of Illinois Press, 1999), 32.

4. Oja, *Making Music Modern,* 47. See also Alan Howard, *Musical Nationalism: American Composers' Search for Identity* (Westport, Conn.: Greenwood Press, 1987); Pollack, *Aaron Copland,* 33–34, 36. See also Barbara L.

Tischler, *An American Music: The Search for an American Musical Identity* (New York: Oxford University Press, 1986).

5. Pollack, *Aaron Copland,* 35–36.

6. Pollack, *Aaron Copland,* 32–33; Copland and Perlis, *Copland,* 27. Pollack suggests that a stylistic trait such as augmented seconds, as found in Copland's earlier *Cavalleria Rusticana,* "bears the obvious imprint of Russian-Jewish melody."

7. Aaron Copland, "Rubin Goldmark: A Tribute," *Julliard Review* 3 (Fall 1956): 15–16.

8. Copland and Perlis, *Copland,* 28.

9. Aaron Copland, "Carlos Chávez—Mexican Composer," in Cowell, *American Composers,* 102. Cf. Aaron Copland, *Our New Music* (New York: Whittlesey House, 1941), 141.

10. Copland, "Carlos Chávez," 102.

11. Aaron Copland, *The New Music 1900–1960,* rev. ed. (New York: W. W. Norton, 1968), 17.

12. Aaron Copland, "The Twentieth Century: Reorientation and Experiment," in *Music and Western Man: The Canadian Broadcasting Corporation,* ed. Peter Garvie (New York: Philosophical Library, 1958), 281.

13. Copland, *The New Music,* 17.

14. Copland, *The New Music,* 17.

15. Aaron Copland, "The Composers of South America," *Modern Music,* January–February 1942, 76.

16. Aaron Copland, "A Modernist Defends Modern Music," *New York Times,* December 25, 1949, sec. 6, p. 11.

17. Aaron Copland, "Music since 1920," *Modern Music,* March–April 1928, 16.

18. Aaron Copland, "The Musical Scene Changes," *Twice a Year* 5–7 (1940–41): 340.

19. Copland and Perlis, *Copland,* 55.

20. Copland, *The New Music,* 53.

21. Aaron Copland, "George Antheil," *Modern Music,* January–February 1925, 27; reprinted in *The New Music.*

22. Copland, *The New Music,* 155.

23. For example, Ferruccio Busoni, in his *Sketch of a New Esthetic of Music* (1907) and *New Aesthetic,* urged composers to free themselves from Romanticism, to not be bound by the conventions of diatonicism and the tonal system, and once having discovered a new method or technique, not to repeat it, but further experiment. Futurist manifestos such as artist Luigi Russolo's pamphlet *The Art of Noises* (1913), rejected all basic assumptions regarding conventional musical parameters and proposed a new musical art that conceived of music purely as sound.

24. Copland, "Carlos Chávez," 102.

25. Aaron Copland, "The Composer in America, 1923–1933," *Modern Music,* January–February 1933, 87.

26. Aaron Copland, *Music and Imagination* (Cambridge: Harvard University Press, 1952), 65; Copland, "The Musical Scene Changes," 340.

27. Aaron Copland, "Nationalism New World Style," unpublished paper, n.d., p. 8, Oral History Project in American Music, Yale University. Hereinafter cited as OHP.

28. Copland, *The New Music,* 18.

29. Pollack, *Aaron Copland,* 34.

30. Music Composition Notebook (MCN) 1: Exercises and Early AC Compositions, 1916–1917, Aaron Copland Collection, Music Division, Library of Congress. Hereinafter cited as ACC.

31. Aaron Copland, "The Reminiscences of Aaron Copland," interview by Vivian Perlis, December 23, 1975–December 8, 1976, Peekskill, New York, Oral History Transcript, p. 40, American Music Series, Yale University, and Oral History Research Office, Columbia University; Copland and Perlis, *Copland.*

32. MCN 2: Exercises and Early AC Compositions, 1917, ACC.

33. MCN 12: Exercises in Harmony (undated); MCN 3: etc. 1918–19; MCN 4: Exercises and AC Transcriptions 1919; Schirmer Manuscript Book (SMB): SMB 3, n.d.; SMB 2, n.d., ACC.

34. MCN 5: Exercises and Early AC Compositions, 1919–20 Exercises; MCN 7: Exercises (undated); SMB 3, n.d.; SMB 4, n.d.; SMB 6, n.d.; SMB 7, n.d., ACC.

35. Copland and Perlis, *Copland,* 27; Arthur Foote and Walter R. Spaulding, *Modern Harmony In Its Theory and Practice* (Boston: Arthur P. Schmidt, 1905).

36. MCN 11: Exercises in Harmony (undated), ACC.

37. Copland, "Nationalism New World Style," 16.

38. Aaron Copland, "The New 'School' of American Composers," *New York Times Magazine,* March 14, 1948, 30.

39. Pollack, *Aaron Copland,* 34–35.

40. Copland, "Rubin Goldmark," 16.

41. Vivian Perlis and Ruth Leon, producers, *Aaron Copland: A Self-Portrait,* Films for the Humanities, 1985, videotape.

42. Copland, "Reminiscences," 48.

43. Copland, *The New Music,* 153.

44. Pollack, *Aaron Copland,* 35.

45. Copland, *The New Music,* 153.

46. Pollack, *Aaron Copland,* 33.

47. Pollack, *Aaron Copland,* 33, 36, 40–42.

48. Many of these unpublished, early works are extant, preserved in ACC.

49. Diaries—Journals 1910–48, p. 8, Binder 1, ACC; cf. Pollack, *Aaron Copland,* 35–36; Copland and Perlis, *Copland,* 24–25.

50. Aaron Schaffer to Aaron Copland, February 2, 1919, ACC.

51. "Night" remained unpublished for seventy years. Boosey & Hawkes finally published it in 1989.

52. Several manuscript sources exist for this work. An incomplete manuscript dated 1920 in Box 1, Folder 1 entitled Humoristic Scherzo: The Cat and the Mouse, an ink copy with lighter pencil marks that appear to have been added later; a complete manuscript copy, also entitled Scherzo humoristique: Le Chat et la Souris; the publisher's proofs, dated November 9, 1921; and the score as published in France by Durand. All sources are very similar with minor changes: chord spellings. The final version contains additional measures, but this mostly increases the dramatic effect of the piece. Cat and Mouse, ARCO 1, Box 1, Folder 1, ACC.

53. Pollack provides another interpretation, *Aaron Copland,* 43.

54. Copland, "Composer from Brooklyn," 522; Copland, "Reminiscences," 48; Copland and Perlis, *Copland,* 27; Copland, *The New Music,* 153.

55. Pollack, *Aaron Copland,* 33–34; Oja, *Making Music Modern,* 46–48.

56. This is a nearly complete version of the song, "Sketch for Song 'Music

I Heard with You,'" MCN 4, p. 25v, Exercises and AC Transcriptions 1919, ACC.

57. Carol J. Oja, "Virgil Thomson's Harvard Years," in *A Celebration of American Music: Words and Music in Honor of H. Wiley Hitchcock,* ed. Richard Crawford, R. Allen Lott, and Carol J. Oja (Ann Arbor: University of Michigan Press, 1990), 339.

58. David Matthews, "Copland and Stravinsky," *Tempo* 95 (Winter 1950): 10–14.

59. Arthur Berger, "Stravinsky and the Younger American Composers," *Score and I.M.A. Magazine,* June 1955, 39–40.

60. Richard Taruskin, *Stravinsky and the Russian Traditions: A Biography of the Works through "Mavra"* (Berkeley and Los Angeles: University of California Press, 1996).

61. Richard Taruskin, "*Chez Pétrouchka:* Harmony and Tonality *chez* Stravinsky," *19th Century Music* 10 (Spring 1987): 271. Arthur Berger made the same observation about the importance of the octatonic scale's bisecting tritone in his germinal "Problems of Pitch Organization in Stravinsky," *Perspectives of New Music* 2 (Fall–Winter 1963): 11–42.

62. Taruskin, "*Chez Pétrouchka,*" 284; Copland and Perlis, *Copland,* 32.

63. Pollack also links the work to Villa-Lobos's *Cat and Mouse* (*O Gato e o Rato,* 1917). Pollack, *Aaron Copland,* 43–44.

CHAPTER TWO

1. Copland, *The New Music,* 153.

2. Copland and Perlis, *Copland,* 83.

3. Schaffer to Copland, August 5, 11, and 14, 1919, September 8 and 23, 1919, October 23, 1919, November 3, 7, and 20, 1919, December 22, 1919, January 19, 1920, February 2 and 13, 1920, ACC; Pollack, *Aaron Copland,* 37.

4. Copland, "Reminiscences," 89.

5. Copland, *The New Music,* 154.

6. Copland and Perlis, *Copland,* 47.

7. See Julia Smith, *Aaron Copland: His Works and Contribution to American Music* (New York: E. P. Dutton, 1955); Copland and Perlis, *Copland;* Arthur Berger, *Aaron Copland* (New York: Oxford University Press, 1953); Tischler, *An American Music;* Alan Howard Levy, *Musical Nationalism: American Composers' Search for Identity* (Westport, Conn.: Greenwood Press, 1987).

8. Mabel C. [Mrs. George Montgomery] Tuttle to Mrs. Kinkeldy, April 9, 1921, Fontainebleau File, Music Division, New York Public Library, New York.

9. Copland and Perlis, *Copland,* 47. Copland, "Reminiscences," 82; see also Copland, *The New Music,* 154. In the notice publicizing Fontainebleau and the application's information booklet, Boulanger is listed as Professor of Harmony. She was professor of composition and taught fugue and counterpoint at the École Normale de Musique. Maurice Ravel's name appears among those of the French committee. Booklet "Palace of Fontainebleau French High School of Musical Studies (École des Hautes Etudes Musicales de France/Conservatoire Americain)" (Melun: Imprimerie Administrative, 1921), n.p., Fontainebleau File, Music Division, New York Public Library, New York.

10. Copland, *The New Music,* 154; Pollack, *Aaron Copland,* 46.

11. Copland, *The New Music,* 155.

12. David Ottenberg, "The Methods and Aesthetics of Nadia Boulanger and Their Influence on Aaron Copland," master's thesis, University of Florida, 1992, 65.

13. Copland, *The New Music,* 155; Aaron Copland, *Copland on Music* (Garden City, N.Y.: Doubleday, 1960), 88.

14. Caroline Potter, "Nadia Boulanger (1887–1979): The Teacher in the Marketplace," in *The Business of Music,* ed. Michael Talbot (Liverpool: Liverpool University Press, 2002), 161–68.

15. Pollack, *Aaron Copland,* 47.

16. Teresa Walters, "Nadia Boulanger, Musician and Teacher: Her Life, Concepts, and Influences," D.M.A. thesis, Peabody Conservatory of Music, Peabody Institute of The Johns Hopkins University, 1981, 48.

17. Walters, "Boulanger, Musician and Teacher," 98.

18. Theresa Walters studied the writings of Boulanger's students about their study and interviewed Boulanger. In "Boulanger, Musician and Teacher," she quotes from *Copland on Music* on how he understood the concept of *la grande ligne.*

19. Levy, *Musical Nationalism,* 54.

20. Walters, "Boulanger, Musician and Teacher," 98.

21. Beginning in 1919 Boulanger wrote articles for *Le Monde musical.* Jérôme Spycket, *Nadia Boulanger,* trans. M. M. Shriver (Stuyvesant, N.Y.: Pendragon Press, 1992), 56.

22. Nadia Boulanger, *Le Monde Musical,* November 1919, 350, as quoted in Walters, "Boulanger, Musician and Teacher," 99.

23. Nadia Boulanger, "Cours d'Interprétation de NB," *Le Monde Musical,* July 1936, 212, as quoted in Walters, "Boulanger, Musician and Teacher," 99.

24. Boulanger, "Cours d'Interprétation," as quoted in Walters, "Boulanger, Musician and Teacher," 212.

25. Here Ottenberg quotes from Virgil Thomson, *A Virgil Thomson Reader;* Ottenberg, "Methods and Aesthetics," 391.

26. Ottenberg, "Methods and Aesthetics," 40.

27. Pollack, *Aaron Copland,* 76–78.

28. Pollack, *Aaron Copland,* 80. Vivian Perlis discovered the manuscript of *Movement* (finally published in 1984) among Copland's papers at the Library of Congress in 1983.

29. The term was first coined by Zarlino, *Le istitutioni harmoniche,* 1558, 3:66, after Lewis Lockwood, *The New Grove Dictionary of Music and Musicians,* s.v. "Soggetto cavato."

30. Aaron Copland, *Two Pieces for String Quartet,* newly engraved edition (n.p.: Boosey & Hawkes, 1991), frontspiece.

31. Glenn Watkins, *Pyramids at the Louvre: Music, Culture, and Collage from Stravinsky to the Postmodernists* (Cambridge: Belknap Press of Harvard University Press, 1994), 1.

32. Aaron Copland, preface to *What to Listen for in Music* (1939; reprint, New York: Mentor/Penguin, 1988).

33. Copland, *What to Listen For,* 105.

34. Copland and Perlis, *Copland,* 51.

35. Smith, *Aaron Copland,* 76; Pollack, *Aaron Copland,* 125.

36. Smith reprinted reviews of the work's premiere. See Smith, *Aaron Copland.*

37. Smith paraphrases the *New York Times* review in *Aaron Copland,* 76.

38. Rosenfeld, as quoted in *Smith, Aaron Copland,* 76. Rosenfeld's article originally appeared in "Musical Chronicle," *The Dial*, March 1925, 258–59.

39. Pollack, *Aaron Copland,* 80 and 86.

40. Neil Butterworth, *The Music of Aaron Copland* (n.p.: Toccata Press, 1985), 28–29.

CHAPTER THREE

1. Louis Gruenberg, "For an American Gesture," *Modern Music,* June 1924, 26–28.

2. Pollack, *Aaron Copland,* 35.

3. Copland, *Copland on Music,* 56; Copland and Perlis, *Copland,* 20; Pollack, *Aaron Copland,* 39.

4. Judith Tick, "The Origins and Style of Copland's *Three Moods for Piano* no. 3, 'Jazzy,'" *American Music* 20 (Fall 2002): 281.

5. Copland and Perlis, *Copland,* 33.

6. Copland, "Reminiscences, "133; Aaron Copland to Nadia Boulanger, August 26, 1924, ACC; Pollack, *Aaron Copland,* 89.

7. Copland and Perlis, *Copland,* 37.

8. Copland, "Nationalism New World Style," 10.

9. Don Gold, "Aaron Copland; the Well-Known American Composer Finds Virtues and Flaws in Jazz," *Down Beat,* May 1, 1958, 16, 39–40.

10. Burton W. Peretti, *The Creation of Jazz* (Urbana: University of Illinois Press, 1992), 94.

11. Aaron Copland to Mr. and Mrs. Koussevitzky, ca. 1930–31, Koussevitzky Collection, Library of Congress; Copland, "Composer from Brooklyn," 550; Smith, *Aaron Copland,* 64.

12. Aaron Copland, "Jazz Structure and Influence," *Modern Music,* January–February 1927, 9.

13. Copland, "Jazz Structure and Influence," 9.

14. For an interpretation of Copland's rhythmic conception of jazz, see Stanley V. Kleppinger, "On the Influence of Jazz Rhythm in the Music of Aaron Copland," *American Music* 21 (2003): 74–111.

15. Copland, "Jazz Structure and Influence," 10.

16. Copland, "Jazz Structure and Influence," 10–11.

17. Copland, "Jazz Structure and Influence," 13–14.

18. George Hutchinson, *The Harlem Renaissance in Black and White* (Cambridge: Belknap Press of Harvard University Press, 1995).

19. Cary D. Wintz, *Black Culture and the Harlem Renaissance* (Houston: Rice University Press, 1988), 94. Davis Levering Lewis took this phrase as the title of his study of the Renaissance, *When Harlem Was in Vogue* (New York: Oxford University Press, 1981).

20. Wintz, *Black Culture,* 87 and 94.

21. Wintz, *Black Culture,* 154.

22. Lewis, *Harlem,* 98–99.

23. Wintz, *Black Culture,* 187.

24. Harold Clurman, Copland's friend, recounted to Arthur Berger that Copland invited him along to many parties, including one at which he met Van Vechten. Berger, *Aaron Copland,* 28.

25. Carol Oja, "New Music and the 'New Negro': The Background of William Grant Still's *Afro-American Symphony,*" *Black Music Research Jour-*

nal 12, no. 2 (1992): 146 n.1. See also Nathan Huggins, *Harlem Renaissance* (New York: Oxford University Press, 1971), 25.

26. David Metzer, "The League of Composers: The Initial Years," *American Music,* Spring 1997, 47, 54, and 68 n. 30.

27. As Judith Tick points out, the manuscript of "Jazzy" is dated July 1921, suggesting that in later years, Copland confused this work with another. Cf. Tick, "Jazzy"; and Copland and Perlis, *Copland,* 36.

28. Tick, "Jazzy," 278; Copland, "Reminiscences," 67.

29. Pollack, *Aaron Copland,* 44.

30. Tick, "Jazzy," 290–91.

31. Copland and Perlis, *Copland,* 374 n. 4.

32. For a definition of "swung" eighths, see Gunther Schuller, *Early Jazz: Its Roots and Musical Development* (New York: Oxford University Press, 1968), 6ff.

33. For more on how African-American jazz musicians accomplished rhythmic development, see Schuller, *Early Jazz,* 89–133.

34. Pollack, *Aaron Copland,* 44.

35. Phillip Ramey, liner notes to *Leo Smit: The Composer for Solo Piano,* Sony Classical SM2K 66 345, a reissue of Smit's recording originally made for Columbia; Tick, "Jazzy," 282–89; Pollack, *Aaron Copland,* 44.

36. "My Buddy" was copyrighted in 1922. At first glance, it seems as though Copland's piece predates the songs. However, one must not rely completely on the copyright date. Donaldson is known to have performed for the troops during World War I.

37. Tick, "Jazzy," 285.

CHAPTER FOUR

1. Copland, *Copland on Music,* 86; Copland, "Reminiscences," 87, and Léonie Rosenstiel, *Nadia Boulanger: A Life in Music* (New York: W. W. Norton, 1982), 170 and 162; Copland, "Composer from Brooklyn," 548; Copland, *The New Music,* 155; Aaron Copland, My Trip Abroad; List of Performances Attended in Paris during 1921 & 1922, ACC; and Copland, "Nationalism New World Style," 155.

2. Copland to Boulanger, August 15, 1922, August 12, 1923, July 23, 1923, ACC; Copland and Perlis, *Copland,* 83.

3. Nancy Perloff, *Art and the Everyday: Popular Entertainment and the Circle of Erik Satie* (Oxford: Clarendon Press, 1991), 18.

4. Copland and Perlis, *Copland,* 71.

5. Perloff, *Art and the Everyday,* 46.

6. Perloff, *Art and the Everyday,* 96, 161ff., 173.

7. Darius Milhaud, *Notes without Music,* trans. Donald Evans, ed. Rollo H. Myers (London: Dennis Dobson, 1952), 117–18.

8. Milhaud, *Notes without Music,* 117–18.

9. Milhaud, *Notes without Music,* 127 and 118.

10. For a study of neoclassicism in France and Germany, from its inception through World War I, see Scott Messing, *Neoclassicism in Music: From the Genesis of the Concept through the Schoenberg/Stravinsky Polemic* (Ann Arbor, Mich.: UMI Research Press, 1988).

11. Copland and Perlis, *Copland,* 71.

12. Copland, *The New Music,* 17.

13. Milhaud, *Notes without Music,* 80–81; cf. Messing, *Neoclassicism in Music.*

14. Copland and Perlis, *Copland,* 90.

15. Malcolm Cowley, *Exile's Return: A Literary Odyssey of the 1920s* (1934; reprint, New York: Penguin, 1979), 83.

16. Copland and Perlis, *Copland,* 90.

17. Perlis and Leon (producers), *Aaron Copland: A Self-Portrait;* Copland, "Reminiscences," 128.

18. Milhaud, *Notes without Music,* 116.

19. Walters, "Boulanger, Musician and Teacher," 241ff. and 291 ff.; see Rosenstiel, *Nadia Boulanger.*

20. Copland, *Copland on Music,* 8; Aaron Copland, "Nadia Boulanger: An Affectionate Portrait," *Harpers,* October 1960, 50; Rosenstiel, *Nadia Boulanger,* 170.

21. Copland, "Nationalism New World Style," 9.

22. Perlis and Leon, *Aaron Copland.*

23. Copland, "Nadia Boulanger," 50. Later, in the Copland-Perlis biography, this passage appears almost verbatim: "I can still remember the eagerness of Nadia's curiosity concerning my rhythms in these early works, particularly the jazz-derived ones. Before long we were exploring polyrhythmic devices together." Copland and Perlis, *Copland,* 67.

24. Smith, *Aaron Copland,* 65.

25. Copland, "Nadia Boulanger," 50.

26. Copland, "Jazz Structure and Influence," 14.

27. Copland, "Jazz Structure and Influence," 14.

28. Copland, "Nationalism New World Style," 7.

29. The original ballet and its 1932 revision were rediscovered by the conductor Oliver Knussen. *Grohg* was originally in three parts, the first consisting of the Introduction and "Cortège Macabre." The second consists of "Dance of the Adolescent," "Dance of the Opium-Eater," and "Dance of the Street Walker." The third consists of "Dance of Mockery," and the Finale/Coda. Roberta Lewise Lindsey's "An Historical and Musical Study of Aaron Copland's First Orchestral Work: 'Grohg, A Ballet in One Act,'" Ph.D. diss., Ohio State University, 1996, is an important study of this work.

30. A photocopy of the 1932 score of *Grohg* is presently available from Copland's publisher Boosey & Hawkes. The holograph is in ACC. The original ballet remained unpublished and unperformed until 1992, when Oliver Knussen conducted the London Sinfonietta at the Aldeburgh Festival. Knussen and the Cleveland Orchestra recorded the work in May 1993 (refer to the 1994 recording *Copland: Grohg/Hear Ye! Hear Ye!* (Argo 443-203-2). *Dance Symphony* was revised in 1932. The score of *Cortège macabre* is now archived in Sibley Library at the Eastman School of Music in Rochester, New York.

31. Lindsey, "Copland's First Orchestral Work," 125.

32. Schuller, *Early Jazz,* 89ff.

33. Cf. Milhaud, *Le boeuf sur le toit.*

34. Cf. Stravinsky, "Dance of the Adolescent," *Rite of Spring.* See also Pieter C. Van den Toorn, *The Music of Igor Stravinsky* (New Haven: Yale University Press, 1983).

35. Walters, "Boulanger, Musician and Teacher," 59.

36. Lindsey transcribed the three waltzes in "Copland's First Orchestral Work," 76–77, 28.

37. Antokoletz, *Twentieth-Century Music,* 249–50.

38. Lindsey, "Copland's First Orchestral Work," 22.

39. Jean Cocteau, *Cock and Harlequin: Notes Concerning Music,* trans. Rollo H. Myers (London: Egoist Press, 1921), 23–24.

CHAPTER FIVE

1. American Family Immigration History Center website, www.Ellisisland.org, accessed May 25, 2004.

2. Cowell, *American Composers,* 8.

3. Edward T. Cone, "Conversation with Aaron Copland," *Perspectives of New Music* 6 (1968): 64.

4. Copland, "Composer from Brooklyn," 549; cf. Copland, *The New Music,* 158.

5. Berger, *Aaron Copland,* 38.

6. Norman Kay, "Copland, All-American Composer," *Music & Musicians* 14 (September 1965): 22.

7. Butterworth, *Music of Aaron Copland,* 34.

8. Larry Starr, "The Voice of Solitary Contemplation: Copland's *Music for the Theatre* Viewed as a Journey of Self-Discovery," *American Music* 20 (Fall 2002): 297–316.

9. James Reese Europe, "A Negro Explains Jazz," reprinted in *Riffs and Chords: A New Jazz Anthology,* ed. Andrew Clark (London: Continuum, 2001), 25–26; also reprinted in *Keeping Time: Readings in Jazz History,* ed. Robert Walser (New York: Oxford University Press, 1999), 12–14.

10. Jelly Roll Morton, "I Created Jazz in 1902," reprinted in Clark, *Riffs and Chords,* 28.

11. Jelly Roll Morton, excerpted from Alan Lomax, *Mister Jelly Roll: The Fortunes of Jelly Roll Morton, New Orleans Creole and "Inventor of Jazz"* (New York: Duell, Sloan, and Pearce, 1949; reprinted in Walser, *Keeping Time*), 19.

12. Anonymous, "Delving into the Genealogy of Jazz (1919)," reprinted in Clark, *Riffs and Chords,* 36.

13. Ernest-Alexandre Ansermet, "Bechet and Jazz Visit Europe, 1919," reprinted in Clark, *Riffs and Chords,* 42–44; see also Walser, *Keeping Time,* 9–11.

14. William Grant Still and Verna Arvey, "Negro Music in the Americas," *Revue Internationale de Musique* (Brussels) 1 (May–June 1938): 283; William Grant Still, "The Music of My Race," (translation of "La Musica de Mi Raza,"), 2, William Grant Still–Verna Arvey Papers, Special Collections Division, University Library, University of Arkansas, Fayetteville, Arkansas. Both are reprinted in Jon Michael Spencer, ed., "The William Grant Still Reader: Essays on American Music," special issue of *Black Sacred Music* 6 (Fall 1992).

15. According to jazz historian Winthrop Sargeant, whose work Copland respected, *hot* is a term used to refer to the "spontaneous improvisation" played by black jazz musicians. This included the music of those such as Louis Armstrong. This term was set in opposition to *sweet,* which was used to refer to the popular dance music of white musicians such as Paul Whiteman. See Winthrop Sargeant, *Jazz, Hot and Hybrid,* 3rd ed. (New York: Da Capo Press, 1975), 46ff.

16. See Sargeant, *Jazz, Hot and Hybrid,* 149ff. for a discussion of pentatonicism in jazz specifically, and in African-American music in general. Cf. Schuller, *Early Jazz,* 43ff. Schuller critiques Sargeant's discussion of African-American melodic idiom and presents insights of his own.

17. Cf. recordings: Johnny Dodds on King Oliver's "Dippermouth Blues"; Barney Bigard, Darnell Howard, and Omer Simeon on Jelly Roll Morton's "Dead Man Blues"; Sydney Bechet on Sydney Bechet and His Blue Note Jazz Men's "Blue Horizon." All can be found on *The Smithsonian Collection of Classic Jazz,* rev. ed.

18. For Pollack's discussion of the grotesque in Copland's use of jazz, see *Aaron Copland,* 114.

19. Smith, *Aaron Copland,* 86.

20. Butterworth, *Music of Aaron Copland,* 33.

21. Kay, "Copland, All-American Composer," 22.

22. Smith, *Aaron Copland,* 84.

23. Butterworth, *Music of Aaron Copland,* 35.

24. Smith, *Aaron Copland,* 85.

25. Aaron Copland, as quoted in Gold, "Aaron Copland," 16.

26. For more on Stravinsky's partitioning the octatonic scale, see Van den Toorn, *Music of Igor Stravinsky,* 50ff. Cf. Berger, "Pitch Organization in Stravinsky," 11–42.

27. Butterworth, *Music of Aaron Copland,* 35.

28. Copland and Perlis, *Copland,* 66ff.

29. Pollack, *Aaron Copland,* 132.

30. Schaffer to Copland, May 23, 1918, ACC.

31. Copland and Perlis, *Copland,* 117.

32. Pollack, *Aaron Copland,* 131.

33. Copland and Perlis, *Copland,* 120.

34. Pollack, *Aaron Copland,* 130.

35. Charles Hamm, *Yesterdays: Popular Song in America* (New York: W. W. Norton, 1979), 258 and 291.

36. Smith, *Aaron Copland,* 85. Smith identifies one of the composers of the songs, Charles B. Lawlor, as a Dublin-born immigrant who came to New York in 1887.

37. Hamm, *Yesterdays,* 296.

38. For more on American popular songs and how they reflect urban New York, see Hamm, *Yesterdays,* 284ff.

39. *Pink Lady* opened March 13, 1911, at the New Amsterdam Theater and rar through the 1911–12 season. Gerald Bordman, *American Musical Theater: A Chronicle,* 2nd ed. (New York: Oxford University Press, 1992), 264–65. See Copland and Perlis, *Copland,* 20. Cf. Copland, *The New Music,* 151ff.

40. Copland and Perlis, *Copland,* 20.

41. This article was presented in the *Magazine of Art* in 1939. It was reprinted in Copland, *The New Music,* 151–68.

42. Copland, *The New Music,* 151.

43. I do not mean to suggest that the lyrics hint that Copland had any form of racial bias or prejudice and that is why he chose this particular songs. On the contrary, I suspect that although the song may have contained pejoratives, it may have been one of the songs performed in Copland's boyhood home. If it were played by his sister or uncle, the pejorative content of the lyrics quite possibly would have gone unquestioned by Copland when he was a boy, and thus, unnoticed by Copland as an adult. One does suspect, however, that

Copland's boyhood was not quite as harmonious as that of the song character's. See Copland and Perlis, *Copland,* 20.

44. For pioneering music scholarship in gay and lesbian studies, see Philip Brett, Elizabeth Woods, and Gary C. Thomas, eds., *Queering the Pitch: The New Gay and Lesbian Musicology* (New York: Routledge, 1994); Lloyd Whitesell and Sophie Fuller, eds., *Queer Episodes in Music and Modern Identity* (Urbana: University of Illinois Press, 2002); Maynard Solomon, "Franz Schubert and the Peacocks of Benvenuto Cellini," *19th Century Music* 12 (Spring 1989): 193–206; Susan McClary, "On the Solomon/Steblein Debate," *19th Century Music* 17 (Summer 1993): 83–88; Kofi Agawu, "Schubert's Sexuality: A Prescription for Analysis?" *19th Century Music* 17 (Summer 1993): 79–82; and Philip Brett, *Benjamin Britten, "Peter Grimes"* (Cambridge: Cambridge University Press, 1983). For more on Ives and masculinity, see Stuart Feder, "Decoration Day: A Boyhood Memory of Charles Ives," *Musical Quarterly* 66 (April 1980): 234–71; and Maynard Solomon, "Charles Ives: Some Questions of Veracity," *Journal of the American Musicological Society* 40 (Autumn 1987): 443–70.

45. Pollack, *Aaron Copland,* 130.

46. George Chauncey Jr., *Gay New York: Gender, Urban Culture, and the Making of the Gay Male World, 1890–1940* (New York: Basic Books, 1994), 190ff.

47. Pollack, *Aaron Copland,* 39, 52, 93, and 183.

48. Chauncey, *Gay New York,* 328, 244–67. See also Eric Garber, "A Spectacle in Color: The Lesbian and Gay Subculture of Jazz Age Harlem," in *Hidden from History: Reclaiming the Gay and Lesbian Past,* ed. Martin Duberman, Martha Vicinus, and George Chauncey Jr. (New York: Meridian, 1990), 318–31. See also Lewis, *Harlem,* 107.

49. Pollack, *Aaron Copland,* 235.

50. As quoted in Pollack, *Aaron Copland,* 130.

51. Jack Babuscio, "Camp and the Gay Sensibility," in *Camp Grounds: Style and Sensibility,* ed. David Bergman (Amherst: University of Massachusetts Press, 1993), 8.

52. Babuscio, "Camp and the Gay Sensibility," 20–29.

53. Copland and Perlis, *Copland,* 120.

54. For more on double entendre, camp, codes, and other strategies used by gay men during the first half of the twentieth century, see Chauncey, *Gay New York,* 286.

55. The term *vaudeville* comes from the French *voix de ville.* Although the original meaning of the term *parody* connotes an imitation or a lampoon, it also refers to a distinctly American form of popular entertainment of the nineteenth century. The burlesque, while meaning parody, was a "girlie" show, or a type of entertainment that featured the enticing public display of women's bodies. The form was popular during the 1860s; however, it was sanitized by Tony Pastor, who eliminated all racy material, thereby creating a new form of American popular entertainment for the 1880s: vaudeville. The vaudeville show thus became a variety show. Bassoons playing the melody, coupled with the pizzicato strings, and the glockenspiel/xylophone do give the movement an air of parody—perhaps a parody of jazz. This interpretation, however, fails to take into account that Copland uses jazz throughout the movement with utmost respect, as if to bear out musically the phrase "imitation is the sincerest form of flattery." Instead of parody or lampoon, the movement suggests comedy, or good humor and good fun.

56. See Catrina Kelly, *Petrushka, the Russian Carnival Puppet* (Cambridge: Cambridge University Press, 1990).

57. Pollack, *Aaron Copland,* 130.

58. Copland, as quoted in Smith, *Aaron Copland,* 87.

59. Copland, *The New Music,* 159.

60. Copland and Perlis, *Copland,* 134.

61. As quoted in Hans Rosenwald, "Contemporary Music," *Music News,* January 1951, 8.

62. Copland and Perlis, *Copland,* 119.

CHAPTER SIX

1. Copland to Boulanger, August 15, 1922, ACC.

2. Copland to Boulanger, July 25, 1923, Vienna, ACC.

3. "C'etait par les oeuvres de Hindemith, de Krenek, et de Hába que j'etais le plus frappé" (author's translation), Copland to Boulanger, August 12, 1923, Vienna, ACC.

4. "Alois Hába est moins hardi malgré son système de quart de ton. Mais son quatour aussi m'a laissé avec une impression très favorable." Copland to Boulanger, August 12, 1923, Vienna, ACC.

5. Aaron Copland, "Playing Safe at Zurich," *Modern Music,* November–December 1926, 28–29.

6. Copland, "Playing Safe at Zurich," 29.

7. Aaron Copland, "Scores and Records," *Modern Music,* March–April 1937, 167–70.

8. Aaron Copland, "Forecast and Review: Baden-Baden, 1927," *Modern Music,* November–December 1927, 33.

9. Aaron Copland, "Contemporaries at Oxford, 1931," *Modern Music,* November–December 1931, 18.

10. "Modern Music at New School," *New York Times,* September 29, 1929, sec. 9, p. 10.

11. Copland, *Our New Music,* 46–47.

12. Copland, *Our New Music,* 49.

13. Copland, *Our New Music,* 49.

14. Copland, *Our New Music,* 51.

15. Copland, *Our New Music,* 47.

16. Copland confirmed this, stating the row "was something like that." Smith, *Aaron Copland,* 99.

17. Pollack, *Aaron Copland,* 138–39.

18. Pollack, *Aaron Copland,* 150.

19. Antokoletz, *Twentieth-Century Music,* 204.

20. Copland and Perlis, *Copland,* 160.

21. Aaron Copland, "What Is Jewish Music?" *New York Herald Tribune,* October 2, 1949, sec. 7, p. 14, cols. 1–3.

22. Copland, "What Is Jewish Music?"

23. Copland, "What Is Jewish Music?"

24. Copland, "What Is Jewish Music?"

25. Copland, "What Is Jewish Music?"

26. Copland and Perlis, *Copland,* 160.

27. Roger Sessions, "An American Evening Abroad," *Modern Music,* November–December 1926, 34.

28. Virgil Thomson, "Aaron Copland (American Composers VII)," *Modern Music,* January– February 1932, 67–68.

29. Thomson, "Copland," 67.

30. Copland, "Composer from Brooklyn," 522–23, 548–50, reprinted in *ASCAP Today* 2 (1968): 4–8.

31. Copland and Perlis, *Copland,* 19.

32. Pollack, *Aaron Copland,* 23–26.

33. Copland as quoted in Pollack, *Aaron Copland,* 26.

34. Karen Mittelman, as quoted in Pollack, *Aaron Copland,* 25.

35. Pollack, *Aaron Copland,* 37.

36. Schaffer to Copland, July 12, 1918, ACC.

37. Schaffer to Copland, February 2, 1919, ACC; Pollack, *Aaron Copland,* 37.

38. Pollack, *Aaron Copland,* 38.

39. Schaffer to Copland, June 30, 1918 or 1919? Schaffer appears to have misdated this letter. It is included among the 1919 letters. ACC.

40. Schaffer to Copland, June 9, 1918, ACC.

41. Pollack, *Aaron Copland,* 27 and 32–33.

42. Hans Nathan, *Folk Songs of the New Palestine, First Series* (New York: Hechalutz and Masada, Young Zionist Organization of America, 1938–39).

43. *Pollack, Aaron Copland,* 328.

44. Pollack, *Aaron Copland,* 27.

45. Copland as quoted in Pollack, *Aaron Copland,* 523.

46. Daniel Gregory Mason, as quoted in Pollack, *Aaron Copland,* 519.

47. Skowronski, *Copland,* 14.

48. Copland and Perlis, *Copland,* 160.

49. Pollack, *Aaron Copland,* 142.

50. Berger, *Aaron Copland,* 39.

51. Smith, *Aaron Copland,* 64.

52. Pollack, *Aaron Copland,* 146.

53. Butterworth, *Music of Aaron Copland,* 45.

54. Butterworth, *Music of Aaron Copland,* 46.

55. Aaron Copland to Nicholas Slonimsky, July 14, 1927, Slonimsky Collection, Music Division, Library of Congress, Washington, D.C.

56. Pollack, *Aaron Copland,* 144.

57. The *lange Gesang* is a folk song genre first extensively studied and described by Béla Bartók during his field studies of folk music. He first heard the genre, an important discovery for Bartók, in the Romanian villages of Komitate Maramures and Ugoesa in 1912. Bartók issued representative examples in "Romanian Folkmusic from Maramures" in 1913. He also found folk song genres of this type in the Ukraine, Algeria, Iran, and Iraq, leading him to the conclusion that these repertoires shared a common eastern ancestry. Bartók identified the *lange Gesang*'s three parts: an initial section partitioned around a single pitch; a richly ornamented middle section, and a recitative-like closing part. The genre has both vocal and instrumental traditions and is linked to Bulgarian, Greek, Albanian, Russian, and French folk music as well. Péter Laki, "Der lange Gesang als Grundtyp in der internationalen Volksmusik," *Studia musicologica* 24, nos. 3–4 (1982): 293.

58. Pollack, *Aaron Copland,* 145.

59. Copland and Perlis, *Copland,* 160.

60. Copland and Perlis, *Copland,* 160.

61. Pollack, *Aaron Copland,* 144 and 379.

62. Copland (Vienna) to Boulanger (Paris), July 23, 1923, ACC.

63. Slonimsky, *Music since 1900,* 238.

64. Copland to Boulanger, July 23, 1923, August 12, 1923, ACC; Copland and Perlis, *Copland,* 90.

65. Copland and Perlis, *Copland,* 160.

CHAPTER SEVEN

1. Copland, "Composer in America, 1923–1933," 91.

2. Copland, "The Musical Scene Changes," 340.

3. This article is the early version of the chapter on radio that appeared in Copland, *Our New Music.*

4. Copland, "The Musical Scene Changes," 341.

5. Copland, *Our New Music,* 142.

6. Elizabeth B. Crist, "Aaron Copland and the Popular Front," *Journal of the American Musicological Society* 56 (Summer 2003): 416ff.; see also her dissertation, "Aaron Copland's Third Symphony (1946): Context, Composition, and Consequence," Ph.D. diss., Yale University, 2000, 88ff.

7. Crist, "Copland and the Popular Front," 410.

8. Aaron Copland. "A Note on Young Composers," *Music Vanguard,* March–April 1935, 15.

9. Copland, "The Musical Scene Changes," 340.

10. Copland, *Our New Music,* 145.

11. Peter Garvie, "Aaron Copland," *Canadian Musician* 6 (1962): 7.

12. Berger, *Aaron Copland,* 27.

13. Copland, "The Musical Scene Changes," 343.

14. For a study of *Gebrauchsmusik* see Stephen Hinton, *The Idea of Gebrauchsmusik: A Study of Musical Aesthetics in the Weimar Republic (1919–1933) with Particular Reference to the Works of Paul Hindemith* (New York: Garland, 1989).

15. Copland, "The Musical Scene Changes," 341.

16. Copland, "The Musical Scene Changes," 341.

17. Copland, "The Musical Scene Changes," 341.

18. Copland, "The Musical Scene Changes," 342.

19. Copland, "The Musical Scene Changes," 341.

20. Copland, "The Musical Scene Changes," 342.

21. In 1970 Copland suggested that film, radio, and the phonograph offered new opportunities to the composer. See Aaron Copland, "An Aaron Copland Photo Album," *HiFi/Musical America,* November 1970, 60.

22. Copland, *The New Music,* 161. Cf. Copland, "Photo Album," 60; and Copland, "Composer from Brooklyn," 522.

23. What Copland listed in the *HiFi/Musical America* article reprinted what appeared in the update to his "Composer from Brooklyn" article, which itself was reprinted in *The New Music 1900–1960,* 160. Cf. Copland, "Photo Album," 60; and Copland, "Composer from Brooklyn," 548–50.

24. Copland, "Contemporaries at Oxford, 1931," 23.

25. Copland, "The Musical Scene Changes," 342.

26. "Aaron Copland," *Musical Events,* February 1962, 19.

27. Skowronski, *Copland,* 16.

28. Copland and Perlis, *Copland,* 237.

CHAPTER EIGHT

1. Copland and Perlis, *Copland,* 184.
2. Copland and Perlis, *Copland,* 171 and 221.
3. Copland and Perlis, *Copland,* 172 and 191.
4. Copland, "The Musical Scene Changes," 343.
5. Much of the following discussion in this section is based on Robbie Lieberman, *My Song Is My Weapon: People's Songs, American Communism, and the Politics of Cultures, 1930–50* (Urbana: University of Illinois Press, 1989); Alexander Bloom, *Prodigal Sons: The New York Intellectuals and Their World* (New York: Oxford University Press, 1986); Michael Denning, *The Cultural Front: The Laboring of American Culture in the Twentieth Century* (London: Verso, 1997); John Patrick Diggins, *The Rise and Fall of the American Left* (New York: W. W. Norton, 1973); and Elizabeth Crist, "Aaron Copland and the Popular Front," *Journal of the American Musicological Society* 56, no. 2 (2003): 409–65.
6. Diggins also identifies an Academic Left, which he sees as a "continuation of the New Left, described as a continuation of the New Left by other means," and active in college classroom and scholarly journals rather than protests and demonstrations. Diggins, *American Left,* 17–20.
7. Diggins, *American Left,* 147–50.
8. Diggins, *American Left,* 45.
9. Bloom, *Prodigal Sons,* 43.
10. Diggins, *American Left,* 84 and 110–11; Lieberman, *My Song Is My Weapon,* xv. See also Arthur Leibman, *Jews and the Left* (New York: John Wiley and Sons, 1979).
11. Lieberman, *My Song Is My Weapon,* xv and 3ff. For more on the American Left and American intellectual history during the 1930s, see Bloom, *Prodigal Sons,* 43ff.
12. Denning, *Cultural Front,* 4, 9, xvi, and xvii.
13. Berger, *Aaron Copland,* 28–29.
14. Pollack, *Aaron Copland,* 186.
15. Arthur Berger, "The Young Composers' Group," *Trend,* April–June 1933, 26. Arthur Berger, "Copland and the Audience of the Thirties," *Partisan Review* 68 (2001): 570.
16. Copland and Perlis, *Copland,* 218.
17. The first generation of writers included Philip Rahv, William Philips, Lionel Trilling, Diana Trilling, Meyer Schapiro, Clement Greenberg, Harold Rosenberg, Dwight Macdonald, Elliott Cohen, and Sidney Hook. The second generation included Irving Howe, Irvin Kristol, Daniel Bell, Delmore Schwartz, Leslie Fielder, Seymour Martin Lipset, Nathan Glazer, Alfred Kazin, Robert Warshaw, Melvin Lasky, Isaac Rosenfeld, and Saul Bellow. Bloom, *Prodigal Sons,* 11ff. and 52; Leibman, *Jews and the Left.*
18. Denning, *Cultural Front,* xix.
19. Crist, "Copland and Popular Front," 415–16.
20. Copland, "Reminiscences," 55.
21. Copland and Perlis, *Copland,* 217.
22. See Stuart Timmons, *The Trouble with Harry Hay: Founder of the Modern Gay Movement* (Boston: Alyson, 1990), 96ff. and 160ff.
23. Denning, *Cultural Front,* 32.
24. Copland and Perlis, *Copland,* 33.

25. Copland, "Reminiscences," 33.

26. Copland and Perlis, *Copland,* 17 and 33; cf. Pollack, *Aaron Copland,* 270–71.

27. Both of Copland's parents were born in Russia. Copland and Perlis, *Copland,* 1ff., 33.

28. Pollack, *Aaron Copland,* 273.

29. Pollack, *Aaron Copland,* 240 and 259; Copland and Perlis, *Copland,* 217–19.

30. Crist, "Copland and the Popular Front," 419 and 421; cf. Denning, *Cultural Front,* 102.

31. Pollack, *Aaron Copland,* 272; Crist, "Copland and the Popular Front," 418; Jennifer DeLapp, "Copland in the Fifties: Music and Ideology in the McCarthy Era," Ph.D. diss., University of Michigan, 1997, 80–82; and Copland and Perlis, *Copland,* 182.

32. Aaron Copland, "The American Composer Gets a Break," *American Mercury,* April 1935, 488–92; Copland, "Note on Young Composers," 14–16; Aaron Copland, "Workers Sing!" *New Masses,* June 5, 1934, 28–29.

33. Copland as quoted in Crist, "Copland and the Popular Front," 422; cf. Copland and Perlis, *Copland,* 229.

34. Pollack, *Aaron Copland,* 277.

35. Copland, "Note on Young Composers," 14.

36. Oja, *Making Music Modern,* 61. Also see her chapters on the critical reception of Edgard Varèse, 25ff.; modern music patrons, 201ff.; and American music criticism of modern music, 297ff.

37. Copland and Perlis, *Copland,* 101.

38. Copland, "Note on Young Composers," 15.

39. Copland, "Note on Young Composers," 16.

40. Copland, "Note on Young Composers," 16.

41. Copland, "Note on Young Composers," 16. N.B.: Copland does not see entrance into commercial music as a solution. This is not entirely due to his politics, however. Kurt Weill—particularly in his collaborations with Bertolt Brecht—wrote for mass media.

42. Pollack, *Aaron Copland,* 273; Copland and Perlis, *Copland,* 192 and 217.

43. Ashley Pettis, "Music," *New Masses,* February 5, 1935, 28.

44. Ashley Pettis, "Music and the Crisis," *New Masses,* March 13, 1934, 28–29.

45. Henry Johnson, "Music: New Recordings," *New Masses,* March 31, 1936, 27.

46. Henry Johnson, "Music Column," *New Masses,* April 14, 1936, 29.

47. Degeyter composed "The Internationale," beloved anthem of the Communist movement around the world.

48. Ann M. Pescatello, *Charles Seeger: A Life in American Music* (Pittsburgh: University of Pittsburgh Press, 1992), 110. See Lieberman, *My Song Is My Weapon;* Carol J. Oja, "Composer with a Conscience: Elie Siegmeister in Profile," *American Music* 6 (Summer 1988): 158–80; Eric A. Gordon, *Mark the Music: The Life and Times of Marc Blitzstein* (New York: St. Martins Press, 1989), 99ff.; Pettis, "Music," 28; Ashley Pettis, "Music: A Music School for Workers," *New Masses,* January 15, 1935, 28.

49. Ashley Pettis, "Second Workers Music Olympiad," *New Masses,* May 22, 1934, 28.

50. "Advertisement for Joint Concert," *New Masses,* February 26, 1935, 26.

51. Ashley Pettis, "Music," *New Masses,* March 6, 1934, 30.

52. Elie Siegmeister, "Musical Life in Soviet Russia," *New Masses,* October 16, 1934, 27–28.

53. Ashley Pettis, "Furtwaengler Resigns," *New Masses,* December 18, 1934, 27.

54. "Advertisement, Downtown Music School (Workers Music School)," *New Masses,* April 9, 1935, 26.

55. Pettis, "Music School for Workers," 28.

56. Tony Clark, "Music: An Interview with Hanns Eisler," *New Masses,* October 15, 1935, 27.

57. Advertisement, "We've Got the Tune, Have You Got the Name?" *New Masses,* January 4, 1938, 27.

58. Copland and Perlis, *Copland,* 233.

59. Copland and Perlis, *Copland,* 223; Pollack, *Aaron Copland,* 273–74.

60. Lieberman, *My Song Is My Weapon,* 28. Pollack asserts that the collective at its height had between sixteen and thirty-four members. Pollack, *Aaron Copland,* 274. In his interview with Carol Oja, Siegmeister identified many members of the group, many of whom used pseudonyms during the 1930s. See Oja, "Composer with a Conscience," 158–80.

61. See Pescatello, *Seeger,* 111.

62. Lieberman, *My Song Is My Weapon,* 29.

63. Oja, "Composer with a Conscience," 165.

64. This group also included Copland, Charles Seeger, Ruth Crawford (Seeger), Cowell, Robinson, Norman Cazden, Blitzstein, Siegmeister, Wallingford Riegger, Herbert Haufrecht, Henry Leland Clarke, Jacob Schaefer, Robert Gross, Alex North. See Pescatello, *Seeger,* 111.

65. Lieberman, *My Song Is My Weapon,* 28. See also Pescatello, *Seeger,* 110.

66. Copland and Perlis, *Copland,* 229–30.

67. Lieberman, *My Song Is My Weapon,* 25.

68. The term "movement culture" is used by Lieberman to describe the outward manifestations of the ideals held by the members of the Left.

69. Lieberman, *My Song Is My Weapon,* xvi.

70. Pettis, "Music and the Crisis," 28–29.

71. Pescatello, *Seeger,* 110.

72. Lieberman, *My Song Is My Weapon,* 29.

73. Lieberman describes mass song style and the music of the Composers' Collective. The collective aimed to supply music for the numerous workers' choruses and other proletarian choral groups. Lieberman, *My Song Is My Weapon,* 29. For more on mass song style, see Carol J. Oja, "Marc Blitzstein's *The Cradle Will Rock* and Mass-Song Style of the 1930s," *Musical Quarterly* 73 (1989): 445–75.

74. Lieberman, *My Song Is My Weapon,* 30.

75. Ashley Pettis wrote a biographical profile of Hanns Eisler in conjunction with an upcoming concert. Ashley Pettis, "Eisler, Maker of Red Songs," *New Masses,* February 26, 1935, 18–19. An article written by Tony Clark on Eisler, published in conjunction with two courses that Eisler was teaching at the New School, also appeared the same year. Clark, "Music," 27.

76. Max Margulis, "Music" *New Masses,* March 5, 1935, 27.

77. Carl Sands, "Copeland's [*sic*] Music Recital at Pierre Degeyter Club," *Daily Worker,* March 22, 1934, p. 5, col. 3. See also Pollack, *Aaron Copland,* 274; Copland and Perlis, *Copland,* 222–23.

78. Charles Seeger's review in *Daily Worker,* as quoted in Pollack, *Aaron Copland,* 274–76.

79. Lieberman, *My Song Is My Weapon,* 29–30.

80. Oja, "Composer with a Conscience," 167.

81. Copland, "Workers Sing!" 28–29.

82. Copland, "Workers Sing!" 28–29.

83. Pescatello, *Seeger,* 110.

84. Copland, "Workers Sing!" 28.

85. Copland, "Into the Streets May First," *New Masses,* May 1, 1934, 16–17.

86. For another analysis of this work see Oja, "Composer with a Conscience," who writes, "Copland's own mass-song style, at least as shown in his setting of the text First of May, published in Workers Song Book 2, tended to be revolutionary in its music as well as its subject matter, especially through the use of bichordal harmonies. Siegmeister took a slightly more conservative route" (168).

87. See Aaron Copland Clippings File, Broughton Tall Collection, Music Division, Library of Congress (hereinafter cited as Broughton Tall Collection); Ashley Pettis, "Singing Workers," *New Masses,* March 20, 1934, 27; Pettis, "Second Workers' Music Olympiad," *New Masses,* May 22, 1934, 29. The entire song was published in the May 1, 1934, issue of *New Masses* and was later reprinted in *Workers' Song Book 2* (1935). Copland, "Into the Streets," 16–17.

88. Seeger, as quoted in Pescatello, *Seeger,* 112.

89. Oja, "Composer with a Conscience," 167.

90. Lieberman, *My Song Is My Weapon,* 29–31 and 39.

91. Lieberman, *My Song Is My Weapon,* 34. The Popular Front was the American version of the People's Front, or United Front; this latter organization was formed in 1937 at the Seventh World Congress of the Communist International to fight fascism.

92. In 1938 the *New Masses* published Roy Gregg's review of a recording of Carl Sandburg. Sandburg performed songs from his *American Song Bag,* singing and accompanying himself on the guitar. See Roy Gregg, "Sandburg, Swing, and Shan-Kar," *New Masses,* January 11, 1938, 29–31; Lieberman, *My Song Is My Weapon,* 39. Pescatello fails to identify the Crawford arrangements. The songs that bear the initials "R.C." were arranged by Ruth Seeger. They are "Those Gamblers Blues," 228, and "Ten Thousand Miles Away From Home," 456. See Carl Sandburg, *The American Song Bag* (1927; reprint, San Diego: Harvest/Harcourt Brace Jovanovich, 1990).

93. Pescatello, *Seeger,* 132ff.

94. For biographies of Aunt Molly Jackson (née Mary Magdalene Garland, 1880–1960), see *The New Grove Dictionary of American Music,* s.v. "Aunt Molly Jackson." See also the October–December 1961 memorial issue of the *Kentucky Folklore Record* devoted entirely to Jackson. It includes a reminiscence by Alan Lomax and a discography by Archie Green. For an article on the authenticity of her version of the Robin Hood ballad, see John Greenway, "Aunt Molly Jackson and Robin Hood: A Study in Folk Re-creation," *Journal of American Folk-lore* 69 (1956): 23–38. Also see Pete Seeger, ed., *Hard Hitting Songs for Hard Hit People: American Folk Songs of the Depression and the Labor Movement of the 1930s* (New York: Oak Publications, 1967).

95. Seeger, as quoted in Pescatello, *Seeger,* 135.

96. See Lieberman, *My Song Is My Weapon,* 36. See also Kenneth J. Bindas, "All of This Music Belongs to the Nation: The Federal Music Project of the WPA and American Cultural Nationalism, 1935–1939." Ph.D. diss., University of Toledo, 1988. This dissertation is also published as *All of This Music Belongs to the Nation: The WPA's Federal Music Project and American Society* (Knoxville: University of Tennessee Press, 1995).

97. Lieberman, *My Song Is My Weapon,* 31.

98. Lieberman, *My Song Is My Weapon,* 39.

99. Elie Siegmeister, as quoted in Oja, "Composer with a Conscience," 167 and 169.

100. Pescatello lists the RA's objectives as "1) to establish an effective land-use program; 2) to resettle destitute low-income families from rural and urban areas and to construct model communities in suburban areas; 3) to offer rural rehabilitation loans and grants to help small farmers purchase land; 4) to move rural populations to new farms and communities." See Pescatello, *Seeger,* 137–38.

101. Seeger as quoted in Pescatello, *Seeger,* 145–46.

102. Denning, *Cultural Front,* 323ff.

103. Lieberman, *My Song Is My Weapon,* 38.

104. Richard Frank, "Negro Revolutionary Music," *New Masses,* May 15, 1934, 29.

105. Frank, "Negro Revolutionary Music," 30.

106. Frank, "Negro Revolutionary Music," 29. As reported in the "Between Ourselves" column. Richard Frank was the pseudonym "of a young native white Southerner who teaches in a Dixie high school. He writes that he has never been out of the South for more than a week. Reading Marx while at college brought him to the Communist position. . . . He is continuing his study of Southern folk-lore."

107. Frank, "Negro Revolutionary Music," 29.

108. Frank, "Negro Revolutionary Music," 29.

109. Frank, "Negro Revolutionary Music," 29.

110. R. D. Darrell, "Native Song," *New Masses,* June 20, 1937, 36.

111. Lawrence Gellert, "Negro Songs of Protest," *New Masses,* March 6, 1934, 30.

112. Lan Adomian, "Black Skin Covern' Po' Workin' Man," *New Masses,* June 23, 1936, 27.

113. Adomian, "Black Skin," 27.

114. Lieberman, *My Song Is My Weapon,* 38.

115. Henry Johnson praised important swing musicians such as Coleman Hawkins, Teddy Wilson, Count Basie, and Benny Goodman. "This genuine and vital music has succeeded in doing many strange things, the most amazing of which is the breaking down of the color line. Although there are not yet any organized black-and-white dance orchestras, there are innumerable places, even in the deep South, where white and colored musicians play together in public after work, defying criticism. Almost any night in Chicago one can find someone like Gene Krupa, Goodman's extraordinary drummer, sitting with a colored band, even Goodman himself plays spasmodically with the orchestra of Fletcher Henderson, who is his chief arranger." Henry Johnson, "Music: The Development of 'Swing,'" *New Masses,* March 3, 1936, 27.

116. Henry Johnson, "Music Column," *New Masses,* April 14, 1936, 29.

117. Johnson, "Music Column," 29.

CHAPTER NINE

1. Lieberman, My *Song Is My Weapon,* 50.

2. Henry Leland Clarke, as quoted in Pescatello, *Seeger,* 117.

3. Berger, *Aaron Copland,* 30.

4. Copland later used *Elegies* (later withdrawn) in *Statements.* Copland and Perlis, *Copland,* 213.

5. Copland, as quoted in Pollack, *Aaron Copland,* 223–24.

6. Copland and Perlis, *Copland,* 218.

7. Crist, "Copland and the Popular Front," 427–29.

8. Pollack, *Aaron Copland,* 217–20.

9. Crist, "Copland and the Popular Front," 427.

10. Crist, "Copland and the Popular Front," 431

11. Crist, "Copland and the Popular Front," 429.

12. Crist, "Copland and the Popular Front," 422–24. She errs in stating that *El Salón México* is the first work in which Copland used folk music. This is not so. He had quoted a folk tune in his 1929 trio *Vitebsk.*

13. Crist, "Copland and the Popular Front," 435.

14. Aaron Copland, "The Story behind *El Salón México,*" *Victor Record Review,* April 1939, 4.

15. Copland and Perlis, *Copland,* 242.

16. Copland, "Story behind *El Salón México,*" 4.

17. Copland, "Story behind *El Salón México,*" 4.

18. See Copland and Perlis, *Copland,* 233ff.; Copland, "Story behind *El Salón México,*" 4. *El Salon México* was later adapted for the film *Fiesta* by Johnny Green. Copland reworked it for concert performances as *Fantasia Mexicana* (*Mexican Fantasy,* 1936) for orchestra. See Skowronski, *Copland,* 15.

19. Copland, Program Notes, Broughton Tall Collection. Frances Toor, *Cancionero Mexicano* (Mexico: Rufino Tamayo, 1931). Toor was an American living in Mexico City. Ruben M. Campos, *El Folk-lore y la Musica Mexicana* (Mexico: La Secretaria de Educacion Publica Talleres Graficos de la Nacion, 1928; reprint, Mexico City: Consejo Nacional para la Cultura y las Artes, 1991).

20. Copland and Perlis, *Copland,* 246.

21. "Al ofrecer esta colección de canciones populares al públic, bien sabemos que es sólo una gota en el ricocaudal que de este género posee México. Sabemos, también, que todos estos corridos, canciones y sones (excepto 'La Vaquilla'), ya son conocidos entre nuestros grupos de cantantes folklóricos y que las canciones revolucionarias, lo son por todo el mundo; pero ni aún éstas, pueden adquirirse por no estar impresas, ni a la venta, en las casas editoras de música." Frances Toor, "Nota de la Editora," *Cancionero Mexicano.* I am indebted to Jerise Fogel for assisting me in this translation.

22. For more on Mexican folk and popular songs, see Bruno Nettl, *Folk and Traditional Music of the Western Continents,* 3rd ed. (Englewood Cliffs, N.J.: Prentice-Hall, 1990), 212ff.; Peter Manuel, *Popular Musics of the Non-Western World* (New York: Oxford University Press, 1988), 52ff.

23. Tullia Magrini, "Aaron Copland: From Practical Music to Unconscious Americanism," *ISME Yearbook* 10 (1983): 137.

24. Copland, "Story behind *El Salón México,*" 5. See also Copland, Program Notes, Broughton Tall Collection; Copland and Perlis, *Copland,* 246.

25. Copland, "Story behind *El Salón México,*" 5. See also Copland, Program Notes, Broughton Tall Collection. See also Copland and Perlis, *Copland,* 245.

26. Copland, Program Notes, Broughton Tall Collection.

27. A Copland triad is a second inversion major triad, voiced to suggest the simultaneous presentation of tonic and dominant. For example, in C major, G would be the bass, which would be heard as a dominant pedal supporting the major third, C-E of the tonic triad.

28. The *sesquialtera* is a proportion used in late medieval Renaissance mensural notation. It marks a change not in tactus, but in the number of subdivisions, from three to two subdivisions. In "El Mosca" three eighths (notated as 6/8) in one measure are played as two eighths in the next measure (notated as 3/4). In this discussion of *El Salón México* the terms *sesquialtera* and *hemiola* will be used as Béhague uses them. See Gerard Béhague, "Latin American Folk Music," in Nettl, *Folk and Traditional Music,* 212.

29. Nettl, *Folk and Traditional Music,* 213.

30. Copland and Perlis, *Copland,* 246.

31. See Berger, *Aaron Copland,* 30 and 32; and Kay, "Copland, All-American Composer," 23.

32. Geoffrey Crankshaw, "Aaron Copland," *Chesterian* 32 (Spring 1958): 99.

33. Zuck, *Musical Americanism,* 8.

34. Crist, "Copland and the Popular Front," 439.

35. Denning, *Cultural Front,* 9; see also 4, 7, 14–20.

36. Copland, "Story behind *El Salón México,*" 4.

37. Aaron Copland, "Mexican Composer," *New York Times,* May 9, 1937, sec. 11, p. 5.

CHAPTER TEN

1. Much of the accepted history of Copland's Americana is in need of revision. Study is currently under way by Elizabeth Crist, who has published articles on Copland in *American Music, JAMS,* and *Journal of Musicology* and is currently working on a book on Copland's Third Symphony. See also Jessica Burr, "Copland, the West and American Identity," in *Copland Connotations: Studies and Interviews,* ed. Peter Dickinson (Woodbridge, Suffolk: Boydell Press, 2002), 22–28; and Beth Ellen Levy, "Frontier Figures: American Music and the Mythology of the American West, 1895–1945," Ph.D. diss., University of California, Berkeley, 2002.

2. This is Lincoln Kirstein's manifesto on American ballet, *Blast at Ballet* (New York: Martin Press, 1938), 11, 46ff., and 310.

3. Kirstein, *Blast at Ballet,* 94.

4. Kirstein, *Blast at Ballet,* 101–2.

5. Kirstein placed himself in the company of prominent and talented Americans creating American ballet works, such as Catherine Littlefield or Ruth Page in Chicago. He pointed out the presence of American ballet companies in San Francisco, Portland, Seattle, Los Angeles, Pittsburgh, Washington, Boston, Baltimore, Newark, and Detroit, healthy signs of the American ballet. For a summary of the ballet's plot, see Pollack, *Aaron Copland,* 314.

6. Kirstein, *Blast at Ballet,* 40ff. Kirstein wanted to create a small company that could be augmented later. This troupe gave their first performance in July 1936 in Bennington, Vermont, and made its first transcontinental tour during the 1938–39 season.

7. Kirstein, *Blast at Ballet,* 42–43.

8. Pollack, *Aaron Copland*, 315–16.

9. Kirstein, *Blast at Ballet*, 46. Kirstein also writes, "The American subject-matter gave me a lot of thought. I had only a small company, so that anything involving pictorial pageantry was out of the question. Trial and error had showed me the danger of competing with the Russians on any ground at all upon which they might choose to perform. Finally, there must be no Spanish, Russian or Italian manual pantomime or character-dancing. We needed something with which they would seem familiar to our hoped-for audiences, something with which they could feel at home, and yet something in which our specifically American-styled dancers could be shown to their best advantage. The familiarity of our subject-matter must never duplicate the familiarity of the Russian formula. The American classic style should never be dulled by a veneer of Russian glamour." Kirstein, *Blast at Ballet*, 43.

10. Copland and Perlis, *Copland*, 280. See also Berger, *Aaron Copland*, 27. Smith and Butterworth also consider this work to be both quintessentially American and Americana, and completely ignore its genesis as a collaborative effort.

11. Copland and Perlis, *Copland*, 284.

12. Copland and Perlis, *Copland*, 278.

13. Copland and Perlis, *Copland*, 237.

14. All musical examples and references refer to the published score of the *Billy the Kid Suite* unless otherwise indicated.

15. These sketches also open a line for future investigation: Copland's recycling of material and self-borrowings. I am presently undertaking a study of another yet unnoticed instance of Copland's self-borrowing. It is well documented that Copland rescored orchestral works for band and two-hand piano, made suites of his ballets, and reworked film scores as concert works. Both Pollack and Daniel Mathers have further shown that Copland self-borrowed as well as salvaged material for an abandoned work and incorporated this material into a new piece. Pollack provides an extensive list of Copland's self-borrowings and recyclings in *Aaron Copland*, 11, 566 n. 25.

16. Copland and Perlis, *Copland*, 271.

17. John White and George Shackley, compilers, *The Lonesome Cowboy: Songs of the Plains and Hills* (New York; G. T. Worth, 1930); Ina Sires, ed., *Songs of the Open Range* (Boston: C. C. Birchard, 1928); Carl Sandburg, ed., *The American Song Bag* (New York: Harcourt, Brace, 1927). See also Pollack, *Aaron Copland*, 320.

18. Copland and Perlis, *Copland*, 284.

19. Pollack, *Aaron Copland*, 628 n.16.

20. Copland and Perlis, *Copland*, 278.

21. John A. Lomax and Alan Lomax, *American Ballads and Folk Songs* (New York: Macmillan, 1934; reprint, New York: Dover, 1994), 383–87. The earlier collection is John A. Lomax, *Cowboy Songs and Frontier Ballads* (New York: Macmillan, 1910). Other collections Copland used also contained variants of this tune. Sandburg, *American Song Bag*, 268. See "Dogie song (Whoopee Ti Yi Yi! Git Along Little Dogies!)," Sires, *Songs of the Open Range*, 44.

22. John A. Lomax published his large collection *Cowboy Songs and Frontier Ballads* in 1910. Jerrold Hirsch notes that Lomax gave little attention to African-American and Mexican cowboy songs in this collection. Jerrold Hirsch, "Modernity, Nostalgia, and Southern Folklore Studies: The Case of John Lomax," *Journal of American Folklore* 105 (Spring 1992): 189.

23. Peter Stanfield, *Horse Opera: The Strange History of the 1930s Singing Cowboy* (Urbana: University of Illinois Press, 2002), 63–65.

24. For a history of the Hollywood film Western, see Scott Simmon, *The Invention of the Western Film: A Cultural History of the Genre's First Half-Century* (Cambridge: Cambridge University Press, 2003); John H. Lenihan, *Showdown: Confronting Modern America in the Western Film* (Urbana: University of Illinois Press, 1980); Peter Stanfield, *Hollywood, Westerns and the 1930s: The Lost Trail* (Exeter: University of Exeter Press, 2001); Will Wright, *Six Guns and Society: A Structural Study of the Western* (Berkeley and Los Angeles: University of California Press, 1975); R. Philip Loy, *Westerns and American Culture, 1930–1955* (Jefferson, N.C.: McFarland, 2001); David Lusted, *The Western* (Harlow, England: Pearson Longman, 2003); and, Andrew Brodie Smith, *Shooting Cowboys and Indians: Silent Westerns, American Culture, and the Birth of Hollywood* (Boulder: University Press of Colorado, 2003).

25. Magrini, "Aaron Copland," 139.

26. See Mark Fenster, "Preparing the Audience, Informing the Performers? John A. Lomax and *Cowboy Songs and Other Frontier Ballads*," *American Music* 7 (Fall 1989): 260–77.

27. See Bill C. Malone, *Country Music, U.S.A.*, rev. ed. (Austin: University of Texas Press, 1985), 137ff. See also Stanfield, *Horse Opera;* and Douglas B. Green, *Singing in the Saddle: The History of the Singing Cowboy* (Nashville: Country Music Foundation Press and Vanderbilt University Press, 2002).

28. Benjamin Filene, "'Our Singing Country': John and Alan Lomax, Leadbelly, and the Construction of an American Past," *American Quarterly* 34 (December 1991): 607.

29. Hirsch, "John Lomax," 185, 186.

30. Hirsch, "John Lomax," 190.

31. See Loy, *Westerns and American Cultures,* chap. 8, "A White Range" and chap. 9, "'These Indians Not Such Bad People'"; Lenihan, *Showdown,* chap. 4, "Racial Attitudes." See also Stanfield, *Horse Opera,* 19; Lusted, *Western,* 35.

32. Denning, *Cultural Front,* 259.

33. Denning, *Cultural Front,* 262.

34. Denning, *Cultural Front,* 267.

35. Levy, "Frontier Figures," 129.

36. Copland, as quoted in Burr, "Copland," 23.

37. Levy, "Frontier Figures," 222–23.

38. Levy, "Frontier Figures," 223.

39. Turner, as quoted in Levy, "Frontier Figures," 11.

40. Stanfield, *Hollywood, Westerns.*

41. William C. King, "New York Composers in the News—a Talk with the Busy Aaron Copland," ca. 1941, Clippings File, Broughton Tall Collection.

42. Copland and Perlis, *Copland,* 279.

43. Copland and Perlis, *Copland,* 279.

44. Copland and Perlis, *Copland,* 280.

45. Copland and Perlis, *Copland,* 280.

46. Copland and Perlis, *Copland,* 247.

47. Although Copland does not mention either Chávez or Revueltas as a direct model, future research on Copland may show an influence, for at the time that American composers were trying to create an American music, Mexican artists and composers were engaged in a similar movement, the Aztec Renaissance.

Bibliography

PRIMARY SOURCES

ARCHIVES

Music Division, New York Public Library, New York, N.Y.
Aaron Copland Collection
Composers Forum Archive
Fontainebleau Collection
Fontainebleau File
Otto Luening Collection

Music Division, Library of Congress, Washington, D.C.
Aaron Copland Collection
Broughton Tall Collection
Koussevitzky Archive
Modern Music Archive
Nicholas Slonimsky Collection
William Treat Upton Collection

American Composers Alliance Archive, American Composers Alliance, New York, N.Y.

American Music Center Archives, American Music Center, New York, N.Y.

William Grant Still–Verna Arvey Papers, Special Collections Division, University Library, University of Arkansas, Fayetteville, Arkansas.

ARTICLES BY AARON COPLAND

"Active Market in New Music Records." *Modern Music,* January–February 1936, 45–47.

"The Aims of Music for Films." *New York Times,* March 10, 1940, sec. 11, p. 7, cols. 4–6.

"America's Young Men of Music." *Music and Musicians* 2 (December 1960): 11, 33.

"America's Young Men of Promise." *Modern Music,* March 1926, 13–20.

"The American Composer Gets a Break." *American Mercury,* April 1935, 488–92.

"The American Composer Today." *U.S.A.* (War Information Office) 2 (1945): 23–27.

"The Art of Darius Milhaud." *Saturday Review,* June 26, 1948, 43.

"A Businessman Who Wrote Music on Sundays." *Modern Music,* November 1960, 18.

"Carlos Chávez—Mexican Composer." In *American Composers on American*

Music: A Symposium, ed. Henry Cowell. Stanford: Stanford University Press, 1933.
"Carlos Chávez—Mexican Composer." *New Republic*, May 2, 1928, 322–23.
"Claire Reis (1889–1978)." *Musical Quarterly* 64 (July 1978): 386–88.
"Composer and Composing." *Saturday Review*, August 27, 1960, 33–35.
"The Composer and His Critic." *Modern Music*, May–June 1932, 143–47.
"The Composer and His Critic." *Perspectives of New Music* 2 (1964): 22–23.
"Composer from Brooklyn." *Magazine of Art*, September 1939, 522–23, 548–50.
"Composer from Brooklyn: An Autobiographical Sketch." *ASCAP Today* 2 (1968): 4–8.
"The Composer in America, 1923–1933." *Modern Music*, January–February 1933, 87–92.
"The Composers Get Wise." *Modern Music*, November–December 1940, 18–21.
"The Composers of South America." *Modern Music*, January–February 1942, 75–82.
"Contemporaries at Oxford, 1931." *Modern Music*, November–December 1931, 17–23.
"The Contemporary Scene: Excerpt from Address, May, 1966." *Saturday Review*, June 25, 1966, 49.
"Copyright Revision and the U. S. Symphonic Composer." *ASCAP Today* 7 (1975): 9.
"Current Chronicle: United States: New York." *Musical Quarterly* 37 (July 1951): 394–96.
"The Dilemma of Our Symphony Orchestras." *Musical Courier*, November 1, 1956, 6, 39.
"Fantasy for Piano: Composer Explains Its Particular Problems." *Tempo* 46 (1958): 13–14.
"Five Post-Romantics." *Modern Music*, May–June 1941, 218–24.
"Forecast and Review: Baden-Baden, 1927." *Modern Music*, November–December, 31–34.
"From A Composer's Notebook." *Modern Music*, May–June 1929, 15–19.
"From the '20's to the '40's and Beyond." *Modern Music*, January–February 1943, 78–82.
"Gabriel Fauré: A Neglected Master." *Musical Quarterly* 10 (October 1924): 573–86.
"George Antheil." *League of Composers' Review (Modern Music)*, January 1925, 26–28.
"The Gifted Listener." *Saturday Review*, September 27, 1952, 41–44, 57.
"An Indictment of the Fourth B." *Music Journal* 10 (November 1952): 13, 30–33.
"Influence, Problem, Tone." *Dance Index* 6 (1947): 249.
"Into the Streets May First." *New Masses*, May 1, 1934, 16–17.
"Jazz Structure and Influence." *Modern Music*, January–February 1927, 9–14.
"Letter on Gustav Mahler." *New York Times*, April 5, 1925, sec. 9, p. 6, cols. 1–2.
"The Lyricism of Milhaud." *Modern Music*, January–February 1929, 14–19.
"Making Music in the Star-Spangled Manner." *Music and Musicians* 8 (August 1960): 8–9.
"The Measure of Kapell." *Saturday Review*, November 28, 1953, 67.
"Memorial to Paul Rosenfeld." *Notes*, 2nd ser. 4 (March 1947): 147–48.

"Mexican Composer—Silvestre Revueltas." *New York Times,* May 9, 1937, sec. 11, p. 5, cols. 2–3.
"Modern Music Fresh and Different: Reply to Henry Pleasants." *New York Times Magazine,* March 13, 1955, sec. 6, pp. 15, 60, 62.
"Modern Orchestration Surveyed by Wellesz." *Modern Music,* November–December 1930, 41.
"A Modernist Defends Modern Music." *New York Times,* December 25, 1949, sec. 6, pp. 11, 30–31.
"Music: As an Aspect of the Human Spirit." *Musical Courier,* February 1, 1955, 54–56.
"Music since 1920." *Modern Music,* March–April 1928, 16–20.
"The Musical Scene Changes." *Twice a Year* 5–7 (1940–41): 340–43.
"Nadia Boulanger: An Affectionate Portrait." *Harpers,* October 1960, 49–51.
"Neglected Works: A Symposium." *Modern Music* 23 (Winter 1946): 3–12.
"The New 'School' of American Composers." *New York Times Magazine,* March 14, 1948, 18, 51–54.
"A Note on Young Composers." *Music Vanguard,* March–April 1935, 14–16.
"On Composing Music Scores for Films." *New York Times,* June 23, 1940, sec. 9, p. 3, cols. 3–4.
"On the Notation of Rhythm." *Modern Music,* May–June 1944, 217–20.
"One Hundred and Fourteen Songs." *Modern Music,* January–February 1934, 59–64.
"Our Younger Generation—Ten Years Later." *Modern Music,* May–June 1936, 3–11.
"The Personality of Stravinsky." In *Igor Stravinsky,* ed. Edwin Corle. New York: Duell, Sloan and Pearce, 1949.
"Pioneer Listener." *New Republic,* April 15, 1936, 291–92.
"Playing Safe at Zurich." *Modern Music,* November–December 1926, 28–29.
"Problemes de la Musique de Film." *Vie Music* 1 (March 1951): 5–6.
"A Quarter-Century Reflection." *American Composers Alliance* 11 (1963): 1.
"Rubin Goldmark: A Tribute." *Julliard Review* 3 (Fall 1956): 15–16.
"Scherchen on Conducting and Ewen on Composers." *Modern Music,* January–February, 1935, 94–96.
"Scores and Records." *Modern Music,* November–December 1936, 39–42.
"Scores and Records." *Modern Music,* January–February 1937, 98–101.
"Scores and Records." *Modern Music,* November–December 1937, 45–48.
"Scores and Records." *Modern Music,* March–April 1937, 167–70.
"Second Thoughts on Hollywood." *Modern Music,* March–April 1940, 141–47.
"Serge Koussevitsky and the American Composer." *Musical Quarterly* 30 (July 1944): 255–69.
"Some Notes on My 'Music for the Theatre.'" *Victor Record Review,* March 1941, 6.
"South American Report." *New York Times,* December 21, 1947, sec. 2, p. 9, cols. 3–7.
"The Story behind *El Salón México.*" *Victor Record Review,* April 1939, 4–5.
"Stravinsky and Hindemith Premiers." *Modern Music,* January–February 1932, 85–88.
"Stravinsky's 'Oedipus Rex.'" *New Republic,* February 29, 1928, 68–69.
"Thomson's Musical State." Book review. *Modern Music,* October–November 1939, 63–65.

"Tips to Moviegoers: Take Off Their Ear-Muffs." *New York Times,* November 6, 1949, sec. 6, pp. 28–32.
"The Twentieth Century: Reorientation and Experiment." In *Music and Western Man: The Canadian Broadcasting Corporation,* ed. Peter Garvie. New York: Philosophical Library, 1958.
"What Is Jewish Music?" *New York Herald Tribune,* October 2, 1949, sec. 7, p. 14, cols. 1–3.
"When Private and Public Worlds Meet." *New York Times,* June 9, 1968, sec. 2, p. 17, cols. 1–4.
"Workers Sing!" *New Masses,* June 5, 1934, 28–29.
"World of the Phonograph." *American Scholar* 6 (1937): 23–37.

BOOKS BY AARON COPLAND

Copland on Music. Garden City, New York: Doubleday, 1960.
Music and Imagination. Cambridge: Harvard University Press, 1952.
The New Music 1900–1960. Rev. ed. New York: W. W. Norton, 1968.
Our New Music. New York: Whittlesey House, 1941.
The Pleasures of Music. Address at the University of New Hampshire, April 16, 1959. Published by the University of New Hampshire, July 1959.
What to Listen for In Music. New York: McGraw-Hill, 1939; reprint: New York: Mentor/Penguin, 1988.

BOOKS BY AARON COPLAND AND VIVIAN PERLIS

Copland: 1900 through 1942. New York: St. Martins/Marek, 1984.
Copland: since 1943. New York: St. Martin's Press, 1989.

INTERVIEWS AND ORAL HISTORIES

"Nationalism New World Style." Unpublished Paper, Composers' Seminar. Transcript, January 24, 1977, Oral History Project in American Music, Yale University.
Copland, Aaron. "The Reminiscences of Aaron Copland." Interview by Vivian Perlis, December 23, 1975–December 8, 1976, Peekskill, New York, Oral History Transcript. American Music Series, Yale University and Oral History Research Office, Columbia University 1977.

DISCOGRAPHY

Copland: The Complete Works for Solo Piano. Leo Smit, piano. Sony Classical SM2K 66 345. 1994.
Copland: Grohg/Hear Ye! Hear Ye! London Sinfonietta conducted by Oliver Knussen. Argo 443-203-2. 1994.
Gershwin: The Birth of Rhapsody in Blue/Paul Whiteman's Historic Aeolian Hall Concert of 1924. Reconstructed and conducted by Maurice Peress. Music Masters Jazz 01612-65144-2. 1986.
Smithsonian Collection of Classic Jazz. Rev. ed. Smithsonian Recordings, 1987.

VIDEOGRAPHY

Vivian Perlis and Ruth Leon (producers). *Aaron Copland: A Self-Portrait.* Films for the Humanities, 1985. Videotape.

PUBLICATIONS BY OTHERS

"An Aaron Copland Photo Album." *HiFi/Musical America,* November 1970, 60.

Advertisement, "All Musical Evening; concert sponsored by The New Masses Lecture Bureau at Washington Irving High School, Thursday, February 15, 1934." *New Masses,* Advertisements for "All Musical Evening" concert sponsored by The New Masses Lecture Bureau at Washington Irving High School. Thursday, February 15, 1934. *New Masses* 10 (1934): 2.

Advertisement, "Downtown Music School (Workers Music School)." *New Masses,* April 9, 1935, 26.

Advertisement, "We've Got the Tune, Have You Got the Name?" *New Masses,* January 4, 1938, 27.

"Advertisement for Joint Concert." *New Masses,* February 26, 1935, 26.

"All-American on the Air." *Modern Music,* May–June 1932, 176.

Adomian, Lan. "Black Skin Covern' Po' Workin' Man." *New Masses,* June 23, 1936, 27.

American Family Immigration History Center website, www.Ellisisland.org, accessed May 25, 2004.

Balaban, Emanuel. "Progress at Rochester." *Modern Music,* May–June 1932, 182–84.

Bauer, Marion, and Claire R. Reis. "Twenty-Five Years with the League of Composers." *Musical Quarterly* 34 (January 1948): 1–14.

Becker, John J. "Imitative versus Creative Music in America." In *American Composers on American Music,* ed. Henry Cowell. Stanford University Press, 1933; reprint, New York: Frederick Unger, 1961.

Berger, Arthur. "Stravinsky and the Younger American Composers." *Score and I.M.A. Magazine,* June 1955, 38–46.

———. "The Young Composers' Group." *Trend,* April–June 1933, 26–28.

Blitzstein, Marc. "Forecast and Review: New York Medley, Winter, 1935." *Modern Music,* January–February 1936, 34–47.

———. "New York Medley, Winter, 1935." *Modern Music,* January–February 1936, 34–40.

Braithwaite, S. H. "Modern Music." *Musical Quarterly* 13 (January 1927): 59–71.

Bulletin of the Eleventh Annual Eastman School Festival of American Music. Rochester, N.Y.: Eastman School of Music of the University of Rochester, 1941.

Burnshaw, Stanley. "What Happened to Stravinsky?" *New Masses,* November 13, 1934, 29.

Busoni, Ferruccio. *Sketch of a New Esthetic of Music* (1907). In *Music in the Western World: A History in Documents,* ed. Piero Weiss and Richard Taruskin. New York: Schirmer Books, 1984.

Butting, Max. "Music of and for the Radio." *Modern Music,* March–April 1931, 15–19.

Campos, Ruben M. *El Folk-lore y la Musica Mexicana.* Mexico City: La

Secretaria de Educacion Publica Talleres Graficos de la Nacion, 1928; reprint, Mexico City: Consejo Nacional para la Cultura y las Artes, 1991.
Carter, Elliott. "The Rhythmic Basis of American Music." *Score and I.M.A. Magazine,* June 1955, 27–32.
———. "Vacation Novelties, New York." *Modern Music,* January–February 1938, 96–103.
Chase, Gilbert, ed. *Music in Radio Broadcasting.* New York: McGraw-Hill, 1946.
Chotzinoff, Samuel. "Music in Radio." In *Music in Radio Broadcasting,* ed. Gilbert Chase. New York: McGraw-Hill, 1946.
Clark, Tony. "Music: An Interview with Hanns Eisler." *New Masses,* October 15, 1935, 27.
Cocteau, Jean. *Cock and Harlequin: Notes Concerning Music.* Trans. Rollo H. Myers. London: Egoist Press, 1921.
"The Composers Organize: A Proclamation." *Modern Music,* January–February 1938, 92–95.
Cone, Edward T. "Conversation with Aaron Copland." *Perspectives of New Music* 6 (1968): 64.
Cowell, Henry, ed. *American Composers on American Music.* Stanford: Stanford University Press, 1933; reprint: New York: Frederick Ungar, 1961.
———. "The Flavour of American Music." *Score and I.M.A. Magazine,* June 1955, 5–8.
———. "Music: Soviet Music Published Here." *New Masses,* November 20, 1934, 28–29.
———. "The Music of Edgar Varèse." *Modern Music,* January–February 1928, 9–18.
———. "Music of and for the Records." *Modern Music,* March–April 1931, 32–34.
———. "New Terms for New Music." *Modern Music,* May–June 1928, 21–28.
Cowley, Malcolm. *Exile's Return: A Literary Odyssey of the 1920s.* 1934; reprint, New York: Penguin, 1979.
Darrell, R. D. "Native Song." *New Masses,* June 20, 1937, 36.
de Schloezer, Boris. "Man, Music and the Machine." *Modern Music,* March–April 1931, 3–9.
Diamond, David. "Premiere in Rochester: Rogers' Frescos." *Modern Music,* January–February 1936, 41–43.
Downes, Olin. "American Composers and Critics: The Daily Review versus the Weekly Essay—the Native Writer's Opportunities and Merits." *New York Times,* May 8, 1932, sec. 8, p. 6.
Dykema, Peter W. *Music as Presented Bb the Radio.* New York: Radio Institute of the Audible Arts, 1935.
Ehrenbourg, Ilya. "Culture and Fascism." *New Masses,* May 29, 1934, 21–24.
Ellis, Peter. "Soviet Musical Satire." *New Masses,* December 25, 1934, 29.
———. "Three Songs about Lenin." *New Masses,* November 20, 1934, 30.
Ewen, David. "The Growth of Radio Music." In *The Music Lover's Handbook,* ed. Elie Siegmeister. New York: William Morrow, 1943.
Finck, Henry T. "What Is American Music?" *Etude* 24 (1906): 356–57.
Finkelstein, Sidney. "Aaron Copland and American Music." *Masses and Mainstream* 7 (March 1954): 50–56.
Foote, Arthur, and Walter R. Spaulding. *Modern Harmony in Its Theory and Practice.* Boston: Arthur P. Schmidt, 1905.

Frank, Richard. "Negro Revolutionary Music." *New Masses,* May 15, 1934, 29.
Gellert, Lawrence. "Negro Songs of Protest." *New Masses,* March 6, 1934, 30.
Gold, Don. "Aaron Copland; the Well-known American Composer Finds Virtues and Flaws in Jazz." *Down Beat,* May 1, 1958, 16, 39–40.
Gold, Michael. "Strike! A Mass Recitation." *New Masses,* July 1926, 19–20.
Goldman, Richard F. "A New Day for Band Music." *Modern Music,* Fall 1946, 261–65.
Graubard, Mark. "The Artist and the Revolutionary Movement." *New Masses,* July 31, 1934, 24.
Gregg, Roy. "Sandburg, Swing, and Shan-Kar." *New Masses,* January 11, 1938, 29–31.
Gruenberg, Louis. "For an American Gesture." *League of Composers Review* [*Modern Music*], June 1924, 26–28.
Hadow, W. H. "Some Aspects of Modern Music." *Musical Quarterly* 1 (January 1915): 57–68.
Hammond, Richard. "Forecast and Review." *Modern Music,* March–April 1931, 35–38.
Hanson, Howard. "American Procession at Rochester." *Modern Music,* March–April 1936, 22–28.
Hayes, Alfred. "Into the Streets May 1st." *New Masses,* May 1, 1934, 16–17.
Heyman, Katherine Ruth. *The Relation of Ultramodern to Archaic Music.* Boston: Small, Maynard, 1921.
Huggins, Nathan Irving. *Harlem Renaissance.* London: Oxford University Press, 1971.
J.L. "New School Symposium." *New Masses,* November 6, 1934, 28.
Johnson, Henry. "Music: New Recordings." *New Masses,* March 31, 1936, 27.
———. "Music: The Development of 'Swing.'" *New Masses,* March 3, 1936, 27.
———. "Music Column." *New Masses,* April 14, 1936, 29.
Kaufman, Schima. "Aaron Copland: Music for Radio." In *The Music Lover's Handbook,* ed. Elie Siegmeister. New York: William Morrow, 1943.
Kirstein, Lincoln. *Blast at Ballet.* New York: Martin Press, 1938.
———. *Mosaic: Memoirs.* New York: Farrar, Straus and Giroux, 1994.
Kolodin, Irving. "American Composers and the Phonograph." *Modern Music,* March–April 1934, 128–37.
Krenek, Ernst. *Music Here and Now.* Trans. Barthold Fies. New York: W. W. Norton, 1939.
Lederman, Minna. *The Life and Death of a Small Magazine (Modern Music, 1924–1946).* Institute for Studies in American Music Monographs no. 18. Brooklyn: Conservatory of Music—Brooklyn College of the City of New York, 1983.
Lieberson, Goddard. "Over the Air." *Modern Music,* May–June 1937, 241–42.
———. "Over the Air." *Modern Music,* November–December 1937, 53.
Lomax, John A. *Cowboy Songs and Frontier Ballads.* New York: Macmillan, 1910.
Lomax, John A., and Alan Lomax. *American Ballads and Folk Songs.* New York: Macmillan, 1934; reprint, New York: Dover, 1994.
Manual, Roland. "Ravel and the New French School." *Modern Music,* January 1925, 17–23.
Margetson, Edward. "Folk Music and Nationalism." *Southern Workman* 56 (November 1927): 487–92.

Margulis, Max. "Music." *New Masses,* March 5, 1935, 27.
Meyer, Alfred. "Yaddo—a May Festival." *Modern Music,* May–June 1932, 172–76.
Milhaud, Darius. *Notes without Music.* Trans. Donald Evans and ed. Rollo H. Myers. London: Dennis Dobson, 1952.
"Modern Music at New School." *New York Times,* September 29, 1929, sec. 9, p.10.
Moton, Robert Russa. "A Universal Language." *Southern Workman* 56 (August 1927): 349–51.
Nathan, Hans, comp. *Folk Songs of the New Palestine, First Series.* New York: Hechalutz and Masada, Young Zionist Organization of America, 1938–39.
Nettl, Paul. "Immigration and American Music." *American-German Review* 9 (December 1942): 6–8, 34.
Osgood, Henry O. *So This Is Jazz.* Boston: Little, Brown, 1926; reprint: New York: Da Capo Press, 1978.
"Palace of Fontainebleau French High School of Musical Studies" (École des Hautes Etudes Musicales de France/Conservatoire Americain). Booklet. Melun: Imprimerie Administrative, 1921.
Patterson, Frank. "American Music." *Franco-American Musical Society Quarterly Bulletin* 6 (1925):11–20.
Pettis, Ashley. "Eisler, Maker of Red Songs." *New Masses,* February 26, 1935, 18–19.
———. "Furtwaengler Resigns." *New Masses,* December 18, 1934, 27.
———. "Marching with a Song." *New Masses,* May 1, 1934, 15–17.
———. "Modern Music: A Dead Art." *New York Times Magazine,* March 13, 1955, sec. 6, pp. 14, 57, 59.
———. "Music." *New Masses,* March 6, 1934, 30.
———. "Music." *New Masses,* February 5, 1935, 28.
———. "Music: A Music School for Workers." *New Masses,* January 15, 1935, 28.
———. "Music: Cosmopolitan Opera." *New Masses,* October 30, 1934, 28–29.
———. "Music: Salomé—Restored." *New Masses,* February 6, 1934, 29.
———. "Music: The First Philharmonic Concert." *New Masses,* October 23, 1934, 28.
———. "Music: The Philharmonic's Varied Course." *New Masses,* December 4, 1934, 27.
———. "Music: Verboten." *New Masses,* April 10, 1934, 18–19.
———. "Music and the Crisis." *New Masses,* March 6, 1934, 28–29.
———. "Second Workers Music Olympiad." *New Masses,* May 22, 1934, 28–29.
———. "Singing Workers." *New Masses,* March 20, 1934, 27.
Pynn, N. A. "American Music? What of It, and Why Not?" *Musician* 41 (1936): 170–79.
R.C.B. "Novelties at Modernist Concert Range from Atonality to Sophisticated Jazz." *Musical America,* January 30, 1926, 4, 23.
Reis, Claire. *American Composers of Today.* New York: International Society for Contemporary Music, U.S. Section, 1930.
———. *Composers, Conductors and Critics.* New York: Oxford University Press, 1955; reprint, Detroit: Detroit Reprints in Music, 1974.
———. *Composers in America.* Rev. ed. New York: MacMillan, 1947.

Rogers, Bernard. "Rochester's American Series." *Modern Music,* May–June 1931, 38–42.

Roldan, Amadeo. "The Artistic Position of the American Composer." In *American Composers on American Music,* ed. Henry Cowell. Stanford: Stanford University Press, 1933; reprint, New York: Frederick Ungar, 1961.

Rosenfeld, Paul. "'Americanism' in American Music." *Modern Music,* May–June 1940, 226–32.

———. "Musical Chronicle." *The Dial,* March 1925, 258–59.

———. *Musical Chronicle (1917–1923).* New York, Harcourt, Brace, 1923.

Rosenstiel, Léonie. *Nadia Boulanger: A Life in Music.* New York: W. W. Norton, 1982.

Rosenwald, Hans. "Contemporary Music." *Music News* 43 (January 1951, 7–8.

Russolo, Luigi. "The Art of Noises" (1913). In *Music in the Western World: A History in Documents,* ed. Piero Weiss and Richard Taruskin. New York: Schirmer Books, 1984.

Sandburg, Carl. *The American Song Bag.* New York: Harcourt, Brace, 1927; reprint, San Diego: Harvest/Harcourt Brace Jovanovich, 1990.

Sands, Carl [Charles Seeger]. "Copeland's [*sic*] Music Recital at Pierre Degeyter Club." *Daily Worker,* March 22, 1934, p. 5, col. 3.

Saunders, William. "The American Opera: Has It Arrived?" *Music and Letters* 13 (1932): 147–55.

Schillinger, Joseph. "Electricity, a Musical Liberator." *Modern Music,* March–April 1931, 26–31.

Seeger, Pete, ed. *Hard Hitting Songs for Hard Hit People: American Folk Songs of the Depression and the Labor Movement of the 1930s.* New York: Oak Publications, 1967.

Seldes, Gilbert. "An Open Letter to Roxy." *Modern Music,* November–December 1932, 3–9.

Sessions, Roger. "An American Evening Abroad." *Modern Music,* November–December 1926, 34.

———. "American Music and the Crisis." *Modern Music,* May–June 1941, 211–17.

———. "Our Attitudes Towards Contemporary Musical Tendencies." *Harvard Musical Review* 2 (January 1914): 3–6, 23.

Siegmeister, Elie. "Musical Life in Soviet Russia." *New Masses,* October 16, 1934, 27–28.

Sires, Ina, ed. *Songs of the Open Range.* Boston: C. C. Birchard, 1928.

Smith, Cecil Michener. "Over the Air." *Modern Music,* May–June 1937, 53.

Smith, Wilson G. "American Composition." *American Art Journal* 47 (1887): 212–14.

Songs of the American West. Ed. Richard E. Lingenfelter, Richard A. Dwyer, and David Cohen. Berkeley and Los Angeles: University of California Press, 1968.

Still, William Grant. "The Music of My Race." Translation of "La Musica de Mi Raza." In "The William Grant Still Reader: Essays on American Music," ed. Jon Michael Spencer, special issue of *Black Sacred Music* 6 (Fall 1992): 102–4.

Still, William Grant, and Verna Arvey. "Negro Music in the Americas." *Revue Internationale de Musique* (Brussels) 1 (May–June 1938): 283.

Taylor, Davidson. "Long Range Policy for Radio." *Modern Music,* January–February 1939, 94–98.

———. "To Order, for Radio." *Modern Music,* November–December 1936, 12–17.

———. "Why Not Try the Air?" *Modern Music,* January–February 1938, 86–91.

Thompson, Randall. "The Contemporary Scene in American Music." *Musical Quarterly* 18 (1932): 9–17.

Thomson, Virgil. "Aaron Copland." *Modern Music,* January–February 1932, 67–73.

———. "Aaron Copland (American Composers VII)." *Modern Music,* January–February 1932, 67–73.

———. *The State of Music.* New York: William Morrow, 1939.

Toor, Frances. *Cancionero Mexicano.* Mexico City: Rufino Tamayo, 1931.

Van Vechten, Carl. *Letters of Carl Van Vechten.* Ed. Bruce Kellner. New Haven: Yale University Press, 1987.

Wellesz, Egon. "Problems of Modern Music." *Musical Quarterly* 10 (January 1924): 1–12.

Weyl, Charles. "The Orchestra on the Air." *Modern Music,* March–April 1931, 20–24.

White, John, and George Shackley, comps. *The Lonesome Cowboy: Songs of the Plains and Hills.* New York: G.T. Worth, 1930.

Whiteman, Paul. *Jazz.* New York: J. H. Sears, 1926.

Wilson, Mortimer. "A Talk about the Making of American Composers." *Musical Courier* 76, no. 13 (1918): 38–39.

SECONDARY SOURCES

"Aaron Copland." *Film Music Notes* 10 (March–April 1951): 3. Reprinted in *Tempo* 21 (Autumn 1951): 1–2.

"Aaron Copland." *Music and Musicians* 12 (May 1964): 11.

"Aaron Copland." *Musical Events,* February 1962, 18–19.

"Aaron Copland." *Musical Events,* May 1964, 24.

"Aaron Copland—Articulate Composer." *Musical Events,* November 1965, 26.

"An Aaron Copland Photo Album." *HiFi/Musical America,* November 1970, 56–63.

"Aaron Copland Reaches Half-Century Mark." *Musical America,* November 15, 1950, 14.

Agawu, Kofi. "Schubert's Sexuality: A Prescription for Analysis?" *19th Century Music* 17 (Summer 1993): 79–82.

Alexander, Charles. *Here the Century Lies: Nationalism and the Arts in Twentieth Century America.* Bloomington: Indiana University Press, 1980.

Antokoletz, Elliott. *Twentieth-Century Music.* Englewood Cliffs, N.J.: Prentice-Hall, 1992.

Apel, Willi. *The Harvard Dictionary of Music.* Cambridge: Harvard University Press, 1944.

The ASCAP Biographical Dictionary. New York: R. R. Bowker, 1980.

Babuscio, Jack. "Camp and the Gay Sensibility." In *Camp Grounds: Style and Sensibility,* ed. David Bergman. Amherst: University of Massachusetts Press, 1993.

Béhague, Gerard. "Latin American Folk Music." In Bruno Nettl, *Folk and Tra-*

ditional Music of the Western Continents. Englewood Cliffs, N.J.: Prentice-Hall, 1990.
Berger, Arthur. *Aaron Copland.* New York: Oxford University Press, 1953.
———. "Copland and the Audience of the Thirties." *Partisan Review* 68 (2001): 570–76.
———. "Problems of Pitch Organization in Stravinsky." *Perspectives of New Music* 2 (Fall–Winter 1963): 11–42. Reprinted in revised form in *Perspectives on Schoenberg and Stravinsky* (Westport, Conn.: Greenwood Press, 1983).
———. "Stravinsky and the Younger American Composers." *Score and I.M.A. Magazine,* June 1955, 38–46.
Bernstein, Leonard. "Aaron Copland." *HiFi/Musical America,* November 1970, 53–55.
Bick, Sally. "Composers on the Cultural Front: Aaron Copland and Hanns Eisler in Hollywood." Ph.D. diss., Yale University, 2001.
Bindas, Kenneth J. *All of This Music Belongs to the Nation: The WPA's Federal Music Project and American Society.* Knoxville: University of Tennessee Press, 1995.
Blanks, F. R. "Aaron Copland, a Vital Force in American Music." *Canon* 12 (August 1958): 413–15.
Bloom, Alexander. *Prodigal Sons: The New York Intellectuals and Their World.* New York: Oxford University Press, 1986.
Bordman, Gerald. *American Musical Theater: A Chronicle.* 2nd ed. New York: Oxford University Press, 1992.
Brant, LeRoy. "America, Involved in Music, Is Becoming Great In Music: From an Interview with Aaron Copland." *Etude* 71 (April 1953): 9; 57.
Brett, Philip. *Benjamin Britten, "Peter Grimes."* Cambridge: Cambridge University Press, 1983.
Brett, Philip, Elizabeth Woods, and Gary C. Thomas, eds. *Queering the Pitch: The New Gay and Lesbian Musicology.* New York: Routledge, 1994.
Bryant, Celia Mae. "Musical Drama: *The Cat and the Mouse. Aaron Copland's Humorous Scherzo.*" *Clavier* 7 (December 1968): 16–18.
Burr, Jessica. "Copland, the West, and American Identity." In *Copland Connotations: Studies and Interviews,* ed. Peter Dickinson. Woodbridge, Suffolk: Boydell Press, 2002.
Butterworth, Neil. *The Music of Aaron Copland.* N.p.: Toccata Press, 1985.
Campbell, Don G. *Master Teacher: Nadia Boulanger.* Washington, D.C.: Pastoral Press, 1984.
Carter, Elliott. "The Rhythmic Basis of American Music." *Score* 12 (June 1955): 27–32.
Chase, Gilbert. *America's Music: From the Pilgrims to the Present.* 3rd ed. Urbana: University of Illinois Press, 1987.
Chauncey, George, Jr. *Gay New York: Gender, Urban Culture, and the Making of the Gay Male World, 1890–1940.* New York: Basic Books, 1994.
Clark, Andrew, ed. *Riffs and Chords: A New Jazz Anthology.* London: Continuum, 2001.
Cone, Edward T. "Conversation with Aaron Copland." *Perspectives of New Music* 6 (1968): 57–72.
Crankshaw, Geoffrey. "Aaron Copland." *Chesterian* 32 (Spring 1958): 97–101.
Crist, Elizabeth B. "Aaron Copland and the Popular Front." *Journal of the American Musicological Society* 56 (Summer 2003): 409–65.

———. "Aaron Copland's Third Symphony (1946): Context, Composition, and Consequence." Ph.D. diss., Yale University, 2000.

———. "Aaron Copland's *Third Symphony* from Sketch to Score." *Journal of Musicology* 18 (Summer 2001): 377–405.

———. "The Compositional History of Aaron Copland's *Symphonic Ode*." *American Music* 18 (Fall 2000): 257–77.

———. "Critical Politics: The Reception History of Aaron Copland's *Third Symphony*." *Musical Quarterly* 85 (Summer 2001): 232–63.

De Long, Thomas A. *Pops: Paul Whiteman, King of Jazz.* N.p.: New Century, 1983.

———. *The Mighty Music Box: The Golden Age of Musical Radio.* Los Angeles: Amber Crest, 1980.

DeLapp, Jennifer. "Copland in the Fifties: Music and Ideology in the McCarthy Era." Ph.D. diss., University of Michigan, 1997.

Denning, Michael. *The Cultural Front: The Laboring of American Culture in the Twentieth Century.* London: Verso, 1997.

Dictionary of American Biography. New York: Charles Scribner's Sons, 1928–58.

Diggins, John P. *The American Left in the Twentieth Century.* New York: Harcourt Brace Jovanovich, 1973.

———. *The Rise and Fall of the American Left.* New York: W. W. Norton, 1973.

Dobrin, Arnold. *Aaron Copland: His Life and Times.* New York: Thomas Y. Crowell, 1967.

Eberly, Philip K. *Music in the Air: America's Changing Tastes in Popular Music, 1920–1980.* New York: Hastings House, 1982.

Feder, Stuart. "Decoration Day: A Boyhood Memory of Charles Ives." *Musical Quarterly* 66 (April 1980): 234–71.

Fenster, Mark. "Preparing the Audience, Informing the Performers? John A. Lomax and *Cowboy Songs and Other Frontier Ballads*." *American Music* 7 (Fall 1989): 260–77.

Filene, Benjamin. "'Our Singing Country': John and Alan Lomax, Leadbelly, and the Construction of an American Past." *American Quarterly* 43 (December 1991): 602–24.

Forte, Allen. *The American Popular Ballad of the Golden Era, 1924–1950.* Princeton: Princeton University Press, 1995.

Freeman, John W. "The Reluctant Composer; a Dialogue with Aaron Copland." *Opera News,* January 26, 1963, 8–12.

Fuller, Parmer. "Copland and Stravinsky: A Study (Based on the Comparison of the Opening Sections of 'Appalachian Spring' and 'Apollon Musagete') of the Traditional and Innovative Techniques Used by the Two Composers in Their Search for a Tonally-Based Musical Language in the Twentieth-Century, Pt. 1." D.M.A. diss., University of California, Los Angeles, 1982.

Garber, Eric. "A Spectacle in Color: The Lesbian and Gay Subculture of Jazz Age Harlem." In *Hidden from History: Reclaiming the Gay and Lesbian Past,* ed. Martin Duberman, Martha Vicinus, and George Chauncey Jr. New York: Meridian, 1990.

Garraty, John A., and Mark C. Carnes, eds. *American National Biography.* New York: Oxford University Press, 1999.

Garvie, Peter. "Aaron Copland." *Canadian Musician* 6 (1962): 3–12.

Goldman, R. F. "Aaron Copland." *Musical Quarterly* (1961): 1–3.

Gordon, Eric A. *Mark the Music: The Life and Times of Marc Blitzstein.* New York: St. Martins Press, 1989.
Green, Douglas B. *Singing in the Saddle: The History of the Singing Cowboy.* Nashville: Country Music Foundation Press and Vanderbilt University Press, 2002.
Greenway, John. "Aunt Molly Jackson and Robin Hood: A Study in Folk Re-creation." *Journal of American Folk-lore* 69 (1956): 23–38.
Griffiths, Paul. *The Thames and Hudson Encyclopaedia of 20th-Century Music.* New York: Thames and Hudson, 1986.
Hamm, Charles. *Yesterdays: Popular Song in America.* New York: W. W. Norton, 1963.
Hershowitz, Alan. "Aaron Copland: The American Composer Shares His Mind." *Music Journal* 39 (March–April 1981): 9–12.
Hinton, Stephen. *The Idea of Gebrauchsmusik: A Study of Musical Aesthetics in the Weimar Republic (1919–1933) with Particular Reference to the Works of Paul Hindemith.* New York: Garland, 1989.
Hirsch, Jerrold. "Modernity, Nostalgia, and Southern Folklore Studies: The Case of John Lomax." *Journal of American Folklore* 105 (Spring 1992): 183–207.
Hitchcock, H. Wiley. "Americans on American Music." *College Music Symposium* 8 (1968): 131–42.
———. "Copland, Aaron, 1900–1990; Copland, since 1943." Book review. *American Music* 8 (Summer 1990): 231–33.
———. *Music in the United States: A Historical Introduction.* 3rd ed. Englewood Cliffs, N.J.: Prentice-Hall, 1988.
Hood, Leon Crist. "The Programming of Classical Music Broadcasts over the Major Radio Networks: An Analysis of the Extent of the Supply by the Four National Radio Networks over the Past Seventeen Years of Programs of Standard Orchestral Music as a Function of the Public Interest in and Demand for Serious Music." Ed.D. diss., New York University, 1955.
Huggins, Nathan Irvin. *Harlem Renaissance.* London: Oxford University Press, 1971.
Hutchinson, George. *The Harlem Renaissance in Black and White.* Cambridge: The Belnap Press of Harvard University, 1995.
Kay, Norman. "Aspects of Copland's Development." *Tempo* 95 (Winter 1950): 23–29.
———. "Copland, All-American Composer." *Music and Musicians* 14 (September 1965): 22–23.
Kelly, Catriona. *Petrushka, the Russian Carnival Puppet.* Cambridge: Cambridge University Press, 1990.
Kendall, Alan. *The Tender Tyrant: Nadia Boulanger, a Life Devoted to Music.* Wilton, Conn.: Lyceum Books, 1976.
Kentucky Folklore Record (Kentucky Folklore Society). October–December 1961.
Key, Susan Margaret. "'Sweet Melody over Silent Wave': Depression-Era Radio and the American Composer." Ph.D. diss., University of Maryland, 1995.
Kleppinger, Stanley V. "On the Influence of Jazz Rhythm in the Music of Aaron Copland." *American Music* 21 (2003): 74–111.
Laki, Péter. "Der lange Gesang als Grundtyp in der internationalen Volksmusik." *Studia musicologica* 24, nos. 3–4 (1982): 293–400.
Leibman, Arthur. *Jews and the Left.* New York: John Wiley and Sons, 1979.

Lenihan, John H. *Showdown: Confronting Modern America in the Western Film*. Urbana: University of Illinois Press, 1980.
Levine, Lawrence W. *Highbrow/Lowbrow: The Emergence of Cultural Hierarchy in America*. Cambridge: Harvard University Press, 1988.
Levy, Alan Howard. *Musical Nationalism: American Composers' Search for Identity.* Westport, Conn.: Greenwood Press, 1987.
Levy, Beth Ellen. "Frontier Figures: American Music and the Mythology of the American West, 1895–1945." Ph.D. diss., University of California, Berkeley, 2002.
Lewis, David Levering. *When Harlem Was in Vogue*. New York: Oxford University Press, 1979.
Lieberman, Robbie. My *Song Is My Weapon: People's Songs, American Communism, and the Politics of Culture, 1930–1950*. Urbana: University of Illinois Press, 1989.
Lindsey, Roberta Lewise. "An Historical and Musical Study of Aaron Copland's First Orchestral Work: 'Grohg,' A Ballet in One Act." Ph.D. diss., Ohio State University, 1996.
Lott, R. Allen. "'New Music for New Ears': The International Composers' Guild." *Journal of the American Musicological Society* 36 (1983): 266–86.
Loy, R. Philip. *Westerns and American Culture, 1930–1955*. Jefferson, N.C.: McFarland, 2001.
Lusted, David. *The Western*. Harlow, England: Pearson Longman, 2003.
McClary, Susan. "On the Solomon/Steblein Debate." *19th Century Music* 17 (Summer 1993): 83–88.
Magrini, Tullia. "Aaron Copland: From Practical Music to Unconscious Americanism." *ISME Yearbook* 10 (1983): 135–40.
Malone, Bill C. *Country Music, U.S.A.* Rev. ed. Austin: University of Texas Press, 1985.
Manuel, Peter. *Popular Musics of the Non-Western World*. New York: Oxford University Press, 1988.
Mathers, Daniel. "Closure in the 'Sextet' and 'Short Symphony' by Aaron Copland: A Study Using Facsimiles and Printed Editions." M.M. thesis, Florida State University, 1989.
Matthews, David. "Copland and Stravinsky." *Tempo* 95 (Winter 1950): 10–14.
Mayer, William. "The Composer in the U. S. and Russia: A Frank Talk between Copland and Khachaturian." *ASCAP* 3 (1969): 22–25.
———. "Copland and Khachaturian—Historic Meeting." *Music Journal* 27 (March 1969): 25–27, 51–53, 56–57, 59.
Mead, Rita. *Henry Cowell's New Music, 1925–1936: The Society, the Music Editions, and the Recordings*. Ann Arbor, Mich.: UMI Research Press, 1981.
Meckna, Michael. "Copland, Sessions, and *Modern Music:* The Rise of the Composer-Critic in America." *American Music* 3 (Summer 1985): 198–204.
Messing, Scott. *Neoclassicism in Music: From the Genesis of the Concept through the Schoenberg/Stravinsky Polemic*. Ann Arbor, Mich.: UMI Research Press, 1988.
Metzer, David Joel. "The Ascendancy of Musical Modernism in New York City, 1915–1929." Ph.D. diss., Yale University, 1993.
———. "The League of Composers: The Initial Years." *American Music* (Spring 1997): 45–69.
———. "The New York Reception of *Pierrot Lunaire:* The 1923 Premiere and Its Aftermath." *Musical Quarterly* 78 (Winter 1994): 669–99.

Moore, MacDonald Smith. *Yankee Blues: Musical Culture and American Identity.* Bloomington: Indiana University Press, 1985.
Nettl, Bruno. *Folk and Traditional Music of the Western Continents.* 3rd ed. Englewood Cliffs, N.J.: Prentice-Hall, 1990.
The New Grove Dictionary of American Music. Ed. H. Wiley Hitchcock. London: Macmillan, 1984.
The New Grove Dictionary of Jazz. Ed. Barry Kernfeld. London: Macmillan, 1988.
The New Grove Dictionary of Music and Musicians. Ed. Stanley Sadie. London: Macmillan, 2001.
Newlin, Dika. "The Piano Music of Aaron Copland." *Piano Quarterly* 28, no.111 (1980): 6–12.
Nicholls, David. *American Experimental Music, 1890–1940.* New York: Cambridge University Press, 1990.
Oja, Carol J. "Composer with a Conscience: Elie Siegmeister in Profile." *American Music* 6 (Summer 1988): 158–80.
———. "The Copland-Sessions Concerts and Their Reception in the Contemporary Press." *Musical Quarterly* 65 (April 1979): 212–29.
———. *Making Music Modern: New York in the 1920s.* New York: Oxford University Press, 2000.
———. "Marc Blitzstein's *The Cradle Will Rock* and Mass-Song Style of the 1930s." *Musical Quarterly* 73 (1989): 445–75.
———. "'New Music and the 'New Negro': The Background of William Grant Still's *Afro-American Symphony.*" *Black Music Research Journal* 12 (Fall 1992): 145–69.
———. "The USA, 1918–1945." In *Modern Times,* ed. Robert P. Morgan. Englewood Cliffs, N.J: Prentice-Hall, 1993.
———. "Virgil Thomson's Harvard Year's." In *A Celebration of American Music: Words and Music in Honor of H. Wiley Hitchcock,* ed. Richard Crawford, R. Allen Lott, and Carol J. Oja. Ann Arbor: University of Michigan Press, 1990.
Olmstead, A. "The Copland-Sessions Letters." *Tempo* 175 (December 1990): 2–5.
Ottenberg, David. "The Methods and Aesthetics of Nadia Boulanger and Their Influence on Aaron Copland." Master's thesis, University of Florida, 1992.
The Oxford English Dictionary. 2nd ed. Oxford: Oxford University Press, 2000. Available online http://dictionary.oed.com/entrance.dtl.
Peretti, Burton W. *The Creation of Jazz: Music, Race, and Culture in Urban America.* Urbana: University of Illinois Press, 1992.
Perloff, Nancy. *Art and the Everyday: Popular Entertainment and the Circle of Erik Satie.* Oxford: Clarendon Press, 1991.
Pescatello, Ann M. *Charles Seeger: A Life in American Music.* Pittsburgh: University of Pittsburgh Press, 1992.
Pollack, Howard. *Aaron Copland: The Life and Work of an Uncommon Man.* Urbana: University of Illinois Press, 1999.
Potter, Caroline. "Nadia Boulanger (1887–1979): The Teacher in the Marketplace." In *The Business of Music,* ed. Michael Talbot. Liverpool: Liverpool University Press, 2002.
Radice, Mark. "Futurismo: Its Origins, Context, Repertory, and Influence." *Musical Quarterly* 73 (1989): 1–17.
Ramey, Phillip. Liner notes. *Leo Smit: The Composer for Solo Piano.* Sony Classical SM2K 66 345.

Robertson, Marta Elaine. "'A Gift to Be Simple': The Collaboration of Aaron Copland and Martha Graham in the Genesis of *Appalachian Spring*." Ph.D. diss., University of Michigan, 1993.

———. "Musical and Choreographic Integration in Copland's and Graham's *Appalachian Spring*." *Musical Quarterly* 83 (Spring 1999): 6–26.

Root, Deane L. "The Pan American Association of Composers (1928–1934)." *Yearbook for Inter-American Musical Research* 8 (1972): 49–70.

Rosenstiel, Léonie. *Nadia Boulanger: A Life in Music*. New York: W. W. Norton, 1982.

Rust, Brian. *Jazz Records, 1897–1942*. 4th ed. New Rochelle, N.Y.: Arlington House, 1978.

Sargeant, Winthrop. *Jazz, Hot and Hybrid*. 3rd ed. New York: Da Capo Press, 1975.

Schuller, Gunther. *Early Jazz: Its Roots and Musical Development*. New York: Oxford University Press, 1968.

———. *The Swing Era: The Development of Jazz, 1930–1945*. New York: Oxford University Press, 1989.

Shirley, Wayne D. *An Analytical Index to Modern Music*. Ed. William and Carolyn Lichtenwanger. New York: AMS Press, 1976.

Simmon, Scott. *The Invention of the Western Film: A Cultural History of the Genre's First Half-Century*. Cambridge: Cambridge University Press, 2003.

Simms, Bryan R. *Music of the Twentieth Century: Style and Structure*. New York: Schirmer Books, 1986.

Skowronski, Joann. *Aaron Copland: A Bio-bibliography*. Westport, Conn.: Greenwood Press, 1985.

Slonimsky, Nicholas. *Music since 1900*. 5th ed. New York: Schirmer Books, 1994.

———, ed. *Baker's Biographical Dictionary of Musicians*. 8th ed. New York: Schirmer Books, 1992.

Smith, Andrew Brodie. *Shooting Cowboys and Indians: Silent Westerns, American Culture, and the Birth of Hollywood*. Boulder: University Press of Colorado, 2003.

Smith, Julia. *Aaron Copland: His Works and Contribution to American Music*. New York: E. P. Dutton, 1955.

Solomon, Maynard. "Charles Ives: Some Questions of Veracity." *Journal of the American Musicological Society* 40 (Autumn 1987): 443–70.

———. "Franz Schubert and the Peacocks of Benvenuto Cellini." *19th Century Music* 12 (Spring 1989): 193–206.

Spycket, Jérôme. *Nadia Boulanger*. Trans. M. M. Shriver. Stuyvesant, N.Y.: Pendragon Press, 1992.

Stanfield, Peter. *Hollywood, Westerns and the 1930s: The Lost Trail*. Exeter, Devon: University of Exeter Press, 2001.

———. *Horse Opera: The Strange History of 1930s Singing Cowboys*. Urbana: University of Illinois Press, 2002.

Starr, Larry. "The Voice of Solitary Contemplation: Copland's *Music for the Theatre* Viewed as a Journey of Self-Discovery." *American Music* 20 (Fall 2002): 297–316.

———. "Copland's Style." *Perspective of New Music* 19, nos 1–2 (1980–81): 68.

St. Barclar, Glen. *Revolutions in Our Time: 20th Century Nationalism*. London: Weidenfeld and Nicolson, 1971.

Stoddard, Hope. "Aaron Copland on the Composer's Craft." *International Musician* 47 (May 1949): 34.

Strauss, Joseph N. "'The Anxiety of Influence' in Twentieth-Century Music." *Journal of Musicology* 9 (Autumn 1991): 430–47.

Summers, H. B. *A Thirty-Year History of Programs Carried on National Radio Networks in the United States, 1926–1956*. Columbus, Ohio: n.p., 1958.

Taruskin, Richard. "*Chez Pétrouchka:* Harmony and Tonality *chez* Stravinsky." *19th Century Music* 10 (Spring 1987): 265–86.

———. "Russian Folk Melodies in *The Rite of Spring.*" *Journal of the American Musicological Society* 33 (1980): 501–43.

———. *Stravinsky and the Russian Traditions: A Biography of the Works through "Mavra."* Berkeley and Los Angeles: University of California Press, 1996.

Thomson, Virgil. *A Virgil Thomson Reader.* Boston: Houghton Mifflin, 1981.

Tick, Judith. "The Origins and Style of Copland's *Mood for Piano* no. 3, 'Jazzy.'" *American Music* 20 (Fall 2002): 277–96.

Timmons, Stuart. *The Trouble with Harry Hay: Founder of the Modern Gay Movement.* Boston: Alyson, 1990.

Tischler, Barbara L. *An American Music: The Search for an American Musical Identity.* New York: Oxford University Press, 1986.

Van den Toorn, Pieter C. *The Music of Igor Stravinsky.* New Haven: Yale University Press, 1983.

Vinton, John, ed. *Dictionary of Contemporary Music.* New York: E. P. Dutton, 1974.

Walser, Robert, ed. *Keeping Time: Readings in Jazz History.* New York: Oxford University Press, 1999.

Walters, Teresa. "Nadia Boulanger, Musician and Teacher: Her Life, Concepts, and Influences." D.M.A. thesis, Peabody Conservatory of Music, Peabody Institute of The Johns Hopkins University, 1981.

Ware, Caroline, K. M. Panikkar, and J. M. Romein. *The Twentieth Century.* Vol. 6 of *History of Mankind: Cultural and Scientific Development.* New York: Harper and Row, 1966.

Warner, Thomas E. *Periodical Literature on American Music, 1620–1920: A Classified Bibliography with Annotations.* New York: Harmonie Park Press, 1988.

Watkins, Glenn. *Pyramids at the Louvre: Music, Culture, and Collage from Stravinsky to the Postmodernists.* Cambridge: Belknap Press of Harvard University Press, 1994.

———. *Soundings: Music in the Twentieth Century.* New York, Schirmer, 1988.

Whitesell, Lloyd, and Sophie Fuller, eds. *Queer Episodes in Music and Modern Identity.* Urbana: University of Illinois Press, 2002.

Wintz, Cary D. *Black Culture and the Harlem Renaissance.* Houston: Rice University Press, 1988.

Wright, Will. *Six Guns and Society: A Structural Study of the Western.* Berkeley and Los Angeles: University of California Press, 1975.

Young, Douglas. "The Piano Music." *Tempo* 95 (Winter 1950): 14–22.

Zuck, Barbara. *A History of Musical Americanism.* Ann Arbor, Mich.: UMI Research Press, 1980.

Index